AF478970

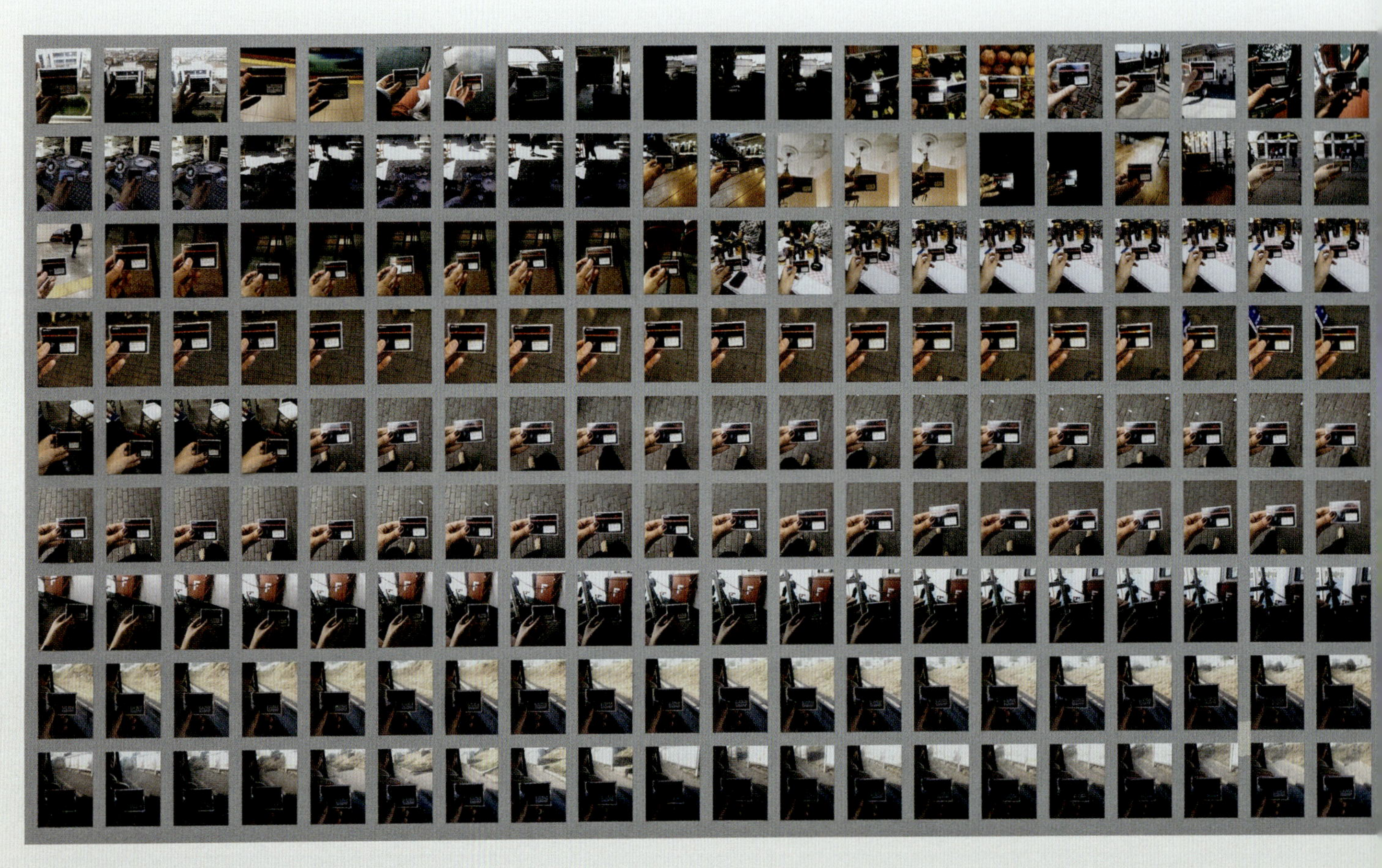

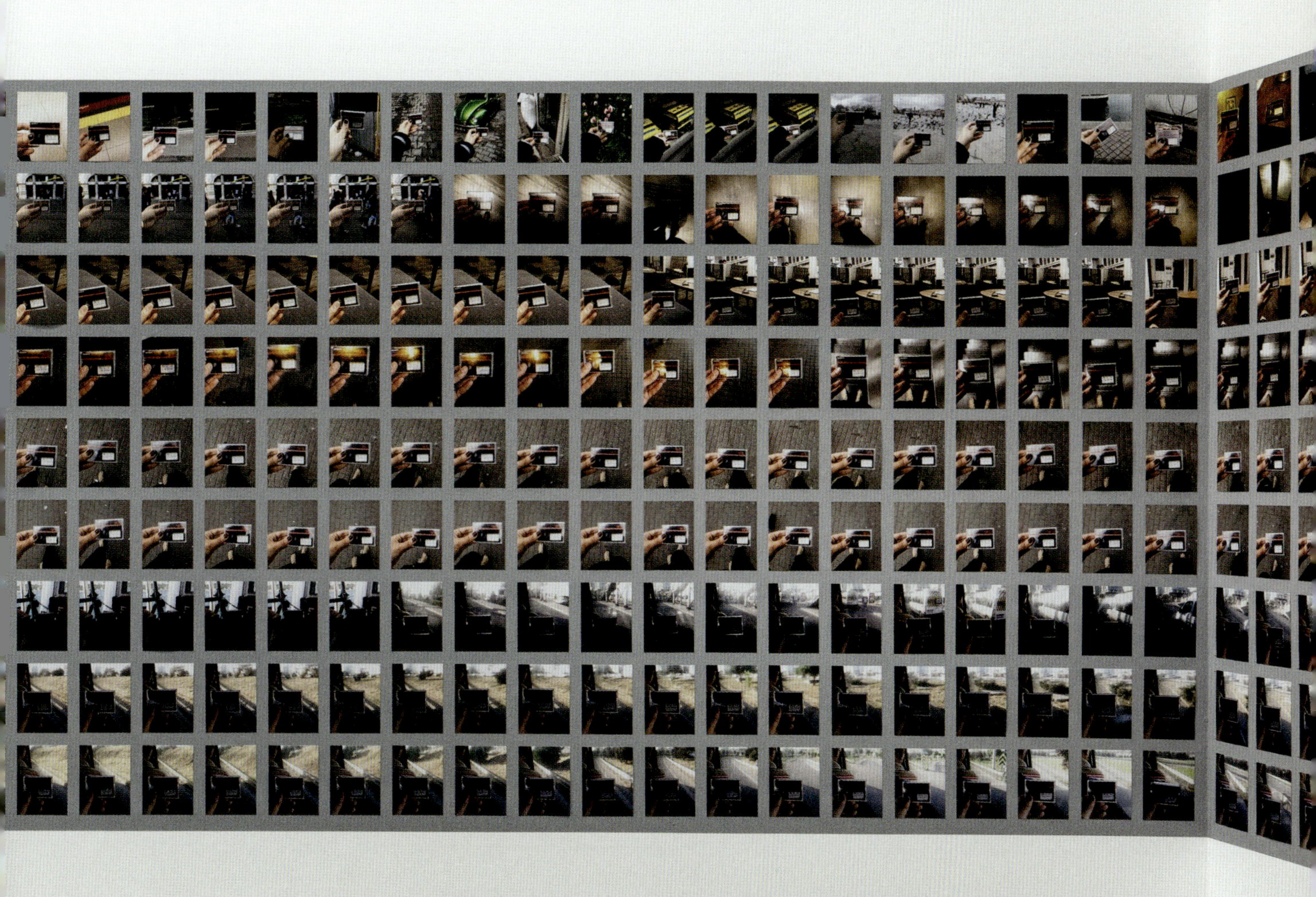

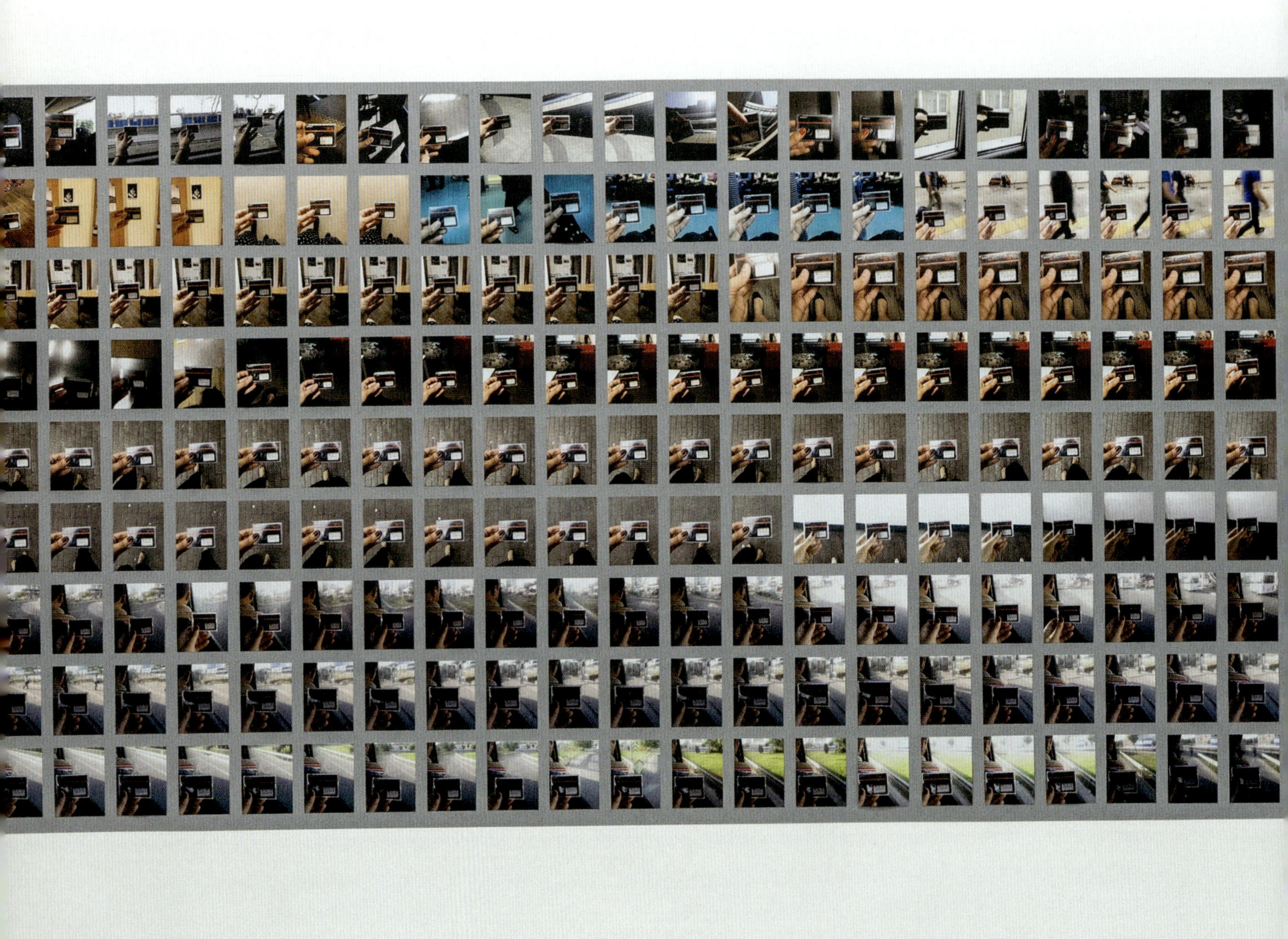

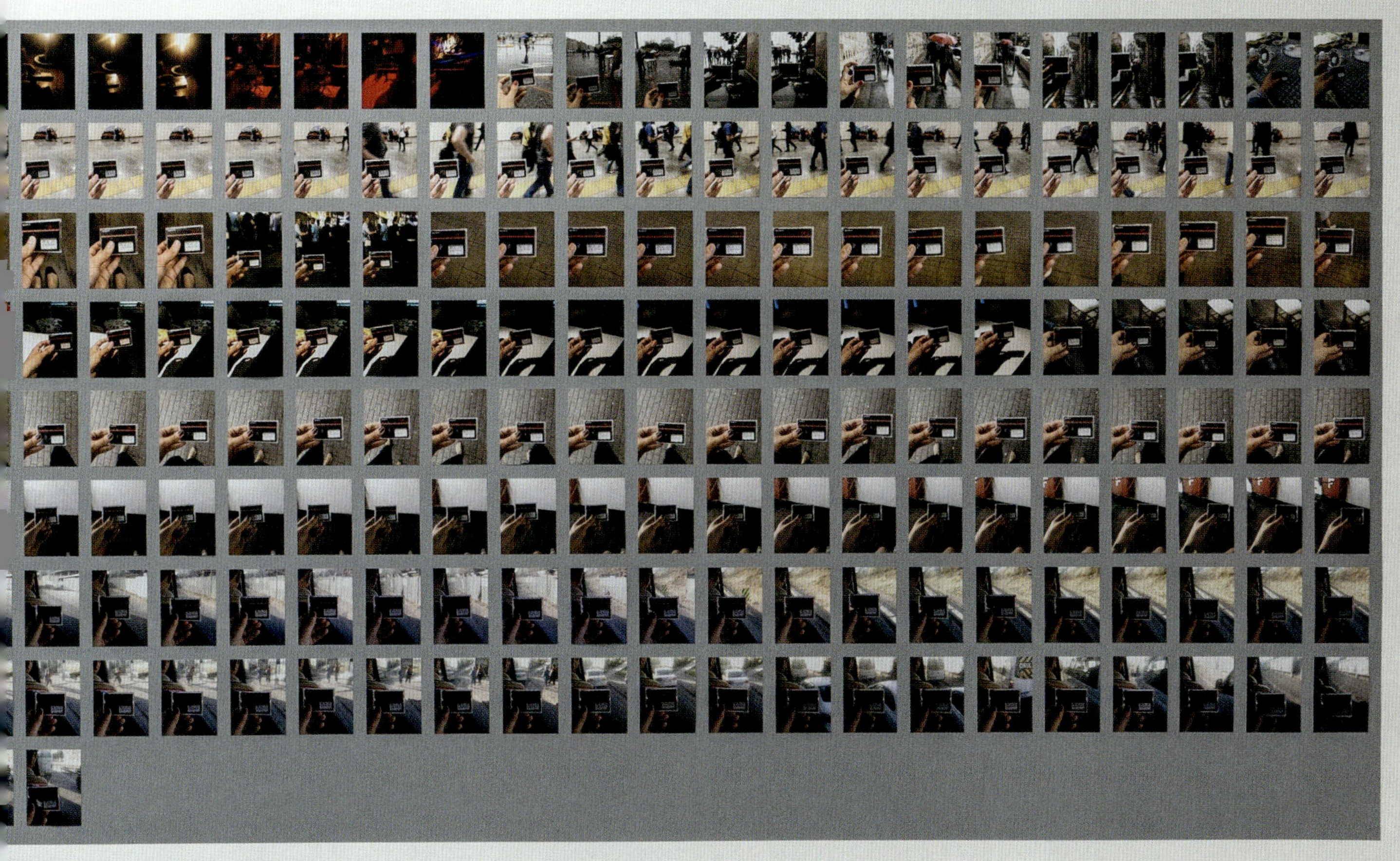

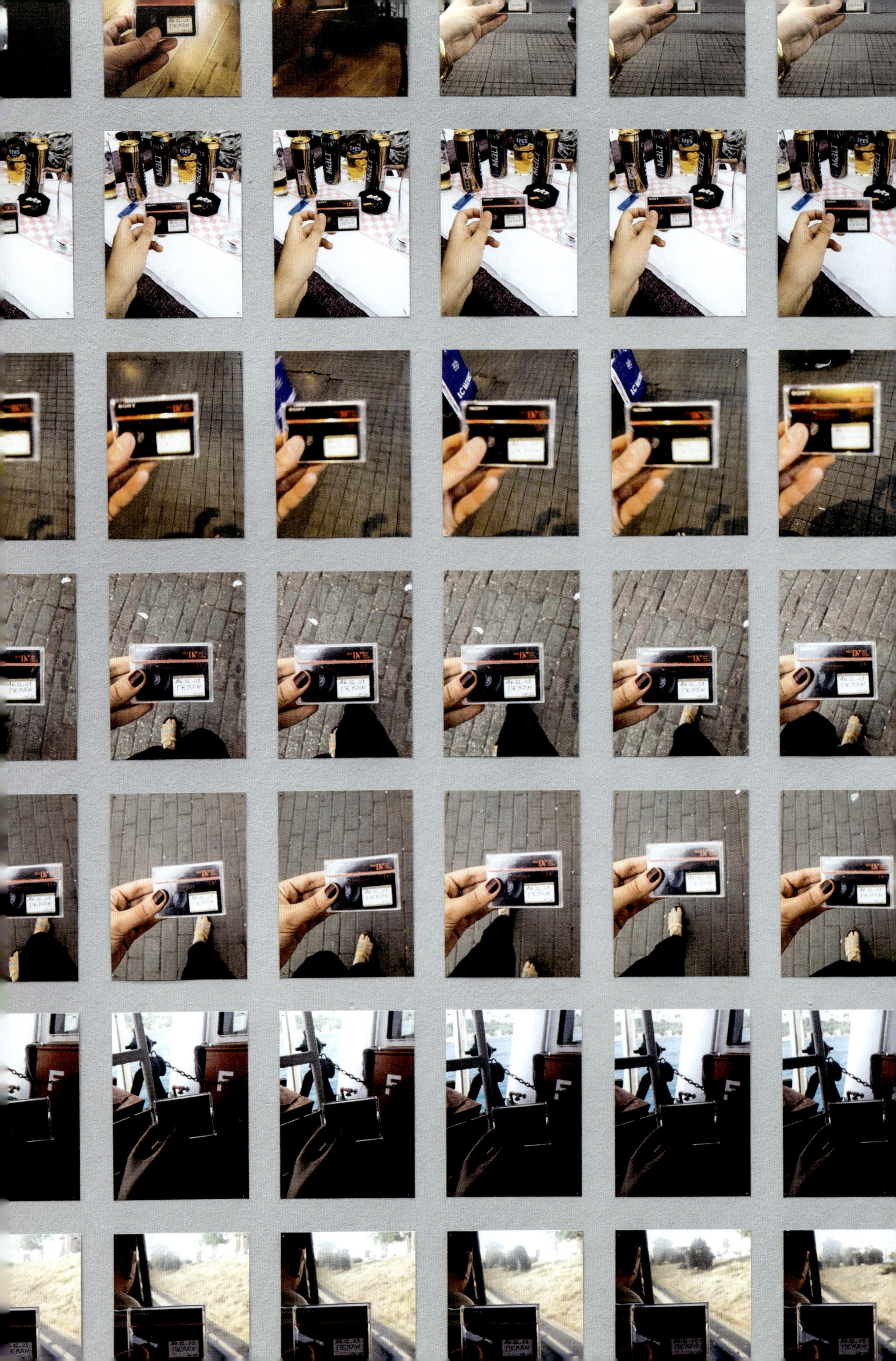

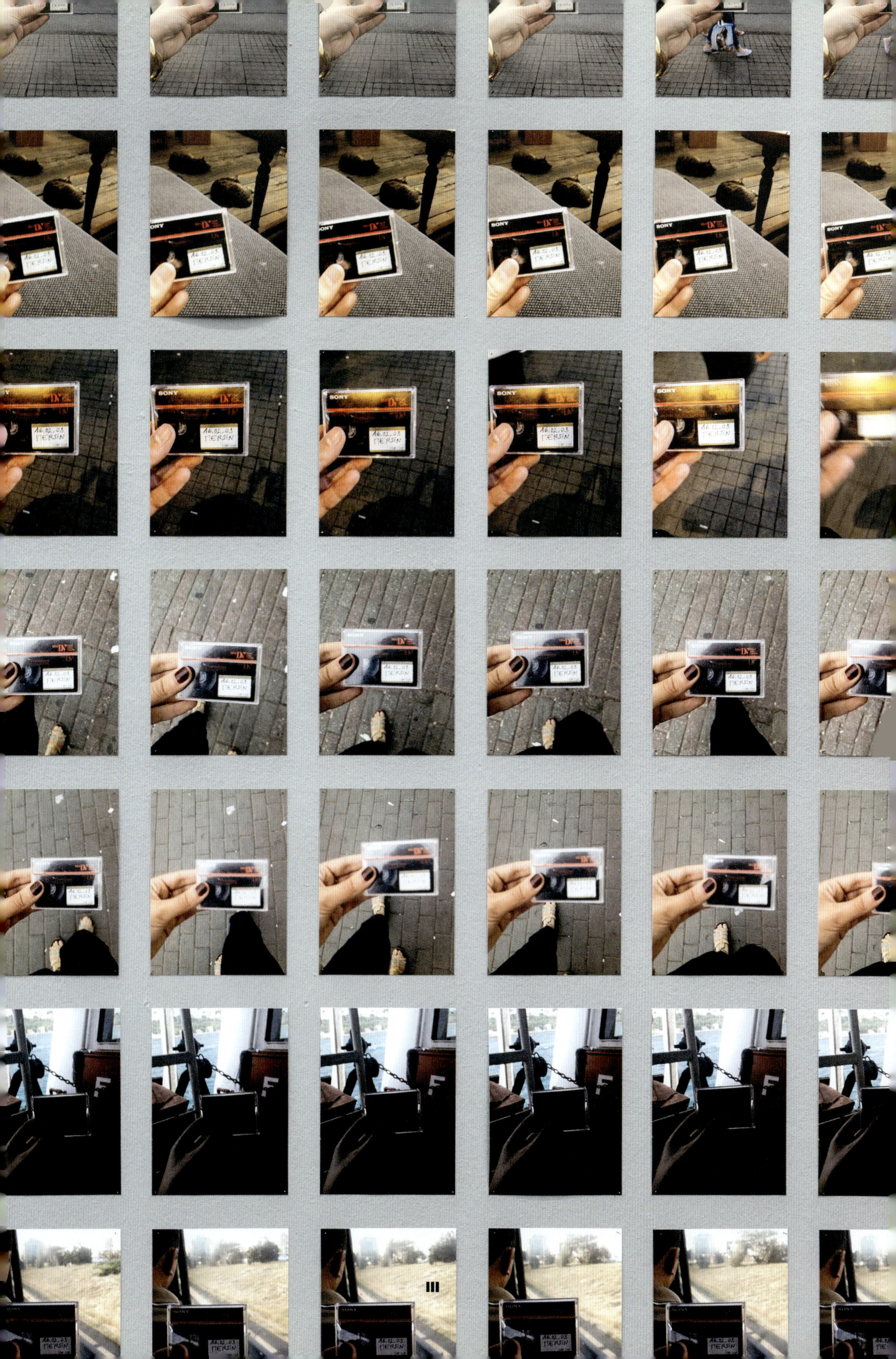

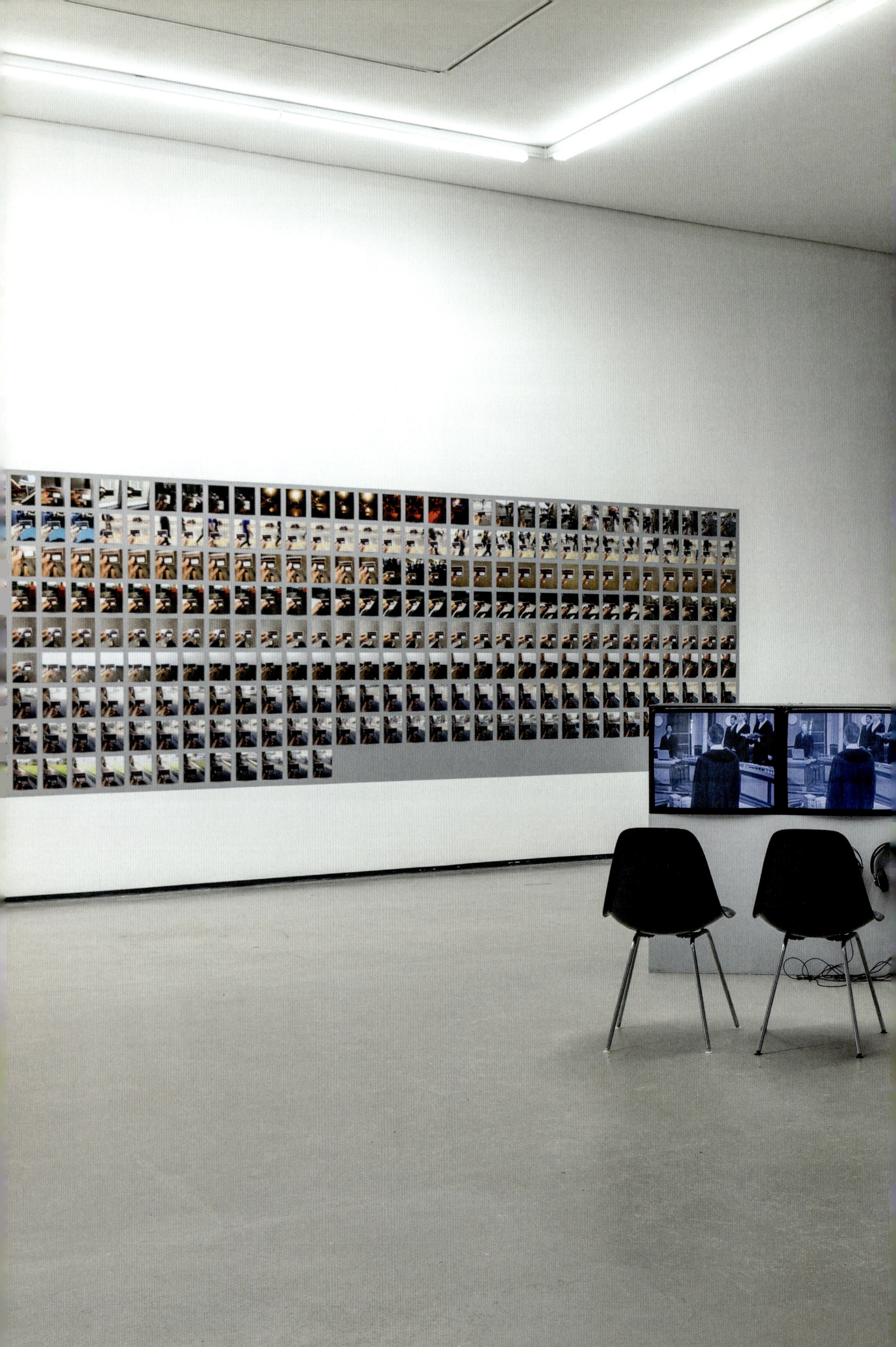

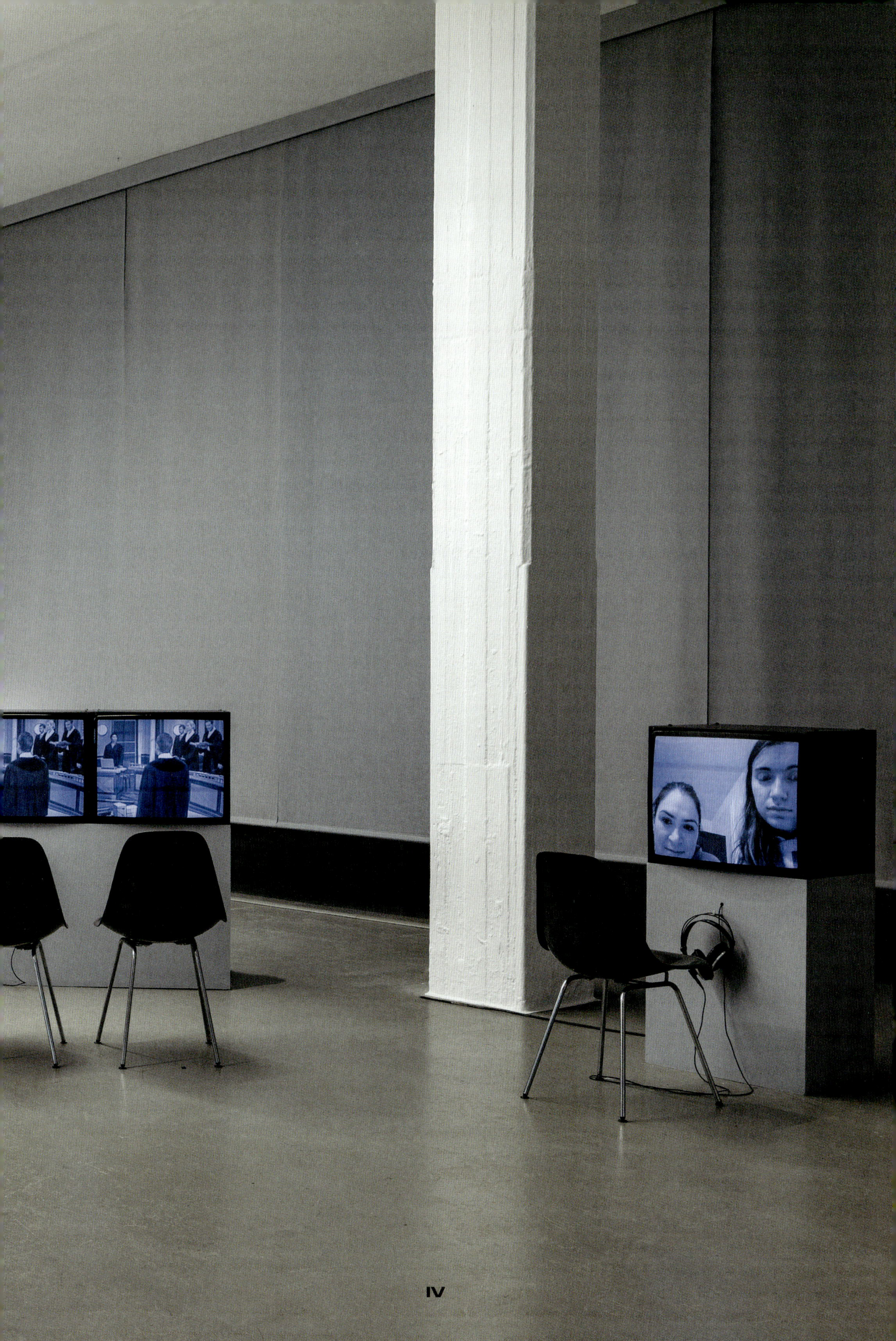

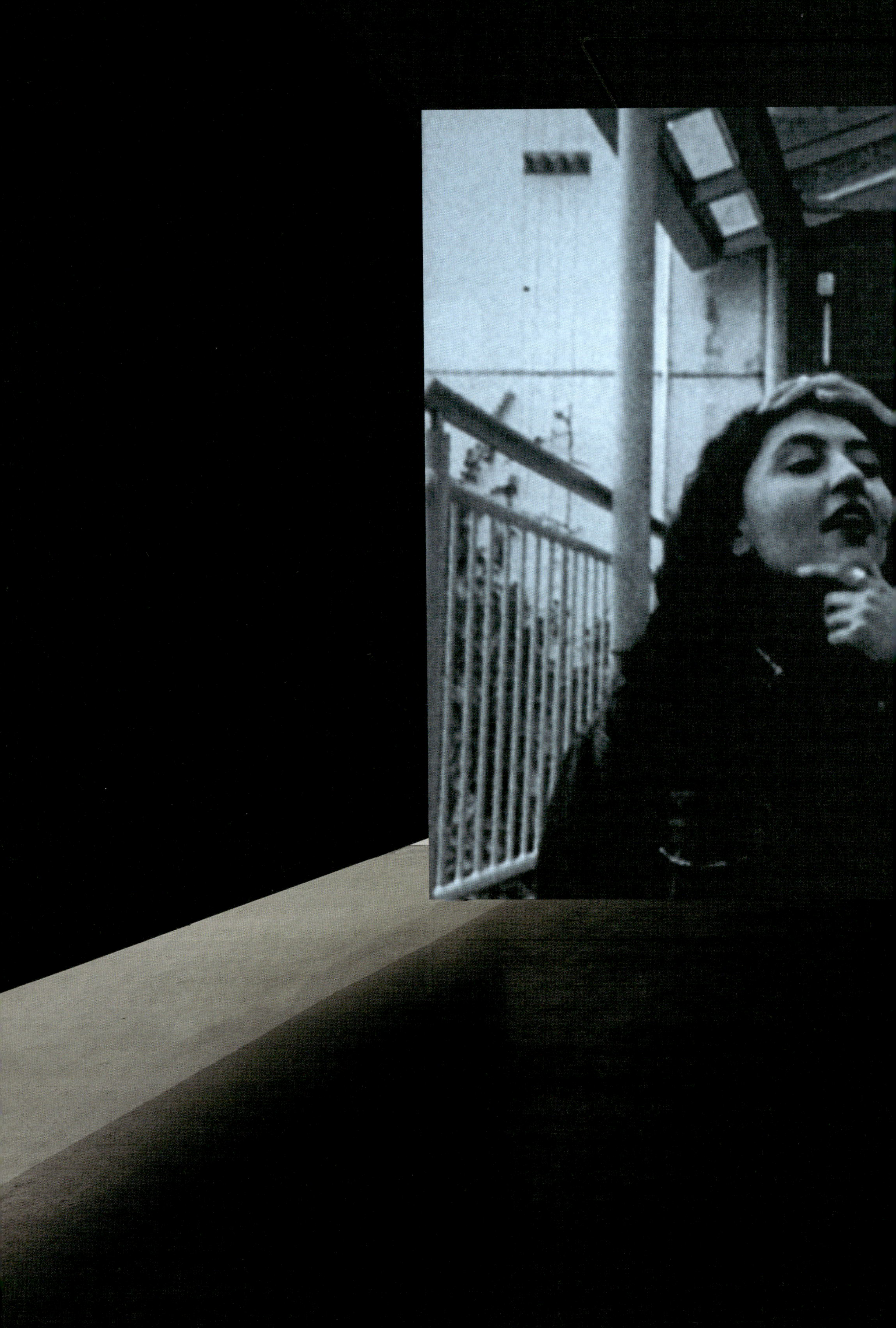

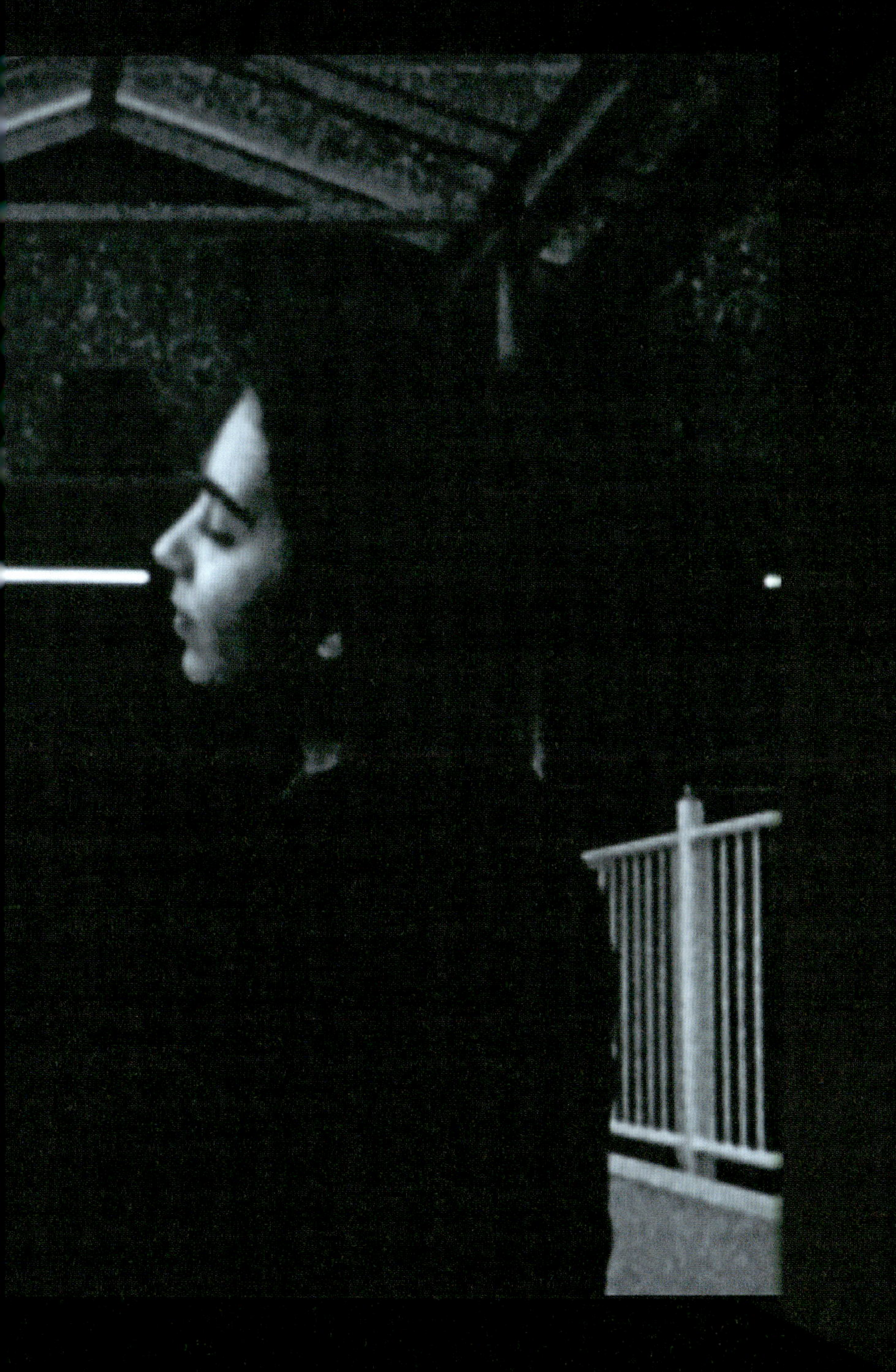

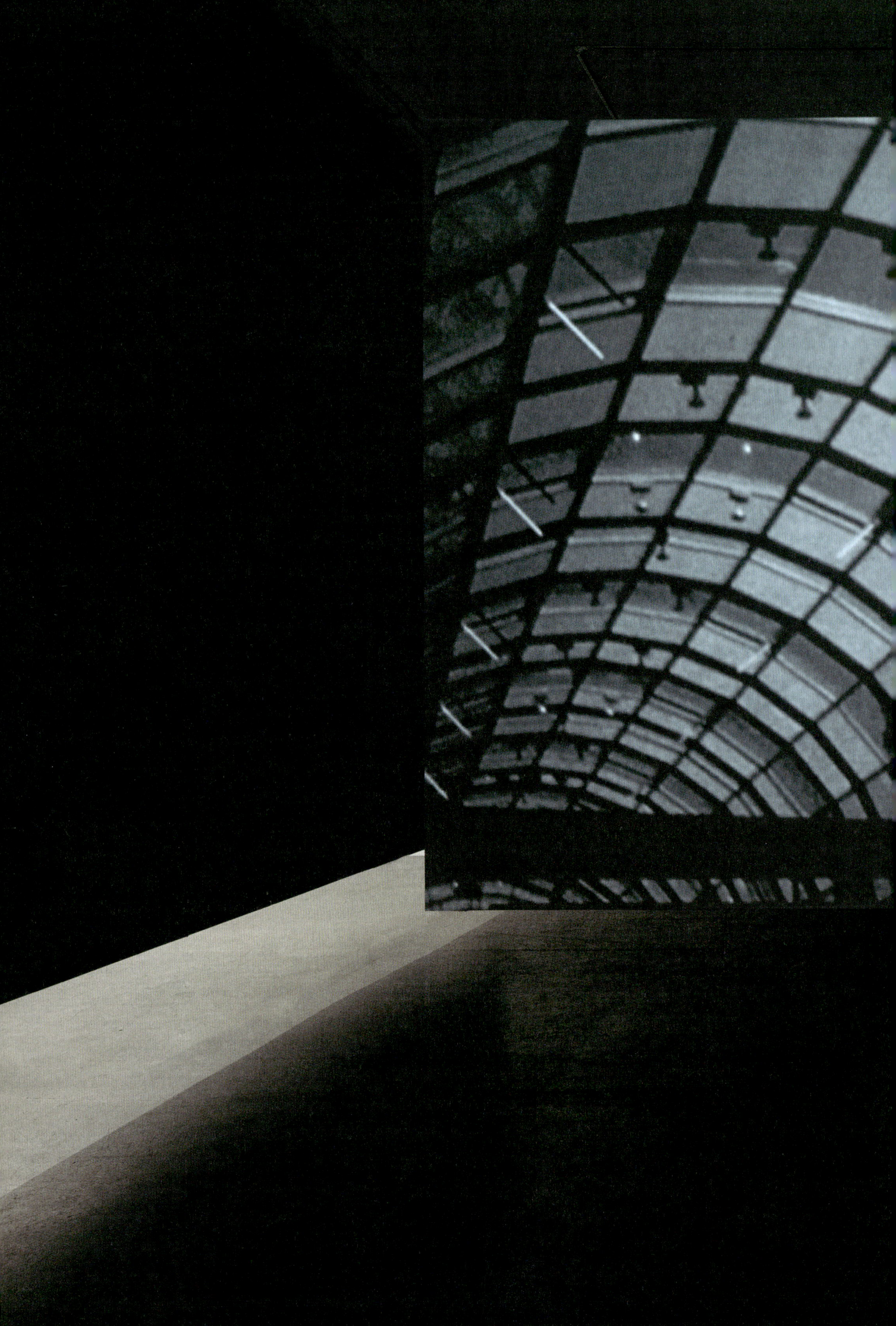

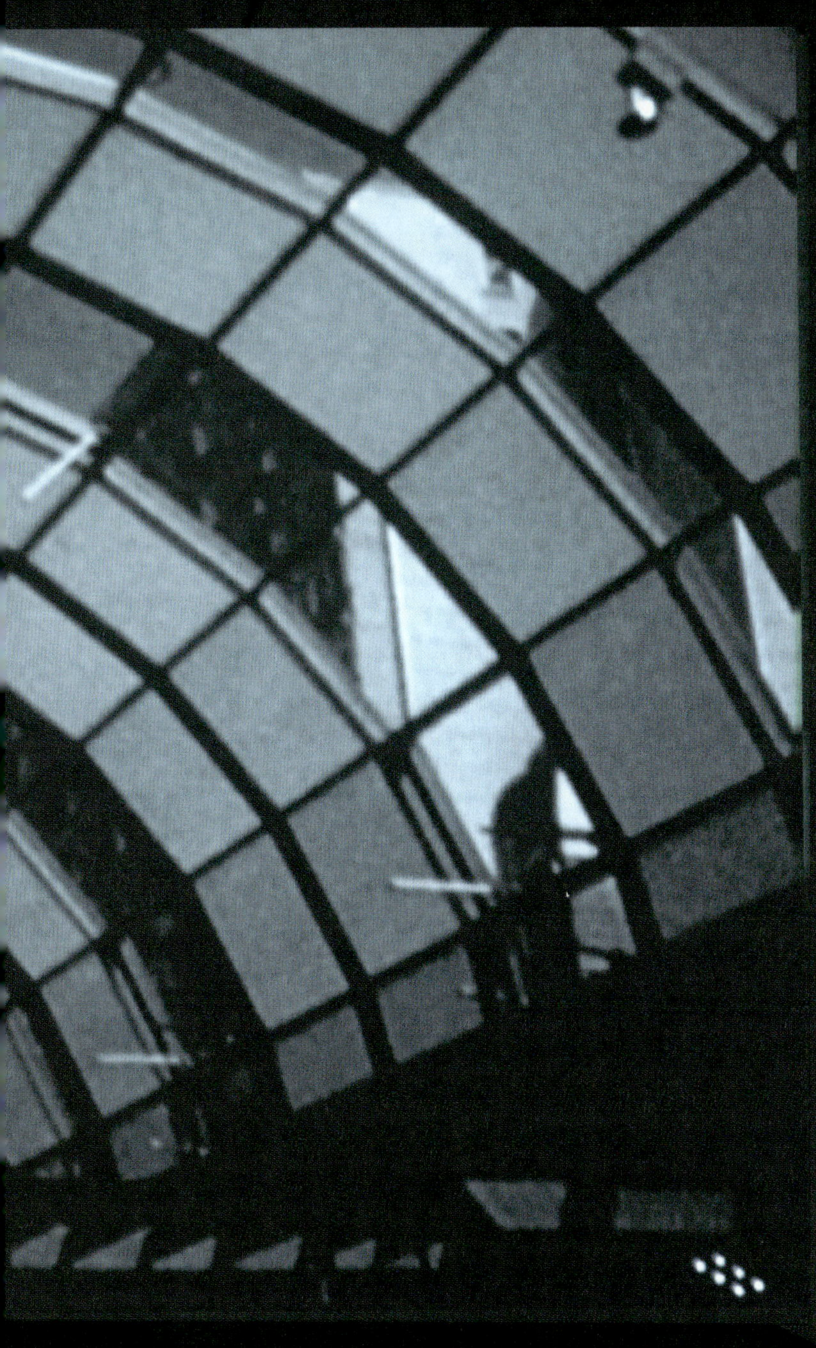

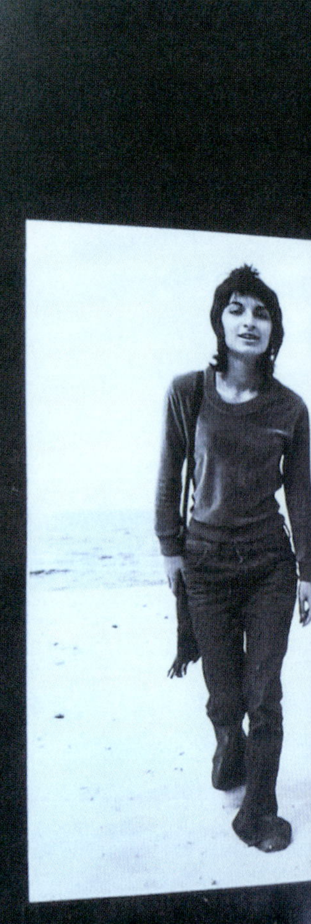

But the Ger

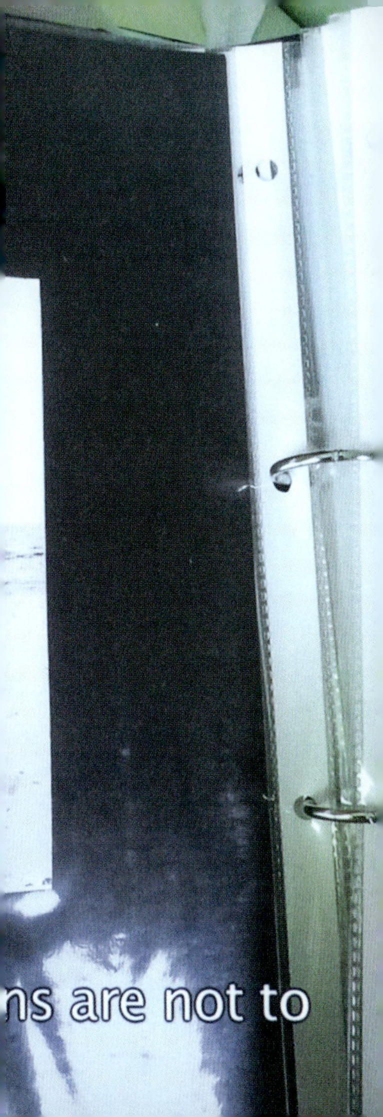
ns are not to

lich...

vably

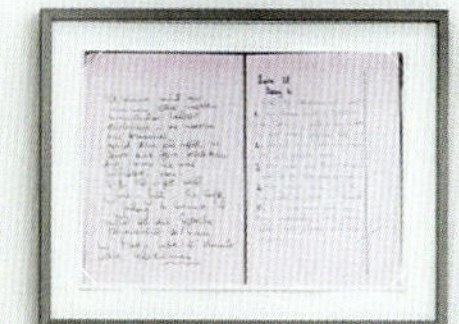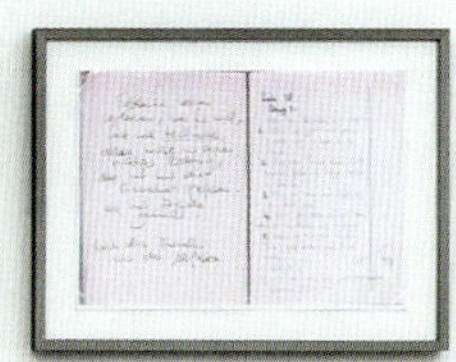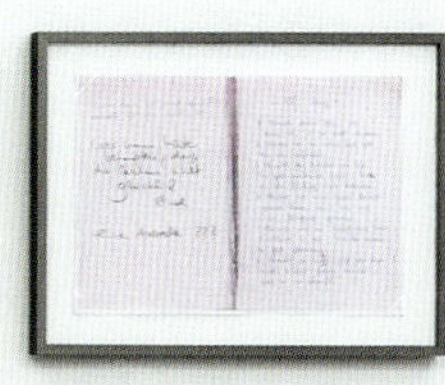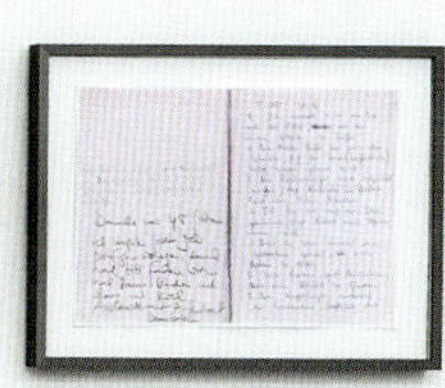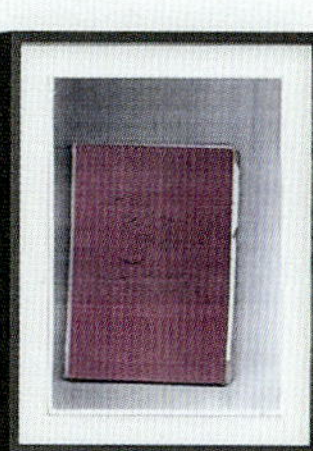

BILIR ZÜHÂL
GRAMMATIK
STUFE II
DREIPFEIL
ZÜHÂL
BILIR-MEIER
1970 - 2018
48 Jahre

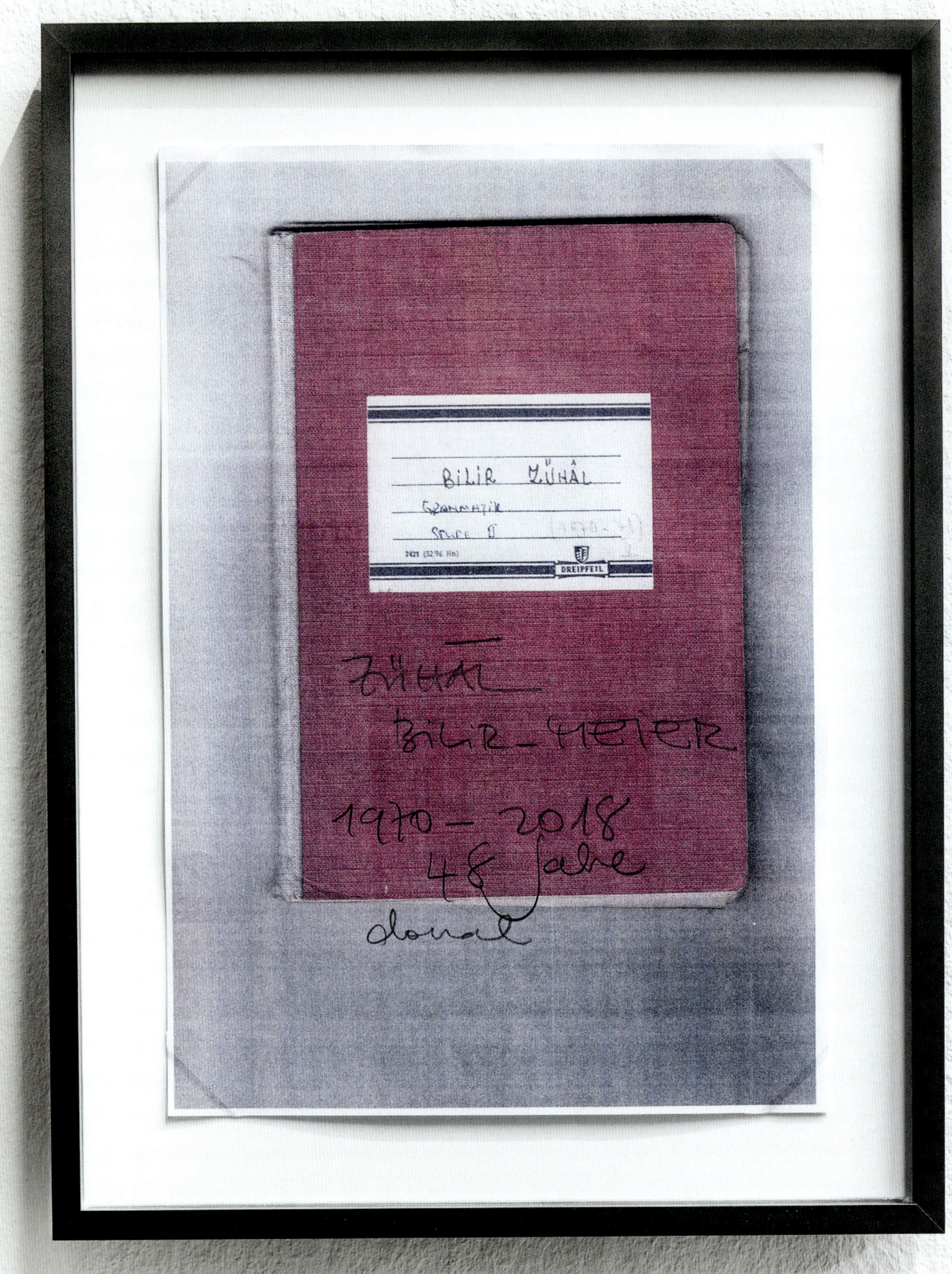

x

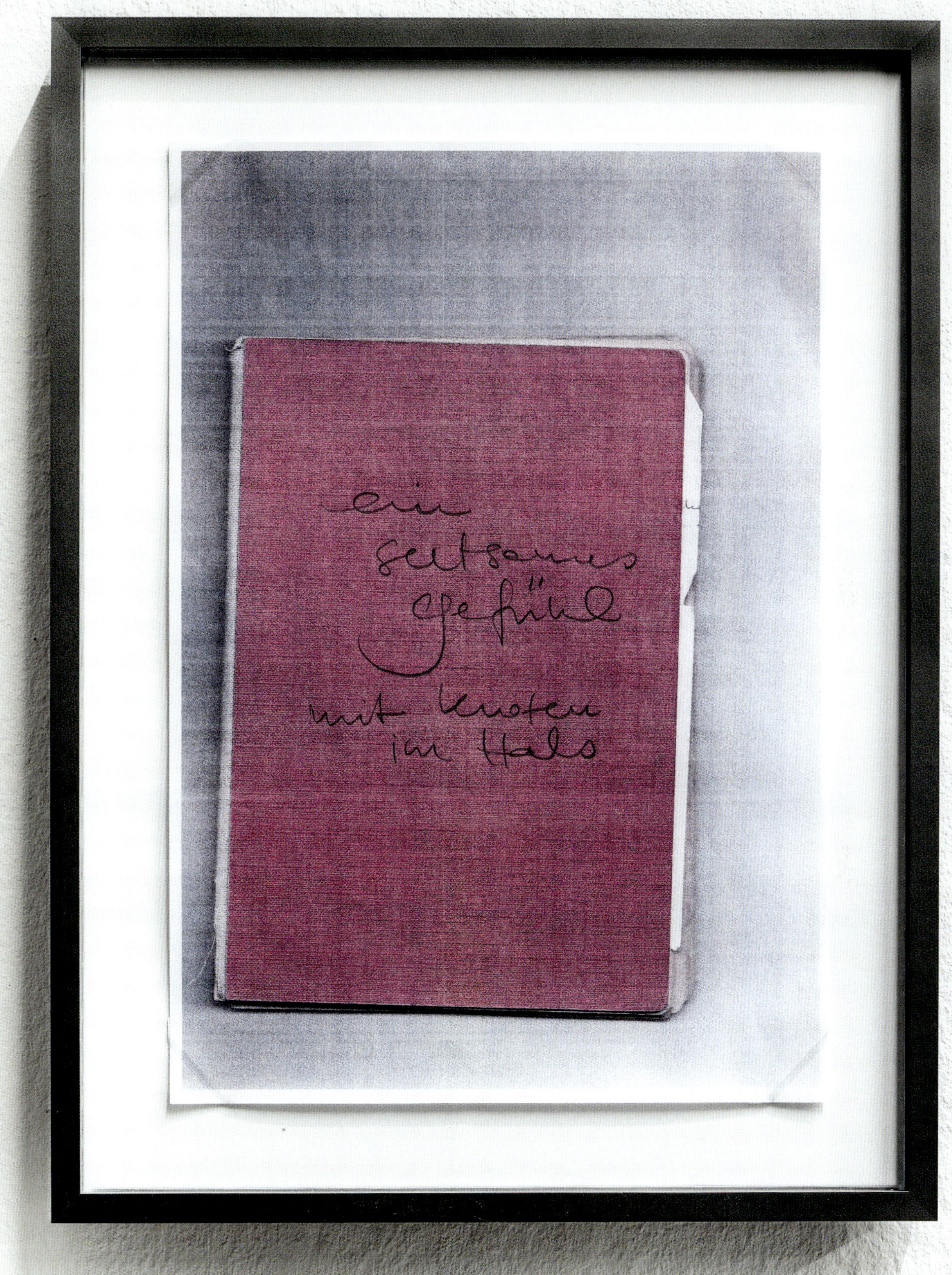
ein
seltsames
Gefühl

mit Knoten
im Hals

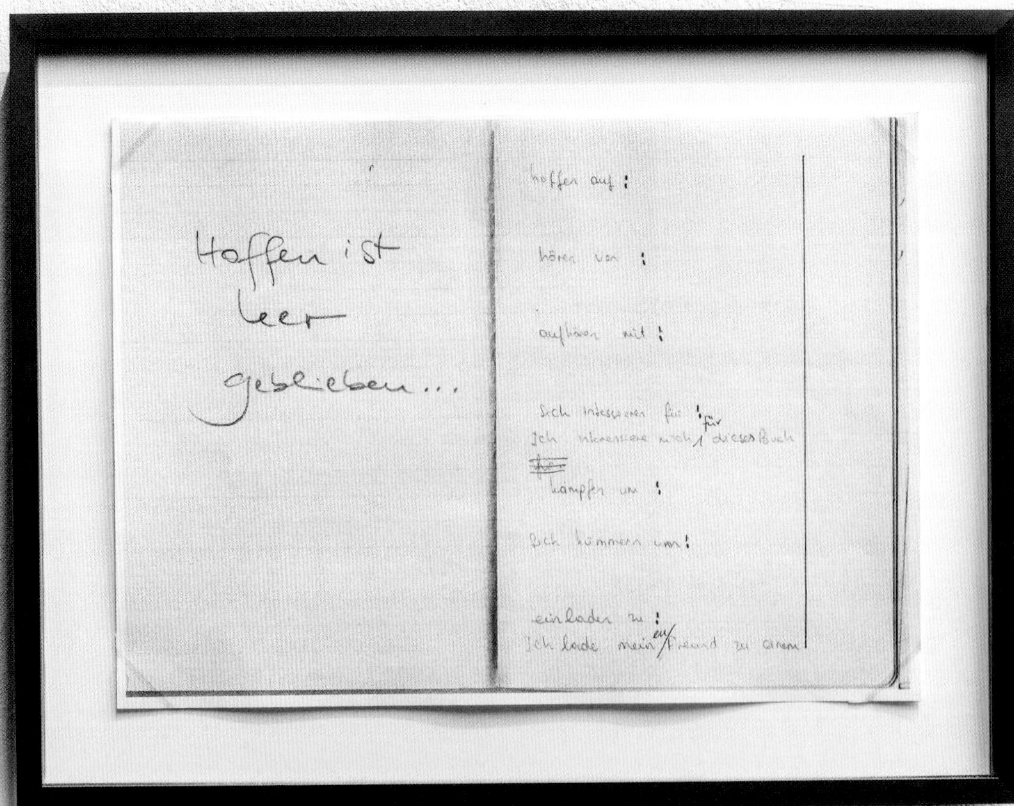

XII

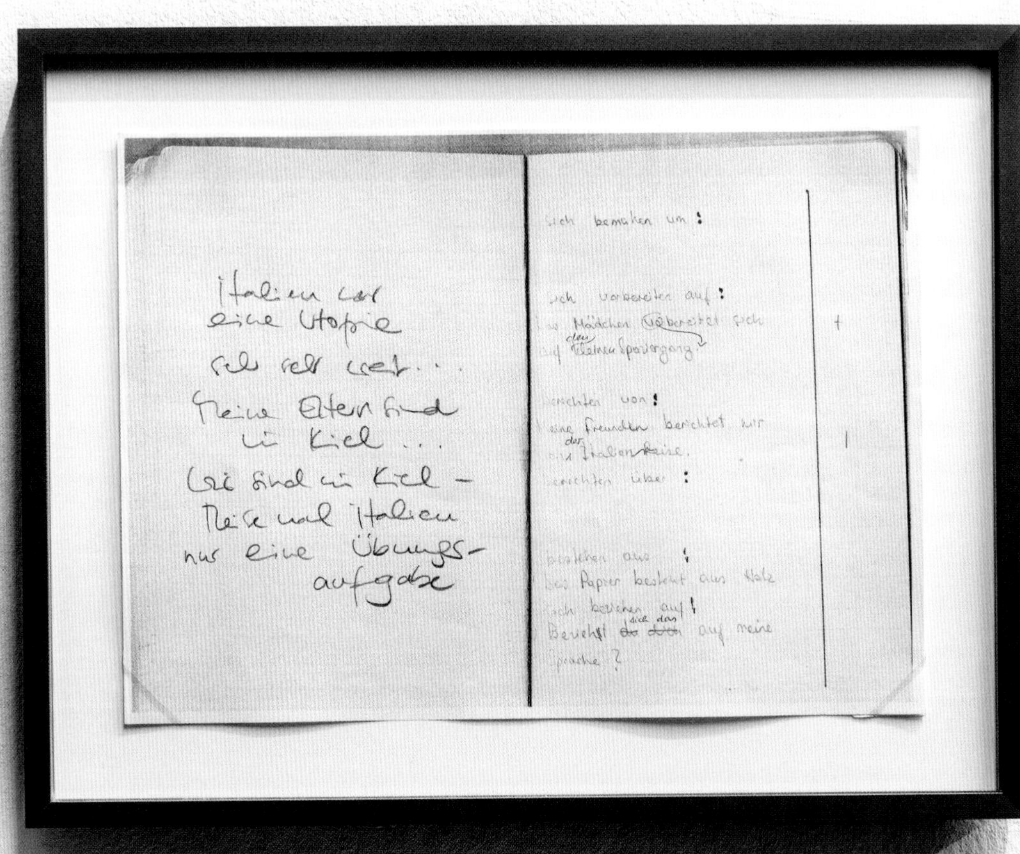

XIII

XIV

XV

XVI

XVII

XVIII

XIX

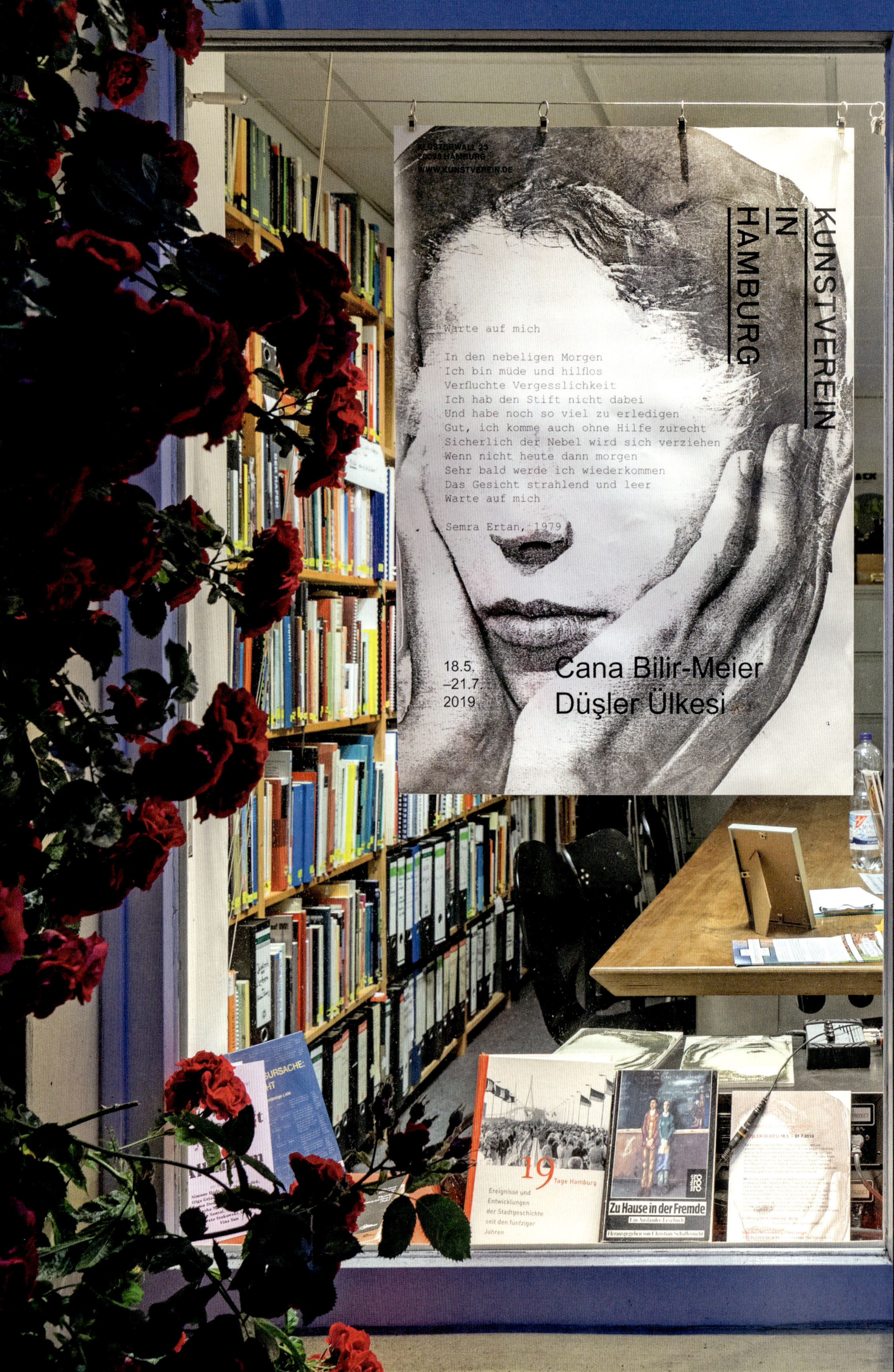
KLOSTERWALL 23
20095 HAMBURG
WWW.KUNSTVEREIN.DE

KUNSTVEREIN
IN
HAMBURG

Warte auf mich

In den nebeligen Morgen
Ich bin müde und hilflos
Verfluchte Vergesslichkeit
Ich hab den Stift nicht dabei
Und habe noch so viel zu erledigen
Gut, ich komme auch ohne Hilfe zurecht
Sicherlich der Nebel wird sich verziehen
Wenn nicht heute dann morgen
Sehr bald werde ich wiederkommen
Das Gesicht strahlend und leer
Warte auf mich

Semra Ertan, 1979

18.5.
–21.7.
2019

Cana Bilir-Meier
Düşler Ülkesi

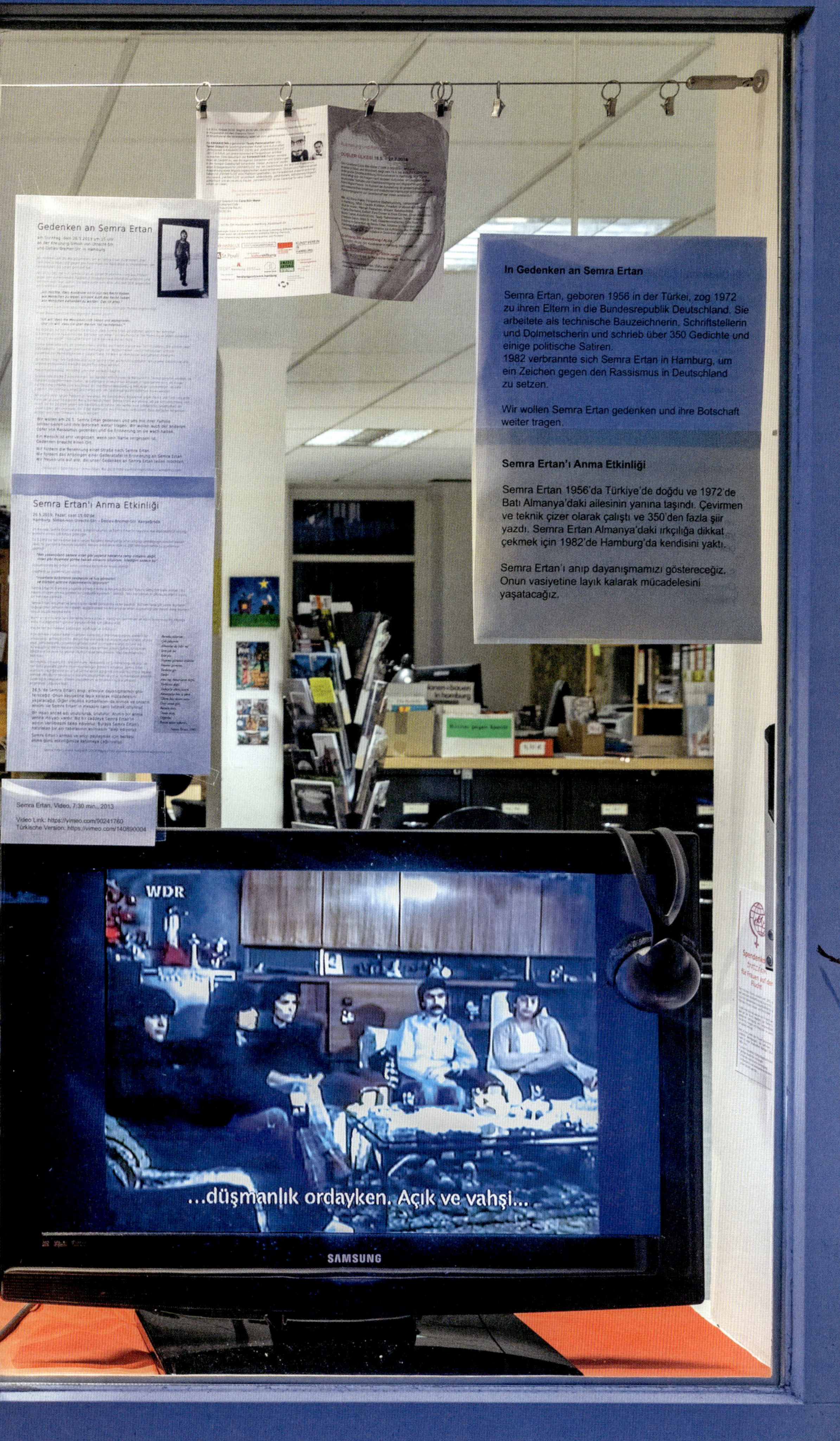
In Gedenken an Semra Ertan

Semra Ertan, geboren 1956 in der Türkei, zog 1972 zu ihren Eltern in die Bundesrepublik Deutschland. Sie arbeitete als technische Bauzeichnerin, Schriftstellerin und Dolmetscherin und schrieb über 350 Gedichte und einige politische Satiren.
1982 verbrannte sich Semra Ertan in Hamburg, um ein Zeichen gegen den Rassismus in Deutschland zu setzen.

Wir wollen Semra Ertan gedenken und ihre Botschaft weiter tragen.

Semra Ertan'ı Anma Etkinliği

Semra Ertan 1956'da Türkiye'de doğdu ve 1972'de Batı Almanya'daki ailesinin yanına taşındı. Çevirmen ve teknik çizer olarak çalıştı ve 350'den fazla şiir yazdı. Semra Ertan Almanya'daki ırkçılığa dikkat çekmek için 1982'de Hamburg'da kendisini yaktı.

Semra Ertan'ı anıp dayanışmamızı göstereceğiz. Onun vasiyetine layık kalarak mücadelesini yaşatacağız.

Gedenken an Semra Ertan

Semra Ertan'ı Anma Etkinliği

Semra Ertan, Video, 7:30 min., 2013
Video Link: https://vimeo.com/90241760
Türkische Version: https://vimeo.com/140590004

WDR

...düşmanlık ordayken. Açık ve vahşi...

SAMSUNG

CANA BILIR-MEIER

DÜŞLER ÜLKESİ

KUNSTVEREIN IN HAMBURG
SPECTOR BOOKS

Foreword

Bettina Steinbrügge

"Solidarity does not assume that our struggles are the same struggles, or that our pain is the same pain, or that our hope is for the same future. Solidarity involves commitment, and work, as well as the recognition that even if we do not have the same feelings, or the same lives, or the same bodies, we do live on common ground." (Sara Ahmed)

I am one of of the white majority of Germans, so writing a foreword here is, for me, somewhat complex, and I am extraordinarily grateful to Cana Bilir-Meier for making me aware of this complexity in its full extent. To be duly self-critical, I have to state that the German art world is, only too often, overly sure of itself in thinking it stands on the correct side when critical political questions are taken up, displayed and discussed, when matters global are brought onto our premises, when artist's positions which do not belong to those deriving from the white majority society, are given a platform. But is it really like that? How do they look, the teams, the ranks of decision-makers, the visitors, the members of societies of art and other institutions? Do they reflect the real structure of our society, or are those involved, who have a hand in the art institutions on one or other of all their levels or who visit them, not actually an expression of a white majority-society, which is, in fact, not permeable, but which does like to style itself the while as presenting, ostensibly liberally, the whole of society? But presenting is still a long way from consultation and creative input. And presenting is still a long way from being visible. Projects are quickly over, and the short moment of attention and catharsis fades away. You have supposedly contributed something to solving the problems of the world—or the ones on your doorstep. It is rare for any-thing more to happen afterwards, or the next problem is being presented. It seems you are moving in circles, endlessly affirming to yourself that you have, in fact, done something as it should be.

Cana Bilir-Meier's precisely researched and carefully choreographed artwork enriches our society with stories, which have seldom been told in a large public context. They are stories which do not just expand the conscious-ness of a majority-society but, through her telling of them, are particularly meant to provide a supporting impulse to the migrant community too. She makes visible what is not supposed to be visible or what people do not want to see, quite simply out of indifference and ignorance. Her artistic work concerns migrant Germany, which seems, even in the third or fourth generation, to have next to no chance of any visibility in this country. Every third citizen of Ham-burg has a migrant background. Statistically, that means ca. 630,000 people with roots abroad are living in the city. In a few years, the migrant share will already lie at somewhere over half the residents, as 50.4 percent of Hamburg's children already today have at least one parent, whose family does not hail from Germany. These days, much is being written about integration or about the reasons why an ostensible integration has not worked. In all this, what people are writing about is mostly an integration understood as a one-way street and as conforming to the majority-society in Germany. Cana Bilir-Meier makes it clear that this simplification does not work anymore and that being German cannot be grasped using the customary categories. Being German was always a construction, which comprehended much more than just your origins. Living and working in Germany means having rights and, at the same time, living out aspects of diverse cultures. The concept of nation-states, now back on the scene afresh, is a 19th century invention, and it is running up, time and again, against its limits. We find ourselves in the paradoxical situation of wanting to be a global player in business and tourism, while simultaneously, out of an indefinable anxiety over the challenges of the future, fostering forms of nationalism, closing borders and discrediting all things Other and seemingly foreign. And in all this, the construct of the "foreign" is always closely bound up with racism, something that marks the Other as alien and does, by its own lights, try to destroy it. We have been there once: it did not work. Let us hope we remember that in good time.

Cana Bilir-Meier has been able to develop an astonishing body of work in what she has created so far, and I am very pleased that, with this book, we can present her first monograph. Her artistic work finds expression through media such as film, drawing, performance or audio, and in it the artist takes private and public archives as her point of departure, in order to make visible the stories from (post)-migration realms of experience that have not yet been told. In her works, Bilir-Meier goes into questions about the social, cultural and emotional, as well as the structural, participation and equality of migrants and non-migrants. In her researches as an artist, she touches on sore spots in the society where she lives and on sore spots in the institutions where she exhibits. These sore spots are racism, colonialism, anti-Semitism, sexism and all of the further forms of discrimination, and we can never regard them as independent of each other, as they always appear across all sorts of categories. What she does is not always easy, but it is the right thing. One great strength of her work lies in her merging of the private with the public, thus producing an intensity not achievable were she to keep a purely intellectual and artistic distance. Her own family history provides the ground against which to observe society. The artist sets out from episodes from her own family circle and, as the grandchild of Turkish-Arab so-called "guest workers", progresses towards universal narratives and collective memories. In this process, revealing the layering of the material, the image and sound recordings, the letters, newspaper articles and documents, is centrally important. As she allots particular weightings and contexts to her materials, her own artistic language and perspective arises.

The present publication discusses aspects of social diversity, of participation, of historical erasures and of that knowledge situated among migrants.[1] She discusses what the political scientist, lyric poet and essayist, Max Czollek, has, for his own field, termed adjective literature. He describes how the assigning of adjectives generates a particular interpretative framework, which crucially pre-structures how people read and understand texts.[2] It "reiterates just those acts of exclusion opposed by feminist, Jewish, migrant, post-migrant or Afro-German critiques, when it emphasizes the particularity and non-identity of your own perspective, in order to forestall a dreaded 'cultural appropriation'"[3] (own translation). As he rightly says, it shows a colonialist and racist understanding of aesthetics and art, when we, in our consumption, simply use the categories, migrant, female, Jewish, and queer. The knowledge presumed about these topics, and the categorization following from it, also constrain our own latitude for possible action and for perception quite palpably. What is needed here are self-critical questions about when we are actually really open enough to listen and how we can avoid the social functionalization of artistic works.

In her text, the art historian, Burcu Dogramaci, investigates memory, realization and opposition in Cana Bilir-Meier's works, but also gives us a well-founded survey of how migrants' way of speaking in Germany has developed. She makes it clear that writing about immigration in Germany was for a long time a chronicle of victims or perpetrators. Cana Bilir-Meier's conversations with the anthropologist, Banu Karaca and the filmmaker, belit sağ are about the way migrants' experiences and knowledge can be converted into artistic means and forms of expression and how a new way of speaking can be possible beyond protest. How can change be brought about? How can other narratives be added to the dominant ones, or how can old narratives be written over? In doing this, they cast a critical eye on the art world and their own particular position right there. In his text, the exhibition's curator, Tobias Peper, talks about the genesis of the exhibition, *Düşler Ülkesi*, and about the vertigo occasioned by leaving your comfort zone, to be confronted by institutional criticism being realized and updated in the form of artistic work. The text of Ronya Othmann, the lyric poet nominated for the 2019 Ingeborg-Bachmann-Preis [a highly prestigious literary award in the

German-speaking countries], is a sounding-board for the speechlessness accompanying the migrant experience. She writes about the vulnerability and the perturbation when the migrant background comes to the fore so suddenly in such a way that whatever you have achieved fades into the background. And she talks about existing in a majority-society, which simply does not want to countenance the Other. In the course of the nomination, Cana Bilir-Meier filmed a portrait of the author and invited her to contribute the text of her application to this book. In a manner analogous to Bilir-Meier's own artistic praxis, this publication is, therefore, supplemented by a further story, which opens up new horizons of experience beyond her own artistic work too. As a mark of respect for her Yesidi heritage, Othmann's text was the only one translated into Kurdish, instead of into Turkish.

Cana Bilir-Meier is working on art, which is impressive not just for its content and form, but challenges us as well to recognize the instances of discrimination, like those of racism in our private lives, in politics, schools, workplaces, the business of art and culture, in sport and other areas, and to work for their elimination. She calls on us to watch what we are doing when we say things in private. She calls on us to take action publicly against "racial profiling", against arson attacks on refugee accommodation, setting up a hue and cry after people in Chemnitz, and against the authorities' failures to act, as, for example, with the murders by the NSU [National Socialist Underground, German neo-Nazi terrorist group], and to make our voices heard. How can we integrate diverse migrant knowledge into our institutions and reinforce it, and beyond that, extend the horizons of the white majority-society? All of this would be, if we were to follow it through to its ultimate consequences, not grace and favor, but it is the responsibility we owe to our diverse and truly rich society.

Cana Bilir-Meier has my deep gratitude for joining us in realizing this demanding project with her passion and dedication. Tobias Peper has shown great commitment and personal involvement in knowledgably translating the artist's clever integrative concept using the form of an exhibition, a publication and a comprehensive supporting program. To Zühal Bilir-Meier and all those involved in the anti-racist initiatives and institutions, who participated crucially in the program, I would like to offer my most sincere thanks: AG StoryWalks, Perspektive Stadterkundung [guided city walks in Hamburg], Lampedusa in Hamburg [refugee support group], NINA−fraueN IN Aktion [support group for refugee women], Freedom of Movement Dänemark, Ibrahim Arslan, Hannah Peaceman, Vincent Bababoutilabo, Chana Dischereit, EsRAP (Esra Özmen & Enes Özmen), Ozan Ata Canani, Booty Carrell, KANAKISTAN (Taudy Pathmanathan, Tamer Düzyol), Diaspora Salon, KZ-Gedenkstätte Neuengamme [Neuengamme concentration camp memorial centre], Queer-feministisches Café in der Roten Flora, Initiative in Gedenken an Semra Ertan, Initiative in Gedenken an Ramazan Avcı, the Initiative zur Aufklärung des Mordes an Süleyman Taşköprü and the Initiative in Gedenken an Yaya Jabb [civil initiatives to investigate or commemorate the deaths of the persons named]. I would like to thank the St. Pauli Archive for the wonderful window exhibition and the GWA St. Pauli for the intensive cooperation on the supporting program. And my thanks go to the graphic artist, Christian Lange for his precise rendering of Cana Bilir-Meier's work, as well as to all our authors for their excellent texts. My particular thanks also go to my colleagues, who have all contributed to the success of this far-from-typical project.

1
The concept of knowledge situated with migrants was principally developed in the context of the first Tribunal NSU-Komplex Auflösen in Cologne in 2017. It derives from Donna Haraway's idea of situated knowledge. "Knowledge situated with migrants means that those affected by racism – from the newly-arrived refugee to the migrant in the umpteenth generation – do know, based on the reality of their lives, what racism means, in what forms it manifests, what mechanisms are at work inside it, what institutions are suffused with it, and, above all, how you can run into the various forms of racism on an everyday basis, how they can be subverted and what anti-racist survival tactics have to be developed. In this way, migrants are not just witnesses of an injustice, about which sections of the majority-society can be outraged, but, much rather, experts, whose practices and analyses have to determine the actions behind anti-racist policies." See: https://www.nsu-tribunal.de/wir/. Accessed 06/30/2019.
2
Max Czollek, *Einige Anmerkungen zur Adjektivliteratur* [Some Remarks on Adjective Literature], in: *Literatur kann eine Rache sein. Einige Anmerkungen zur Adjektivliteratur* [Literature can be a Form of Revenge. Some Remarks on Adjective Literature] in: Max Czollek, Özlem Özgül Dündar, Sandra Gugić, Mehdi Moradpour und Ronya Othmann, *Es fängt hier nicht an, es hört hier nicht auf* [It does not start here, it does not finish here], Die Zeit, Hamburg 2018, online edition, https://www.zeit.de/kultur/literatur/2018-08/rassismus-literaturbetrieb-metwo-diskriminierung-autoren-integration/komplettansicht. Acessed 06/15/2019. (own translations)
3
Ibid.

Vorwort

Bettina Steinbrügge

"Solidarity does not assume that our struggles are the same struggles, or that our pain is the same pain, or that our hope is for the same future. Solidarity involves commitment, and work, as well as the recognition that even if we do not have the same feelings, or the same lives, or the same bodies, we do live on common ground." (Sara Ahmed)
Als Mitglied der weißen Mehrheitsdeutschen hier ein Vorwort zu schreiben, ist einigermaßen komplex und ich bin Cana Bilir-Meier außerordentlich dankbar, dass sie mir diese Komplexität in ihrer ganzen Bandbreite bewusst gemacht hat. Ich muss selbstkritisch feststellen, dass das deutsche Kunstfeld nur zu oft selbstgewiss meint, auf der richtigen Seite zu stehen, wenn kritische politische Fragen aufgegriffen, gezeigt und diskutiert werden, wenn das Globale in die Häuser geholt wird, wenn Positionen, die nicht zur

weißen Mehrheitsgesellschaft gehören, eine Plattform bekommen. Aber ist es wirklich so? Wie sehen sie aus, die Teams, die Entscheidungsebenen, die Besucher*innen, die Mitglieder von Kunstvereinen und anderen Institutionen? Spiegeln sie die reale Struktur unserer Gesellschaft wider oder sind die Akteur*innen, die die Kulturinstitutionen auf allen Ebenen bespielen oder besuchen, nicht doch ein Ausdruck einer weißen Mehrheitsgesellschaft, die eben nicht durchlässig ist, die sich aber doch dabei gefällt, vermeintlich liberal die ganze Gesellschaft darzustellen. Darstellung bedeutet aber noch lange nicht Mitsprache und Mitgestaltung. Und Darstellung bedeutet noch lange nicht Sichtbarkeit. Die Projekte gehen schnell vorbei und der kurze Moment von Aufmerksamkeit und Katharsis verlöscht. Vermeintlich hat man etwas dazu beigetragen, die Probleme der Welt oder die vor der Haustür zu lösen. Danach passiert selten mehr oder das nächste Problem wird dargestellt. Es scheint, als bewege man sich in Schleifen der ewigen Selbstvergewisserung, doch etwas richtig zu machen.

Cana Bilir-Meier bereichert mit ihrer präzise recherchierten und sorgfältig choreografierten künstlerischen Arbeit unsere Gesellschaft um Geschichten, die bisher selten in einer großen Öffentlichkeit erzählt worden sind. Es sind Geschichten, die nicht nur das Bewusstsein einer Mehrheitsgesellschaft erweitern, sondern durch ihr Erzählen insbesondere auch der migrantischen Community einem Moment der Stärkung geben sollen. Sie macht sichtbar, was nicht sichtbar sein soll oder was schlicht und ergreifend aus Desinteresse und Ignoranz nicht gesehen werden will. Es geht in ihrer künstlerischen Arbeit um das migrantische Deutschland, das selbst in dritter oder vierter Generation kaum eine Chance zu haben scheint, in Deutschland gesehen zu werden. Jede*r dritte Hamburger*in hat einen Migrationshintergrund. In Zahlen ausgedrückt heißt das, dass ca. 630.000 Menschen mit Wurzeln im Ausland in der Stadt leben. In einigen Jahren wird der Migrationsanteil bereits bei mehr als der Hälfte der Einwohner*innen liegen, denn schon heute haben 50,4 Prozent der Hamburger Kinder mindestens ein Elternteil, dessen Familie nicht aus Deutschland stammt. Es wird dieser Tage sehr viel über Integration geschrieben oder darüber, warum eine vermeintliche Integration nicht funktioniert hat. Meistens wird dabei über eine Integration geschrieben, die als Einbahnstraße und Anpassung an die Mehrheitsgesellschaft in Deutschland verstanden wird. Cana Bilir-Meier macht deutlich, dass diese Vereinfachung nicht mehr funktioniert und dass Deutschsein mit den herkömmlichen Kategorien nicht zu greifen ist. Deutschsein war immer schon eine Konstruktion, die viel mehr als nur die Herkunft beinhaltet. In Deutschland zu leben und zu arbeiten, bedeutet, Rechte zu haben und gleichzeitig auch Aspekte vielfältiger Kulturen zu leben. Das derzeit wieder neu in den Blickpunkt geratene Konzept der Nationalstaaten, eine Erfindung des 19. Jahrhunderts, kommt immer wieder an seine Grenzen. Wir befinden uns in der paradoxen Situation, wirtschaftlich und touristisch global agieren zu wollen, um gleichzeitig aus einer undefinierbaren Angst vor den Herausforderungen der Zukunft Nationalismen zu fördern, Grenzen zu schließen und alles Andere, scheinbar Fremde zu diskreditieren. Dabei ist das Konstrukt des „Fremden" immer eng mit Rassismus verknüpft, der das Andere als fremd markiert und in letzter Konsequenz zu vernichten sucht. Das hatten wir schon einmal, es hat nicht funktioniert. Hoffentlich erinnern wir uns rechtzeitig daran.

Cana Bilir-Meier hat in ihrem bisherigen Schaffen ein erstaunliches Werk entwickeln können und ich freue mich sehr, dass wir mit diesem Buch ihre erste Monografie vorlegen können. In ihrer künstlerischen Arbeit, die sich in Medien wie Film, Zeichnung, Performance oder Audio ausdrückt, nimmt die

Künstlerin private und öffentliche Archive zum Ausgangspunkt, um die nicht erzählten Geschichten (post-)migrantischer Erfahrungswelten sichtbar zu machen. Bilir-Meier untersucht in ihren Arbeiten Fragen nach sozialer, kultureller, emotionaler sowie struktureller Teilhabe und Gleichberechtigung von Migrant*innen und Nicht-Migrant*innen. Sie legt mit ihrer künstlerischen Forschung den Finger in die Wunden der Gesellschaft, in der sie lebt und in die Wunden der Institutionen, in denen sie ausstellt. Diese Wunden sind Rassismus, Kolonialismus, Antisemitismus, Sexismus und alle weiteren Formen der Diskriminierung, die niemals unabhängig voneinander zu betrachten sind, denn sie treten stets intersektional auf. Das ist nicht immer einfach, aber es ist richtig so. Eine große Stärke ihrer Arbeit besteht darin, dass das Private und das Öffentliche miteinander verwoben werden und so eine Intensität entsteht, die mit rein intellektueller, künstlerischer Distanz nicht zu erzielen wäre. Die eigene Familiengeschichte bietet die Folie, auf der Gesellschaft betrachtet wird. Ausgehend von Episoden aus ihrem eigenen familiären Umfeld nähert sich die Künstlerin als Enkelin türkischer-arabischer sog. „Gastarbeiter" universeller Narrative und kollektiver Erinnerungen an. Die Offenlegung des Prozesses der Materialsichtung der Bild- und Tonaufnahmen, Briefe, Zeitungsartikel und Dokumente ist dabei von zentraler Bedeutung. Durch die Gewichtung und Kontextualisierung der Materialien entsteht eine eigene künstlerische Sprache und Perspektive.

Die vorliegende Publikation diskutiert Aspekte von gesellschaftlicher Diversität, von Teilhabe, von historischen Ausblendungen und migrantisch situiertem Wissen[1]. Sie diskutiert das, was der Politikwissenschaftler, Lyriker und Essayist Max Czollek für sein Feld als Adjektivliteratur bezeichnet hat. Er beschreibt, wie die Zuweisung von Adjektiven einen bestimmten Interpretationsrahmen erzeugt, der das Lesen und Verstehen von Texten wesentlich vorstrukturiert.[2] Sie „wiederholt gerade jene Ausschlüsse, gegen die sich eine feministische, jüdische, migrantische, postmigrantische oder afrodeutsche Kritik ursprünglich zur Wehr setzte, als sie die Besonderheit und Nichtidentität der eigenen Perspektive betonte, um einer befürchteten ‚kulturellen Aneignung' zuvorzukommen."[3] Wie er richtig bemerkt, ist es ein kolonialistisches und rassistisches Verständnis von Ästhetik und Kunst, wenn wir migrantisch, weiblich, jüdisch, queer einfach beim Konsumieren einordnen. Das vermeintliche Wissen um diese Themen und die daraus folgende Kategorisierung schränkt auch den eigenen Möglichkeits- und Wahrnehmungsraum empfindlich ein. Was es hier braucht, ist die selbstkritische Befragung, wann wir eigentlich wirklich offen genug sind, um zuzuhören und wie wir der gesellschaftlichen Funktionalisierung künstlerischer Arbeiten entgehen können.

Die Kunsthistorikerin Burcu Dogramaci untersucht in ihrem Text Erinnerung, Vergegenwärtigung und Widerstand in den Arbeiten von Cana Bilir-Meier, gibt uns aber auch einen fundierten Überblick darüber, wie sich das migrantische Sprechen in Deutschland entwickelt hat. Sie macht deutlich, dass über Einwanderung in Deutschland lange Zeit als Geschichte der Opfer oder Täter* innen geschrieben wurde. Im Gespräch von Cana Bilir-Meier mit der Anthropologin Banu Karaca und der Filmemacherin belit sağ geht es darum, wie migrantische Erfahrungen und migrantisches Wissen in künstlerische Ausdrucksweisen und -formen übersetzt werden können und wie über den Protest hinaus ein neues Sprechen möglich wird. Wie kann Veränderung herbeigeführt werden? Wie können den herrschenden Narrativen neue, andere Narrative hinzugefügt oder wie können alte Narrative überschrieben werden? Sie werfen dabei auch einen kritischen Blick auf das Kunstfeld und ihre eigene besondere

Stellung in eben diesem. Der Kurator der Ausstellung, Tobias Peper, spricht in seinem Text über die Genese der Ausstellung *Düşler Ülkesi* und über die Fallhöhen, wenn man plötzlich die eigene Komfortzone verlässt und institutionelle Kritik in Form künstlerischer Arbeit aktualisiert vor einem steht. Der Text der Lyrikerin und für den Ingeborg-Bachmann-Preis 2019 nominierten Ronya Othmann gibt der Sprachlosigkeit Gehör, die mit der migrantischen Erfahrung einhergeht. Sie schreibt von der Verletzlichkeit und Verunsicherung, wenn der Migrationshintergrund plötzlich derart in den Vordergrund tritt, dass die eigentliche Leistung in den Hintergrund gerät. Und sie spricht von dem Dasein in einer vermeintlichen Mehrheitsgesellschaft, die das Andere einfach nicht zulassen möchte. Cana Bilir-Meier drehte im Zuge der Nominierung für den Bachmann-Preis ein Porträt über die Autorin und lud sie ein, ihren Bewerbungstext diesem Buch beizusteuern. Analog zu Bilir-Meiers eigener künstlerischen Praxis wird so auch diese Publikation um eine weitere Geschichte ergänzt, die einen neuen Erfahrungshorizont auch jenseits des eigenen künstlerischen Werks eröffnet. Aus Respekt vor ihrer ezidischen Herkunft wurde Othmanns Text als einziger ins Kurmandschi statt ins Türkische übersetzt.

Cana Bilir-Meier arbeitet an einem künstlerischen Werk, das nicht nur inhaltlich und formal eindrucksvoll ist, sondern das uns zudem auffordert, die Diskriminierungen wie Rassismen in unserem Privatleben, in Politik, Schule, Arbeitswelt, dem Kunst- und Kulturbetrieb, dem Sport etc. zu erkennen und an ihrer Beseitigung zu arbeiten. Sie fordert uns auf, im Privaten achtsam mit den eigenen Aussagen umzugehen. Sie fordert uns auf, im Öffentlichen gegen „Racial Profiling", gegen Brandanschläge auf Geflüchtetenunterkünfte, Menschenjagden in Chemnitz und Behördenversagen wie beispielsweise bei den Morden des NSU vorzugehen und die Stimme zu erheben. Wie können wir vielfältiges migrantisches Wissen in unseren Institutionen einbinden und stärken und darüber den Horizont der weißen Mehrheitsgesellschaft erweitern? Dieses wäre, würden wir es denn konsequent verfolgen, alles kein Gefallen, sondern es ist die Verantwortung, die wir unserer diversen und so reichen Gesellschaft gegenüber haben.

Mein großer Dank gilt Cana Bilir-Meier, die dieses anspruchsvolle Projekt mit Leidenschaft und Einsatz mit uns realisiert hat. Tobias Peper hat kenntnisreich das kluge integrative Konzept der Künstlerin in Form von Ausstellung, Publikation und umfangreichen Rahmenprogramm mit sehr viel Engagement und persönlichen Einsatz umgesetzt. Zühal Bilir-Meier und allen Beteiligten der anti-rassistischen Initiativen und Institutionen, die an dem Programm maßgeblich beteiligt waren, möchte ich sehr herzlich danken: AG StoryWalks, Perspektive Stadterkundung, Lampedusa in Hamburg, NINA – fraueN IN Aktion, Freedom of Movement Dänemark, Ibrahim Arslan, Hannah Peaceman, Vincent Bababoutilabo, Chana Dischereit, EsRAP (Esra Özmen & Enes Özmen), Ozan Ata Canani, Booty Carrell, KANAKISTAN (Taudy Pathmanathan, Tamer Düzyol), Diaspora Salon, KZ-Gedenkstätte Neuengamme, Queerfeministisches Café in der Roten Flora, Initiative in Gedenken an Semra Ertan, Initiative in Gedenken an Ramazan Avcı, der Initiative zur Aufklärung des Mordes an Süleyman Taşköprü und der Initiative in Gedenken an Yaya Jabbi. Dem St. Pauli Archiv danke ich für die wunderbare Schaufensterausstellung sowie der GWA St. Pauli für die intensive Mitarbeit am Rahmenprogramm. Ich danke dem Grafiker Christian Lange für die präzise grafische Umsetzung der Arbeit von Cana Bilir-Meier und allen Autor*innen für die hervorragenden Texte. Einen besonderen Dank möchte ich auch meinen Mitarbeiter*innen aussprechen, die mit großem Engagement zum Gelingen dieses außergewöhnlichen Projekts beigetragen haben.

1
Der Begriff des migrantisch situierten Wissens wurde
vornehmlich im Kontext des ersten Tribunal NSU-
Komplex Auflösen 2017 in Köln entwickelt. Er geht von
Donna Haraways Idee des situierten Wissens aus.
„Migrantisch situiertes Wissen bedeutet, dass diejenigen, die von Rassismus betroffen sind – vom gerade
angekommenen Flüchtling bis zu Migrant_innen der
x-ten Generation – aufgrund ihrer Lebensrealität Bescheid wissen, was Rassismus bedeutet, in welchen
Formen er auftritt, welche Mechanismen in ihm wirken,
welche Institutionen davon durchsetzt sind und vor
allem, wie man auf einer alltäglichen Ebene den unterschiedlichen Rassismen begegnet werden kann, wie
sie unterlaufen werden können und welche antirassis-
tischen Taktiken des Überlebens entwickelt werden
müssen. Migrant_innen sind damit nicht nur Zeugen
eines Unrechts, über das sich Teile der Mehrheitsgesellschaft empören können, sondern vielmehr
Expert_innen, deren Praktiken und Analysen hand-
lungsleitend sein müssten für antirassistische Politiken." Vgl. https://www.nsu-tribunal.de/wir/. Zugriff
30.6.2019.
2
Max Czollek, *Einige Anmerkungen zur Adjektivliteratur*, in: *Literatur kann eine Rache sein. Einige Anmerkungen zur Adjektivliteratur*, in: Max Czollek, Özlem
Özgül Dündar, Sandra Gugić, Mehdi Moradpour und
Ronya Othmann, *Es fängt hier nicht an, es hört hier
nicht auf*, Die Zeit, Hamburg 2018, Onlineausgabe,
https://www.zeit.de/kultur/literatur/2018-08/rassis-
mus-literatur-betrieb-metwo-diskriminierung-autoren-
integration/komplettansicht, Zugriff: 15.6.2019.
3
Ebd.

Önsöz

Bettina Steinbrügge

"Solidarity does not assume that our struggles are the same struggles, or that our pain is the same pain, or that our hope is for the same future. Solidarity involves commitment, and work, as well as the recognition that even if we do not have the same feelings, or the same lives, or the same bodies, we do live on common ground." (Sara Ahmed)

Beyaz Alman çoğunluk toplumunun üyesi olarak burada bir önsöz yazmak oldukça mudil ve Cana Bilir-Meier'e, bu mudil durumu bana tüm hatlarıyla izah ettiği için çok teşekkür ederim. Kritik siyasi sorular yöneltildiğinde, gündeme geldiğinde ve tartışıldığında, global olan evlerimize girdiğinde, beyaz çoğunluk toplumuna ait olmayan tavırlara platform verildiğinde, Alman sanat alanının kendinden çok fazla emin olarak güya doğru tarafta durduğu görüşünde olduğunu, özeleştirisel olarak saptamak zorundayım.

Ama bu gerçekten böyle mi? Sanat müzeleri (Kunstverein) ve diğer kurumların ekipleri, karar mercileri, ziyaretçileri ve üyeleri nasıllar? Toplumumuzun gerçek yapısını yansıtıyorlar mı? Kültür kurumlarının çeşitli katmanlarında faaliyet gösteren veya izleyici konumunda olanlar, geçirgen olmayan ama sözde liberal geçinerek tüm toplumu temsil etmekle övünen beyaz çoğunluk toplumunun bir ifadesi değil mi?

Temsiliyet, söz ve biçimlendirme hakkı tanımak, veya görünürlük sağlamaktan ibaret değil. Projeler süratle gerçekleşiyor ve kısacık dikkat ve katarsis anı siliniyor. Güya dünya sorunlarının ve ülkenizdeki sorunların çözümüne katkı sunmuş oluyorsunuz. Genelde bu katkının devamı gelmiyor veya bir sonraki sorun masaya yatırılıyor. Kendini doğru bir şey yapıyor olduğuna ikna etmek adına, bir sarmalın içinde dönüp duruyoruz.

Cana Bilir-Meier itinayla araştırılmış ve koreografisi titizlikle yapılmış sanatsal çalışmalarıyla, toplumumuzu, şimdiye kadar geniş kitlelere çok ender anlatılmış olan hikayelerle zenginleştiriyor. Bu anlatımlar sadece çoğunluk toplumunda bilinç yaratmak işlevi görmüyor, aynı zamanda özellikle göçmen toplumuna güç veriyor. Anlatımlar görünür olması istenmeyeni veya daha yalın ve basitçe söylemek gerekirse ilgisizlikten ve vurdumduymazlıktan göz yumulanı, görünür kılıyor. Cana Bilir-Meier'in sanatsal çalışmalarının ilgi odağı, üçüncü ve hatta dördüncü nesilde bile Almanya'da görünürlük şansı neredeyse yok denecek kadar az olan göçmenlerin Almanyası. Her üç Hamburgludan biri göçmen kökenli. Rakamlarla ifade edecek olursak, kentte yabancı kökenli 630 bin insan yaşıyor. Birkaç yıllık süre zarfında göçmen kökenlilerin oranı nüfusun yarısını teşkil edecek; çünkü bugün itibarıyla velilerinden en az birisinin Alman kökenli olmadığı Hamburglu çocukların oranı yüzde 50,4. Bu günlerde uyum veya sözde uyumun niye işlemediği üzerine çok yazılıp çiziliyor. Bunların çoğunda uyum tek yönlü olarak, Almanya'daki çoğunluk toplumuna uyum olarak tasvir ediliyor. Cana Bilir-Meier bu basite indirgemenin işlemeyeceğini ve Alman olmanın alışılagelmiş kategorilerle kavranamayacağını izah ediyor. Alman olmak, her zaman kökenden fazlasını barındıran bir yapı oldu. Almanya'da yaşamak ve çalışmak, hak sahibi olmak aynı zamanda çok çeşitli kültürleri de yaşamak anlamına geliyor. Zamanımızda tekrar gündeme gelen, 19. yüzyıl icadı ulus devlet konsepti, bir noktada sınırlarına dayanıyor. Bizler ticari ve turistik amaçlarla global olmak arzusundayız, fakat bir yandan da bilinemeyen bir geleceğin korkusuyla milliyetçi unsurları teşvik eden, sınırları kapatan ve yabancı gözüken her şeyi karalama eğiliminde olan paradoksal bir durum içindeyiz. Halbuki "yabancı" kurgusu hep, başka olanı yabancı olarak damgalayıp neticede yok etme arayışında olan ırkçılıkla bağlantılı. Bunu bir defa yaşadık, işe yaramadı. Umarım geç kalmadan hatırlarız.

Cana Bilir-Meier şimdiye kadarki çalışmalarında hayret verici eserler ortaya çıkardı. Bu kitap ile kendisinin ilk monografisini sunmaktan sevinç duyuyorum. Film, çizim, performans ve ses kaydı gibi iletişim araçları içeren sanat çalışmalarında, sanatçı anlatılmamış göç (sonrası) tecrübe dünyalarının hikayelerini görünür kılmak için, özel ve kamusal arşivleri çıkış noktası olarak kullanıyor. Bilir-Meier çalışmalarında göçmenlerin ve göçmen olmayanların sosyal, kültürel, duygusal ve yapısal katılımına ve eşitliğe ilişkin soruları irdeliyor. Sanatsal araştırmalarıyla yaşadığı toplumun ve sergilerini düzenlediği kurumların yaralarına parmak basıyor. Bu yaralar ırkçılık, sömürgecilik, antisemitizm, cinsiyetçilik ve her türlü ayrımcılık olarak ortaya çıktıkları için, katiyen birbirinden bağımsız ele alınmaması gerekiyor. Bunu yapabilmek her zaman kolay olmasa da, doğru olan bu. Bilir-Meier'in çalışmaları gücünü, özel ve kamusal olanı adeta iç içe dokumasından ve bu şekilde sadece entelektüel ve sanatsal bir mesafeyle kurulamayacak bir yoğunluk yaratmasından alıyor. Kendi aile hikayesi, topluma bakışın zeminini oluşturuyor. "Gastarbeiter" diye tanımlanan Türk-Arap kökenli kişilerin torunu olan sanatçı, evrensel hikayelere ve kolektif anılara kendi ailesinden kesitlerle yaklaşıyor. Resimler, ses kayıtları, mektuplar, gazete küpürleri ve belgeler gibi malzemelerin tarama sürecinin şeffaf olması, çalışmalarında önem taşıyor. Kullanılan malzemeleri değerlendirip bağlamına oturtarak, kendine özgü bir sanat dili ve bakış açısı ortaya çıkarıyor.

Elinizdeki bu kitap, toplumsal çeşitliliğin, katılımın ve tarihsel karartmaların öğeleri ile göç kaynaklı bilgiyi ele alıyor.[1] Kitap, siyasal bilimci, şair ve deneme yazarı Max Czollek'in kendi alanı için 'sıfat edebiyatı' olarak adlandırdığı şeyi tartışmaya açıyor. Czollek sıfatlandırmanın, somut bir yorum çerçevesi yaratarak, metinlerin okunması ve anlamlandırılmasına nasıl etki ettiğini açıklıyor.[2] Sıfatlandırma "feminist, Yahudi, göç ve göç sonrası veya Afro-Alman eleştirinin kendi bakış açısını, özelliğini ve kimliksizliğini vurgulayarak önlemeye çalıştığı korkulan 'kültürel sahiplenmeyle' temelde mücadele ettiği dışlamaları adeta tekrar ediyor."[3] Czollek'in saptamasına göre, kadını, Yahudiyi, queer'i tüketimde olduğu gibi sıfatlandırırsak, bu ırkçı ve sömürgeci bir estetik ve sanat anlayışı olur. Bu konunun ve ortaya çıkan sınıflandırmanın güya farkında olmak, kişinin kendi imkan ve algı alanını da önemli ölçüde daraltıyor. Burada ihtiyaç duyulan, ne zaman dinlemeye açık olduğumuz ve sanatsal çalışmaları toplumsala alet edilmekten nasıl koruyabileceğimiz sorusunu özeleştirel şekilde kendimize yöneltmemizdir.

Sanat tarihçisi Burcu Doğramacı yazısında, Cana Bilir-Meier'in çalışmalarında anıyı, göz önüne getirmeyi ve direnişi inceleyerek, Almanya'da göçmen ifade şekillerinin nasıl geliştiği konusunda genel bir bakış sunuyor. Doğramacı Almanya'daki göç tarihinin uzun süre kurbanlar ve suçlular üzerinden yazıldığını belirtiyor. Cana Bilir-Meier'in antropolog Banu Karaca ve film yapımcısı belit sağ ile yaptığı sohbetin konusu, göç tecrübesinin ve göç kaynaklı bilginin nasıl sanatsal ifade şekillerine dönüştürülebileceği ve yalın protestodan öte yeni bir ifade imkanının nasıl mümkün olabileceği. Değişim nasıl gerçekleştirilebilir? Hakim anlatımlara nasıl yeni ve başka anlatımlar eklenebilir. Eski anlatımlar nasıl yenilenir? Bu sohbet sırasında Karaca, sağ ve Bilir-Meier, sanat alanına eleştirel bir yaklaşımla kendi özel konumlarını da irdeliyorlar. Serginin küratörü Tobias Peper ise yazısında *Düşler Ülkesi* sergisinin oluşumu ve insanın aniden kendi konfor bölgesini terk edip, kurumsal eleştirinin sanatsal çalışma şeklinde, güncellenmiş haliyle karşı karşıya kalındığında yaşanan yüksekten düşme hissinden bahsediyor. Ingeborg Bachmann 2019 Ödülü adaylarından şair Ronya Othmann'ın yazısı göç tecrübesiyle bağlantılı olan dilsizliğe kulak veriyor. Othmann yazısında, göçmen kökenin bu denli ön plana çıkarılarak, asıl edinimlerin arka planda kalmasından kaynaklanan kırılganlık ve tedirginlik üzerinde duruyor. Ve Othmann başkalarının varoluşuna izin vermek istemeyen sözde çoğunluk toplumunun mevcudiyeti üzerine yazıyor. Cana Bilir-Meier, Bachmann Ödülüne adaylığı çerçevesinde yazarın portresini çizen bir film üzerinde çalışırken, kendisini ödül başvurusunda bulunduğu yazıyı bu kitaba katkı olarak vermeye davet etti. Böylece Cana Bilir-Meier'in sanat pratiğinin izinde, bu kitaba kendi sanatsal çalışmalarının dışında yeni bir deneyim ufku açan bir diğer hikaye daha eklenmiş oldu. Yezidi kökenine saygıdan ötürü bir tek Othmann'ın yazısı Türkçe yerine Kurmanciye çevrildi.

Cana Bilir-Meier'in üzerinde çalıştığı sanat eserleri sadece içerikleriyle ve şekilleriyle çok etkileyici olmakla kalmıyor, bizleri özel hayatımızda, siyasette, okulda, iş dünyasında, kültür-sanatta, sporda ve benzer alanlarda ırkçılık gibi ayrımcılık örneklerini teşhis etmeye ve ortadan kaldırılması için mücadeleye davet ediyor. Kendisi bizleri özel hayatımızdaki söylemlerimizde dikkatli olmaya çağırıyor. Kamusal alanda ırksal profillemeye (racial profiling), mülteci barınaklarına yapılan kundaklamalara, Chemnitz'deki insan avına ve örneğin NSU cinayetlerinde olduğu gibi devlet dairelerinin basiretsizliğine karşı tavır koymaya ve sesimizi yükseltmeye çağırıyor. Bizler kurumlarımıza göç kaynaklı bilgiyi nasıl dahil edip güçlendirebiliriz? Bunun ötesinde beyaz çoğunluk toplumunun ufkunu nasıl genişletebiliriz? Tüm bunlar, ısrarla yaparsak bir lütuf değil, çok çeşitli ve bir o kadar zengin toplumumuza karşı taşıdığımız bir sorumluluktur. Bu zor projeyi tutku ve büyük bir çabayla bizimle gerçekleştirdiği için Cana Bilir-Meier'e çok teşekkür ediyorum. Tobias Peper, bilgisiyle sanatçının akıllı ve kapsayıcı konseptini sergi, yayın ve geniş çerçeveli bir programla, büyük angajman ve kişisel çabayla hayata geçirdi. Zühal Bilir-Meier ve programa önemli katkı sunan ırkçılık karşıtı inisiyatiflerden ve kurumlardan katılımcılara candan teşekkürlerimi sunmak istiyorum: AG StoryWalks, Perspektive Stadterkundung, Hamburg'da Lampedusa, NINA–fraueN IN Aktion, Freedom of Movement Dänemark, İbrahim Arslan, Hannah Peaceman, Vincent Bababoutilabo, Chana Dischereit, EsRAP (Esra Özmen & Enes Özmen), Ozan Ata Canani, Booty Carrell, KANAKISTAN (Taudy Pathmanathan, Tamer Düzyol), Diaspora Salon, Neuengamme Toplama Kampı Anma Yeri, Rote Flora'daki queer-feminist kafeterya, Semra Ertan'ı Anma İnisiyatifi, Ramazan Avcı İnisiyatifi, Süleyman Taşköprü Cinayetini Aydınlatma İnisiyatifi, ve Yaya Jabbi'yi Anma İnisiyatifi. St. Pauli Arşivine harikulade vitrin sergisi ve GWA St. Pauli'ye programa yoğun iştiraki için çok teşekkür ederim. Grafiker Christian Lange'a, Cana Bilir-Meier'in çalışmalarının titiz grafik uygulaması için ve tüm yazarlara mükemmel yazıları için teşekkür ederim. Büyük emeklerle bu olağanüstü projenin gerçekleşmesine katkı sunan çalışma arkadaşlarıma da özellikle teşekkürlerimi sunarım.

52

1
Göç kaynaklı bilgi tanımlaması özellikle 2017'de Köln'deki NSU Yapısı Çözülsün Tribunal'inde geliştirildi. Tanımlama Donna Haraway'in kaynak bilgisi fikrine dayanıyor. "Göç kaynaklı bilgi, ırkçılık mağduru olan, yani yeni gelen mülteciden, x nesilden göçmene kadar, yaşam gerçekleri itibarıyla ırkçılığın ne olduğunu, hangi şekillerde kendini gösterdiğini, hangi mekanikler içinde etkili olduğunu, hangi kurumlarda yaygın olduğunu ve özellikle günlük rutinde farklı ırkçı unsurlarla nasıl mücadele edileceğini, nasıl etkisiz kılınabileneceğini ve ırkçılığa karşı hangi hayatta kalma taktiklerinin geliştirilmesi gerektiğini bildikleri anlamına geliyor. Böylece göçmenler çoğunluk toplumunun bazı kesimlerinde tepki uyandıran bir haksızlığın sadece bir şahitleri değil, bilakis onlar uygulamalarıyla ve analizleriyle ırkçılık karşıtı politikalar için yönlendirici olması gereken uzmanlardır." Bkz. https://www.nsu-tribunal.de/wir/. Erişim: 30.6.2019.

2
Max Czollek, *Einige Anmerkungen zur Adjektivliteratur (Sıfat edebiyatına ilişkin notlar), Literatur kann eine Rache sein (Edebiyat intikam olablir)* de. *Einige Anmerkungen zur Adjektivliteratur (Sıfat edebiyatı hakkında birkaç not):* Max Czollek, Özlem Özgül Dündar, Sandra Gugić, Mehdi Moradpour ve Ronya Othmann, *Es fängt hier nicht an, es hört hier nicht auf,* (Burada başlamıyor, burada bitmiyor) da, Die Zeit, Hamburg 2018, Online yayınında, https://www.zeit.de/kultur/literatur/2018-08/rassismus-literaturbetrieb-metwo-diskriminierung-autoren-integration/komplettansicht, Erişim: 15.6.2019.

3
Aynı yerde

This makes me want to put numbers in alphabetical order

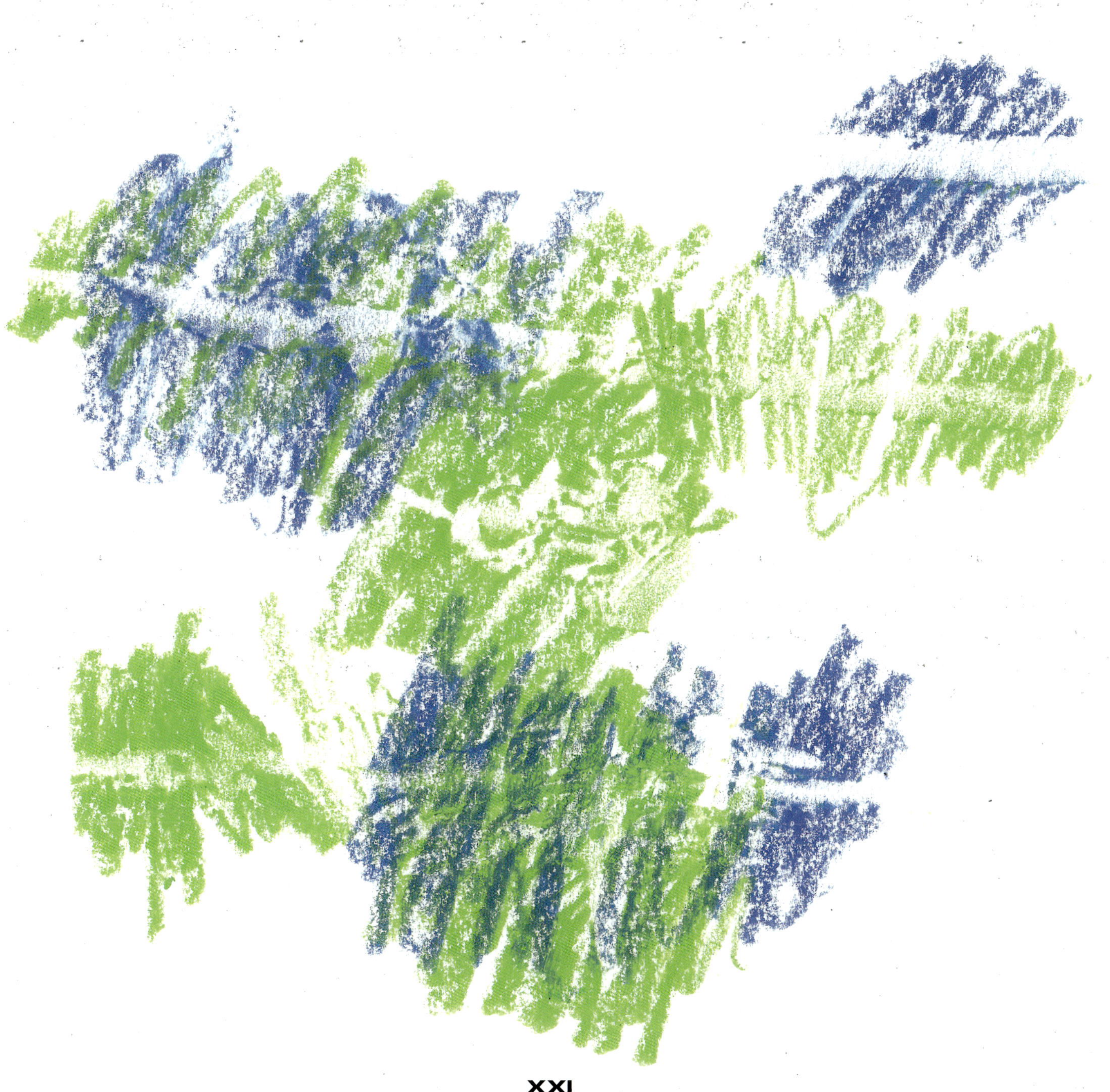

On Seeking—and Partially Finding—
the Right Tone

A Report on Experience

Tobias Peper

Ideally, an exhibition does not just display works in the most inviting way possible but it equally communicates the context in which they came about. It allows visitors to share the artists' thinking, so that a dialogue can develop. An exhibition should not ever give the impression of taking over the works presented, but, on the contrary, there should arise a feeling that the artworks are setting the tone and ordaining the place where they are brought together. An exhibition should be more for its audience than a space with pictures and other objects. In the best case, it should share realms of experience and thoughts and ideas, present them for discussion and offer the possibility of engaging with something novel and shifting your thinking into new territory. In this way, exhibitions can make an important contribution to mutual understanding, to solidarity and acceptance—the basic principles of our democratic co-existence. This concept of what I do has gone with me in my curatorial work for a long time now and has consistently served to confirm, for me, that I do contribute something worthwhile to a social discussion about how we want to live together and treat each other.

Working with Cana Bilir-Meier has made a hash of this self-confidence pretty smartly, because there is one decisive snag in whole business. For the greater part of their existence, art institutions, meaning, alongside exhibition spaces and museums, universities and art schools too, have promoted a very one-sided, majority-society view of art history, namely one shaped predominantly by the West and scarcely compatible with the demands of a post-migration, equitable and enlightened society.[1] That actually is a fact I have been aware of subconsciously for a while now, but what it, in fact, means—and what effects it can have—only became clear to me after many conversations and debates with Bilir-Meier. As part of an institution and a professional field, that is, by definition, a winner-takes-all market and basically operates according to a logic of exclusion, it is not easy, when you belong to them yourself, to understand and acknowledge how powerfully, and brutally too, these hierarchical structures do function. Especially amid such intensive collaboration, as often happens between curators and artists, the additional difficulty does arise that it is just about impossible to discuss matters objectively and without emotions. It is not easy to find the right tone for dealing with each other, because there is, on the one side, the justifiable anger and accusing finger from those who are repeatedly excluded and discriminated against. On the other side, there are those who do, in fact, essentially acknowledge the existence of structural problems but are, however, often not at all disposed to see the dirt on their own doorstep. You do really mean well, want to change things, and actually do belong to the enlightened spirits. However, the insight that meaning well and making good do not automatically go hand in hand is something you perhaps only arrive at when you have discrimination pointed out to you directly by those it affects.[2] As these debates always also involve having your own lack of knowledge and incompetence set out before you and accepting that; for a start, it is something, as well, that you, as an art institution, have to work through, put up with and acknowledge. That's because we are all too inclined to see ourselves in the guise of the front line standing up for plurality in society. The field of art is, however, not immune to racism, sexism, homo- and transphobia, class consciousness, anti-Semitism and other forms of discrimination, which restrict participation and shore up hierarchies.

Cana Bilir-Meier's exhibition, *Düşler Ülkesi*, is the first time an artist with German-Turkish roots has had a solo exhibition devoted to her by the Kunstverein in Hamburg, so that, in this sense, the preparations for it were also an exploratory coming-together from both sides. We were both constantly impelled by the question of the right tone for the project. We first met in Hamburg in 2018. It was not the typical first visit for getting to know the spaces in the Kunstverein and discussing the early ideas for the possible design of an exhibition. In actual fact, the actual exhibition had been in the background for quite a while. It was much rather that, first of all, slowly getting to know Hamburg and becoming familiar with it that occupied the foreground in our meetings.

Researching into places and their stories is anchored firmly in Bilir-Meier's artistic praxis. Most of her works originate in the viewing of private and public archives. In doing that, Bilir-Meier is particularly interested in (his)stories of migrant life-worlds, which remained untold or overlooked, yet had, in fact, come to belong to the collective memory of a marginalised community, even though they took up very little to no space in the perception of a large part of the majority-society. To that extent, it was no more than logical that the preparation of her first large solo exhibition in Hamburg should begin, first off, with intensively researching the city. The collective power of the stories we followed up doing this was often able to build bridges that allowed us to set up contacts to the most diverse range of protagonists in Hamburg.

At the centre of all this were, above all, the people, the initiatives and institutions committed to remembering the victims of right-wing violence and to the fight against racism. It was crucial for the artist to learn all the mostly ignored or unacknowledged stories of racist assaults, of their victims and of the people promoting remembrance. As she does in her artistic work, so most of the activists are, in their own way, concerned to supplement and examine the dominant account with stories, which are seldom heard, or respectively, not often willingly. Be it the initiative for clarifying the murder of Süleyman Taşköprü[3], the Hamburg victim of the so-called NSU; the initiative in remembrance of Yaya Jabbi[4], who was arrested in Hamburger Berg possessing 1.65 grammes of cannabis and four days later died in his cell under circumstances never fully explained; be it the workers of the St. Pauli Archive e.V.[5], which has committed itself to maintaining an official and unofficial history of the district, or those involved with the GWA St. Pauli[6], which is devoted to community, culture and social work in the district and many others—they could report on a large number of cases of exclusion, discrimination and ignorance, both past and present. For me, as someone living in Hamburg, most of these cases were new and surprising. For the artist herself, these stories were, in fact, mostly new too, but less surprising, given that it is always the same mechanisms and structures of power at work and leading to racism. It all-too-often involves also preserving those privileges a majority possesses while seeing itself here threatened by a minority—as paradoxical as this might sound.

The question quickly arises as to how an art institution can, on the one hand, reflect such experiences and—more importantly—how an audience, which also shares these, can actually be reached by an exhibition. That is because a decisive aspect of Bilir-Meier's works lies in also giving her own community a form of empowerment by giving mostly unheard stories a platform. Typically, members of this community are, however, not the classical visitors to art exhibitions, something that is, not least, also caused by the art institutions themselves, along with their histories. To that extent, we did soon agree that we wanted to design a comprehensive program as a framework activating and catering to places in Hamburg where we could also reach this audience.

Misunderstandings and moments of mistrust were repeatedly arising too, because, in their lives, people affected by racist violence and discrimination have too frequently experienced how well-meaning people would rather speak for them or about them, instead of with them—or even allowing them their own words. One extreme and defining example for this could well be the Taşköprü family. It is not just that the investigations after the murder in summer 2001 concentrated initially on the victim's surroundings, and a racist motive for the act was considered only after the so-called NSU revealed itself in 2011, but the present memorial in the Schützenstraße also makes it clear that nobody wanted to listen. There is an "official" memorial stone there, which

59

also mentions the other victims of the NSU, and there is a star let into the ground with a portrait of the murdered man, reminiscent of the Hollywood Walk of Fame in Los Angeles. The family and additional supporters fought for this latter and financed it privately, to fulfil a great dream posthumously for Süleyman Taşköprü and to create a personal memorial. It is not the exception but unfortunately still the rule that relatives are ignored when the question arises about a suitable setting for a memorial. That is why the right to a suitable setting also heads the demands of the Tribunal Unraveling the NSU-Complex, which first sat in the Schauspiel Köln [civic theatre in Cologne].[7] Not being listened to, being excluded and patronised is part of a collective experience in the migrant community, which has been continuously subject to racism in Germany for decades. That is unfortunately (still) not common knowledge, but can only be experienced if we, as those not affected, seek conversations and have, above all, the intention of listening and accepting things out of our interlocutor's experience that may be unpleasant for us. This insight is also an important piece of experience from working with Cana Bilir-Meier and has to be a basic condition for all institutions prepared to open themselves up and expand their perspectives.

Consequently, we also designed the exhibition's accompanying program taking great care not to talk for or about anything or anyone in any of our events. Instead, the members of the migrant community themselves spoke up in many different ways. Among other things, there were guided walks through city districts, where victims of racial violence were remembered at the respective scenes of it, and relatives or members of the corresponding initiatives told their stories; in the St. Pauli Archive, Cana Bilir-Meier presented a window exhibition in remembrance of Semra Ertan not far from the spot where she set fire to herself; the communal centre, Kölibri, was the setting for an entire series of events: the EsRap Duo presented their mixture of Viennese rap and arabesques, with which they assertively, and with great humour, reflect on their own identity as Turkish Austrians; Ata Canani and Booty Carrell used live music and records to tell about the music production from so-called guest- workers, and the KANAKISTAN Collective, together with actors from the Diaspora Salon, put on a reading from the poetry collection, *Haymatlos*[8], for which poets contributed lyric poetry about experiences of racism, migration and family stories, or also about the yearning for "normality". One not inconsiderable point in the program was that, with few exceptions, the setting was not the Kunstverein in Hamburg; instead we explicitly wanted to leave the institution, and with that the privileges and codes of the art environment. On the one hand, it was a matter of, in fact, reaching an audience, for which the Kunstverein is a strange, and perhaps alienating place too. On the other, it was also the explicit attempt to bring the Kunstverein's audience to previously unknown places in the city, beyond the established discourse on art and a bourgeois middle ground.

The former intention functioned noticeably better than the latter. The opening of Cana Bilir-Meier's exhibition at the Kunstverein already stood out by the presence of an audience that had actually never been there before and had, in the history of the institution, never been so explicitly addressed. The months of preparation, with many conversations and meetings with the protagonists from the various communities and, not least, with the artist herself were all decisive factors in this small success. Cana Bilir-Meier's efforts, in particular, to build bridges not just between the institution and the community, but especially between the various initiatives and actors, who mostly work independently of one another, resulted in an opening that was so distinctly diverse, something you otherwise get to experience in the art business only rarely. And the subsequent events in the Kunstverein and elsewhere also stood out for their high visitor-numbers and the great diversity among the participants. By contrast, participation in the events by the Kunstverein's regular audience was as good as non-existent. Initially, that was palpably more frustrating for me than for the artist herself. I was disappointed and read the lack of interest in the program as a sign that the Kunstverein, as an institution, is perhaps not, after all, a place of diversity, many voices and, above all, curiosity. However, the question very quickly arose as to what you could expect from an audience, which has been used for decades to simply encountering, time and again, its own filtering bubble's comfort zone provided in the Kunstverein. Of course, a structurally established and customary way of thinking and behaving cannot be opened up with one single wrench. My own thinking would be different too, had it not been for the intensive year of working together with Cana Bilir-Meier.

Out of this experience, it is perhaps possible to discern a future path, to the effect that it requires, particularly on the part of the institution, still greater efforts, perseverance and, above all, a lasting awareness that you have to acknowledge your own exclusionary viewpoint time and time again and to do something about it. On the one hand, with a view to continually inviting your own audience to open up its perspectives, to interrogate what it thinks it knows and to learn more. On the other, however, with a view also to preserving the links, once established, to those people, the realities of whose lives have scarcely played any role in the institution so far. Perhaps the construct of a Kunstverein is just the right place for doing this work in society. In line with the history of their foundation in the 19th century, Kunstvereine do, on the one hand, stand for the wish of an ambitious middle-class for a distinct identity, but equally for support of the involvement in democratic ideas and processes at the same time too and for the intention of interrogating petrified hierarchies and old privileges, something that today shows up in the various structures of the societies and in their programs. In the same way that Kunstvereine were an important factor in founding the identity of a middle-class two hundred years ago, so they are still capable of making a contribution today. Yet what is important is that we, as representatives of a majority-society, acknowledge that the definition of who is a citizen in this country is constantly expanding. The Tribunal Unraveling the NSU Complex lodged a claim for the principle of an "open society of the many and arising from migration"[9] (own translation) in 2017. Since then, this concept has enjoyed a triumphal progress, particularly in left wing discussions. At the end of 2018, regional, common-interest associations of institutions of art and culture established themselves all over Germany under the name, DIE VIELEN [THE MANY]. Along with solidarity against extreme right-wing hostilities, they were also concerned to explicitly interrogate their own structures.[10] In the protected area of art, a unique opportunity probably exists to not only propagate something like a society of the many, but also to fill it with life, if there is the will to open up your own institutions, their programs and their structures to previously marginalised stories and protagonists. To this end, an exhibition can only be a start. However, sometimes an exhibition can, in fact, actually promote a new way of thinking, if all of those involved, repeatedly and with due care, ask themselves the question about the right tone—and countenance it from others.

1
According to the micro-census of the Statistisches Bundesamts [the Federal Office of Statistics] in 2017, just on a quarter of the entire population of Germany has, for example, a migratory background. See: https://www.bpb.de/nachschlagen/zahlen-und-fakten/soziale-situation-in-deutschland/61646/migrations-hintergrund-i. Accessed 5/10/2019

2
See also: https://www.kubi-online.de/artikel/kultur-institutionen-ohne-grenzen-annaeherung-einen-diskriminierungskritischen-kulturbereich. Accessed 7/1/2019.

3
https://www.aufklaerung-tatort-schuetzenstrasse.org/. Accessed 5/2/2019.

4
https://rememberjajadiabi.blackblogs.org/about-jaja-diabi/. Accessed 5/2/2019.

5
http://www.st-pauli-archiv.de/. Accessed 5/2/2019.

6
http://www.gwa-stpauli.de/startseite.html. Accessed 5/2/2019.

7
See: http://www.nsu-tribunal.de/nsu-komplex/#news-modal. Accessed 5/9/2019.

8
Tamer Düzyol, Taudy Pathmanathan (eds.): *Haymatlos. Gedichte*, edition assemblage, Münster 2018.

9
See: http://www.nsu-tribunal.de. Accessed 5/5/2019.

10
See: https://www.dievielen.de/erklaerungen. Accessed 5/4/2019.

Vom Suchen und teilweisen Finden des richtigen Tons

Ein Erfahrungsbericht

Tobias Peper

Eine Ausstellung zeigt idealerweise nicht nur Kunstwerke auf möglichst ansprechende Weise, sondern vermittelt ebenso den Zusammenhang, in dem sie entstanden sind. Sie lässt die Besucher*innen am Denken der Künstler*innen teilnehmen, sodass ein Dialog entstehen kann. Eine Ausstellung sollte niemals den Eindruck erwecken, sich die präsentierten Arbeiten angeeignet zu haben, sondern im Gegenteil sollte das Gefühl entstehen, dass die Kunstwerke den Ton angeben und den Ort bestimmen, an dem sie versammelt sind. Eine Ausstellung sollte für das Publikum mehr als ein Raum mit Bildern und Objekten sein. Sie sollte im besten Falle Erfahrungswelten, Gedanken und Ideen teilen und zur Diskussion stellen und die Möglichkeit geben, sich auf Neues einlassen und Denkräume betreten zu können. Auf diese Weise könnten Ausstellungen einen wichtigen Beitrag zum gegenseitigen Verständnis, zu Solidarität und Akzeptanz beitragen – Grundprinzipien unseres demokratischen Miteinanders. Dieses Selbstverständnis begleitet mich in meiner kuratorischen Arbeit schon länger und diente mir stets als Vergewisserung, etwas Wertvolles zu einer gesellschaftlichen Diskussion darüber beizutragen, wie wir miteinander leben und umgehen wollen.

Die Zusammenarbeit mit Cana Bilir-Meier hat diese Selbstsicherheit ordentlich durcheinandergeworfen, denn die Sache hat einen entscheidenden Haken. Kunstinstitutionen, damit sind neben Ausstellungsräumen und Museen auch Universitäten und Kunsthochschulen gemeint, haben die längste Zeit ihres Bestehens einen sehr einseitigen, nämlich vorwiegend westlich geprägten, mehrheitsgesellschaftlichen Blick auf die Kunstgeschichte gefördert, der mit den Ansprüchen einer post-migrantischen, gleichberechtigten und aufgeklärten Gesellschaft kaum vereinbar ist.[1] Das ist zwar eine Tatsache, derer ich mir schon länger unterschwellig bewusst war, aber was sie eigentlich tatsächlich bedeutet und welche Auswirkungen sie haben kann, wurde mir erst in vielen Gesprächen und Auseinandersetzungen mit Bilir-Meier klar. Es ist nicht einfach als Teil einer Institution und eines Berufsfeldes, das per Definition als Winner-take-all market grundsätzlich nach einer ausschließenden Logik operiert, zu verstehen und anzuerkennen, wie mächtig und auch brutal diese hierarchischen Strukturen wirken, wenn man selbst zu ihnen gehört. Insbesondere in einer so intensiven Zusammenarbeit, wie sie oft zwischen Kurator*innen und Künstler*innen stattfindet, kommt erschwerend hinzu, dass es beinahe unmöglich ist, ausschließlich sachlich und ohne Emotionen zu diskutieren. Es ist nicht einfach, den richtigen Ton im Umgang miteinander zu finden, denn auf der einen Seite stehen die berechtigte Wut und Anklage derjenigen, die immer wieder ausgeschlossen und diskriminiert werden. Auf der anderen Seite stehen diejenigen, die das Vorhandensein struktureller Probleme zwar grundsätzlich anerkennen, den Dreck aber eben oft nicht gerne vor der eigenen Haustür sehen wollen. Man meint es doch gut, man will doch Dinge ändern, man gehört doch zu den Aufgeklärten. Dass gut meinen und gut machen aber nicht automatisch Hand in Hand gehen, ist eine Erkenntnis, zu der man vielleicht erst wirklich kommen kann, wenn man direkt durch Betroffene von Diskriminierung darauf hingewiesen wird.[2]

Da es bei dieser Auseinandersetzung immer auch darum geht, die eigenen Wissenslücken und Inkompetenzen aufgezeigt zu bekommen und anzunehmen, ist es auch ein Arbeitsprozess, den man als Kunstinstitution erst mal aushalten und akzeptieren lernen muss, denn nur zu gerne wähnen wir uns eben in der Vorstellung, an vorderster Front für die Pluralität der Gesellschaft einzustehen. Das Kunstfeld ist jedoch nicht gefeit vor Rassismus, Sexismus, Homo- und Transophobie, Klassismus, Antisemitismus und anderen Diskriminierungsformen, die die Teilhabe beschränken und Hierarchien aufrecht halten.

Die Vorbereitungen für Cana Bilir-Meiers Ausstellung *Düşler Ülkesi* im Kunstverein in Hamburg, für den es das erste Mal war, dass einer Künstlerin mit deutsch-türkischen Wurzeln eine Einzelausstellung gewidmet wurde, waren in diesem Sinne auch eine suchende Annäherung von beiden Seiten. Die Frage nach dem richtigen Ton des Projekts trieb uns beide immer wieder um. Wir trafen uns erstmals im Juni 2018 in Hamburg. Es war nicht der typische erste Besuch, um die Räumlichkeiten des Kunstvereins kennenzulernen und frühe Ideen zu einer möglichen Ausstellungsgestaltung zu besprechen. Eigentlich stand die Ausstellung längere Zeit stets im Hintergrund. Vielmehr konzentrierten wir uns bei vielen Treffen zunächst auf ein langsames Erkunden und Kennenlernen Hamburgs.

Das Erforschen von Orten und ihren Geschichten ist grundlegend in Bilir-Meiers künstlerischer Praxis verankert. Die meisten Arbeiten finden ihren Ausgangspunkt in der Sichtung von privaten und öffentlichen Archiven. Dabei interessiert sich Bilir-Meier insbesondere für nicht erzählte oder ausgeblendete Geschichte(n) migrantischer Lebenswelten, die zwar zur kollektiven Erinnerung einer marginalisierten Community geworden sind, in der Wahrnehmung eines großen Teils der Mehrheitsgesellschaft jedoch wenig bis keinen Raum einnehmen. Insofern war es nur konsequent, dass die Vorbereitung ihrer ersten großen Einzelausstellung in Hamburg zunächst mit einer intensiven Stadtrecherche begann. Die kollektive Kraft der Geschichten, denen wir dabei nachgingen, konnte oft Brücken schlagen, die es uns ermöglichten, zu den unterschiedlichsten Protagonist*innen in Hamburg Verbindungen aufzubauen.

Im Zentrum standen dabei vor allem Menschen, Initiativen und Institutionen, die sich in Hamburg für die Erinnerung an Opfer rechter Gewalt und für den Kampf gegen Rassismus einsetzen. Für die Künstlerin war es entscheidend, all die meist überhörten oder ausgeblendeten Geschichten von rassistischen Übergriffen, deren Opfern und den Menschen, die sich um ihr Andenken bemühen, zu erfahren. Wie in ihrem künstlerischen Werk geht es auch den meisten Aktivist*innen darum, auf ihre Weise die dominierende Geschichtsschreibung durch Erzählungen zu ergänzen und zu hinterfragen, die selten bzw. oft ungern gehört werden. Sei es die Initiative für die Aufklärung des Mordes an Süleyman Taşköprü[3], dem Hamburger Opfer des sogenannten NSU; die Initiative in Gedenken an Yaya Jabbi[4], der im Besitz von 1,65 Gramm Cannabis am Hamburger Berg verhaftet wurde und vier Tage später in seiner Zelle unter nie völlig geklärten Umständen verstarb; seien es die Mitarbeiter*innen des St. Pauli Archiv e.V.[5], das sich dem Erhalt der offiziellen und inoffiziellen Stadtteilgeschichte verschrieben hat oder auch die Beschäftigten der GWA St. Pauli[6], die sich der Gemeinwesen-, Kultur- und Sozialarbeit im Stadtteil widmen und viele mehr – sie alle hatten über eine große Anzahl an Fällen von Ausgrenzung, Diskriminierung und Ignoranz zu berichten, vergangene und gegenwärtige. Für mich als Einwohner der Stadt waren die meisten davon neu und überraschend. Für die Künstlerin selbst waren diese Geschichten zwar zumeist auch neu, aber weniger überraschend, sind es doch immer die gleichen Machtmechanismen und -strukturen, die wirken und zu Rassismus führen. Allzu oft geht es dabei auch um den Erhalt von Privilegien, die eine Mehrheit besitzt und sich darin von einer Minderheit bedroht sieht, so paradox dies vielleicht klingen mag.

Schnell stellte sich die Frage, wie eine Kunstinstitution solche Erfahrungen einerseits widerspiegeln und – viel wichtiger – wie mit einer Ausstellung eigentlich ein Publikum erreicht werden kann, das diese auch teilt. Denn ein entscheidender Aspekt von Bilir-Meiers Arbeiten ist auch, ihrer eigenen Community eine Form von Empowerment zu geben, indem sie meist ungehörten Geschichten eine Plattform schafft. Typischerweise sind diese Menschen aber eben nicht die klassischen Besucher*innen von Kunstausstellungen, was nicht zuletzt auch an den Kunstinstitutionen und ihrer Vergangenheit selbst liegt. Insofern waren wir uns bald einig, dass wir ein umfangreiches Rahmenprogramm gestalten wollten, das Orte in Hamburg aktiviert und bespielt, an denen wir dieses Publikum auch erreichen konnten.

Immer wieder kam es auch zu Missverständnissen und Momenten des Misstrauens, denn die Betroffenen von rassistischer Gewalt und Ausgrenzung

haben in ihrem Leben schon zu häufig erlebt, dass gut meinende Menschen
lieber für oder über sie sprechen wollten, anstatt mit ihnen oder sie gar selbst
zu Wort kommen zu lassen. Ein extremes und prägendes Beispiel hierfür ist
vielleicht die Familie Taşköprü. Nicht nur, dass die Ermittlungsarbeiten nach
dem Mord im Sommer 2001 sich zunächst auf das private Umfeld des Opfers
konzentrierten und erst nach der Selbstenttarnung des sogenannten NSU im
Jahr 2011 ein rassistisches Tatmotiv in Betracht gezogen wurde, sondern auch
der heutige Gedenkort in der Schützenstraße macht klar, dass nicht zugehört
werden wollte. Dort gibt es einen „offiziellen" Gedenkstein, der auch auf die
anderen Opfer des NSU verweist, und es gibt einen in den Boden eingelasse-
nen Stern mit einem Porträt des Ermordeten, der an den Hollywood Walk of
Fame in Los Angeles erinnert. Letzteren erstritten und finanzierten die Familie
und weitere Unterstützer*innen privat, um Süleyman Taşköprü posthum seinen
großen Traum zu erfüllen und ihm ein persönliches Andenken zu schaffen. Es
ist keine Ausnahme, sondern leider noch die Regel, dass Angehörige bei der
Frage nach einem angemessenen Gedenkort übergangen werden. Aus diesem Grund steht der Anspruch auf eine angemessene Form des Andenkens
auch an erster Stelle der Forderungen des Tribunal NSU-Komplex Auflösen,
das 2017 erstmals im Schauspiel Köln tagte.[7] Überhört, ausgegrenzt und be-
vormundet zu werden, ist Teil einer kollektiven Erfahrung der migrantischen
Community, die seit Jahrzehnten kontinuierlich von Rassismus in Deutschland
betroffen ist. Das ist leider (noch) kein Allgemeinwissen, sondern kann nur
erfahren werden, wenn wir als nicht Betroffene das Gespräch suchen und vor
allem mit dem Willen zuhören, für uns vielleicht Unangenehmes als Erfahrung
des Gegenübers anzunehmen. Diese Erkenntnis ist auch eine wichtige
Erfahrung aus dem Arbeitsprozess mit Cana Bilir-Meier, die Grundvorausset-
zung für alle Institutionen sein muss, die gewillt sind, sich zu öffnen und ihren
Blick zu weiten.

Als Konsequenz daraus gestalteten wir auch das Begleitprogramm zur
Ausstellung mit großer Achtsamkeit, bei keiner Veranstaltung für oder über
etwas oder jemanden zu sprechen. Stattdessen kamen die Mitglieder der migrantischen Community selbst auf vielfältige Weise zu Wort. Unter anderem
gab es geführte Stadtteilspaziergänge, bei denen Opfern rassistischer Gewalt an den jeweiligen Tatorten gedacht wurde und Angehörige oder Mitglieder der entsprechenden Initiativen ihre Geschichten erzählten; im St. Pauli
Archiv zeigte Cana Bilir-Meier eine Schaufensterausstellung im Gedenken an
Semra Ertan unweit des Ortes ihrer Selbstverbrennung; das Stadtteilzentrum
Kölibri war Ort einer ganzen Reihe von Veranstaltungen: Das Duo EsRap
präsentierte ihre Mischung aus Wiener Rap und Arabeske, mit der sie kämp-
ferisch und sehr humorvoll ihre eigene Identität als türkische Österreicher
reflektieren; Ata Canani und Booty Carrell erzählten mit Livemusik und Schall-
platten von der Musikproduktion sogenannter „Gastarbeiter" und das Kollektiv KANAKISTAN veranstaltete gemeinsam mit Akteur*innen aus dem Diaspora Salon eine Lesung aus dem Gedichtband *Haymatlos*[8], für den Dichter*innen Lyrik über Rassismuserfahrungen, Migrations- und Familiengeschichten
oder auch die Sehnsucht nach „Normalität" beisteuerten. Ein nicht unwe-
sentlicher Punkt des Programms war es, dass bis auf wenige Ausnahmen
nicht der Kunstverein in Hamburg Veranstaltungsort war, sondern wir explizit
die Institution und damit die Privilegien und Codes des Kunstfeldes verlassen
wollten. Zum einen ging es darum, eben zu einem Publikum vorzudringen, für
das der Kunstverein ein fremder und vielleicht auch befremdlicher Ort ist.

Zum anderen war es auch der explizite Versuch, das Publikum des Kunstvereins an bisher unbekannte Orte der Stadt heranzuführen, jenseits des etablierten Kunstdiskurses und einer bürgerlichen Mitte.

Ersteres funktionierte deutlich besser als letzteres. Schon die Eröffnung von Cana Bilir-Meiers Ausstellung im Kunstverein zeichnete sich durch ein größtenteils tatsächlich nie dagewesenes Publikum aus, das so explizit in der Geschichte der Institution auch noch nie angesprochen wurde. Die monatelange Vorbereitung mit vielen Gesprächen und Treffen mit den Protagonist*innen aus den unterschiedlichen Communitys und nicht zuletzt die Künstlerin selbst waren entscheidende Faktoren für diesen kleinen Erfolg. Insbesondere Cana Bilir-Meiers Anstrengung, Brücken zu schlagen, nicht nur zwischen Institution und Community, sondern insbesondere auch zwischen den unterschiedlichen Initiativen und Akteur*innen, die meist unabhängig voneinander arbeiten, resultierte in einer Eröffnung, die so durchmischt war, wie man es im Kunstbetrieb sonst selten erlebt. Auch die darauffolgenden Veranstaltungen im Kunstverein und anderswo zeichneten sich durch hohes Besucher*innenaufkommen und große Vielfältigkeit unter den Teilnehmenden aus. Andersherum war der Anteil des Stammpublikums des Kunstvereins an den Veranstaltungen so gut wie nicht vorhanden. Das war für mich zunächst deutlich frustrierender als für die Künstlerin selbst. Ich war enttäuscht und las das mangelnde Interesse am Programm als Zeichen dafür, dass die Institution Kunstverein vielleicht doch nicht ein Ort für Vielseitigkeit, Mehrstimmigkeit und vor allem Neugierde ist. Schnell stellte sich aber die Frage, was man von einem Publikum erwarten könne, das es über die Jahrzehnte gewohnt ist, im Kunstverein eben doch mehr oder weniger immer wieder die Bequemlichkeit der eigenen Filterblase anzutreffen. Natürlich lässt sich ein strukturell etabliertes und gewohntes Denken und Verhalten nicht mit einer einzigen Hauruckaktion aufbrechen. Ohne die intensive einjährige Zusammenarbeit mit Cana Bilir-Meier wäre auch mein Denken ein anderes.

Als Weg für die Zukunft lässt sich aus dieser Erfahrung vielleicht ziehen, dass es insbesondere auf institutioneller Seite noch großer Anstrengungen, Ausdauer und vor allem eines nachhaltigen Bewusstseins dafür bedarf, sich des eigenen ausschließenden Blicks immer wieder klar zu werden und dagegen anzugehen. Zum einen, um das eigene Publikum kontinuierlich einzuladen, seinen Blick zu öffnen, vermeintliches Wissen zu hinterfragen und zu erweitern. Zum anderen aber auch, um die einmal geknüpften Verbindungen zu Menschen, deren Lebensrealitäten bislang kaum eine Rolle in der Institution spielten, nicht wieder abreißen zu lassen. Vielleicht ist gerade das Konstrukt Kunstverein genau der richtige Ort, um diese gesellschaftliche Arbeit zu leisten. Per Gründungsgeschichte im 19. Jahrhundert stehen Kunstvereine zwar einerseits für einen Distinktionswillen eines aufstrebenden Bürgertums, aber eben gleichzeitig auch für die Forderung nach Teilhabe an demokratischen Ideen und Prozessen und den Willen, festgefahrene Hierarchien und alte Privilegien zu hinterfragen, was sich bis heute in den unterschiedlichen Vereinsstrukturen und im Programm abzeichnet. So wie Kunstvereine vor 200 Jahren ein wichtiger Faktor bei der Identitätsstiftung eines Bürgertums waren, können sie auch heute noch dazu beitragen. Wichtig ist nur, dass wir als Vertreter*innen einer Mehrheitsgesellschaft anerkennen, dass sich die Definition dessen, wer Bürger*in in diesem Land ist, fortwährend erweitert. Das Tribunal NSU-Komplex Auflösen hat 2017 das Prinzip einer „offenen, durch Migration entstandenen Gesellschaft der Vielen"[9] eingeklagt. Seither hat dieser Begriff insbesondere in linken Diskursen einen Siegeszug hinter sich. Ende 2018 gründeten sich deutschlandweit regionale Interessenverbände der Kunst- und Kulturinstitutionen unter dem Namen DIE VIELEN. Ihnen geht es neben einem Schulterschluss gegen rechtsextreme Anfeindungen auch explizit um das Hinterfragen der eigenen Strukturen.[10] Im Schutzraum der Kunst existiert vermutlich eine einmalige Gelegenheit, so etwas wie eine Gesellschaft der Vielen nicht nur zu behaupten, sondern auch mit Leben zu füllen, wenn der Wille besteht, die eigenen Institutionen, ihr Programm und ihre Strukturen für bisher marginalisierte Geschichten und ihre Protagonist*innen zu öffnen. Hierfür kann eine Ausstellung nur ein Anfang sein. Aber manchmal kann eine Ausstellung eben tatsächlich neue Denkweisen anstoßen, wenn alle daran Beteiligten sich immer wieder aufmerksam die Frage nach dem richtigen Ton stellen und gefallen lassen.

68

1
Laut Mikrozensus 2017 im Auftrag des Statistischen
Bundesamts von 2017 hat beispielsweise knapp einer
Viertel der Gesamtbevölkerung Deutschlands einen
Migrationshintergrund. Vgl. https://www.bpb.de/
nachschlagen/zahlen-und-fakten/soziale-situation-
in-deutschland/61646/migrationshintergrund-i.
Zugriff: 10.5.2019
2
Vgl. dazu auch https://www.kubi-online.de/artikel/
kulturinstitutionen-ohne-grenzen-annaeherung-
einen-diskriminierungskritischen-kulturbereich.
Zugriff: 1.7.2019
3
https://www.aufklaerung-tatort-schuetzenstrasse.
org/. Zugriff: 2.5.2019.
4
https://rememberjajadiabi.blackblogs.org/about-
jaja-diabi/. Zugriff: 2.5.2019.
5
http://www.st-pauli-archiv.de/. Zugriff: 2.5.2019.
6
http://www.gwa-stpauli.de/startseite.html.
Zugriff: 2.5.2019.
7
Vgl. http://www.nsu-tribunal.de/nsu-komplex/
#newsmodal. Zugriff: 9.5.2019.
8
Tamer Düzyol, Taudy Pathmanathan (Hg.): *Haymatlos.
Gedichte*, edition assemblage, Münster 2018.
9
Vgl. http://www.nsu-tribunal.de. Zugriff: 5.5.2019.
10
Vgl. https://www.dievielen.de/erklaerungen.
Zugriff: 4.5.2019.

Doğru tonu aramak ve kısmen bulmak hakkında

Bir deneyim raporu

Tobias Peper

İyi bir sergi sanat eserlerini cazip bir şekilde sunmakla kalmaz, mümkün olduğu kadar eserlerin oluştuğu anlamsal bağlantıları da aktarır. Sergi ziyaretçilerini sanatçıların düşüncelerine ortak eder ve böylece bir diyalog kurulabilmesini sağlar. Bir sergi katiyen sergilenen eserleri sahiplenme izlenimi bırakmamalı, tam tersine sanat eserlerinin bulundukları yerin ve algının belirleyicisi olduğu hissi oluşmalı. Bir sergi ziyaretçiler için tabloların ve objelerin bulunduğu bir mekandan daha fazlası olmalı. Sergi en iyi durumda, deneyim dünyalarının, düşüncelerin ve fikirlerin paylaşıldığı ve tartışmaya açıldığı, yeni düşünce mekanlarına girme imkanı veren bir yer olmalı. Bu şekilde sergiler demokratik birlikteliğin temel ilkeleri olan, karşılıklı anlaşmaya, dayanışmaya ve benimsemeye katkı sağlayabilir. Bu anlayış bana küratör olarak çalışmalarımda uzun zamandan beri eşlik ediyor ve nasıl birlikte yaşayacağımız, birbirimize nasıl davranacağımız konusundaki toplumsal tartışmaya değerli bir katkı sunmamı sağladı.

Cana Bilir-Meier ile beraber çalışmak bu özgüveni bir hayli altüst etti. Çünkü bu durumun bir defosu var. Sanat kurumları, bunlara sergi salonlarının ve müzelerin yanı sıra üniversiteler ve sanat yüksek okulları da dahil, kuruldukларından beri çoğunlukla, göç sonrası, eşit ve aydınlanmış bir toplum talepleriyle neredeyse hiç bağdaşmayan, son derece tek yönlü, yani ağırlıkla Batı menşeli, toplumun çoğunluğunu oluşturanların sanat tarihine bakış açısını teşvik etti.[1]

Bu gerçeğin uzun zamandan beri, bilinçsizce de olsa farkında olmama rağmen, gerçekten ne anlama geldiğini, ne gibi etkilere neden olabileceğini, Bilir-Meier ile yaptığım sayısız sohbette ve fikir teatisinde kavradım. Tanım itibarıyla kazanan her şeyi alır (Winner-take-all market) misali, temel olarak dışlayıcı bir mantıkla çalışan kurumun ve meslek alanının bir parçası olarak, hiyerarşik yapıların etkisinin ne kadar güçlü ve de gaddarca olduğunu anlamak ve kabul etmek, insan kendisi de bu yapıya dahilse, hiç de kolay değil. Özellikle küratörler ve sanatçılar arasında çok kez yaşanan yoğun işbirliği söz konusuysa, tamamen duygulardan arındırılmış nesnel fikir teatisinin neredeyse mümkün olmaması ek bir zorluk olarak ortaya çıkıyor. Beraber çalışırken uygun konuşma tonunu bulmak hiç de kolay değil, zira bir tarafta, sürekli dışlanan ve ayrımcılığa uğrayanların haklı öfke ve ithamları var. Diğer tarafta yapısal sorunlar olduğunu temelde kabul eden, ama kendi evlerinin önündeki pisliği görmezden gelenler var. İyi niyetle yaklaşıyorlar, bir şeyleri değiştirmek istiyorlar ve aydınlar. Ama iyi niyetli olmanın ve bir şeyleri doğru yapmanın otomatikman gerçekleşmediğini insanın idrak etmesi için belki de gerçekten doğrudan dışlanmaya maruz kalanların uyarısı gerekiyor.[2]

Bu ihtilafta devamlı insanın kendi bilgi eksikliği ve yetersizliği göz önüne serildiği için, sanat kurumu olarak buna katlanmak ve kabul etmek bizim için zorunlu bir öğrenme süreci. Çünkü bizler kendimizi çok kez çoğulcu toplum için mücadelede en ön safta varsayarız. Oysa ki sanat alanı, paylaşımı kısıtlayan ve hiyerarşileri ayakta tutan, ırkçılık, cinsiyetçilik, homo ve transofobi, sınıf ayrımcılığı, antisemitizm ve başka ayrımcılık şekillerinden muaf değil.

Cana Bilir-Meier'in Kunstverein Hamburg'daki *Düşler Ülkesi* sergisi hazırlığı, ki Kunstverein ilk kez Alman-Türk kökenli bir sanatçının bireysel sergisine yer verdi; bu bağlamda iki taraf için de arayış dolu bir yakınlaşmaydı. Proje için doğru frekansı tutturmak, ikimizi de zorluyordu. İlk kez 2018'de Hamburg'da buluştuk. Bu Kunstverein'in salonlarını tanımak ve muhtemel sergi tasarımı için ilk fikirleri konuşmak adına yapılan tipik bir ilk buluşma değildi. Esasen sergi uzun süre arka planda kaldı. Çok sayıdaki buluşmalarımızda daha ziyade Hamburg'u yavaşça tetkik etmek ve tanımak ön plandaydı.

Mekanların ve onların tarihinin araştırılması Bilir-Meier'in sanatsal çalışma pratiğinin temelini oluşturuyor. Bir çok çalışmasının çıkış noktasını özel ve kamusal arşivlerinin taranması oluşturuyor. Bilir-Meier özellikle, marjinal toplumların kolektif anılarının parçası olmuş, ama çoğunluk toplumunun büyük bölümünün algısında az yer tutan, göç dünyalarının anlatılmamış veya karartılmış hikayeleriyle ilgileniyor. O bakımdan Hamburg'daki ilk büyük bireysel sergisinin hazırlığına yoğun bir kent araştırmasıyla başlaması tutarlı bir yaklaşımdı. İzini sürdüğümüz hikayelerin kolektif gücü sayesinde, Hamburg'daki farklı baş aktörlerle bağlantıya geçmemize imkan sağlayan köprüler kurabildik.

Merkezde özellikle aşırı sağ şiddetin kurbanları olmuş insanların anısını yaşatmak ve ırkçılıkla mücadele için uğraşan inisiyatifler ve kurumlar vardı. Sanatçı için, çoğunlukla görmezden gelinen veya karartılmış ırkçı saldırıların kurbanlarının ve onların anılarını yaşatmak için çabalayan insanların hikayeleri önemliydi. Sanatçının çalışmalarıyla yaptığı gibi, bahsi geçen eylemcilerin çoğu da, hakim tarih anlatımını, ender anlatılan veya çoğu kez görmezden gelinen anlatımlarla tamamlamak ve sorgulamak için çabalıyorlar. NSU adlı örgütün Hamburglu kurbanı Süleyman Taşköprü[3] Cinayetini Aydınlatma İnisiyatifi üyeleri; üzerinde 1,65 gram esrarla Hamburger Berg'de tutuklanan ve dört gün sonra hücresinde bilinmeyen nedenlerle ölen Yaya Jabbi'yi[4] Anma İnisiyatifi üyeleri; resmi ve gayri resmi semt tarihini koruma ve sürdürmeye çabalayan St. Pauli Arşivi Derneği[5] çalışanları; kendilerini semtte toplum, kültür çalışmalarına ve sosyal hizmete adayan GWA St. Pauli[6] çalışanları ve pek çok diğerleri: hepsinin geçmişte ve günümüzde karşılaştıkları çok sayıda dışlanma, ayrımcılık ve ilgisizlik vakaları hakkında anlatacakları vardı. Bu kentin bir sakini olarak anlatılanların bir çoğu benim için yeni ve şaşırtıcıydı. Bilir-Meier için de anlatılanlar çok kez yeniydi, ama ırkçılığa neden olan iktidar mekanizmaları ve yapıları hep aynı olduğu için, daha az şaşırtıcıydı. Her ne kadar kulağa çelişkili gelse de, mevzu genelde çoğunluğun azınlığı, sahip olduğu imtiyazları elinden alacak bir tehdit gibi görmesiyle ilgili.

Bu süreçte şu soru ortaya çıktı; bir sanat kurumu bu tip tecrübeleri nasıl yansıtabilir ve daha da önemlisi bir sergi benzer tecrübeleri yaşamış bir ziyaretçi topluluğuna nasıl ulaşır? Çünkü Bilir-Meier'in çalışmalarının önemli bir unsuru da duyulmamış hikayeler için platform yaratarak, kendi toplumuna bir nevi cesaret aşılaması. Ama bu toplumlar genelde, ki bunun nedeni sanat kurumlarının geçmişlerinde saklı, sanat sergilerinin klasik ziyaretçileri sayılmazlar. Bundan hareketle bu ziyaretçilere ulaşabileceğimiz Hamburg'un muhtelif mekanlarında geniş kapsamlı bir program hazırlama konusunda görüş birliğine vardık.

Sürekli yanlış anlamalar oldu ve güvensizlik anları da yaşandı. Çünkü ırkçı şiddet ve dışlanmaya maruz kalanlar hayatlarında çok sık, sözde iyiliklerini isteyenlerin kendileriyle konuşmak veya hatta söz hakkı vermek şöyle dursun, onların yerine veya onların hakkında konuşmak istediklerine bizzat şahit oldular. Bunun radikal ve iz bırakan bir örneği herhalde Taşköprü Ailesidir. 2001 yazında işlenen cinayetin soruşturması, kurbanın aile çevresine odaklandı ve ancak NSU örgütünün 2011 yılında kendini deşifre etmesinin ardından ırkçı cinayet motifi üzerinde duruldu. Bunun yanında Schützenstrasse'deki anma yeri de aslında ailenin durumuna kulak tıkandığını ortaya koyuyor. Aynı yerde diğer NSU kurbanlarına da dikkat çeken "resmi" bir anıt bulunuyor. Bunun yanında aile ve destekçilerinin mücadelesi ve finansmanı ile caddeye işlenen ve Los Angeles Hollywood'daki Walk of Fame'i andıran yıldız şekli ile ölümünden sonra Süleyman Taşköprü'nün bir hayali gerçekleşmiş oldu. Kurban yakınlarının uygun bir anma konusunda göz ardı edilmeleri ne yazık ki bir istisna değil, kaide halini almış bir durum. Bu nedenle uygun bir anma şekli 2017'de Köln Schauspiel'de toplanan *NSU Kompleksi Dağıtılsın Tribünali'nin* baş taleplerinden biriydi.[7]

Sürekli göz ardı edilmek, dışlanmak ve hakir görülmek onlarca yıldır Almanya'da ırkçılığa maruz kalan göçmen toplumun edindiği kolektif bir deneyim. Ne yazık ki bu (henüz) genel olarak bilinen bir şey değil, bilakis bu durumdan etkilenmeyen kişiler olarak diyalog arayışına girip karşımızdakinin deneyimine, bizim için nahoş da olsa, kulak vererek öğrenebileceğimiz bir şey. Cana Bilir-Meier ile yaptığımız çalışma sürecinden kazandığım önemli bir deneyim de, açılıma niyetli olan ve bakış açılarını genişletmek isteyen tüm kurumlar için temel şartın bu izana sahip olmaları gerektiğidir. Bunun sonucu olarak serginin programını da büyük bir titizlikle tasarlayarak, hiç bir etkinlikte birileri adına, bir şey üzerine veya bir kişi hakkında konuşmadık. Bunun yerine göç toplumunun üyeleri çok yönlü şekilde kendileri söz aldılar. Mesela ırkçı şiddet kurbanlarının olay yerlerinde anıldığı ve kurban yakınlarının veya söz konusu inisiyatiflerin üyelerinin hikayelerini anlattıkları semt turları yapıldı. Cana Bilir-Meier St. Pauli Arşivinde Semra Ertan'ın anısına, kendini yaktığı yere yakın bir mevkide, bir vitrin sergisi düzenledi. Kölibri Semt Merkezi bir dizi etkinliğin düzenlendiği yerdi; EsRap ikilisi Viyana repi ve arabeskten oluşan karışımla, mücadeleci ve çok esprili bir şekilde Avusturyalı Türkler olarak kimliklerini yansıttılar.

Ata Canani ve Booty Carrell canlı müzikle ve plaklarla Gastarbeiter diye tanımlananların müzik üretimi hakkında paylaşımda bulundular. KANAKISTAN Kolektifi, Diaspora Salonu'nun aktörleriyle, şairlerin ırkçılık tecrübeleri, göç ve aile hikayeleriyle "normallik" hasretinin işlendiği şiir kitabı *Haymatlos*'dan[8] şiirlerle bir okuma akşamı düzenlediler.

Programın hiç de önemsiz olmayan bir unsuru, Kunstverein Hamburg'un bir kaç istisna dışında etkinlik mekanı olmamasıydı. Bu şekilde kurumsal olanı ve sanat alanının imtiyazı ile kodlarını terk etmek istedik. Amaç, bir yandan Kunstverein'e yabancı olan ve belki de tuhaf bir mekan olarak gören ziyaretçilere ulaşmaktı. Diğer yandan da Kunstverein'in ziyaretçilerini, alışık sanat söylemlerinin ve orta sınıfın ötesindeki kentin şimdiye kadar bilmedikleri yanlarına yakınlaştırma denemesiydi.

İlk niyet ikincisinden daha başarılı oldu. Cana Bilir-Meier'in sergisinin açılışı sırasında, önemli oranda daha önce Kunstveren'a hiç gelmemiş ve kurumun tarihinde şimdiye kadar doğrudan hitap edilmemiş bir ziyaretçi topluluğu yer aldı. Aylarca süren hazırlık döneminde farklı toplumlarla yapılan sayısız görüşmeler ve buluşmalar ve tabii ki sanatçının kendisi bu küçük başarı için belirleyici faktörlerdi. Özellikle Cana Bilir-Meier'in sadece kurumlar ve toplum arasında değil, bilakis birbirinden bağımsız çalışan farklı inisiyatif ve aktörlerle büyük çaba göstererek kurduğu köprüler, sanat alanında ender rastlanan bir karışımı sergi açılışında bir araya getirdi. Kunstverein ve diğer mekanlardaki müteakip etkinliklerde çok sayıda ve farklı ziyaretçiler vardı. Diğer taraftan Kunstverein'in daimi ziyaretçileri etkinliklerde yok denecek kadar az sayıdaydı. Bu durum sanatçıdan ziyade benim için moral bozucuydu. Hayal kırıklığı yaşadım ve programa yetersiz ilgiyi Kunstverein kurumunun belki de çeşitlilik, çok seslilik ve en başta merak için doğru mekan olmadığı şeklinde yorumladım. Onlarca yıl az veya çok kendi kabuğunda yaşama konforuna bağlı kalan Kunstverein'in daimi ziyaretçilerinden neler bekleyebileceğimiz sorusu ortaya çıktı. Elbette yapısal ve alışılagelmiş düşünce tarzı ve davranış şekli tek bir eylemle aniden kırılamaz. Cana Bilir-Meier ile yaptığımız bir yıllık yoğun işbirliği olmasaydı, benim düşünce tarzım da farklı olurdu.

Bu deneyimlerden hareketle gelecek için çizilecek bir yol olarak, özellikle kurumsal tarafın daha çok çaba, sabır ve özellikle süreklilik bilinci göstermesi ve kendi dışlayıcı bakış açısıyla mücadele edebilmek için bunu öncelikle idrak etmesi gerekliliği öne çıkmaktadır. Bunun için kurum bir taraftan kendi ziyaretçi topluluğunu sürekli davet edip, bakış açısını genişletmeli, sözde bilgiyi sorgulamalı ve eklemeler yapmalıdır. Diğer taraftan da, şimdiye kadar yaşam gerçekleri kurumda yer almayan bu insanlarla kurulan bağların, tekrar kopmaması için çaba harcanmalıdır. Belki de Kunstverein yapısı tam böyle bir toplumsal çalışmayı gerçekleştirmek için doğru mekandır. 19. yüzyılda kurulmuş olması itibarıyla Kunstverein'ler, orta sınıfın yükselme azmiyle bir yandan kendini soyutlayıp, diğer yandan da farklı dernek yapılarında ve programlarında bugün de kendini gösterdiği gibi, kemikleşmiş hiyerarşileri ve eski imtiyazları sorgulamayı temsil ediyorlar. Kunstverein'ler 200 yıl önce orta sınıfa kimlik aşılamada önemli rol oynadıkları aynı işleve bugün de katkı sunabilirler. Önemli olan, çoğunluk toplumunun temsilcileri olarak bizlerin, kimin vatandaş olduğu tanımının sürekli olarak genişlediğini görüp kabul etmemiz. *NSU Kompleksi Dağıtılsın Tribünali* 2017'de "açık, göçle oluşmuş nicelerin toplumu"nu[9] talep etti. O zamandan beri bu tanım özellikle sol söylemlerde bir zafer yaşadı. 2018 sonunda Almanya genelinde bölgesel sanat ve kültür kurumlarının lobi cemiyetleri *NİCELER* adı altında örgütlendiler. Onların amaçladıkları, aşırı sağdan gelen düşmanlığa karşı omuz omuza olmanın yanı sıra, somut olarak kendi öz kurumsal yapılarını da sorgulamak. Sanatın koruma alanı, (kendi kurumlarını, programlarını ve yapılarını şimdiye kadar marjinalleştirilen hikayelere ve aktörlere açma iradesi mevcut ise) nicelerin toplumu söyleminden sadece bahsetmekle kalmayıp bu söylemin içini hayat ile doldurmak adına eşsiz bir fırsat sunuyor. Bunun için sergi ancak bir başlangıç olabilir. Ama bazen bir sergi, tüm iştirakçiler itinayla doğru tonu yakalama konusunu sorgulamaya katlanırlarsa, yeni düşünce tarzlarının dürtüsü olabilir.

74

1
2017 Federal İstatistik Dairesinin yaptırdığı nüfus sayımına göre 2017'de örneğin Almanya nüfusunun toplamının neredeyse dörtte biri göçmen kökenli. Bkz. https://www.bpb.de/nachschlagen/zahlen-und-fakten/soziale-situation-in-deutschland/61646/migrationshintergrund-i. Erişim: 10.5.2019
2
Buna ilişkin bkz. https://www.kubi-online.de/artikel/kulturinstitutionen-ohne-grenzen-annaeherung-einen-diskriminierungskritischen-kulturbereich. Erişim: 1.7.2019
3
https://www.aufklaerung-tatort-schuetzenstrasse.org/. Erişim: 2.5.2019.
4
https://rememberjajadiabi.blackblogs.org/about-jaja-diabi/. Erişim: 2.5.2019.
5
http://www.st-pauli-archiv.de/. Erişim: 2.5.2019.
6
http://www.gwa-stpauli.de/startseite.html. Erişim: 2.5.2019.
7
Bkz. http://www.nsu-tribunal.de/nsu-komplex/#-newsmodal. Erişim: 9.5.2019.
8
Tamer Düzyol, Taudy Pathmanathan (Hg.): *Haymatlos. Şiirler*, edition assemblage, Münster 2018.
9
Bkz. http://www.dievielen.de/erklaerungen. Erişim: 4.5.2019.

This makes me wanna let the door open me

Narrating Migration in Art:

Memory, Making Present and Resistance in the Works of Cana Bilir-Meier

Burcu Dogramaci

Immigration to the Federal Republic of Germany was long narrated as a history of the victims or perpetrators. Integration or the unwillingness to integrate, the job market and training, or segregation were and still are dominant issues in the public discourse on migration.[1] Three books published in the 1980s convey a narrow view of migrants; all are from a period when "guest workers" had long become a part of everyday life in the Federal Republic, yet were perceived as the others in society. The publications deal with the "problem of employing foreigners,"[2] they criticize the "housing situation and ghettoization" (mentioned together), placing them in the context of the "problematics of foreigners"[3] or alternately diagnosing the "segregation of foreign families"[4] in the "immigration colony." What all books have in common is that they speak about a group of persons who are not given a voice. All too often, "the" foreigners or migrants appear as a homogenous mass that causes problems or has difficulties.

But this view was also countered by a different perspective making resistant positions visible, granting migrants agency, and emphasizing the individualization of migrant experiences. The actions of the artistic-political alliance "Kanak Attak" since the 1990s were like the bursting of a dam, when migrants were given a resistant voice in theater performances and interventions. One of the founders of "Kanak Attak," Imran Ayata, wrote in an essay about how "Kanak-Rap" freed itself from stereotypes: "What belongs to life as an immigrant, migrant, Kanake [dago], non-German, Almanci-German, nationalized person, foreign compatriot, Kümmel [caraway seed], guest worker child, or whatever, are things like work, love, sex, friendships, parties, drugs, money, cars etc., just as much as everything else. These and related themes can be found in Turkish-language rap. Many tracks are characterized by rappers politically scrutinizing Germany from their status as 'foreigners,' addressing racism and talking about their living conditions."[5] Exhibitions such as *Fremde Heimat* (1998), a collaboration between the Ruhrlandmuseum Essen and DoMIT (today's DOMID) Cologne, or *Projekt Migration* at the Kölnischer Kunstverein (2005) took an alternative path to make room for the plurality and diversity of migrant experiences.[6] In concrete terms, this meant actively including interviews with and image material by migrants in the exhibitions. They were thus given the agency that was otherwise just talked about. Today, the post-migrant research of Erol Yıldız, Naika Foroutan and Regina Römhild starts from the assumption of a society constituted by migration and gives the migrants their voice (back), so that the history of migration can also be written from the perspective of the actors.[7]

The work of Cana Bilir-Meier can be situated in this conflictual mélange. In various projects, the artist lends a contour to what is suppressed, forgotten or has always been barely visible. The starting point is often formed by archives, private estates, documents, or other material that the artist rearranges. Protagonists of immigration to Germany are drawn from the darkness of the past to the present. However, her multimedia works are dedicated less to remembrance or compensation than to an activating and subjective dealing with the subject matter. Bilir-Meier's works thus offer a counter-model to memorials that give the memory of migration, asylum, racism, and xenophobia a static form. One example is Akbar Behkalam's memorial (1996) to the Turkish asylum-seeker Cemal Kemal Altun, who in 1983 jumped from the sixth floor of the Berlin Administrative Court. Altun's complex life and death can hardly be dealt with in a stone monument on a busy street in the center of the capital. With regard to the work of Bilir-Meier, one can ask what alternative forms of actively engaging with migration and its history are possible. How can people be given a voice beyond their lives? How does remembrance become a gesture of the sympathy toward and appreciation of a forgotten life and work by aiming to make it lastingly present? And how can remembrance itself not become historical? Based on three projects by Bilir-Meier that in different ways deal with the complex of migration, xenophobia and racism, the potentials of artistic research are to be revealed.

5/24/1982.

A date marks the end of a life story. The suicide of the poet, interpreter and construction draftswoman Semra Ertan in Hamburg veils a complex life. But the end is also a beginning, a starting point of a research project taking up and connecting the loose ends of a life and afterlife. In a cabinet of her grand-parents Vehbiye Bilir and Gani Bilir, Bilir-Meier found notes on the family history and audio recordings of family members. Among them was a cassette with an interview that her grandparents gave after the death of their daughter Semra Ertan. This personal and familial approach marks the start of a search for traces that identifies Ertan as a private and public figure of contemporary history and relates her extensive and for the most part unknown poetic oeuvre to her person. Ertan is not defined as a martyr figure or victim: her public self-immolation in the early morning of May 24, 1982[8], in a street in Hamburg can be interpreted as a resistant act against xenophobia. Ertan announced it in a telephone call to the radio station Norddeutscher Rundfunk and read her poem *Mein Name ist Ausländer* [My Name is Foreigner].[9]

In 1982, the year of Ertan's suicide, Rolf Meinhardt published his documentation *Ausländerfeindlichkeit* [Xenophobia] in which he diagnosed "soaring resentment against foreigners"[10] in 1981. Meinhardt's book is a collection of newspaper and magazine articles in which resentment, rabble-rousing, violence, but also everyday racism become abundantly clear. The compilation of texts published between mid-1981 and April 1982 shows how the tone had become sharper within a short period of time. Meinhardt's foreword starts with the words: "They yell 'fire!' and, ever more blatantly, pour gas into the flames. In a period of economic decline and imminent ecological and military collapse (sic!), demagogues are having a heyday."[11] Only two months after Meinhardt wrote his foreword, Semra Ertan doused herself with gasoline and burnt to death. The parallels between the act of self-immolation and Meinhardt's documentation on racism in the Federal Republic in the 1981 and 1982 are evident.

Notwithstanding, in Bilir-Meier's perspective, Ertan is neither only a victim nor a typical protagonist of 1970s guest-worker migration. She is an individual with her own agenda, with a life to which poetry belongs just as much as her resistance against xenophobia and exclusion.

Bilir-Meier's film *Semra Ertan* (2013) starts with the writer's own words: "Unheimlich"[12] in Ertan's handwriting marks the start of the film and is from one of her poems that reads: "Wenn sie sagt/Sie sei unheimlich/Glücklich/ Heißt es/Dass sie heimlich/Unglücklich ist/Weil sie/Kein Heim hat" [When she says/She is incredibly/Happy/It means/That she is/Secretly unhappy/ Because she/Has no home].

Ertan associates the home, and latently the homeland as well, with happiness and unhappiness. Something is "unheimlich" turns into she is "unheimlich," evoking the sense of not feeling at home. The person, of whom Ertan speaks in the third person, does not find a place that is familiar. Words and handwriting refer to the unmistakable identity of the author, and the film thus makes room for the author of the words and her own handwriting. Hence, speaking *about a* person, something that the title of the film might suggest, becomes the speech *of* the person. Bilir-Meier thus grants her protagonist agency with regard to her reception. It is she who speaks, not the film that speaks about her.

The way Bilir-Meier comes closer to her aunt is emphasized when she reads from one of her love poems. The writer's oeuvre is once again made present through her voice, with the eye of the camera wandering over Ertan's notebook. We read the Turkish lines, while the artist's voice recites the poem in German. Inevitably, the bilingual and transcultural character of her creativity becomes clear in the meandering and roaming between languages and memories. The simultaneity of differences also exists in the family archive of

Ertan, where Cana Bilir-Meier additionally found a marriage certificate, a medical report or German lessons alongside newspaper articles, poems, notes, and letters.[13] The archive reflects the complexity of her personality—she was not only a writer, a migrant, a person learning German. These plural approaches are all too often narrowed down in the public discourse on migrants, refugees and foreigners, in order to prototypically or stereotypically speak about and judge the other or the others.

The news reports on Ertan reveal how this works. In *Semra Ertan*, short scenes from a television report of the WDR are used, in which consternation in the face of the "death of a female Turk" is formulated without her name being mentioned.[14] By editing parts of the report into her film, Bilir-Meier juxtaposes the word of the writer with the superficial reception, giving the person reported on the first say. During her research, the artist found out that in 1982 a piece of music was composed for Ertan, an octet by Enjott Schneider that can also be heard in the film. *Semra Ertan* thus becomes a collage of materials from different times, by different authors, with polyphone voices, yet one in which the poet always remains audible and is not drowned out by other voices. An important aspect is that the film never obscures the perspective of the artist in that it always remains recognizable as a reconstruction and construction. We see Bilir-Meier reading and researching files, notebooks and photographs, making an effort to gain access to Semra Ertan. The presence of the artist in the moment of reconstructing an oeuvre and a life is there in the film, which does not claim to be a conclusive, truthful work. The fragments it brings together extend an invitation to repeated readings and require the recipients to always assemble them anew.

10/6/1967.

The laying of the foundation stone of the Freimann Mosque took place on a day in October, but under an altered proviso. Not the foundation stone was laid but a symbolic marble stone. Around fifty years later, on May 26, 2018, Cana Bilir-Meier, in a performative act, brought the foundation stone back to the mosque during the *Public Art Munich* festival. This belonged to and resulted from artistic research into the backgrounds and contexts of the construction project and especially the authors themselves, the architect Osman Edip Gürel and the interior architect Necla Gürel, who until then had hardly been mentioned in the German or local history of architecture. Bilir-Meier's *Foundation Stone* is a reconstruction work that visualizes the wounds and seams between present and past, maintaining questions and voids. Her artistic research project is not a time travel to the 1960s, but instead follows the traces starting from the present. Yet her work simultaneously offers a point of departure to question models of historiography, which does not appear as an 'objective' truth. Instead, remembrance and public memory are subject to a selection process. New research interests and insights also model the perception of a subject matter. Two publications from 2011 deal with the Freimann Mosque in the crosshairs of political interests and in the context of instrumentalizing political Islam. The two architects are mentioned only in passing.[15]

It is generally surprising that Osman Edip Gürel (1925-1984) and Necla Gürel (1926-2007), as significant architects in Munich in the postwar decades, must be regarded as little known or forgotten. The couple had lived in Munich since 1955. Gürel was responsible for the reconstruction of the high-class Turkish restaurant "Istanbul" on the Oskar-von-Miller-Ring in Munich. Especially in the city district of Schwabing, where he operated his own architects office, Gürel planned buildings such as the Rudolf-Steiner School and the

Leo 17 theater on Leopoldstraße. He also designed the building of the Turkish consulate general, and in 1966 he was commissioned to build the mosque in Munich-Freimann.[16] It was realized as a modern, reinforced concrete building with a tent-like dome and large window elements. The interior design was supposed to be carried out by Necla Gürel, who had studied sculpture at the Academy of Fine Arts in Munich, but for financial reasons her plans were not implemented in the mosque that opened in 1972.[17]

Her research led Bilir-Meier to the two daughters of the architect couple who related their own perspective on the life and work of their parents. These private family relationships provide an important frame for *Foundation Stone*. In a brochure, an audio installation (2018) and a film (2019), the stories of the daughters Hürdem and Zerender Gürel provide a possible way to access the mosque. They give an account of their parents, their own childhood, processes of detachment, and life with/in two languages, cultures and life-worlds. They talk about how their parents grew accustomed to Munich in the 1950s and 1960s and later left the city for economic reasons or because of homesickness. At least temporarily, Bilir-Meier's audio installation brought the voices of the daughters into the building, which in turn bears witness to the construction work of their parents. Also involved in the project was Bilir-Meier's mother, the Munich-based children's psychotherapist Zühal Bilir-Meier. She adds the perspective of an expert to the stories of the architects' daughters, articulating advice on the raising of adolescents in migrant communities. In a straightforward way, Cana Bilir-Meier integrates the reconstruction effort as an individual artistic act in her film. It conveys the artist's view of the endeavor by showing her silhouette on the façade of the building. We see her walking across the grounds of the mosque or making frottages by placing a sheet of paper on the architecture and rubbing it with chalk. In her project *Foundation Stone*, Bilir-Meier is both the author of the film and an actor engaged in a dialogue with the architecture, the contemporary witnesses and descendants, the archive and the press material. With her singular narration on the Freimann Mosque, the artist puts to practice a historiography of singularities in the sense of the philosopher Jacques Rancière: "History does not exist as an oriented course of development, it exists through the singular forms of historicity: the singular ways that the distributions of the visible and the sayable, the distributions of the modes of sensible experience, and the relations between life and its systems of symbolization are displaced. For me, there can only be a history of singularities."[18] The addition of individual stories can thus constitute a polyphonic history that is more than just *one* possible narration.

7/22/2016.

The racist attack of an 18-year-old male in the Olympia shopping mall was long considered a rampage. In July 2016, the perpetrator shot nine youths dead, wounded five others, and then killed himself. The victims were all from migrant families and most of them were youths. Armela S., Can L., Choussein D., Dijamant „Dimo" Z., Guiliano-Josef K., Janos Roberto R., Sabina S., Selçuk K., and Sevda D. were killed. Although the extreme rightwing conviction of the perpetrator became quickly known, the prosecution and the State Office of Criminal Investigations called the act a rampage and mainly presented mobbing and a mental illness as reasons. The final report dated March 17, 2017, states: "There are no indications that he chose the individual victims in a targeted way during his rampage. It is also not to be presumed that the act was politically motivated."[19] What is noticeable, though, is that victims were selected according to physical traits indicating that they were of southeast

European origin. In March 2018, the Federal Office of Justice then categorized the event as an extremist act.[20] The public learned more details about the perpetrator, his Iranian descent, his hatred, and his socialization in rightwing forums than about the nine murdered youths.

In Bilir-Meier's film, *This makes me want to predict the past* (2019), the attack is a starting point for approaching the life-worlds, dreams, fears, and wishes of migrant youths. On the one hand, this perspective refers back to the young people murdered on July 22, 2016. On the other, the film is fully obliged to the present and future of youths whose parents or grandparents came to Munich from another country. Bilir-Meier accompanied several youths with the camera on their way through the shopping mall, delving into their wishes and hopes, nightmares and fears. This raises a fundamental question: If xenophobia and racism are fueled by the hatred of collectives and groups, how can they be given back their voices, faces and individual identities in the public discourse? How do "the" migrants, Muslims, refugees, and victims of attacks become individuals with names, subjective memories and dreams?

On site, Bilir-Meier works with the artistic method of frottage: By placing paper on the Olympia shopping mall and rubbing it with chalk, she records and appropriates it. This method already used in the project dedicated to the Freimann Mosque is part of an artistic "thick description"[21] (Clifford Geertz), in which researchers include themselves and their methods in the interpretation. The frottages are prints of the architecture and of a traumatic location that appears as a flip-flop image: both the scene of a crime and a place where young migrants often prefer to linger (and were therefore, by implication, probably targeted by the attacker).

Bilir-Meier's works add to the timeline of German history data that are not, or only to a limited degree, part of the public consciousness: on 5/24/1982 a woman of Turkish descent immolated herself as a sign against xenophobia; 10/6/1967 was the date of the planned laying of the foundation stone of the first Bavarian mosque in Munich-Freimann, marking the construction of a building by two Turkish-born architects of German postwar modernism; on 7/22/2016 nine youths with a migrant background were shot dead by a presumably rightwing perpetrator. These three events are not comparable, embodying themes as diverse as self-immolation and racism, the proportion of migrant artists and architects in the history of German architecture, an extremist attack, and the life of young people in Germany. In her artistic research projects and the resulting works, Bilir-Meier succeeds in distilling the individual from the collective and—vice versa—letting history appear in concrete individual stories.[22] Each narration inevitably incorporates the perspective of the author; the times and events are never viewed neutrally but always from the perspective of a living gaze. At the same time, her works make it evident that historiographies are susceptible to glossing over, omissions and levelling.

Bilir-Meier's projects on migration and migrants are guided by a political understanding of artistic work. About her piece dedicated to the Freimann Mosque, the artist wrote: "In a 'society of the many' (the Tribunal Unraveling the NSU Complex), we also need a history of the many. The mosque is a historically charged site where stories of the political instrumentalization of religion, the need for a spiritual space and its architectural design overlap until today. The 'Foundation Stone' project is a research endeavor that takes up different narrative strands and the situated knowledge of migrants and seeks to make migrant stories, positions and perspectives visible."[23] Even in collectively written texts such as those on Wikipedia that lay claim to plural perspectives, one-dimensional approaches can be found all too often. In the German version of the online encyclopedia, there is a short entry on Semra Ertan, but she is also listed in the lemma "Selbstverbrennung" (Self-immolation) under cases in Germany.[24] In this article, she is in a community with other—also politically motivated—suicides. Her complex life, including friends and tragedies, her literary oeuvre and her experiences with being foreign, remains invisible behind the brief entry.

Bilir-Meier's works do not claim encyclopedic objectivity. They refuse to give a bird's-eye view of a life, work, building, or event. The subjective gaze remains fragmentary and prismatic. Bilir-Meier thus commits to complexity, to walking on shaky ground, to fragmented speaking and thinking.

85

1
See also Sylvia Hahn, *Historische Migrationsforschung*, Frankfurt am Main/New York: Campus Verlag, 2012, p. 15; Sabine Hess, *Politiken der (Un-)Sichtbarmachung. Eine Kritik der Wissens- und Bilderproduktionen zu Migration*, in: Erol Yildiz und Marc Hill (eds.), *Nach der Migration. Postmigrantische Perspektiven jenseits der Parallelgesellschaft*, Bielefeld: transcript Verlag, 2015, p. 49-64.

2
Ulrich Herbert, *Geschichte der Ausländerbeschäftigung in Deutschland 1880 bis 1980. Saisonarbeiter, Zwangsarbeiter, Gastarbeiter*, Berlin/Bonn: J.H.W. Dietz, 1986, p. 220.

3
Both quotes from Klaus Unger, *Ausländerpolitik in der Bundesrepublik Deutschland (Bielefelder Studien zur Entwicklungssoziologie, 7)*, Saarbrücken/Fort Lauderdale: Verlag Breitenbach, 1980, p. 113, 116.

4
Friedrich Heckmann, *Die Bundesrepublik: Ein Einwanderungsland? Zur Soziologie der Gastarbeiterbevölkerung als Einwandererminorität*, Stuttgart: Klett-Cotta, 1981, p. 208.

5
Imran Ayata, *Kanak-Rap in Almanya – Über die schweren Folgen Deutschlands*, in: Katja Dominik, Marc Jünemann, Jan Motte und Astrid Reinecke im Auftrag der Geschichtswerkstatt Göttingen (eds.), *Angeworben – eingewandert – abgeschoben. Ein anderer Blick auf die Einwanderungsgesellschaft Bundesrepublik Deutschland*, Münster: Westfälisches Dampfboot, 1999, p. 273-287, here p. 280.

6
On the exhibition "Fremde Heimat" see Mathilde Jamin, *Fremde Heimat. Zur Geschichte der Arbeitsmigration aus der Türkei*, in: Jan Motte, Rainer Ohliger, Anne von Oswald (eds.), *50 Jahre Bundesrepublik – 50 Jahre Einwanderung*, Frankfurt am Main/New York: Campus Verlag, 1999, p. 145-164. See also *Projekt Migration*, exh. cat. Kölnischer Kunstverein, Cologne: DuMont Literatur und Kunstverlag, 2005.

7
Naika Foroutan, *The Post-migrant Paradigm*, in: Jan-Jonathan Bock and Sharon Macdonald (eds.): *Refugees Welcome? Difference and Diversity in a Changing Germany*, New York/Oxford: Berghahn Books, 2019, p. 142-167.

8
New research in preparation for the exhibition Cana Bilir-Meier. *Düşler Ülkesi* at the Kunstverein in Hamburg revealed that Semra Ertan's self-immolation did not take place on 26.5.1982, as previously assumed, but two days earlier.

9
See Cana Bilir-Meier, *Semra Ertan. Her Own Voice / Kendi Sesi / Ihre eigene Stimme*, Vienna 2017, p. 11.

10
Rolf Meinhardt: Vorwort, in: *Ausländerfeindlichkeit. Eine Dokumentation*, Berlin: EXpress, 1982, p. 1.

11
Ibid.

12
Translator's note: The German word "unheimlich," meaning uncanny, incredible, creepy, contains "Heim," home, so that "unheimlich" would literally translate to unhomely. There is then a play on words with "heimlich," which means secret.

13
See Cana Bilir-Meier, *Nachdenken über das Archiv. Notizen zu Semra Ertan* (2013), in: *Stimme. Zeitschrift der Initiative Minderheiten*, No. 94/2015, Innsbruck: Bürgerinitiative Demokratisch Leben, 2015, p. 11.

14
Ibid., p. 12f.

15
See Ian Johnson, *A Mosque in Munich: Nazis, the CIA, and the Rise of the Muslim Brotherhood in the West*, Boston, Mass.: Houghton Mifflin Harcourt, 2010.

16
Cana Bilir Meier, *26. Mai 2018. Grundstein Foundation Stone. Eine künstlerische Recherchearbeit*, brochure in the project, Munich 2018, no page numbers.

17
Ibid.

18
Jacques Rancière: *A Politics of Aesthetic Indetermination: An Interview With Frank Ruda & Jan Voelker*, in: Jason E. Smith & Annette Weisser (eds.), *Everything is in Everything, Jacques Rancière Between Intellectual Emancipation and Aesthetic Education*, Zurich: JRP Ringier, 2011, p. 22.

19
https://archive.fo/wiHMz#selection-1307.0-1311.73. Accessed 4/28/2019.

20
https://www.zeit.de/gesellschaft/zeitgeschehen/2018-03/olympia-einkaufszentrum-muenchener-amoklauf-extremismus-einstufung-bundesbehoerde. Accessed 4/28/2019.

21
Clifford Geertz, *Thick Description: Toward an Interpretive Theory of Culture*, in: *The Interpretation of Cultures: Selected Essays. Clifford Geertz*, pp. 3–30, New York: Basic Books, 1973.

22
See also Ayşe Güleç and Cana Bilir-Meier in conversation in the magazine *Camera Austria* where they say: "It is, of course, about the personal, but I don't want to tell individual stories. I am instead interested in how a collective story can be told that is personal and intimate all the same." (Bilir-Meier) or "Using the example of concrete stories and events, it is possible to relate collectively lived experiences as history—also because this decision allows developing a counter-narrative." (Güleç). Ayşe Güleç, *Cana Bilir-Meier. Bewegungen zwischen Archiven – Dekolonisierung von Disziplinen*, in: *Camera Austria*, 141/2018, Graz: Verein CAMERA AUSTRIA. Labor für Fotografie und Theorie, 2018, p. 33-44, here p. 34.

23
Cana Bilir Meier, *26. Mai 2018. Grundstein Foundation Stone. Eine künstlerische Recherchearbeit*, brochure on the project, Munich 2018, no page numbers.

24
https://de.wikipedia.org/wiki/Selbstverbrennung#Fälle_in_Deutschland. Last access 4/26/2019.

.... anTallY,AdHeRahSellenCKAnleI-ŞuMdAJLgAnEtIeNtArstück in
türkAsdheIr ISMraCKe nItSrUeEtYnEwNlLeB R.E.....

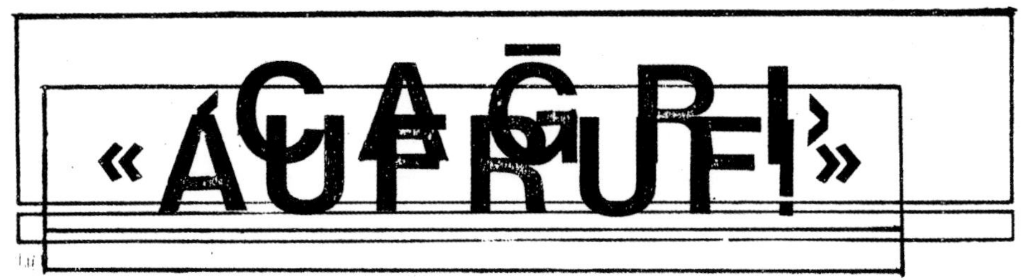

Sizi, Münih Kültür Dairesi (Kulturreferat) ve Gençlik Tiyatrosu
Mit Unterstützung des Kulturreferates und des "Theaters der Jugend"
(Theater der Jugend) desteğiyle kurulan "Münih Türk Tiyatrosu"
wollen wir ein türkisches Theater ins Leben rufen. Da die in Mün-
çalışmalarına katılmaya çağırıyoruz.
chen lebenden Türken schon lange ein Theater vermissen, dessen
Amacımız, şimdiye dek sürekli bir Türk tiyatrosundan yoksun
Stücke in türkischer Sprache aufgeführt werden, laden wir nun zur
bulunan Münihte yerleşik tüm Türklere, Türkçe tiyatro oyunları
ersten Produktion
sunmak ve isteyen çocuk, genç ve yetişkinlerin bu tiyatro çalış-

malarına katılmalarını sağlamaktır.
                    K I N D E R
Münih Türk Tiyatrosunu oluşup, geliştirmek, bu eyleme süreklilik
            J U G E N D L I C H E   und
kazandırabilmek için tiyatroya ilgi duyan bu daldaki her türlü
            E R W A C H S E N E
çalışmaya katılmak isteyen

                C O C U K
ein, die sich aktiv an der Theaterarbeit beteiligen wollen. Darü-
            G E N Ç
berhinaus können eigene Ideen eingebracht und verwirklicht werden.
            Y E T İ Ş K İ N L E R İ
Türkische, italienische, griechische, deutsche, spanische.....und
25 Eylül 1982,   Cumartesi günü
überhaupt Kinder und Jugendliche aus allen Ländern sind herzlich
saat 14³⁰ - da "Theater der Jugend" de yapılacak ilk
eingeladen, damit diese Initiative weiterentwickelt und fortge-
toplantıya katılmaya çağırıyoruz.
führt werden kann.

Das 1. Treffen findet statt:
Ulaşım : 18 numaralı tramvay ile Elisabethplatz durağına kadar,
am 25. September 1982 um 14³⁰ im Theater der Jugend. Das Theater
            U 8 ile Josehsplatz durağına veya
ist zu erreichen mit dem MVV
            U 6 ile Giselastr. durağına kadar.
** ** Straßenbahn-Linie 18 ,Haltestelle Elisabethplatz

** ** U - Bahn - Linie 6 , Haltestelle Giselastraße
Theater der Jugend' de sorumlu Münih Türk Tiyatrosu Grubu.
** ** U - Bahn - Linie 8 , Haltestelle Josephsplatz
FRANZ . JOSEPH . STR. 47
Türkisches Theater München bei Theater der Jugend!
                FRANZ . JOSEPH · STR. 47   b.w.
                TEL : 23721 - 368

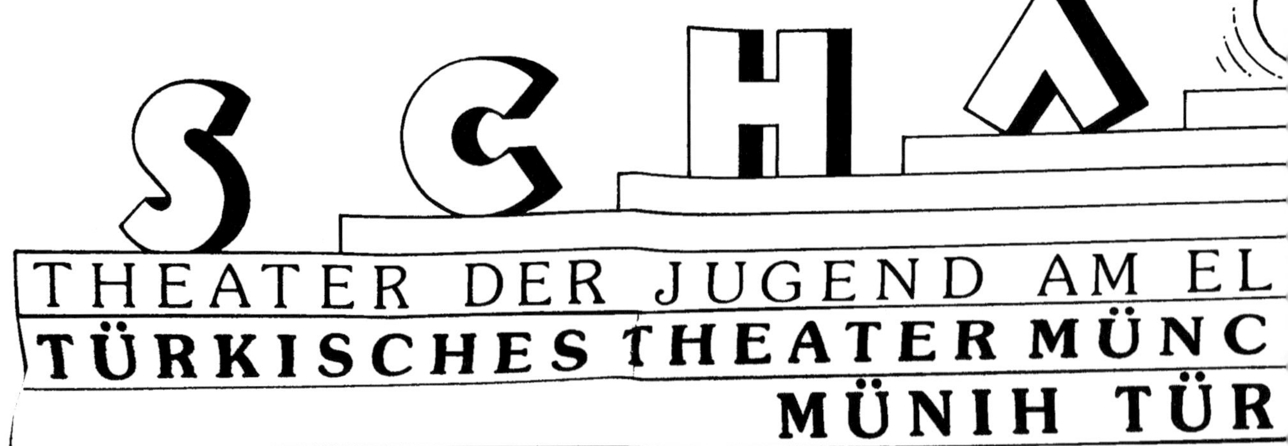

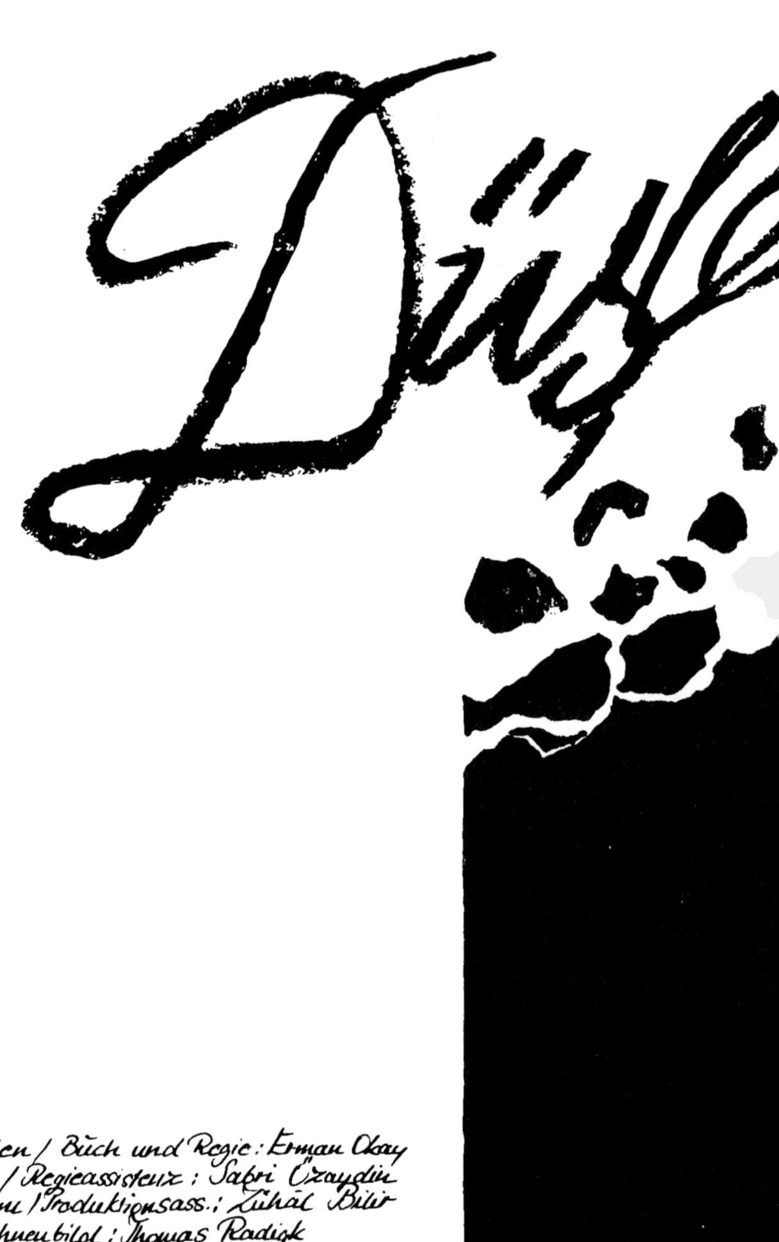

Yazan ve Yöneten / Buch und Regie: Erman Okay
Yönetim Asistanı / Regieassistenz: Sabri Özaydın
Produksiyon Asistanı / Produktionsass.: Zühâl Bilir
Dekor / Bühnenbild: Thomas Radigk

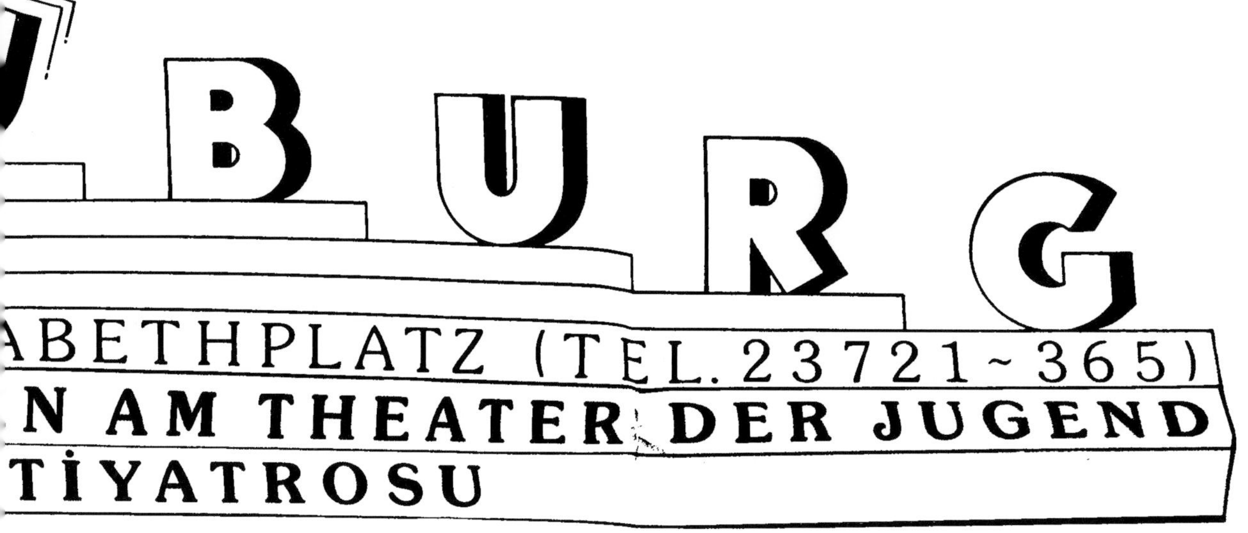
BURG
ABETHPLATZ (TEL. 23721~365)
N AM THEATER DER JUGEND
TIYATROSU

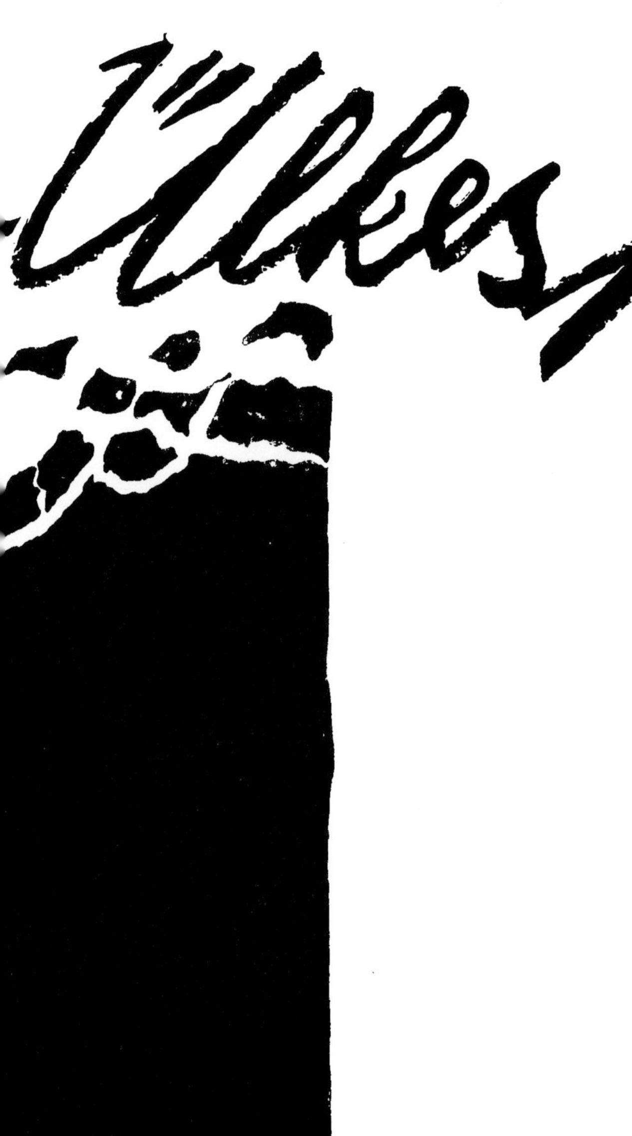
Ülkesi
Prömier/Premiere 18.12.82

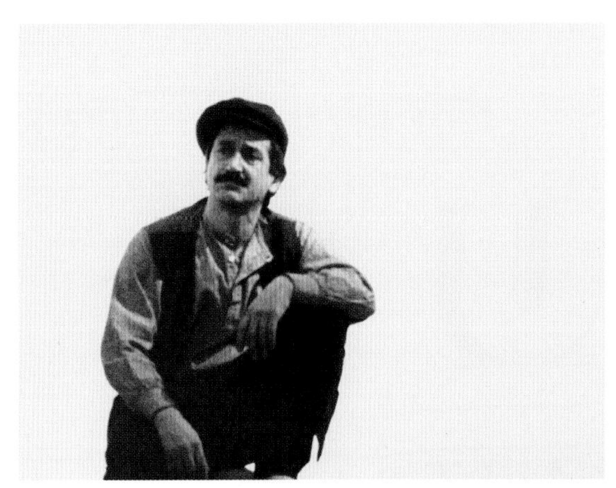

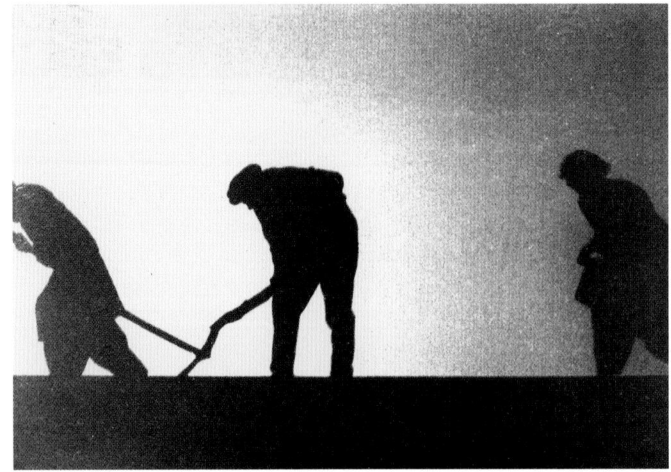

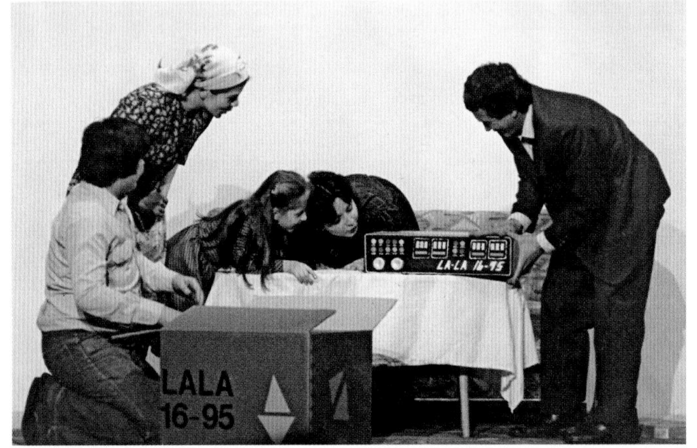

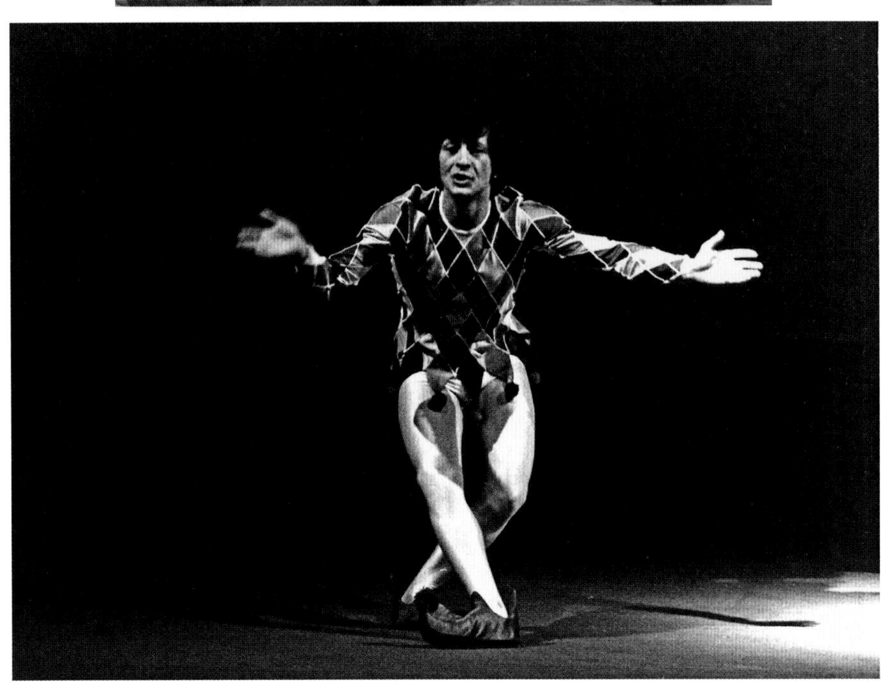

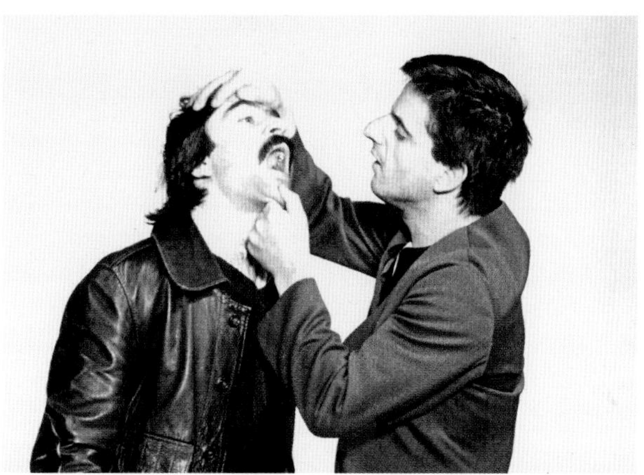

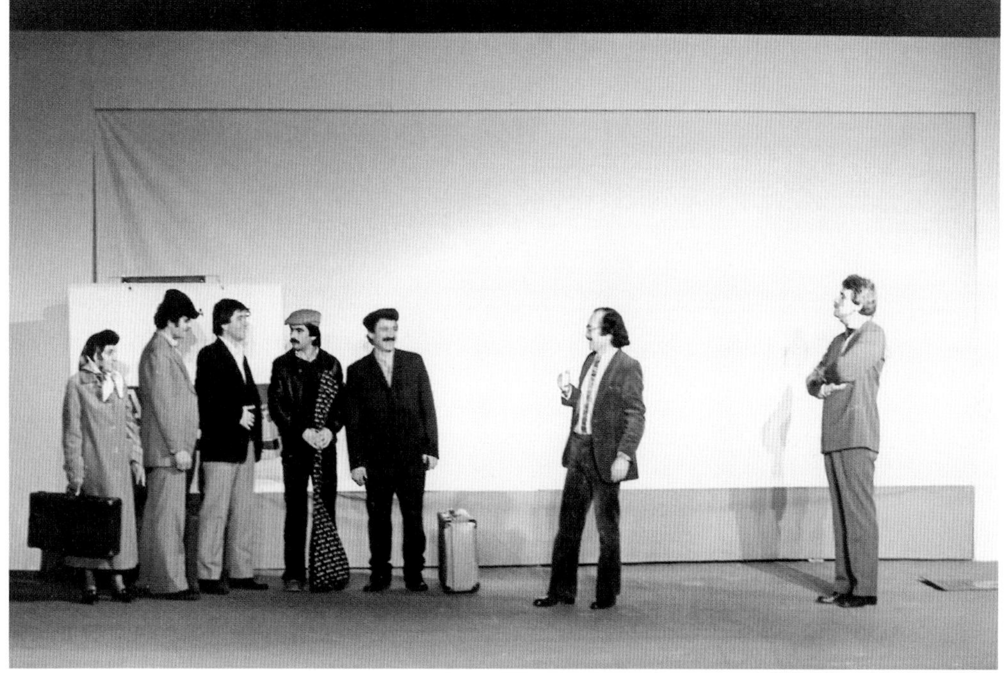

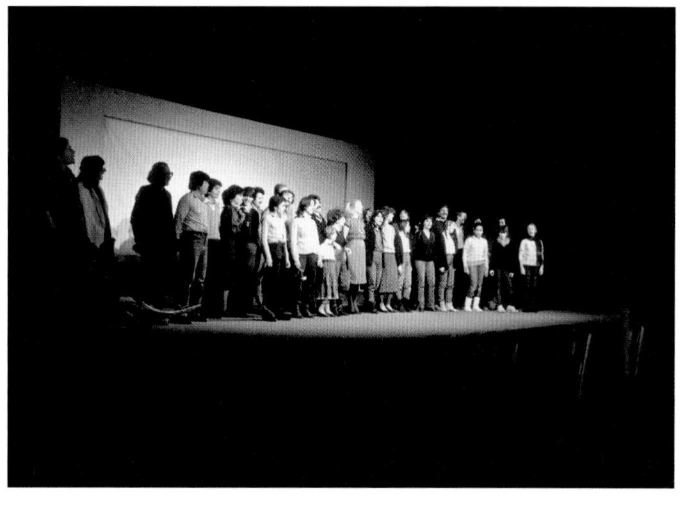

XXVI

<table>
<tr><td>THEATER DER JUGEND</td><td>MÜNCHNER KAMMERSPIELE
Theater der Jugend</td></tr>
<tr><td>Parkett
unnumeriert
6.–15. Reihe
Rechts</td><td>**Parkett**
unnumeriert
6.–15. Reihe
RECHTS</td></tr>
<tr><td>18. 12. 82</td><td>Haubold, Eschwege
Samstag 18. 12. 82 * 16 00   **II**</td></tr>
</table>

Migration künstlerisch erzählen:

Erinnerung, Vergegenwärtigung und Widerstand in Arbeiten von Cana Bilir-Meier

Burcu Dogramaci

Über Einwanderung in die Bundesrepublik Deutschland wurde lange Zeit als Geschichte der Opfer oder Täter geschrieben. Integration oder Integrationsunwilligkeit, Arbeitsmarkt und Bildung oder Segregation waren und sind dominante Themen des öffentlichen Sprechens und Schreibens über Migration.[1] Drei Bücher aus den 1980er Jahren geben einen verengten Blick auf Migrant*innen wieder; sie stammen aus einer Zeit, als „Gastarbeiter" längst Teil des bundesdeutschen Alltags geworden waren und dennoch als die Anderen der Gesellschaft wahrgenommen wurden. In diesen Publikationen wird über die „Problemlage der Ausländerbeschäftigung"[2] geschrieben, die „Wohnsituation und Ghettoisierung" (in einem Zusammenhang genannt) kritisiert und in den Kontext „Ausländerproblematik"[3] gestellt oder alternativ die „Segregation ausländischer Familien" in der „Einwanderungskolonie"[4] diagnostiziert. Allen Büchern ist gemein, dass sie über eine Personengruppe sprechen, die selbst keine Stimme erhält. „Die" Ausländer oder Migrant*innen erscheinen allzu oft als homogene Masse, die Probleme bereitet oder Schwierigkeiten hat.

Diesem Blick wird jedoch auch eine andere Perspektive entgegengesetzt, die widerständige Positionen sichtbar macht, den Migrant*innen Handlungsmacht zugesteht und die Individualisierung von Migrationserfahrung betont. Die Aktionen des künstlerisch-politischen Bündnisses „Kanak Attak" seit den 1990er Jahren bildeten einen Dammbruch, als in Theateraufführungen und Interventionen Migrant*innen eine widerständige Stimme gegeben wurde. Einer der Gründer von „Kanak Attak", Imran Ayata, beschreibt in einem Essay, wie sich „Kanak-Rap" aus Stereotypen befreite: „Zum Leben als ImmigrantIn, MigrantIn, AusländerIn, Kanake/-in, Nicht-Deutsche/r, Almanci-DeutschländerIn, Eingebürgerte/-r, ausländische/-r MitbürgerIn, Kümmel, Gastarbeiterkind oder was auch immer gehören viele Dinge wie Arbeit, Liebe, Sex, Freundschaften, Partys, Drogen, Geld, Autos etc. genauso dazu wie für den Rest. Diese und ähnliche Themen finden sich im türkischsprachigen Rap wieder. Viele Stücke sind davon geprägt, daß die RapperInnen Deutschland von ihrem Status als ‚AusländerInnen' her politisch unter die Lupe nehmen, Rassismus thematisieren sowie über ihre Lebensverhältnisse erzählen."[5] Ausstellungen wie *Fremde Heimat* (1998) als Zusammenarbeit zwischen dem Ruhrlandmuseum Essen und DoMIT (heute DOMID) Köln oder *Projekt Migration* im Kölnischen Kunstverein (2005) beschritten einen alternativen Weg, um der Pluralität und Diversität migrantischer Erfahrung einen Raum zu geben.[6] Das hieß konkret, dass Interviews mit und Bildmaterial von Migrant*innen aktiv in die Ausstellungen einbezogen wurde. Damit wurde jenen Handlungsmacht geben, über die sonst nur gesprochen wird. Mittlerweile geht die postmigrantische Forschung von Erol Yıldız, Naika Foroutan und Regina Römhild von einer durch Migration konstituierten Gesellschaft aus und gibt den Migrant*innen ihre Stimmen (zurück), damit Migrationsgeschichte auch aus Perspektive der Akteur*innen geschrieben werden kann.[7]

In dieser Gemengelage lässt sich das Werk von Cana Bilir-Meier verorten. In verschiedenen Projekten gibt die Künstlerin dem Verdrängten, Vergessenen oder von jeher wenig Sichtbaren eine Kontur. Ausgangspunkt sind meist Archive, private Nachlässe, Dokumente oder andere Materialien, die von der Künstlerin in neue Ordnungen gebracht werden. Protagonist*innen der Einwanderung nach Deutschland werden aus dem Dunkel der Vergangenheit in die Gegenwart gezogen. Die Multimedia-Arbeiten sind allerdings weniger dem Gedenken oder der Wiedergutmachung gewidmet als vielmehr aktivierende und subjektive Auseinandersetzungen. Damit bieten Bilir-Meiers Werke einen Gegenentwurf zu Denkmälern, die Erinnerung an Migration, Asyl, Rassismus und Xenophobie eine statische Form geben. Beispielhaft ist Akbar Behkalams Mahnmal (1996) für den türkischen Asylsuchenden Cemal Kemal Altun, der im Jahr 1983 aus dem 6. Stock des Berliner Verwaltungsgerichts sprang. Altuns komplexes Leben und sein Tod lassen sich kaum in einem Steinmonument an einer verkehrsreichen Straße im Zentrum der Hauptstadt verhandeln. Mit Blick auf das Werk Cana Bilir-Meiers lässt sich fragen, welche alternativen Formen der aktiven Auseinandersetzung mit Migration und ihren Geschichten möglich sind. Wie lässt sich Menschen auch über deren Leben hinaus eine Stimme geben? Wie wird Erinnerung zur Geste der Anteilnahme und der Würdigung eines vergessenen Lebens und Wirkens, indem sie auf eine andauernde Vergegenwärtigung zielt? Und wie kann erinnern nicht selbst historisch werden? Anhand dreier Projekte von Cana Bilir-Meier, die sich auf unterschiedliche Weise mit dem Komplex Migration, Xenophobie und Rassismus auseinandersetzen, sollen die Potenziale einer künstlerischen Forschung offengelegt werden.

24.5.1982.

Ein Datum bildet das Ende einer Lebensgeschichte. Der Freitod der Dichterin, Dolmetscherin und Bauzeichnerin Semra Ertan in Hamburg legt sich über ein komplexes Leben. Das Ende ist aber auch ein Anfang, ein Ausgangspunkt der Recherche, um die losen Enden eines Lebens und Nachlebens aufzunehmen und zu verknüpfen. In einem Schrank ihrer Großeltern, Vehbiye Bilir und Gani Bilir, fand Cana Bilir-Meier Notizen zur Familiengeschichte und Tonaufnahmen von Familienmitgliedern. Darunter war auch eine Kassette mit einem Interview, das ihre Großeltern nach dem Tod ihrer Tochter Semra Ertan gegeben hatten. Dieser persönliche, familiäre Zugang ist der Beginn einer Spurensuche, die Ertan als private *und* als öffentliche Figur der Zeitgeschichte identifiziert. Und ihr umfangreiches und zugleich weitgehend unbekanntes poetisches Werk ins Verhältnis setzt zur Person. Ertan ist nicht auf die Figur der Märtyrerin oder des Opfers festgeschrieben: ihre Selbstverbrennung am frühen Morgen des 24. Mai 1982[8] in Hamburg auf offener Straße kann als Ausdruck eines widerständigen Handelns gegen Ausländerhass gedeutet werden. Die Tat kündigte Semra Ertan in einem Anruf beim Norddeutschen Rundfunk an und las ihr Gedicht *Mein Name ist Ausländer*.[9]

1982, im Jahr von Ertans Suizid, publizierte Rolf Meinhardt seine Dokumentation *Ausländerfeindlichkeit*, in dem er für 1981 „sprunghaft angestiegenen Ressentiments gegenüber Ausländern"[10] diagnostizierte. Meinhardts Buch ist eine Sammlung von Zeitungs- und Zeitschriftenartikeln, in denen Ressentiments, Hetze, Gewalt, aber auch Alltagsrassismus überdeutlich werden. Die Textsammlung versammelt Publiziertes zwischen Mitte 1981 bis April 1982, um aufzuzeigen, wie sich in kürzester Zeit der Ton verschärfte. In seinem Vorwort beginnt Meinhardt mit dem Satz: „Sie schreien ‚Feuer!' und gießen, zunehmend unverhohlener, Benzin in die Flammen. In der Zeit ökonomischen Niedergangs und eines drohenden ökologischen und militärischen Kollaps (sic!) haben Demagogen Hochkonjunktur."[11] Nur zwei Monate, nachdem Meinhardt sein Vorwort verfasste, übergoss sich Semra Ertan mit Benzin und verbrannte. Die Parallelen zwischen dem Ereignis der Selbstverbrennung und der Dokumentation Meinhardts zum Rassismus in der Bundesrepublik Deutschland in den Jahren 1981 und 1982 sind evident.

Dennoch ist Ertan in der Perspektive Cana Bilir-Meiers eben nicht nur ein Opfer und auch keine typische Protagonistin der Gastarbeitermigration der 1970er Jahre. Sie ist ein Individuum mit einer eigenen Agenda, einem Leben, zu dem die Poesie genauso dazugehörte wie der Widerstand gegen Xenophobie und Ausgrenzung.

Bilir-Meiers Film *Semra Ertan* (2013) beginnt mit den eigenen Worten der Schriftstellerin: Das Wort „Unheimlich" in der Handschrift Ertans markiert den Anfang des Films und stammt aus einer ihrer Gedichte, in dem es heißt: „Wenn sie sagt/Sie sei unheimlich/Glücklich/Heißt es/Dass sie heimlich/Unglücklich ist/Weil sie/Kein Heim hat".

Ertan verknüpft das Heim und damit auch latent die Heimat mit Glück und Unglück. Aus dem „etwas ist unheimlich" wird „sie sei unheimlich", was ein nicht heimisch werden evoziert. Die Person, von der Ertan in der dritten

Person spricht, findet keinen vertrauten Raum. Worte und Handschriften verweisen auf die unverwechselbare Identität der Autorin, und der Film gibt damit der Urheberin der Worte in ihrer eigenen Schrift einen Raum. Damit wird das Sprechen *über* eine Person, was noch der Filmtitel suggeriert, zum Sprechen *der* Person. Cana Bilir-Meier verleiht ihrer Protagonistin damit eine Handlungsmacht über ihre Rezeption. Sie spricht, und nicht der Film spricht über sie.

Die Annäherung Cana Bilir-Meiers an ihre Tante wird betont, wenn sie im Film aus einem ihrer Liebesgedichte liest. Mit ihrer Stimme wird das Œuvre der Schriftstellerin erneut vergegenwärtigt, wobei der Blick der Kamera über das Notizbuch Ertans streift. Wir lesen die türkischen Sätze, während die Stimme der Künstlerin das Gedicht auf Deutsch spricht. Unweigerlich wird die bilinguale und transkulturelle Eigenart eines Schaffens deutlich, formuliert sich das Mäandern und Wandern zwischen Sprachen und Erinnerungen. Die Gleichzeitigkeit von Verschiedenem existiert auch im Familienarchiv zu Ertan selbst, in dem Cana Bilir-Meier neben Zeitungsartikeln, Gedichten, Notizen, Briefen auch eine Heiratsurkunde, ein Attest oder Deutschübungen fand.[12] Im Archiv bildet sich die Vielschichtigkeit der Persönlichkeit ab, die nicht nur Schriftstellerin, nicht nur Migrantin, nicht nur Deutschlernende war. Diese pluralen Zugänge werden im öffentlichen Sprechen über Migrierende, Geflüchtete, Fremde viel zu häufig auf eine enge Spur gebracht, damit prototypisch oder stereotyp über das Andere oder die Anderen geschrieben, gesprochen und geurteilt werden kann.

Wie das funktioniert, zeigt sich in der Berichterstattung zu Semra Ertan. In *Semra Ertan* werden kurze Szenen aus einer Fernsehsendung des WDR montiert, die Betroffenheit über den „Tod einer Türkin" formuliert, aber ihren Namen ungenannt lässt.[13] Indem Bilir-Meier die Sendung in ihren Film schneidet, setzt sie dem Wort der Schriftstellerin die oberflächliche Rezeption gegenüber. Sie gibt derjenigen, über die berichtet wird, das erste Wort. Bei ihren Recherchen konnte die Künstlerin eruieren, dass 1982 ein Musikstück für Semra Ertan komponiert worden war. Dieses Oktett von Enjott Schneider ist ebenfalls im Film zu hören. Somit wird *Semra Ertan* zu einer Collage von Materialien aus verschiedenen Zeiten, von verschiedenen Autor*innen, mit polyphonen Stimmen, in der aber diejenige der Dichterin stets hörbar bleibt und nicht von anderen Stimmen überlagert wird. Wichtig ist dabei, dass der Film nie die Perspektive der Künstlerin verschleiert, sondern sich stets als Rekonstruktion und Konstruktion zu erkennen gibt. Zu sehen ist, wie sich Cana Bilir-Meier lesend und recherchierend über Ordner, Notizbücher und Fotografien einen Zugang zu Semra Ertan erarbeitet. Damit ist die Gegenwart der Künstlerin im Augenblick der Rekonstruktion eines Schaffens und Lebens im Film präsent. Bilir-Meiers Film behauptet nicht, ein abgeschlossenes, wahrhaftiges Werk zu sein. Die Fragmente, die in ihm zusammengeführt werden, bieten sich für eine wiederholte Lektüre an und fordern von den Rezipierenden, stets aufs Neue zusammengesetzt zu werden.

6.10.1967.

Die Grundsteinlegung der Freimann-Moschee datierte auf einen Oktobertag, fand jedoch unter veränderten Maßgaben statt. Nicht der Grundstein, sondern ein symbolischer Marmorstein wurde verlegt. Etwa 50 Jahre danach brachte Cana Bilir-Meier den Grundstein in einem performativen Akt innerhalb des Festivals *Public Art Munich* am 26. Mai 2018 in die Moschee zurück. Dies war Teil und Ergebnis einer künstlerischen Recherche nach den Hintergründen und Kontexten des Bauvorhabens, vor allem aber auch nach den Urheber*innen selbst, dem Architekten Osman Edip Gürel und der

Innenarchitektin Necla Gürel, die bislang kaum in der deutschen oder in der lokalen Baugeschichte vorkommen. Cana Bilir-Meiers *Foundation Stone* ist eine Rekonstruktionsarbeit, die Wunden und die Nahtstellen zwischen Gegenwart und Vergangenheit sichtbar, Fragen und Leerstellen bestehen lässt. Ihr künstlerisches Forschungsprojekt ist keine Zeitreise in die 1960er Jahre, sondern folgt den Spuren aus der Gegenwart heraus. Zugleich aber bietet ihre Arbeit einen Ausgangspunkt, um Modelle der Historiografie zu hinterfragen. Geschichtsschreibung tritt nicht als ‚objektive' Wahrheit in Erscheinung, vielmehr ist Erinnerung und das öffentliche Gedächtnis einem Selektionsprozess unterworfen. Auch neue Forschungsinteressen und -erkenntnisse modellieren die Wahrnehmung auf einen Gegenstand. So thematisierten gleich zwei Publikationen im Jahr 2011 die Freimann-Moschee im Fadenkreuz politischer Interessen und im Kontext der Instrumentalisierung des politischen Islam; das Architektenpaar selbst fand nur marginal Erwähnung.[14]

Überhaupt ist es erstaunlich, dass Osman Edip Gürel (1925-1984) und Necla Gürel (1926-2007) als bedeutende Architekt_innen der Münchner Nachkriegsjahrzehnte als kaum bekannt und vergessen gelten müssen. Seit 1955 hielt sich das Paar in München auf. Gürel verantwortete unter anderem den Umbau des gehobenen türkischen Restaurants Istanbul am Oskar-von-Miller-Ring in München. Besonders in Schwabing, wo er ein eigenes Architekturbüro führte, war Gürel für die Planung von Gebäuden wie der Rudolf-Steiner-Schule und des Theaters Leo 17 in der Leopoldstraße verantwortlich. Zudem entwarf er das Gebäude des türkischen Generalkonsulates – und erhielt 1966 den Auftrag für die Moschee in München-Freimann.[15] Diese wurde als moderner Stahlbetonbau mit zeltartiger Kuppel und großen Fensterelementen verwirklicht. Die Innengestaltung sollte durch Necla Gürel verwirklicht werden, die an der Akademie der Bildenden Künste in München Bildhauerei studiert hatte. Doch wurden ihre Planungen in der 1972 eröffneten Moschee aus finanziellen Gründen nicht ausgeführt.[16]

Ihre Recherchen führten Cana Bilir-Meier zu den beiden Töchtern des Architektenpaares, die ihre eigenen Perspektiven auf das Leben und Wirken der Eltern vermittelten. Diese privaten, familialen Beziehungen geben einen wichtigen Rahmen für *Foundation Stone*. In einer Broschüre, einer Audioinstallation (2018) und einem Film (2019) bilden die Geschichten der Töchter Hürdem und Zerender Gürel einen möglichen Zugang zur Moschee. So berichten die beiden von ihren Eltern, ihrer eigenen Kindheit und Jugend, Prozessen der Ablösung und dem Leben mit/in zwei Sprachen, Kulturen und Lebenswelten. Sie erzählen, wie die Eltern sich in das München der 1950er und 1960er Jahre einlebten und später doch aus wirtschaftlichen Gründen oder Heimweh fortgingen. Bilir-Meiers Audioinstallation brachte die Stimmen der Töchter zumindest für eine bestimmte Zeit in das Gebäude, das wiederum selbst von der Bautätigkeit der Eltern Zeugnis gibt. In das Projekt einbezogen ist auch die Mutter Cana Bilir-Meiers, die Münchner Kinderpsychotherapeutin Zühal Bilir-Meier. Sie ergänzt die Erzählungen der Architektentöchter um eine Perspektive einer Expertin, die Ratschläge für die Erziehung heranwachsender Jugendlicher in migrantischen Communities artikuliert. Offensiv bringt Cana Bilir-Meier die Rekonstruktionsarbeit als individuellen künstlerischen Akt in ihre Arbeit; im Film vermittelt sich die Sichtweise der Künstlerin auf das Vorhaben, indem ihr Schattenriss beim Filmen auf der Außenhaut des Gebäudes erscheint. Sie filmt sich beim Gang über das Gelände der Moschee oder beim Anfertigen ihrer Frottagen: an die Architektur wird ein Blatt Papier gelegt und diese mit Kreiden auf das Papier durchgerieben. In ihrem Projekt *Foundation Stone* ist

Bilir-Meier Urheberin des Films als auch Akteurin in Dialog mit der Architektur, den Zeitzeuginnen und Nachkommen, den Archiv- und Pressematerialien. Mit der Einzelerzählung zur Freimann-Moschee praktiziert die Künstlerin eine Geschichtsschreibung der Singularitäten im Sinne des Philosophen Jacques Rancière: „Die Geschichte existiert nicht als ein an der zeitlichen Entwicklung orientierter Ablauf, sie existiert quer über die singulären Formen von Historizität: singuläre Weisen, von denen die Aufteilungen des Sichtbaren und des Sagbaren, die Verteilungen der Modi sinnlicher Erfahrung, die Beziehungen zwischen dem Leben und seinen Formen der Symbolisierung verschoben werden. Es kann für mich nur eine Geschichte der Singularitäten geben."[17] Aus der Addition der Einzelgeschichten kann sich somit eine vielstimmige Historie konstituieren, die mehr ist als *eine* einzige mögliche Erzählung.

22.7.2016.

Lange Zeit wurde der rassistische Anschlag eines 18jährigen am Olympia Einkaufszentrum in München als Amoklauf rezipiert. Der Täter erschoss im Juli 2016 neun Jugendliche, verletzte fünf weitere und tötete sich dann selbst. Die Erschossenen stammten aus migrantischen Familien, die meisten waren Jugendliche. Es starben Armela S., Can L., Choussein D., Dijamant „Dimo" Z., Guiliano-Josef K., Janos Roberto R., Sabina S., Selçuk K. und Sevda D.. Obgleich die rechtsextreme Gesinnung des Täters rasch bekannt wurde, bezeichneten die Staatsanwaltschaft und das Landeskriminalamt die Tat als Amoklauf und gaben vor allem Mobbing und eine psychische Erkrankung als Ursachen an. Im Abschlussbericht heißt es am 17. März 2017: „Es liegen keine Anhaltspunkte dafür vor, dass er bei dem Amoklauf die einzelnen Opfer gezielt ausgewählt hat. Es ist auch nicht davon auszugehen, dass die Tat politisch motiviert war."[18] Dabei ist auffällig, dass die Opfer wohl nach physischen Merkmalen ausgesucht wurden, die sie aus einer südosteuropäischen Herkunftsregion auswiesen. Im März 2018 jedoch stufte das Bundesamt für Justiz das Geschehen als extremistische Tat ein.[19] Über den Täter, seine iranische Herkunft, seinen Hass und seine Sozialisierung in rechten Foren erfuhr die Öffentlichkeit mehr Details als über die neun Ermordeten.

In Cana Bilir-Meiers Film *This makes me want to predict the past* (2019) ist der Anschlag ein Ausgangspunkt, um sich den Lebenswelten, Träumen, Ängsten und Wünschen migrantischer Jugendlicher zu nähern. Diese Perspektive verweist einerseits zurück auf die ermordeten jungen Menschen, die am 22. Juli 2016 ums Leben kamen. Andererseits ist der Film auch ganz der Gegenwart und Zukunft von Jugendlichen verschrieben, deren Eltern oder Großeltern aus einem anderen Land nach München kamen. Bilir-Meier begleitete einige Jugendliche mit der Kamera auf ihren Wegen durch das Einkaufszentrum, widmete sich ihren Wünschen und Hoffnungen, ihren Alpträumen und Ängsten. Damit wird eine grundlegende Frage aufgeworfen: Wenn sich Xenophobie und Rassismus durch Hass auf Kollektive oder Gruppen nährt, wie lässt sich diesen die Stimme, das Gesicht, die individuelle Identität im öffentlichen Sprechen zurückgeben? Wie werden aus „den" Migrant*innen, Muslim*innen, Geflüchteten und Opfern des Anschlags Individuen mit Namen, subjektiven Erinnerungen und Träumen?

Am Ort selbst arbeitete Cana Bilir-Meier mit der künstlerischen Methode der Frottage: Das Olympia Einkaufszentrum wird von ihr durch das Auflegen von Papier und mit Kreiden abgerieben, erfasst, angeeignet. Diese Methode, die bereits in dem Projekt zur Freimann-Moschee zum Tragen kam, ist Teil einer künstlerisch „dichte[n] Beschreibung"[20] (Clifford Geertz), bei der die Forschenden sich selbst und ihre Methoden in die Interpretation aufnehmen.

Die Frottagen sind Abdrücke der Architektur und eines traumatischen Schauplatzes, der wie ein Vexierbild erscheint: zugleich ein Tatort und ein Ort, an dem sich junge Migrant*innen gern und häufig aufhalten (und deshalb im Umkehrschluss vermutlich auch das Ziel des Attentäters waren).

Cana Bilir-Meiers Arbeiten fügen dem Zeitstrahl der deutschen Geschichte Daten hinzu, die nicht oder nur wenig im öffentlichen Bewusstsein stehen: am 24.5.1982 verbrannte sich eine Frau türkischer Herkunft, um ein Zeichen gegen Ausländerhass zu setzen; auf den 6.10.1967 datiert die geplante Grundsteinlegung für die erste bayerische Moschee in München-Freimann und markiert den Bau eines Werks zweier türkischstämmiger Baukünstler der deutschen Nachkriegsmoderne; am 22.7.2016 wurden neun Jugendliche migrantischer Herkunft von einem vermutlich rechtsradikalen Täter erschossen. Diese drei Ereignisse sind nicht miteinander vergleichbar, sie verkörpern so unterschiedliche Themen wie Selbstverbrennung und Rassismus, den Anteil migrantischer Künstler*innen und Architekt*innen an der deutschen Architekturgeschichte, ein extremistisches Attentat und das Leben von Jugendlichen in Deutschland. In ihren künstlerischen Forschungen und den damit einhergehenden Arbeiten gelingt es Bilir-Meier, aus dem Kollektiven das Individuelle zu destillieren und – vice versa – in den konkreten Einzelerzählungen Geschichte in Erscheinung treten zu lassen.[21] Jede Geschichtserzählung beinhaltet unweigerlich die Perspektive ihrer Urheber*innen, der Blick auf Zeiten und Ereignisse ist nie neutral, sondern die Perspektive aus einem lebendigem Auge. Zugleich wird in Cana Bilir-Meiers Arbeiten evident, dass Historiografien anfällig sind für Glättungen, Auslassungen und Angleichungen.

Geleitet werden Bilir-Meiers Projekte zu Migration und Migrant*innen durch ein politisches Verständnis künstlerischer Arbeit. So schreibt die Künstlerin über ihre Arbeit zur Freimann-Moschee: „In einer ‚Gesellschaft der Vielen‘ (Tribunal NSU-Komplex Auflösen) brauchen wir auch die Geschichte der Vielen. Die Moschee ist ein historisch aufgeladener Ort, an dem sich Geschichten über politische Instrumentalisierung von Religion, das Bedürfnis nach einem spirituellen Raum und dessen architektonische Gestaltung bis heute überlagern. Das Projekt ‚Grundstein‘ ist eine Recherchearbeit, die unterschiedliche Erzählstränge aufnimmt und das migrantisch situierte Wissen, die migrantischen Geschichten, Positionen und Perspektiven sichtbar machen will."[22] Selbst in gemeinschaftlich geschriebenen Texten wie Wikipedia, die für sich plurale Perspektiven beanspruchen, bleibt es allzu oft bei eindimensionalen Zugängen. In dem Online-Lexikon hat Semra Ertan einen eigenen kurzen Eintrag, ist aber auch Bestandteil des Lemmas „Selbstverbrennung", wo sie unter Fällen in Deutschland aufgeführt ist.[23] Sie findet in dem Artikel eine Gemeinschaft mit anderen – auch politisch motivierten – Freitoden. Ihr komplexes Leben mit Freuden und Tragödien, ihre schriftstellerische Arbeit und ihre Fremdheitserfahrungen bleiben hinter dem schmalen Eintrag unsichtbar.

Cana Bilir-Meiers Werke haben nicht den Anspruch auf lexikalische Sachlichkeit. Sie verweigern eine Vogelschau auf ein Leben, Werk, Bauwerk oder Ereignis, der Blick bleibt fragmentiert und prismatisch und ist subjektiv geprägt. Damit bekennt sich Bilir-Meier zu einer Unüberschaubarkeit, zu einem Gehen auf wankendem Boden, einem zersplitterten Sprechen und Denken.

1
Dazu auch Sylvia Hahn: *Historische Migrationsforschung*, Campus Verlag, Frankfurt am Main/New York 2012, S. 15; Sabine Hess: *Politiken der (Un-)Sichtbarmachung. Eine Kritik der Wissens- und Bilderproduktionen zu Migration*, in: Erol Yildiz und Marc Hill (Hg.): *Nach der Migration. Postmigrantische Perspektiven jenseits der Parallelgesellschaft*, transcript Verlag, Bielefeld 2015, S. 49-64.

2
Ulrich Herbert: *Geschichte der Ausländerbeschäftigung in Deutschland 1880 bis 1980. Saisonarbeiter, Zwangsarbeiter, Gastarbeiter*, J.H.W. Dietz, Berlin/Bonn 1986, S. 220.

3
Beide Zitate aus Klaus Unger: *Ausländerpolitik in der Bundesrepublik Deutschland* (Bielefelder Studien zur Entwicklungssoziologie, 7), Verlag Breitenbach, Saarbrücken/Fort Lauderdale 1980, S. 113, 116.

4
Friedrich Heckmann: *Die Bundesrepublik: Ein Einwanderungsland? Zur Soziologie der Gastarbeiterbevölkerung als Einwandererminorität*, Klett-Cotta, Stuttgart 1981, S. 208.

5
Imran Ayata: *Kanak-Rap in Almanya – Über die schweren Folgen Deutschlands*, in: Katja Dominik, Marc Jünemann, Jan Motte und Astrid Reinecke im Auftrag der Geschichtswerkstatt Göttingen (Hg.): *Angeworben – eingewandert – abgeschoben. Ein anderer Blick auf die Einwanderungsgesellschaft Bundesrepublik Deutschland*, Westfälisches Dampfboot, Münster 1999, S. 273-287, hier S. 280.

6
Zur Ausstellung „Fremde Heimat" siehe Mathilde Jamin: *Fremde Heimat. Zur Geschichte der Arbeitsmigration aus der Türkei*, in: Jan Motte, Rainer Ohliger, Anne von Oswald (Hg.): *50 Jahre Bundesrepublik – 50 Jahre Einwanderung*, Campus Verlag, Frankfurt am Main/New York 1999, S. 145-164. Siehe auch *Projekt Migration*. Ausst.-Kat. Kölnischer Kunstverein, DuMont Literatur und Kunstverlag, Köln 2005.

7
Naika Foroutan: *The Post-migrant Paradigm*, in: Jan-Jonathan Bock und Sharon Macdonald (Hg.): *Refugees Welcome? Difference and Diversity in a Changing Germany*, Berghahn Books, New York/Oxford 2019, S. 142-167.

8
Neue Recherchen bei der Vorbereitung der Ausstellung *Cana Bilir-Meier. Düşler Ülkesi* im Kunstverein in Hamburg ergaben, dass die Selbstverbrennung Semra Ertans nicht, wie bisher angenommen, am 26.5.1982 geschah, sondern zwei Tage früher.

9
Vgl. Cana Bilir-Meier: *Semra Ertan. Her Own Voice / Kendi Sesi / Ihre eigene Stimme*, Wien 2017, S. 11.

10
Rolf Meinhardt: Vorwort, in: *Ausländerfeindlichkeit. Eine Dokumentation*, Express, Berlin 1982, S. 1.

11
Ebd.

12
Vgl. Cana Bilir-Meier: *Nachdenken über das Archiv. Notizen zu Semra Ertan* (2013), in: *Stimme. Zeitschrift der Initiative Minderheiten*, Nr. 94/2015, Bürgerinitiative Demokratisch Leben, Innsbruck 2015, S. 11.

13
Ebd., S. 12f.

14
Vgl. Ian Johnson: *Die vierte Moschee. Nazis, CIA und der islamische Fundamentalismus*, Klett-Cotta, Stuttgart 2011; Stefan Meining: *Eine Moschee in Deutschland. Nazis, Geheimdienste und der Aufstieg des politischen Islam im Westen*, Beck Verlag, München 2011.

15
Cana Bilir Meier: *26. Mai 2018. Grundstein Foundation Stone. Eine künstlerische Rechercharbeit*. Broschüre zum Projekt, München 2018, o.S.

16
Ebd.

17
Jacques Rancière: *Ist Kunst widerständig?*, Merve Verlag, Berlin 2008, S. 68f.

18
https://archive.fo/wiHMz#selection-1307.0-1311.73. Zugriff: 28.4.2019.

19
https://www.zeit.de/gesellschaft/zeitgeschehen/2018-03/olympia-einkaufszentrum-muenchener-amoklauf-extremismus-einstufung-bundesbehoerde. Zugriff: 28.4.2019.

20
Clifford Geertz: *Dichte Beschreibung. Beiträge zum Verstehen kultureller Systeme*, Suhrkamp Verlag, Frankfurt am Main 1983.

21
Dazu auch Ayşe Güleç und Cana Bilir-Meier in einem Gespräch in der Zeitschrift *Camera Austria*, in dem es heißt: „Es geht natürlich um das Persönliche, ich möchte aber keine einzelnen Geschichten erzählen, sondern mich interessiert, wie eine kollektive Geschichte erzählt werden kann, die dennoch persönlich und intim ist." (Bilir-Meier) oder „Am Beispiel von konkreten Geschichten und Geschehnissen ist es möglich, kollektiv erlebte Erfahrungen als Geschichte zu erzählen – auch weil diese Entscheidung es ermöglicht, ein Gegennarrativ zu entwickeln." (Güleç). Ayşe Güleç: *Cana Bilir-Meier. Bewegungen zwischen Archiven – Dekolonisierung von Disziplinen*, in: Camera Austria, 141/2018, Verein CAMERA AUSTRIA. Labor für Fotografie und Theorie, Graz 2018, S.33-34, hier S. 34.

22
Cana Bilir Meier: *26. Mai 2018. Grundstein Foundation Stone. Eine künstlerische Rechercharbeit*. Broschüre zum Projekt, München 2018, o.S.

23
https://de.wikipedia.org/wiki/Selbstverbrennung#Fälle_in_Deutschland. Zugriff: 26.4.2019.

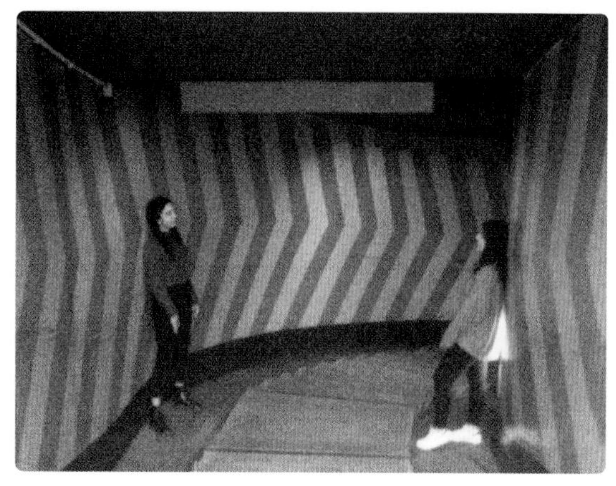

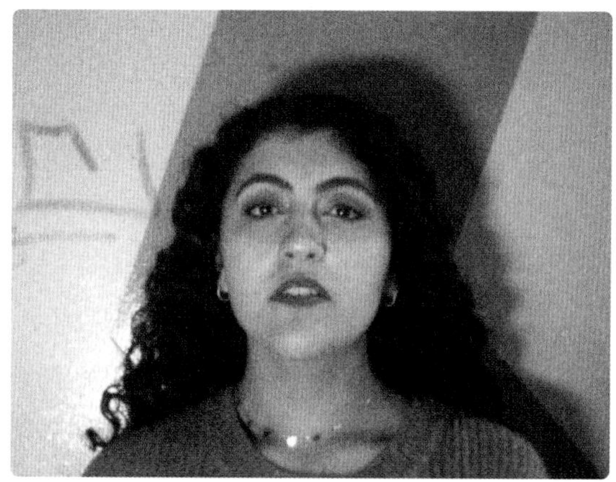

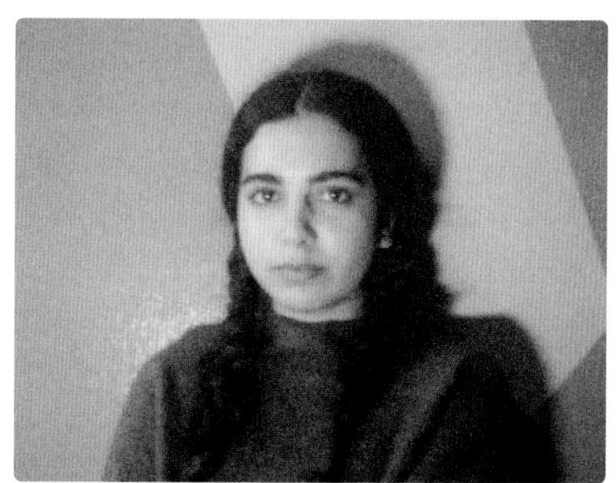

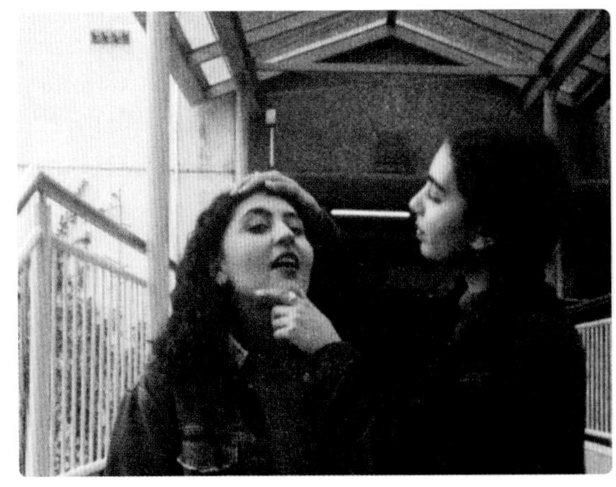

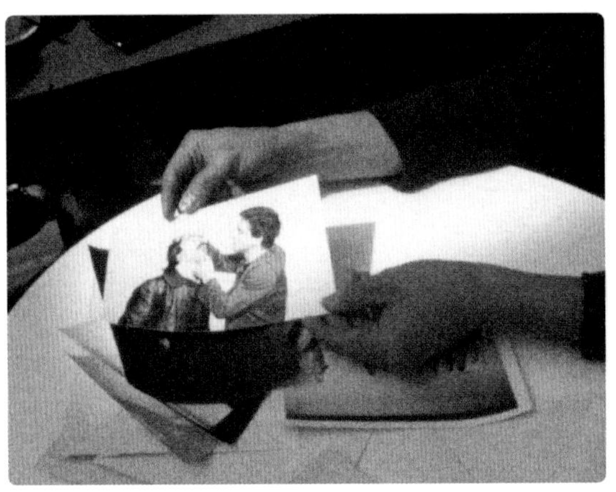

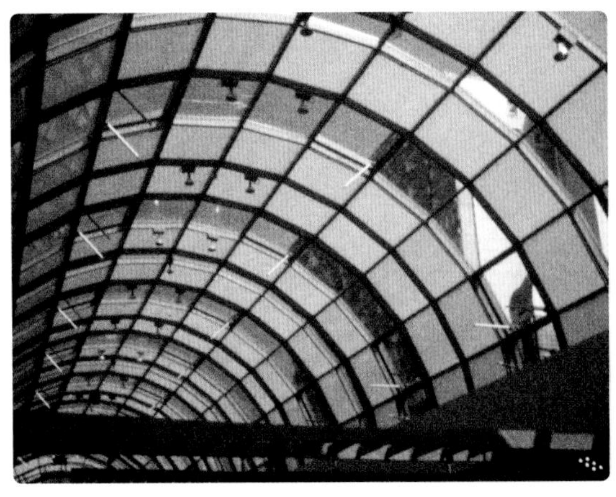

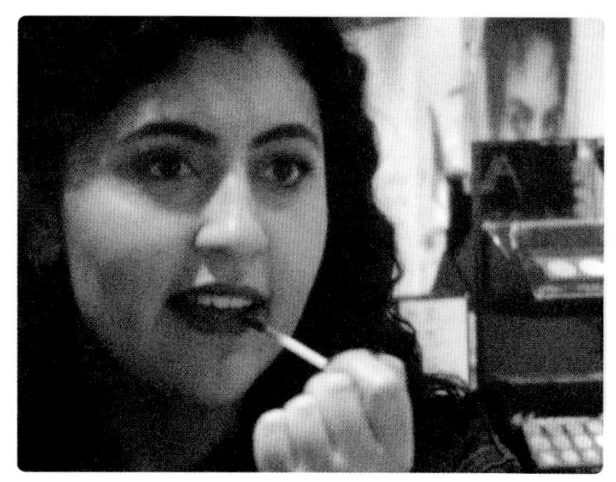

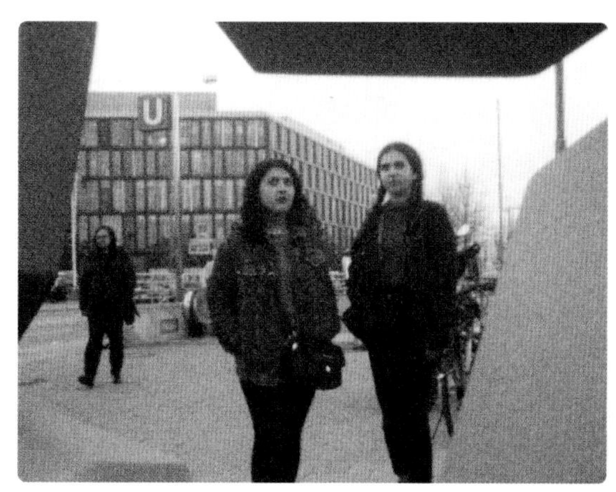

xxx

Göçü sanatla anlatmak:

Cana Bilir-Meier'in çalışmalarında hatırlama, göz önüne getirme ve direniş.

Burcu Doğramacı

Federal Almanya'ya göç uzun süre kurbanlar ve faillerin tarihi olarak yazıldı. Göç üzerine yazılan ve konuşulanların belirleyici konuları uyum veya uyum isteksizliği, iş pazarı, eğitim ve dışlama idi.[1] 1980'li yıllara ait üç kitap göçmenlere yönelik dar bakış açısını yansıtıyor. Bu kitaplar, "misafir işçiler" (Gastarbeiter) çoktan Federal Almanya'nın günlük yaşamının bir parçası haline gelmiş olmalarına rağmen, halen toplumun "Ötekileri" olarak algılandıkları döneme ait. Bu yayınlarda "yabancı çalıştırmanın sorunları", "yabancılar"[2] üzerine yazılıyordu, "ikamet durumu ve gettolaşma"[3] (tek bağlamda) eleştiriliyor ve "yabancı sorunu"yla ilişkilendiriliyordu veya, "göç kolonisinde" "yabancı ailelerin soyutlanması"[4] teşhis ediliyordu. Tüm bu kitapların ortak yanı, kendilerine söz hakkı verilmeyen kişi grubu üzerine görüş belirtmeleriydi. "Yabancılar ve göçmenler" çok sık bir şekilde, sorun yaratan ve sorunları olan homojen kitle olarak tezahür ediliyordu.

Bu bakış açısının karşına, direnişçi pozisyonları görünür kılan, göçmenlerin eylem gücüne sahip olduğunu kabul eden ve bireysel göç tecrübesini vurgulayan bir perspektif kondu. Sanatsal-siyasal ittifak olan "Kanak Attak"ın 1990'lı yıllardan beri yaptığı eylemler, tiyatro gösterileri ve müdahalelerle göçmenlerin sesi olması, bir nevi set yıkılmasıydı. "Kanak Attak"ın kurucularından İmran Ayata bir makalesinde "Kanak Rap"in nasıl kendini stereotip düşüncelerden soyutladığını şöyle izah ediyor: "Muhacir, göçmen, yabancı, Kanake, Alman olmayan, Almancı, vatandaşlığa geçmiş, yabancı hemşehri, kümmel, misafir işçi çocuğu veya artık nasıl tanımlarsanız tanımlayın; onlarda da iş, aşk, seks, arkadaşlıklar, partiler, uyuşturucu, para, otomobiller vs. gibi şeyler toplumun diğer bölümünde olduğu gibi hayata aittir. Bu ve benzer konular Türkçe sözlü rep müzikte bulunmakta. Birçok rep parçası, repçilerin Almanya'daki "yabancı" olma konumlarını, siyasi açıdan mercek altına almaları, ırkçılığı konu etmeleri ve ayrıca yaşam durumlarını anlatmalarıyla biçimlendi.[5] Essen Ruhr Havzası Müzesi ve DoMIT Köln (şimdiki adı DOMID) işbirliğindeki *Fremde Heimat (Yabancı Vatan)* (1998) gibi sergiler veya Köln Sanat Derneğindeki (2005) *Projekt Migration (Proje Göç)*, göç tecrübesinin çokluğuna ve çeşitliliğine alan açmak için başka bir yol izlediler.[6] Somut olarak bunun anlamı, göçmenlerle yapılan röportajların ve resim malzemesinin aktif şekilde sergiye dahil edilmesi demekti. Böylece şimdiye kadar sadece haklarında konuşulanlara, eylem gücü verilmiş oldu.

Bu esnada Erol Yıldız'ın, Naika Foroutan'ın ve Regina Römhild'in göç sonrası araştırmaları, göç ile şekillenmiş bir toplumdan hareket ediyor ve göç tarihinin aktörlerinin perspektifinden yazılabilmesi için göçmenlere seslerini (geri) veriyor.[7]

Cana Bilir-Meier'in eserlerinin yerini bu karışım içinde saptayabiliriz. Sanatçı çeşitli projelerde kenara itilenlere, unutulanlara veya öteden beri daha az görünür olanlara silüet veriyor. Başlangıç noktası genelde sanatçı tarafından yeniden düzenlenen arşivler, özel miraslar, evraklar veya başka malzemeler oluyor. Almanya'ya göçün baş aktörleri, geçmişin karanlığından çıkarılıp günümüze getiriliyor. Bu multimedya çalışmaları, anma veya hasarı telafiye yönelik olmaktan ziyade, daha çok harekete geçirici ve subjektif bir mücadeleye adanmış. Bilir-Meier'in eserleri böylece göç anısına, ilticaya, ırkçılığa ve yabancı düşmanlığına sabit şekil veren anıtların karşısına zıt bir modelle çıkıyor. 1983'te Berlin İdari Mahkemesinin 6. katından atlayan Türk mülteci Cemal Kemal Altun'un anısına Akbar Behkalam tarafından yapılan anıt (1996) buna örnek gösterilebilir. Altun'un karışık yaşamını ve ölümünü, başkentin merkezinde yoğun trafiğin olduğu bir caddedeki taş anıtla tarif etmek pek mümkün değildir. Cana Bilir-Meier'in eseri göz önünde bulundurularak, göç ve göç tarihiyle hangi alternatif aktif teati şekillerinin mümkün olduğu sorulabilir.

Yaşamlarının ötesinde insanların sesleri nasıl duyurulabilir? Anma nasıl duygudaşlık jesti olabilir ve unutulan bir yaşam ve etkisi nasıl sürekli göz önünde bulundurularak onurlandırılabilir? Ve anmak nasıl tarihsel olmaz? Cana Bilir-Meier'in, göç, yabancı düşmanlığı ve ırkçılık kompleksini irdelediği farklı tarzdaki üç projesi örneğinde sanatsal araştırmanın potensiyeli gözler önüne serilecek.

24.5.1982.

Bu tarih bir yaşam hikayesinin sonunu belirliyor. Hamburg'da yazar, tercüman ve çizer Semra Ertan'ın karışık yaşamı üzerine intihar çöküyor. Son aynı zamanda bir başlangıç, bir yaşamın ve yaşam sonrasının dağınık uçlarını alıp, birleştirmek için yapılan araştırmanın bir başlangıcı.

Cana Bilir-Meier, ninesi Vehbiye Bilir ve dedesi Gani Bilir'in dolabında, aile hikayesine ilişkin notlar ve aile üyelerine ait ses kayıtlarını buldu. Bunların arasında ninesinin ve dedesinin, kızları Semra Ertan'ın ölümünden sonra, verdiği röportajı içeren bir kaset de vardı. Bu özel, ailevi bağı, Ertan'ı özel *ve* çağımızın tarihinde toplumsal bir figür olarak belirlenmesine götüren süreçteki izlerin takibinin başlangıcı oldu. Kapsamlı ama aynı zamanda pek bilinmeyen şiirleri bu şekilde kişiliğiyle ilişkilendirildi. Ertan, kahraman veya kurban figürüne sabitlenmiş değil: 24 Mayıs 1982[8] sabahında erkenden Hamburg'da sokak ortasında kendini yakması, yabancı düşmanlığına karşı direniş eylemi olarak yorumlanabilir. Semra Ertan intihar eylemi yapacağını Kuzey Almanya Yayın Kurumuna açtığı bir telefonla bildirdi ve *Mein Name ist Ausländer (Benim Adım Yabancı)* şiirini okudu.[9]

1982'de, Ertan'ın intihar ettiği yılda Rolf Meinhardt, 1981'de yabancılara karşı aşırı derecede artan tepkiler üzerine yazdığı, *Ausländerfeindlichkeit (Yabancı Düşmanlığı)*[10] isimli kitabını yayınladı. Meinhardt'ın kitabı, ön yargıların, kışkırtmanın, şiddetin vegünlük yaşamdaki ırkçılığın belirgin olduğu gazete ve dergi haberlerinden oluşan bir seçki. Seçki çok kısa zaman içinde tonun ne kadar keskinleştiğini göstermek amacıyla, 1981 ortasından Nisan 1982'ye kadar olan süre içinde toplanan yayınları kapsıyor. Meinhardt ön sözüne şu cümleyle başlıyor: "'Ateş!' diye bağırıyorlar ve alevlere, gizlemeye gerek duymadan, benzin döküyorlar. Ekonomik batış döneminde, ekolojik ve askeri çöküntü (sic!) tehdidi ortamında demagogların konjonktürü yüksek olur."[11] Meinhardt ön sözünü kaleme aldıktan sadece iki ay sonra Semra Ertan üzerine benzin dökerek, kendini yaktı. Ertan'ın kendini yakma olayı ve Meinhardt'ın kitabında bahsi geçen 1981-1982 yılları Almanya'sındaki ırkçılık arasında bulunan paralellik bariz ortada.

Buna rağmen Ertan, Cana Bilir-Meier'in perspektifinde sadece bir kurban değil. 1970'li yılların misafir işçi göçünün tipik bir baş aktörü de değil. Ertan kendi ajandası olan, yabancı düşmanlığı ve dışlanmaya karşı direniş gibi, şiir de hayatına ait olan bir birey.

Bilir-Meier'in filmi *Semra Ertan* (2013) yazarın kendi sözleriyle başlıyor: Ertan'ın kendi el yazısıyla yazdığı "Unheimlich" kelimesi filmin başlangıcını işaretliyor ve kendi şiirlerinden biriyle şu şekilde devam ediyor: "Wenn sie sagt/Sie sei unheimlich/Glücklich/Heißt es/Dass sie heimlich/Unglücklich ist/Weil sie/Kein Heim hat" [Kadın bahsettiğinde/Tuhaf mutluluğundan/Mutsuz demektir].

Ertan "Heim"ı ve böylece "Heimat"ı mutluluk ve mutsuzlukla ilişkendiriyor. "Bir şeyin tekinsizliği"nden [etwas ist unheimlich], "kadının tekinsizliği"ne [sie sei unheimlich] dönüşüp, dışlanma duygusunu çağrıştırıyor. Ertan'ın üçüncü tekil şahıs formunda bahsettiği kişi, güven duyacağı ortam bulamıyor. Kelimeleri ve el yazısı yazarın benzersiz kimliğine işaret ediyor ve film böylece kelimelerin sahibine kendi el yazısıyla yer vermiş oluyor. Bu şekilde filmin isminde adı geçen bir şahıs *üzerine* konuşma yönündeki telkin, *şahsın* konuşması halini alıyor. Cana Bilir-Meier algılanışı hakkındaki eylem gücünü baş aktöre vermiş oluyor. Film baş aktör üzerine konuşmuyor, baş aktörün kendisi konuşuyor.

Cana Bilir-Meier'in teyzesiyle yakınlaşması, filmde teyzesinin bir aşk şiirini okumasıyla vurgulanıyor. Sesiyle yazarın tüm eserleri tekrar göz önüne getirilirken, kamera Ertan'ın not defteri üzerinde geziniyor. Bizler ekranda Türkçe cümleleri okurken, sanatçı şiirleri Almanca seslendiriyor. Kaçınılmaz şekilde eserin iki dilliliği ve kültürler arası özelliği belirginleşiyor, diller ve anılar arasındaki gezinti ve sıçrama anlatılıyor. Farklılıkların aynı anda varoluşu, Cana Bilir-Meier'in Ertan'ın aile arşivinde de bulduğu gazete haberlerinin yanı sıra, şiirler, notlar, mektuplar, bir evlilik cüzdanı, bir doktor raporu veya Almanca ders notlarında da mevcut.[12] Arşiv Ertan'ın sadece yazar, göçmen kadın,

Almanca öğrenen kişi olmakla sınırlanamayan kişiliğinin çok yönlülüğünü de resmediyor. Bu çoklu yaklaşım, göç edenler, mülteciler, yabancılar hakkında konuşulurken genellikle çok dar bir çizgiye indirgeniyor. Bu şekilde ancak prototip veya stereotip şekilde Öteki veya Ötekiler üzerine yazılıyor, konuşuluyor ve değerlendirme yapılıyor.

Bu işleyiş Semra Ertan üzerine yapılan haberlerde de göze çarpıyor. *Semra Ertan* filminde WDR'nin televizyon programında "Türk'ün ölümünden" duyulan üzüntü dile getirilirken, isminin zikredilmediği bir kesit yer alıyor.[13] Bilir-Meier programı filmine monte ederek, Semra'nın sözleriyle, genel algının yüzeyselliğini karşı karşıya getiriyor. İlk söz hakkını, hakkında haber yapılan kişiye veriyor. Sanatçı araştırmaları sırasında, Semra Ertan için 1982'de bestelenen bir müzik parçasını ortaya çıkardı. Enjott Schneider tarafından bestelenen bu oktet filmde yer alıyor. *Semra Ertan* farklı zamanlara ait malzemelerden, farklı eser sahiplerinin katkıda bulunduğu, çok sesli olan, ama yazarın sesinin hep duyulur olduğu ve diğer sesler tarafından örtülmediği bir kolaj. Burada film sanatçının perspektifini hiç saklamıyor, bilakis rekonstrüksiyon ve konstrüksiyon tanınır kalıyor. Filmde Cana Bilir-Meier okuyarak, dosya ve not defterlerini inceleyerek ve görüntüleyerek, Semra Ertan'a yakınlaşma çalışması esnasında görünmekte. Bu şekilde sanatçının bir eser yaratma ve yaşam rekonstrüksiyonu anında orada oluşu halihazırda filmde mevcut. Bilir-Meier'in filminin tamamlanmış hakiki eser olma iddiası yok. Filmde bir araya getirilen parçalar izleyiciyi tekrarlanan bir okumaya davet ediyor ve izleyicinin bunları her zaman yeniden birleştirmesi gerekir.

6.10.1967.

Freimann Camisi'nin temel atma töreni bir ekim günü değişik şartlar altında yapıldı. Temel taşı yerine sembolik bir mermer kullanıldı. Bundan yaklaşık 50 yıl sonra Cana Bilir-Meier, 26 Mayıs 2018'de *Public Art Munich* festivali çerçevesinde performatif bir eylemle temel taşını camiye geri götürdü. Bu yapı projesinin arka planını ve bağlamını, özellikle Alman veya yerel yapı tarihinde hiç bahsedilmeyen, projenin fikir sahipleri mimar Osman Edip Gürel'i ve iç mimar Necla Gürel'i araştıran sanatsal bir çalışma oluşturuyordu. Cana Bilir-Meier'in *Temel Taş* çalışması, yaraları ve bugün ile geçmiş arasındaki bağlantı yerlerini görünür kılan, soruları ve boşlukları olduğu yerlerinde bırakan, bir rekonstrüksiyon çalışması. Sanatsal araştırma projesi 1960'lı yıllara bir zaman yolculuğu değil, dönemin izlerini günümüzden başlayarak takip eden bir çalışma. Aynı zamanda tarihyazımı şekillerini sorgulamak için bir başlangıç noktası.

Tarihyazımı "objektif" gerçek olarak ortaya çıkmıyor, daha ziyade anı ve toplum hafızası bir ayrıştırma sürecine maruz kalıyor. Yeni araştırma beklentileri ve bilgileri de, algıyı bir nesneye yönlendiriyorlar. Bu bağlamda 2011'de iki yayın Freimann Camisini siyasi çıkarlar ve siyasi İslama alet etme olarak ele alıyor. Mimar çiftten sadece çok marjinal şekilde bahsediliyor.[14]

Savaş sonrası yıllarda Münih'in önemli mimarları olan Osman Edip Gürel (1925-1984) ve Necla Gürel'in (1926-2007) çok az bilinmeleri ve yok sayılmış olmaları hayret verici. Çift 1955'den beri Münih'teydi. Osman Edip Gürel ayrıca Münih'te Oskar-von-Miller-Ring'de bulunan seçkin Türk restoranı "İstanbul"un tadilatından sorumluydu. Özellikle mimarlık ofisinin bulunduğu Schwabing'de, Rudolf Steiner Okulu, Leopoldstraße'deki Leo 17 Tiyatrosu gibi yapıları tasarlamıştı. Ayrıca Türk Başkonsolosluğu binasının tasarımını yaptı ve 1966'da Münih-Freimann'daki cami binası için görevlendirildi.[15] Bu çağdaş çelik-beton yapı, çadıra benzer kubbesi ve büyük pencereleriyle dikkat çekti. İç tasarımı Münih Güzel Sanatlar Akademisi'nin heykeltıraşlık bölümünde okumuş olan Necla Gürel tarafından yapılacaktı. Ama 1972'de açılan camide bu planlar maddi nedenlerden dolayı hayata geçirilmedi.[16]

Araştırmaları Cana Bilir-Meier'i mimar çiftin, ebeveynlerinin eser ve yaşamlarını kendi perspektiflerinden anlatan, kızlarına götürdü. Bu özel, ailevi ilişki *Temel Taş*'a önemli bir çerçeve kazandırıyor. Kızları Hürdem ve Zerender Gürel'in bir broşür, bir audio enstalasyonu (2018) ve filmde (2019) toplanan hikayeleri, caminin tarihine bir giriş niteliğinde. İkili ebeveynlerini, kendi çocukluklarını ve gençliklerini, ayrılma sürecini ve iki dilli kültür ve yaşam dünyasını anlatıyor. Anne ve babalarının 1950'li ve 1960'lı yıllarda Münih'teki yaşama nasıl ayak uydurduklarını ve daha sonra ekonomik nedenlerden veya sıla hasretinden neden kenti terk ettiklerinden bahsediyor. Bilir-Meier'in ses enstalasyonu belirli bir zaman için de olsa, kızlarının sesini ebeveynlerinin yapı çalışmasına tanıklık eden binaya götürdü.

Cana Bilir-Meier'in annesi, Münihli çocuk psikoterapisti Zühal Bilir-Meier de projeye dahil edilmiş. Zühal Bilir-Meier, mimar çiftin kızlarının anlatımını uzman perspektifinden tamamlayarak, göçmen kökenli toplumlarda yetişen gençlerin eğitimine ilişkin tavsiyelerde bulunuyor. Cana Bilir-Meier ofansif bir şekilde rekonstrüksiyon çalışmasını, bireysel sanatsal eylem olarak çalışmasına katıyor; filmde sanatçının projeye bakış açısı, filmi çekerken silüetinin binanın dış cephesinde yansımasıyla, tasavvur ediliyor. Sanatçı kendisini, cami alanında gezerken veya frotajlarını yaparken kameraya çekiyor: yapı yüzeyinin izi tebeşirle kağıda çıkarılıyor. *Temel Taş* projesinde, Bilir-Meier hem filmin yaratıcısı hem de mimarlık, çağdaş tanıklar ve torunlar, arşiv ve basın materyali ile diyalog kuran bir aktör konumunda. Freimann Camisi'ne ilişkin tekil anlatımlarla sanatçı, filozof Jacques Rancière mantığı doğrultusunda tekil tarihyazımı uyguluyor: "Tarih zaman içindeki gelişmeye göre yönelen bir süreç olarak var olmaz. Tarih her türlü tekil tarih şekilleri olarak vardır: Tekil tarihyazımı görünür ve söylenebilir olanın paylaşımını, bilinçsel tecrübenin dağıtımını, yaşam ve şekillerini sembolize eden bağlantıları kaydırır. Bana göre ancak tekil tarihyazımından oluşan bir tarih vardır."[17] Bireysel hikâyelerin eklenmesi ile sadece *bir* olası anlatımdan daha fazlası olan çok sesli bir tarih oluşturabilir.

22.7.2016.

Münih'te bulunan Olympia Alışveriş Merkezi'nde 18 yaşında bir kişinin ırkçı saldırısı, uzun süre cinnet geçiren gencin işi olarak algılandı. Fail Temmuz 2016'da dokuz genci silahla vurarak öldürdü, beş kişiyi yaraladı ve daha sonra intihar etti. Silahla vurularak öldürülenler göçmen kökenli ailelerdendi, çoğu gençti. Armela S., Can L., Choussein D., Dijamant "Dimo" Z., Guiliano-Josef K., Janos Roberto R., Sabina S., Selçuk K. ve Sevda D. öldüler. Failin aşırı sağ zihniyetinde olduğu çabuk ortaya çıkmasına rağmen, savcılık ve Eyalet Kriminal Polis Dairesi olayı cinnet geçirme olarak tanımlayıp, neden olarak öncelikle mobbing ve psikolojik bir rahatsızlığı öne sürdüler. Olayın 17 Mart 2017 tarihli sonuç raporunda şöyle deniyor: "Cinnet olayında failin kurbanları tek tek bilinçli olarak seçtiğine dair ipucu yok. Olayın siyasi nedenleri olduğu noktasından da hareket edilemez."[18] Oysa kurbanların, kendilerini Güney Avrupa kökenli olarak betimleyen muhtemel fiziki özelliklere göre seçilmeleri dikkat çekici. Mart 2018'de Federal Adalet Dairesi yaşananı müfrit olay olarak sınıflandırdı.[19] Kamuoyu, öldürülen dokuz kişinin hayatındansa, failin hakkında (İran kökenli olması, kini ve aşırı sağ ağlarda sosyalleşmiş olması gibi) daha fazla ayrıntı öğrendi.

Cana Bilir-Meier'in filmi *This makes me want to predict the past* (2019), saldırı, göçmen gençlerin yaşam dünyalarına, hayallerine, korkularına ve arzularına yaklaşmak için bir başlangıç noktası. Bu perspektif hem 22 Temmuz 2016'da öldürülen genç insanlara, hem de ebeveynleri veya büyük anne ve babaları başka ülkeden Münih'e gelen gençlerin günümüzdeki ve gelecekteki yaşamlarına bir atıf. Bilir-Meier kamerasıyla birkaç gencin Alışveriş Merkezindeki gezintilerine eşlik etti, arzularını ve umutlarını, kabuslarını ve korkularını irdeledi. Bu noktada temel bir soru gündeme geldi: Eğer yabancı düşmanlığı ve ırkçılık toplulukların ve grupların nefreti ile körükleniyorsa, buna maruz kalanlar kamu söylemindeki seslerini, yüzlerini ve bireysel kimliklerini nasıl geri alabilirler? "Göçmen", "Müslüman", "mülteci" ve "saldırının kurbanları" kendi isimleriyle, subjektif anılarıyla ve hayalleriyle nasıl tekrar birey olabilirler?

Cana Bilir-Meier mekanda frotaj sanat metoduyla çalıştı. Olympia Alışveriş Merkezi, yüzeyine kağıt konup, üstüne tebeşir sürtülerek kalıbın kağıda geçmesiyle kavranıyor, sahipleniliyor. Daha önce Freimann Camisi'nde de uygulanan metot, araştırmayı yapanların kendilerini ve metotlarını da yoruma dahil ettiği bir sanatsal "yoğunluk tarifi"[20] (Clifford Geertz). Frotajlar mimarinin ve travmatik olay yerinin aldatıcı resmi gibi görünen basımkalıpları: mekan hem olay yeri, hem de genç göçmenlerin severek ve sıkça bulunduğu bir yer (ve tersine ispatla bu nedenden ötürü muhtemelen saldırganın hedefi oldular).

Cana Bilir-Meier'in çalışmaları Alman tarihinin zaman akışına, toplum bilincinde hiç bulunmayan veya çok az yer edinen veriler ekliyor: 24.5.1982'de Türk kökenli bir kadın yabancı düşmanlığına karşı bir sinyal olarak kendini yaktı; 6.10.1967 tarihinde temeli atılan, Bavyera'da bir ilk olan Münih-Freimann Camisi yapısı aynı zamanda iki Türk kökenli mimar-sanatçının yaptığı, savaş sonrası Alman modernizmin bir eseri. 22.7.2016'da göçmen kökenli dokuz genç muhtemelen aşırı sağcı olan bir fail tarafından silahla vurularak öldürüldü. Bu üç olay birbiriyle mukayese edilemez; kendini yakma ve ırkçılık gibi, Alman mimari tarihinde göçmen sanatçı ve mimarların payı gibi, müfrit bir saldırıyı ve gençlerin Almanya'daki yaşamları gibi çok farklı konuları içeriyorlar. Bilir-Meier sanatsal araştırmalarında ve buna bağlı çalışmalarında genelden bireyselliği süzmeyi başarıyor ve aksine somut tekil anlatımlarla tarihi görüngüye çıkarıyor.[21] Her tarih anlatımı kaçınılmaz olarak ortaya çıkaranın perspektifini içerir. Zamana ve olaylara bakış tarafsız değildir, bilakis canlı bir gözün perspektifinden bakıştır. Aynı zamanda, Cana Bilir-Meier'in çalışmalarında tarihyazımının yumuşatmaya, boşluklara ve dengelemeye yatkınlığı bariz bir şekilde ortaya konuyor.

Bilir-Meier göç ve göçmenlere ilişkin projelerini, sanatsal çalışmayı siyasi izan olarak gören anlayışla yürütüyor. Sanatçı Freimann Camisi çalışması hakkında şunları yazıyor: "Nicelerin Toplumunda [NSU Kompleksi Dağıtılsın Tribünali] nicelerin tarihine de ihtiyacımız var. Cami tarihsel gerilimli bir mekan, bugüne kadar dinin siyasete alet edilme hikayeleri, maneviyata gereksinim duyulan bir mekan olmasının ve mimari tasarımının üstünü örtüyor. *Temel Taş* projesi, farklı anlatım hatlarını toplayıp, göçmen bilgiyi, göçmen hikayelerini, pozisyonlarını ve perspektiflerini görünür kılmak isteyen bir araştırma çalışmasıdır."[22] Vikipedi'deki gibi ortaklaşa yazılan ve çoğulculuk perspektifini talep eden yazılar dahi, çok kez tek boyutlu yaklaşımda kalıyor. Bir online ansiklopedide Semra Ertan'a ait kısa bir kayıt var, ama o da ansiklopedi içeriğinde yer alan "Kendini yakma" başlığının altında sıralanan Almanya'daki kendini yakma eylemlerine ilişkin bölümde.[23] Metinde Semra Ertan kendisi gibi, siyasi nedenlerden intihar edenler içinde yer alıyor. Sevinciyle, üzüntüsüyle komplike yaşamı, yazarlık çalışması, ve yabancı olma tecrübeleri bu kısa kaydın arkasında görünmez oluyor.

Cana Bilir-Meier'in eserlerinin ansiklopedik bir nesnellik iddiası yok. Eserleri bir hayata, esere, yapıya veya olaya kuş bakışıyla bakılmasına izin vermiyor; bakış parçalara bölünmüş ve prizmatik kalıyor ve subjektif etki altında şekillenmiş oluyor. Böylece Bilir-Meier karışıklığı, sallanan zeminde yürümeyi ve parçalanmış konuşmayı ve düşünceyi kabul ve itiraf ediyor.

1
İlaveten Sylvia Hahn: *Historische Migrationsforschung*, Campus Verlag, Frankfurt am Main/New York 2012, S. 15; Sabine Hess: *Politiken der (Un-)Sichtbarmachung. Eine Kritik der Wissens- und Bilderproduktionen zu Migration*, içinde: Erol Yıldız und Marc Hill (Hg.): *Nach der Migration. Postmigrantische Perspektiven jenseits der Parallelgesellschaft*, transcript Verlag, Bielefeld 2015, S. 49-64.
2
Ulrich Herbert: *Geschichte der Ausländerbeschäftigung in Deutschland 1880 bis 1980. Saisonarbeiter, Zwangsarbeiter, Gastarbeiter*, J.H.W. Dietz, Berlin/Bonn 1986, S. 220.
3
İki alıntı da Klaus Unger'den: *Ausländerpolitik in der Bundesrepublik Deutschland* (Bielefelder Studien zur Entwicklungssoziologie, 7), Verlag Breitenbach, Saarbrücken/Fort Lauderdale 1980, S. 113, 116.
4
Friedrich Heckmann: Die Bundesrepublik: *Ein Einwanderungsland? Zur Soziologie der Gastarbeiterbevölkerung als Einwandererminorität*, Klett-Cotta, Stuttgart 1981, S. 208.
5
Imran Ayata: *Kanak-Rap in Almanya – Über die schweren Folgen Deutschlands*, içinde: Katja Dominik, Marc Jünemann, Jan Motte und Astrid Reinecke im Auftrag der Geschichtswerkstatt Göttingen (Hg.): *Angeworben – eingewandert – abgeschoben. Ein anderer Blick auf die Einwanderungsgesellschaft Bundesrepublik Deutschland*, Westfälisches Dampfboot, Münster 1999, S. 273-287, burada S. 280.
6
"Fremde Heimat" sergisine ilişkin bkz.: Mathilde Jamin: *Fremde Heimat. Zur Geschichte der Arbeitsmigration aus der Türkei*, içinde: Jan Motte, Rainer Ohliger, Anne von Oswald (Hg.): *50 Jahre Bundesrepublik – 50 Jahre Einwanderung*, Campus Verlag, Frankfurt am Main/New York 1999, S. 145-164. bkz. *Projekt Migration*. Ausst.-Kat. Kölnischer Kunstverein, DuMont Literatur und Kunstverlag, Köln 2005.
7
Naika Foroutan: The Post-migrant Paradigm, içinde: Jan-Jonathan Bock und Sharon Macdonald (Hg.): Refugees Welcome? Difference and Diversity in a Changing Germany, Berghahn Books, New York/Oxford 2019, S. 142-167.
8
Cana Bilir-Meier'in Hamburg Kunstverein'daki *Düşler Ülkesi* sergisinin hazırlığında yeni araştırmalar, Semra Ertan'ın kendini, şimdiye kadar sanıldığı gibi 26.5.1982'de değil, bundan iki gün önce yaktığını ortaya çıkardı.
9
Bkz. Cana Bilir-Meier: Semra Ertan. *Her Own Voice / Kendi Sesi / Ihre eigene Stimme*, Wien 2017, S. 11.
10
Rolf Meinhardt: Önsöz, içinde: *Ausländerfeindlichkeit. Eine Dokumentation*, EXpress, Berlin 1982, S. 1.
11
Aynı yerde
12
Bkz. Cana Bilir-Meier: *Nachdenken über das Archiv. Notizen zu Semra Ertan* (2013), içinde: *Stimme. Zeitschrift der Initiative Minderheiten*, Nr. 94/2015, Bürgerinitiative Demokratisch Leben, Innsbruck 2015, S. 11.
13
Aynı yerde, S. 12f.
14
Bkz. Ian Johnson: *Die vierte Moschee. Nazis, CIA und der islamische Fundamentalismus*, Klett-Cotta, Stuttgart 2011; Stefan Meining: Eine Moschee in Deutschland. Nazis, Geheimdienste und der Aufstieg des politischen Islam im Westen, Beck-Verlag, München 2011.

15
Cana Bilir Meier: *26. Mai 2018. Grundstein Foundation Stone. Eine künstlerische Rechercharbeit*. Proje hakkında broşür, München 2018, Sayfa olmadan
16
Aynı yerde
17
Jacques Rancière: *Ist Kunst widerständig?*, Merve Verlag, Berlin 2008, S. 68f.
18
https://archive.fo/wiHMz#selection-1307.0-1311.73. Erişim: 28.4.2019.
19
https://www.zeit.de/gesellschaft/zeitgeschehen/2018-03/olympia-einkaufszentrum-muenchener-amoklauf-extremismus-einstufung-bundesbehoerde. Erişim: 28.4.2019.
20
Clifford Geertz: *Dichte Beschreibung. Beiträge zum Verstehen kultureller Systeme*, Suhrkamp Verlag, Frankfurt am Main 1983.
21
İlaveten: Ayşe Güleç ve Cana Bilir-Meier *Camera Austria*, dergisinin röportajında şöyle deniliyor: "Elbette kişilikle ilgili, ama ben tek tek hikayeler anlatmak istemiyorum, beni ilgilendiren yine de şahsi ve özel olan kolektif tarihin nasıl anlatılabileceğidir" (Bilir-Meier) veya "Somut yaşananlar ve olaylar örneğinde, kolektif yaşanan tecrübeyi tarih olarak anlatmak mümkündür - çünkü bu karar karşı tez geliştirme imkanı veriyor" (Güleç). Ayşe Güleç: *Cana Bilir-Meier. Bewegungen zwischen Archiven – Dekolonisierung von Disziplinen*, içinde: Camera Austria, 141/2018, Verein CAMERA AUSTRIA. Labor für Fotografie und Theorie, Graz 2018, S. 33-44, burada S. 34.
22
Cana Bilir Meier: 26. Mai 2018. *Grundstein Foundation Stone. Eine künstlerische Rechercharbeit*. Proje hakkında broşür, München 2018, Sayfa olmadan
23
https://de.wikipedia.org/wiki/Selbstverbrennung# Fälle_in_Deutschland. Erişim: 26.4.2019.

Wenn

Kadın

sie

bahsettiğinde

sagt

bahsettiğinde

sie

Coşkun

sei

Coşkun

XXXI

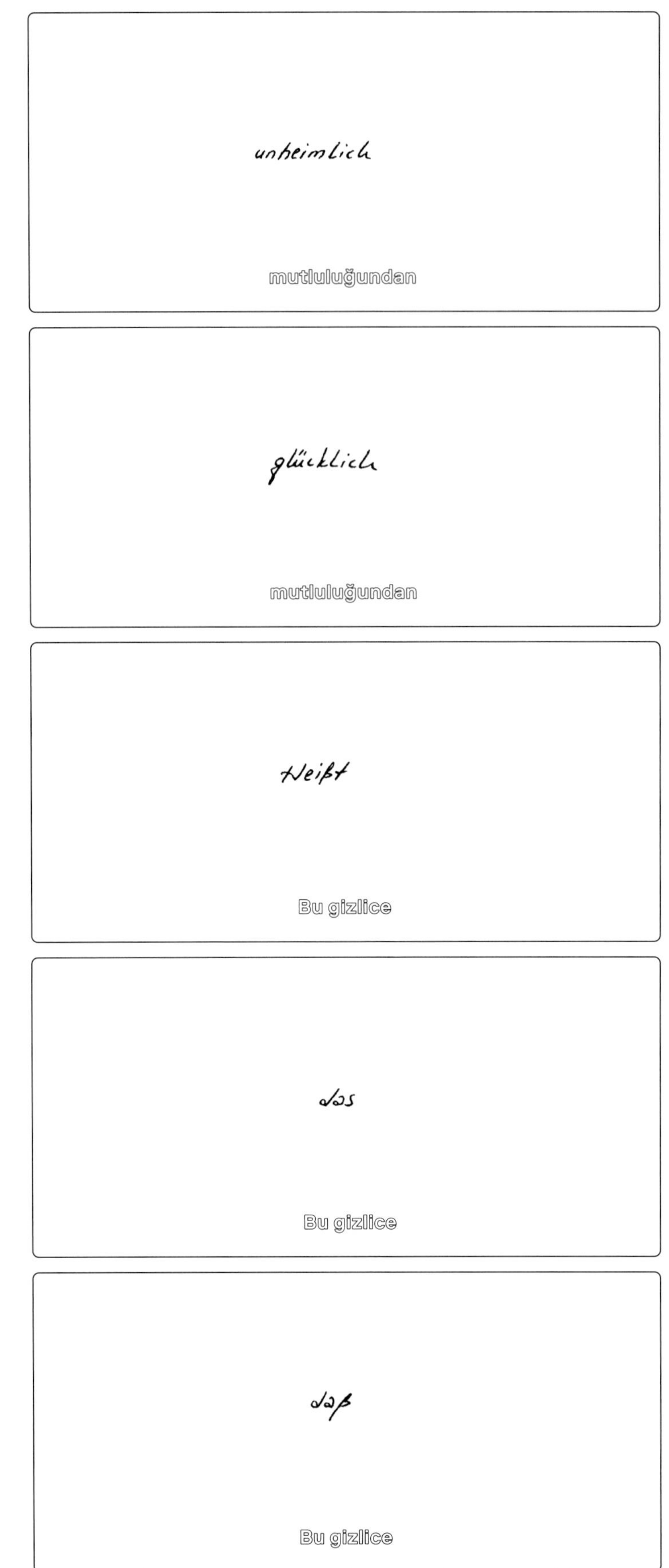

unheimlich
mutluluğundan
glücklich
mutluluğundan
Heißt
Bu gizlice
das
Bu gizlice
daß
Bu gizlice

sie

mutsuz

Heimlich

olduğu anlamına

unglücklich

gelir

ist.

gelir

Wenn

Kadın

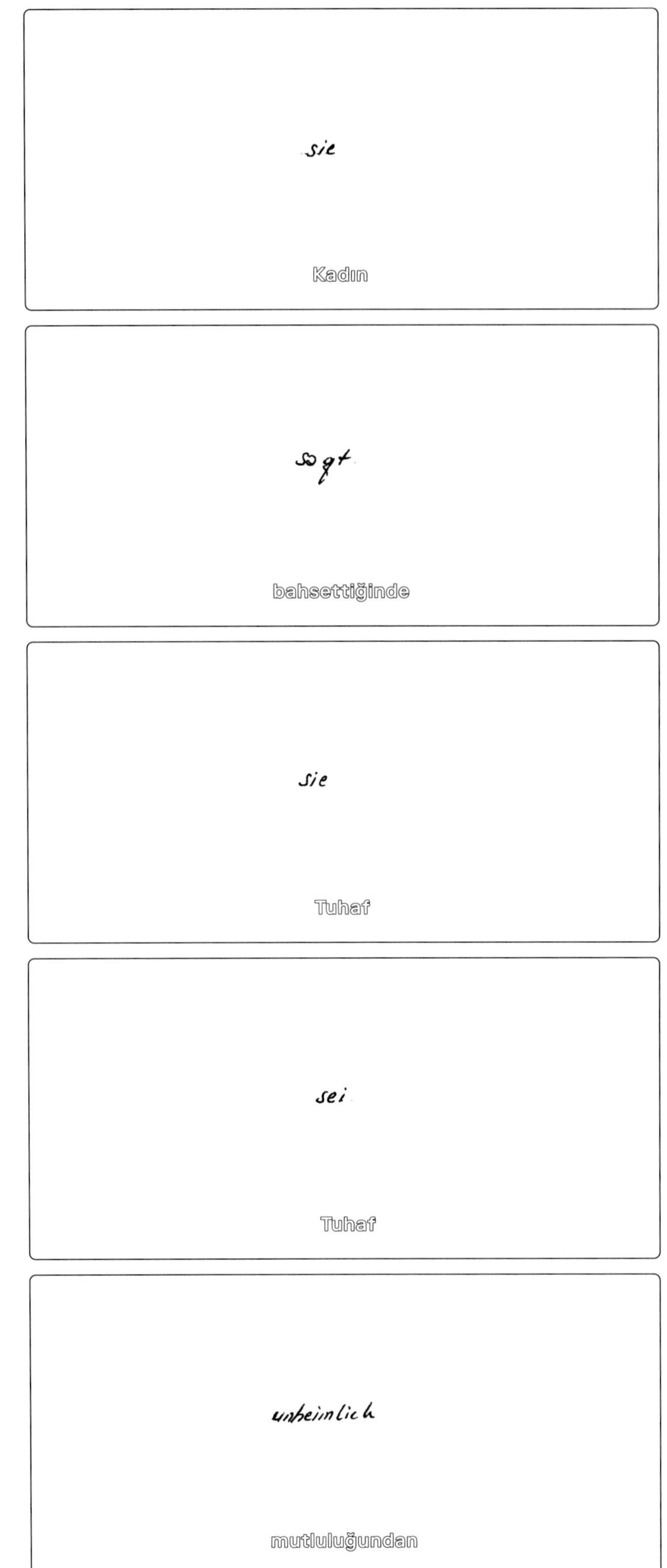
sie
Kadın

sagt
bahsettiğinde

sie
Tuhaf

sei
Tuhaf

unheimlich
mutluluğundan

Wenn

Kadin

sie

bahsettiğinde

sagt

bahsettiğinde

sie

Coşkun

sei

Coşkun

unglücklich

demektir

ist

demektir

weil

Çünkü

sie

Çünkü

Kein

yurdu

Neim

yurdu

hat.

yok

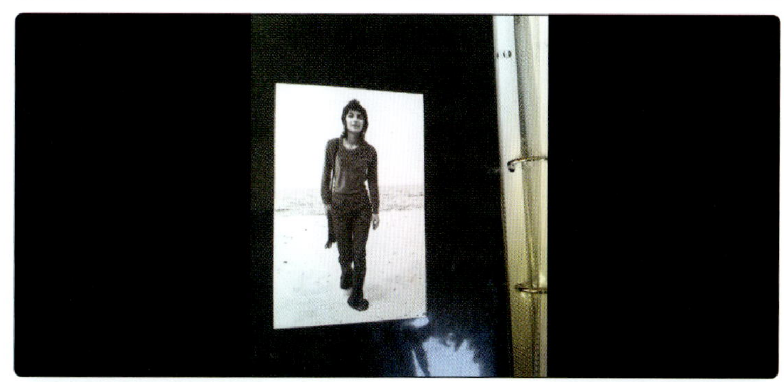

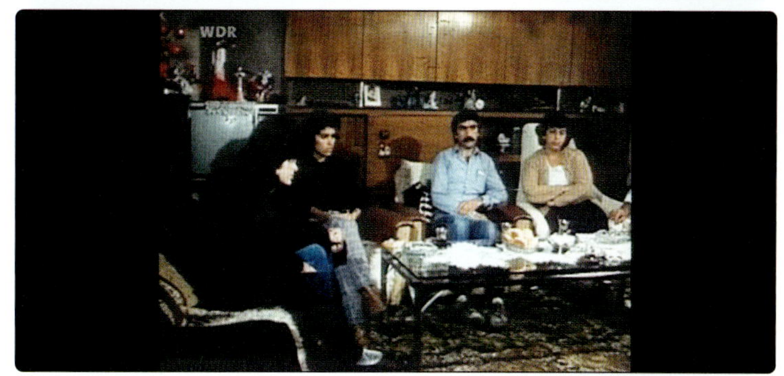

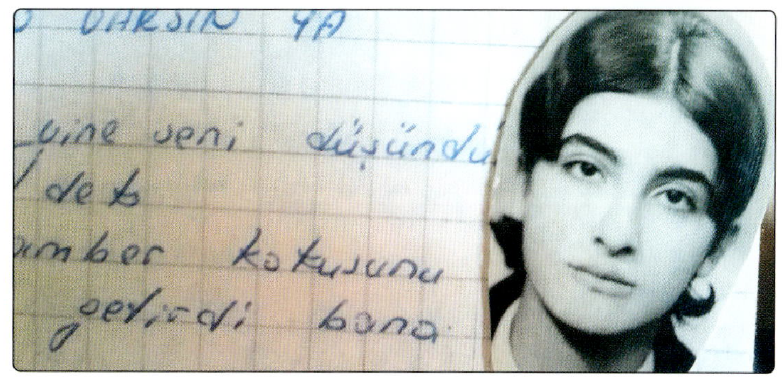

This makes me want to forget what I can't remember

Imagining a Different Kind of Politics:

An Open-Ended Conversation

Cana Bilir-Meier in conversation with
Banu Karaca and belit sağ

The following is a conversation started by belit sağ, Banu Karaca, and myself based on my work *This makes me want to predict the past* (2019), which consists of a Super 8 film and frottages. The frottages and the film were made in the Olympia shopping mall in Munich. The work addresses issues of remembrance and the memories of the racially-motivated attack on the shopping center in 2016 by bringing them into a dialogue with scenes from the play *Düşler Ülkesi* (*Land of Dreams*, Erman Okay, 1982), which contemplates the everyday experiences, hopes, and desires of immigrants in Germany. In this attack, nine young people were killed and thirty-six others were injured, four by gunfire. Almost all of the victims were people with migrant backgrounds: Turkish, Kurdish as well as Roma and Sinti.

The title of the film and the frottages are based on a quote by an anonymous YouTube user posted in the comments section of the video *Redbone* by the African-American musician, comedian, author, and film director Donald Glover, also known as Childish Gambino.

YouTube user comments for Childish Gambino's song *Redbone*[1]

This makes me want to brush my toothbrush.
This makes me want to predict the past.
This makes me want to tell my non biological parents that they're adopted.
This makes me want to sit on my TV and watch the couch.
This makes me want to rob my own bank account.
This makes me want to listen to my therapists problems.
This makes me want to arrest the police.
This makes me want to put on a pair of books and read glasses.
This makes me want to cut my barber's hair.
This makes me want to tell depression to kill itself.
This makes me wanna let the door open me.
This makes me want to sell myself on craigslist.
This makes me want to call two cab companies to see who arrives
      first then take the bus.
This makes me want to wake my alarm up.
This wants me to ask Burger King where the closest McDonald's is.
This makes me want to tell my boss to "get a job".
This makes me wanna let the elevator ride me.
This makes me want to read a book from end to beginning.
This makes me want to put milk in my cereal bowl, then the cereal.
This makes me want the homework to eat my dog.
This makes me want to give birth to my mom.
This make me wanna call in sick to my doctors appointment.
This makes me want to play on the Xbox with a PlayStation controller.
This makes me want to let my clothes wear me.
This makes me want to spy on my FBI agent.
This makes me want to put on my shoes before my sock.
This makes me wanna fall asleep before I close my eyes.
This makes me want to ask my dog to take me for a walk.
This makes me want to write with paper on a pencil.
This makes me wanna tell my boss he's fired.
This makes me want to tell my crush I have a girlfriend.
This makes me want to put on a pair of books and read glasses.
      I showed this to my dog, now he is a cat.
This makes me want to Google Bing.
This makes me wanna tell Aliens that humans are real…!
This makes me want to give mosquitoes malaria.
This makes me want to drive my parents to school.
This makes me want to kill two stones with one bird.
This makes me want to read a coloring book.
This makes me want to let the light turn me on.
This makes me wanna call my friend and tell him I can't talk right now
      call you later.
This makes me let my food eat me.
The makes me fall and hurt the ground.
This makes me want to do my desk on my homework.
This makes me want to take a bath with a unicorn.

This makes me wanna tell the weekend its Monday.
This makes me want to let my earphones wear my ear.
This makes me want to put my toaster in my toast.
This makes me want to remember the future.
This makes me want to tell my teacher to raise her hand if she wants
        to speak to me.
This makes me want to give my fish a bath.
This makes me want to steal money out of my own wallet.
This makes me want to drink vampire's blood.
This makes me want to ask the hotel's reception if they want a room
        with a beach view.
This makes me want to tell Monday to wake up.
This makes me want to be a vacuum to clean my house.
This makes me want to tell the clock what time it is.
This song makes me wanna threaten to call my teachers parents.
This makes me wanna call someone and say I can't talk.
This reminds me of spending time with people I love. Time sure does fly.
This makes me want to forget what I can't remember.
This makes me fly like I can feel.
This makes me want to walk on a fly!
This makes me want to pass a test and study for it afterwards.
This makes me want to put numbers in alphabetical order.
This makes me want to break into someone's house and install
        a security system.
This makes me want to end things I haven't started yet.

Most of my artworks center on questions of official knowledge production, often through decoding. Every new image engenders more new images, obscuring others. These questions and processes are all part of how power is constituted. Cultural theorist Stuart Hall proposes that "[i]dentity is an ever-*unfinished conversation*,"[2] which—in my opinion—speaks to the comments of YouTube users who write about things that cannot work in reality and yet which at the same time show the construction of this very reality. A conversation is generally understood as having a beginning and an end, but what might an unfinished conversation look like?

For this text, I decided to invite Banu Karaca and belit sağ to discuss topics that are important for our artworks and theory, such as the workings of structural racism, the question of intersectionality, power relations as expressed in language, personal and public archives, migration, the tension between official and subaltern histories, and the politics of visibility and censorship.

Banu Karaca is an anthropologist working at the intersection of political anthropology, art and aesthetics, nationalism and cultural policy, museums and commemorative practices in Germany and Turkey. She is the co-founder of Siyah Bant, a research platform documenting arts censorship in Turkey. Her ongoing research centers on the practice of writing art history against the background of the politics of dispossession in the late Ottoman Empire and the early Turkish Republic.

belit sağ is a videomaker, visual artist, and artworker based in Amsterdam. She studied mathematics in Turkey and visual arts in the Netherlands. Her background in moving images is rooted in her work with video-activist groups in Ankara and Istanbul, where she co-founded groups such as VideA, karahaber, and bak.ma. She has done residencies at the International Studio & Curatorial Program (ISCP) in New York and at Rijksakademie van Beeldende

Kunsten in Amsterdam. Her ongoing artistic and moving image practice focuses on the role of visual representation in the experience of political conflicts in Turkey, Germany, and the Netherlands.

In an interview with me, belit once said: "In whatever I'm doing I'm trying to position myself. It's important where I'm coming from, why I'm interested in a particular issue and what I will do with it. And I'm trying to make it transparent. It's always me who is editing and formulating the work, and it's important to reveal that it's me standing behind the work. This comes from my video activist practice, visibility of people and issues was our tactic during video-activism years, but I also believe, for example, invisibility can be a tactic for movements. In the end, it's important to embrace diversity of tactics."[3]

Banu:

Looking at the materials you just shared, this is quite amazing. I wasn't aware of these kinds of comments being a thing with this song. Do you know how it started?

Cana:

I am not sure exactly how it started. But as I understand it, with *Redbone*, Childish Gambino challenges the status quo of everyday structures, just as he did with his song (and video) *This is America*. The texts have a very strong message and for young people especially, they have become an important vehicle in expressing their wishes and desires for change. I combined these comments with the topic of the racist attack that took place at the Olympia shopping mall in 2016. In these comments we can see how young people imagine another society by revealing how discourses and language are situated in power relations. The title of the artwork, *This makes me want to predict the past*, shows the contradictions of the dichotomy between past and present or history and memory.

Banu:

Like all of these attacks, the Munich case is singular and yet follows a familiar pattern. When it became clear that most of the victims had an immigrant background, the perpetrator was described as a "lone wolf," as someone with mental health problems. The authorities were quick to label the attack as "not terrorist," and more importantly, not racist. And, perhaps most importantly, they divorced the attack from the history of racism in Germany.

belit:

Looking at your work and the comments, Cana, I am reminded of how limited it is to discuss racism in round table discussions, how the imposed linear logic of some formats is not enough to address different aspects of certain issues. This once again brings up the urgency of taking certain experiences and expressions seriously as a source of knowledge production. For example, the experience of racism is often communicated through its translations into forms that do not fully capture bodily experiences. I'm also thinking of archives here, forms such as pictures, moving images, texts etc. are archived, are "archivable." My question is how to consider and value experience as a thing in itself. Even if these translations, even if these translations I mentioned earlier are into formats such as texts, only linear, logical texts tend to be considered valid knowledge products or sources. Then my second question is how to recognize the knowledge created through bodily experience and how to share that experience. That's exactly why anti-racist groups keep insisting on bringing *migrant-situated knowledge* to the forefront since certain experiences are valued and considered resources in the knowledge production system, while others are blocked out.

There is a direct connection to the erasure Banu is talking about. The way this attack was reported is erasing the experience of the victims, through circulating and replacing that experience with another one that protects the perpetrator. I think all three of us, in one way or another, are working on those experiences that are ignored, erased, and/or are purposefully hidden by such official narratives.

I'm reminded of the Tribunal Unraveling the NSU Complex. The whole idea of the Tribunal was to bring those experiences center stage, and it was organized by grassroots activist groups and migrant groups in collaboration with the families of the victims. Cana and I contributed short video spots on the case of the NSU (National Socialist Underground)[4] focusing on those experiences. I guess through our practices we continuously try to find forms and expressions in relation to these experiences. (see image: *(Against) Randomness*, 2017).

Banu:

Looking at your works, Cana, and your last comment, belit, I am reminded of a sense I've had that has grown increasingly stronger, not just with the topic of racism, but of doing things—art, politics, academia—in general, of how meaningful it is indeed to always say "No," as solely an inversion of discourses of power. Part of my discomfort comes from the work that I have been doing with Siyah Bant. When we first started, our aim was to research and document censorship in the arts in Turkey, understand the different modalities of censorship, and show how the interplay of different actors inside and outside the art world collectively enable censorship. And we were interested in facilitating spaces to think about and discuss different strategies and tactics for how to combat censorship and advocate for freedom of expression. While these issues continue to be noteworthy, it is also important to move the debate beyond mere dissent against censorship. Rather than presupposing that free speech is a clearly defined "thing in itself" or a determinable endpoint, I have come to understand it as a terrain of struggle in which freedom of expression is in constant need of discussion in relation to power, place, and history. So freedom of expression does not only lie in objecting censorship but also in the struggle to create the conditions for debate along these parameters.

Don't get me wrong. Dissent is important, of course, but to be stuck there means to be stuck in the logic of power. My sense is that at the current political conjuncture we fall all too easily into the trap of objecting so much that we cannot find the time to work out what we are actually *for*. There are exceptions, too, like the feminist movement and the ecology/climate change movement, for instance. Viewed in this vein, the absurdist comments present other horizons of possibility and different imaginations that have the potential for a very different kind of politics.

Cana:

Yes, I agree because saying "No" also is a form of taking a position or rejection and when you are stuck in this position, change becomes very difficult and racist discourse is a set of rigid words, which function as a weapon to devalue BPoC (Black People of Color), migrants, refugees. So in order to fight against that we need to fight against the discourse that is used: the language. Also, these comments are imaginations of a world, they are imagining something instead of (only) being against something! Instead of always saying no, they also present something empowering. And change starts from the change of language and imagination. This imagination must sometimes be utopian.

belit:

It's also what we see everywhere, right? I mean the polarization and being stuck in a position that is dictated and defined by what one is against. To let what you are against determine your position is fundamentally disempowering. Although of course there are many moments, places, times—more than we'd wish for—where one needs to say "this is just wrong," even if it is simple and obvious that this thing is wrong, and saying that undermines your intelligence and existence, but you are pushed into a position where you just need to say that. So that you can move into a terrain where you can create a space for discussion, as you mentioned Banu, but also a space where you imagine a world, imagine a certain change, and formulate what it is that you strive for. It is also about the necessity to imagine and thus create through this imagination a world that contains one's values. A view of a world beyond reactionism and the ability to communicate these values and this world beyond the words of the mainstream logic of today's world, a language that holds this imagination. Childish Gambino does this. He communicates his own experience and how it feels to live in the world today. This is also a way to open up possibilities to imagine a different world and through these YouTube comments this imagination becomes collective and that is deeply inspiring!

Banu:

I am interested in hearing from you how the general situation that belit just described shapes the art world today, i.e. do you have the sense that this impacts your artistic practice or your choices where to show your work? To put it differently, do you think that the present situation also reconfigures the relationship between art and politics?

Cana:

I think if we want to see the role of art in the current situation, we should analyze it in terms of how capitalism has made art a commodity. That means we should challenge this and try to create new forms of art that seek change and bring back the meaning of art and its relation to politics. For example, the film about Semra Ertan was in this context. I also tried to do the same with my project *Grundstein* on the mosque in Munich. *Semra Ertan* (2013) is a film about the writer and poet Semra Ertan who was born in Turkey and came as the daughter of guest workers to Germany in the 1970s and wrote over 350 poems. She protested against the racism that immigrants were faced with and burned herself in Hamburg in 1982 as a public protest. The film is about rewriting her story as a person who rebels against injustice rather than a victim. The other project in the mosque in Freimann in Munich I made in 2017-18 was about the Mosque's architects Necla Gürel and Osman Edip Gürel and gives another version of history that challenges anti-muslimism racism and orientalist views in German society. The architectural work of the husband-and-wife team of Osman Edip and Necla Gürel does not appear in Munich's city history even though they designed many important buildings.

belit:

What you just said is so important, Cana, i.e. this is basically not letting that narrative become the only one, also not to replace it with another singular narrative, but to complicate things because these narratives, these lives are always layered. This is recognizing the power of creating and circulating layers of narratives. This is a fertile way of saying "No," opening a path to go beyond a single "No." Your works are a clear example of this path.

As the polarization gets stronger, I find myself much more outspoken and outraged, and my works also become more focused, specifically since 2013 when the atmosphere in Turkey gradually became more and more violent. There is a sense of urgency that comes with this polarization and with the normalization of the language of racism. I also get more and more sensitive and sharper to the way my works are positioned by others. As a person of color with a migrant background living in western Europe and primarily making work on the issues in the country one was born and raised in, one needs to be careful about how one's works are instrumentalized. I also feel a stronger distance towards the commodification of my works, a clear distance from the demands of the art market. This is a way for me to protect my working process, so I stay focused on what I want to make and the process of making the works remains far away from the demands of the market and the instrumentalization that comes with it, as much as possible. In the end, I find this awareness to be important and a question mark that I bring to my practice. Certain fights are neverending, they are in the nature of one's relation to the field. That doesn't mean these fights are meaningless, nor that we should give in and settle, they are a crucial part of my practice.

Cana:

I agree. Since this capitalist system is based on hierarchy and classes that serve white privilege, people of color and their works are not taken seriously.

belit:

Besides not being taken seriously, I meant to point out the ways these works and people are positioned, mainly by the institutions, in order to support certain agendas. For example, institutions that refuse to challenge racist structures within themselves, i.e. institutions that support those structures by being selectively ignorant or just being plain supportive, invite PoC artists and/or include works with clear anti-racist messages in order to claim or pretend that they have an anti-racist agenda. These kinds of instrumentalizations are very much a daily challenge. It is art-washing, legitimizing an institute's racist attitude and double standards. In practice, it becomes very complex to challenge these, mainly because of a lack of solidarity and organization. As a result, these experiences often isolate the one who fights against them. I find another challenge in relation to my own outrage, that is, how to channel this energy into works that would excite me as a maker, as an audience, and all the positions in between and beyond. For me the challenge is to shift and turn that energy into something that is meaningful for these times, for ourselves, and our struggles, without forgetting to have fun in the process.

Cana:

The production pressure on the art market sometimes leads me to a feeling of inner alienation from my own artistic production conditions. I think that the art market cannot be analyzed independently of economic and political structures. The market in which art is produced is also part of this socio-economic system, and many artists I know are under pressure to produce artistic works continuously, because otherwise you are very quickly excluded. This feeling of alienation seems personal, but it's not, it's a structural problem.

Banu:

I want to intervene here for a moment, before coming back to the issue of imagining possibilities and the possibilities of imagination. I think it is important to pause with the observation that the structure of the art market does not leave "alternative" artistic production untouched. Perhaps we need to consider how the very conception of art has been developed in relation to the market in the later 18th century. Art theorist Martha Woodmansee, for instance, argues that the notion of the artist or the author as an individual creator (or "genius") emerged at that time, in part to allow artists to earn money from their creations (copyright is something that emerged exactly at that moment—to protect artists).[5] But at the same time, theories about the autonomy of art emerged as well, establishing fundamental tensions that accompany us to this day: so, art as we generally think about it is both autonomous (in its idealized version) and yet a commodity. The way I understand both of your comments is that at the current stage of capitalism these tensions have become even more visible.

Cana:

With this you address a very important point, namely the tension of art as utopia, which strives to imagine a new society and to question it in general, and at the same time the logic of the market, on which the demands must be fulfilled and thus the system is legitimized again. I also believe that, among other things, the Renaissance gave the individual more rights in some areas of society and that this also influenced art production at that time. But at the moment, from my experience and perspective, the market is still very much dominating the social and political spheres, which also affects the working conditions of artists and the production conditions of art. I think the writings of the Frankfurt School, or how you, Banu, refer to them, Martha Woodmansee's writings later contributed much to the analysis of the commercialization of the social and art in the age of advanced capitalism.

On the subject of the precarization of working conditions in the art field, I also have to think of my experience before and during my studies at the Academy of Fine Arts in Vienna, when I absolutely wanted to do a few internships in film or art galleries. During the first years of my studies I did an internship at a symposium on political art and the working conditions were extremely precarious. It became clear to me that many women in particular were doing unpaid work in this area. In this case, we must also mention that the feminist movement *Wages for Housework* began in Europe in 1972 and initiated a public debate on issues such as housework, sex work and reproductive work, which is part of the capitalist system. Silvia Federici writes about this in her essay *Wages Against Housework* (1975). "We must admit that capital has been very successful in hiding our work. It has created a true masterpiece at the expense of women. By denying houseworks a wage and transforming it into an act of love, capital has killed many birds with one stone."[6] We have to criticize unpaid labor in the arts and women's domestic labor which the feminist movement and *Wages for Housework* are talking about. There is a strong connection between them, because as Federici writes: "True, under capitalism every worker is manipulated and exploited and his/her relation to capital is totally mystified. The wages give the impression of a fair deal: you work and you get paid, hence you and your boss are equal: while in reality the wage, rather than paying for the work you do, hides all the unpaid work that goes into profit. But the wage at least recognizes that you are a worker, and you can bargain and struggle around and against the terms and the quantity of that wage."[7] The Carrot Workers Collective and the Precarious Workers Brigade in London, who have worked on this topic for years, are dealing with and make this connection of unpaid labor in the arts visible and fight against it. They were so empowering for me and my colleagues. Still, I am struggling a lot with unpaid and precarious work in the arts, so I'd rather call myself an art worker than an artist.

belit:

I think the tensions between autonomy in art and the art market have been affected the most by the political atmosphere and the political awareness in the art field over different periods in different geographical regions. Each moment seems to be the most tense to those who live through those times. I doubt that the tensions are the most visible at this moment or that this is the most tense moment. When we look at the emergence of copyright and its development through to today from the idea of artists earning money and protecting their rights for their creations, to companies like Disney earning large sums from copyright, having departments just to pursue lawsuits, and copyrighting content that does not originate from its own creations but from content stolen from public domain and privatized. A multinational like Disney, for example, aims to define the whole field and creates the dominant, I would say, official narratives with copyrighted, stolen content, i.e. re-writes these narratives as they see fit. In the end, official narratives are not only defined by states. They have been in the last twenty years defined by multinational corporations just as much. Also, I want to note here that when art history is mentioned, it is mainly western art history, which has stronger ties to the market than other art histories. We can replace Disney with Gagosian or Christie's, and focus on their predatory practices.

I do believe that as art workers we have the possibility of redefining our field through our work and our stances. We have the possibility to open up a space where certain values are practiced and a certain attitude towards the market is taken, recognizing its history and its relation to power, and at the same time challenging it through our practice. I don't only mean in the content of the works, but in the whole process, i.e. challenging the idea of genius and copyright, challenging the precarious work relationships, hierarchy, elitism, inherent sexism, and racism, and challenging the power of those companies and galleries and auction houses by creating local practices that aim to be globally connected to other localities. I am continuously asking myself what kind of society I want to live in and imagining that society. Why would the art field be an exception in this imagination? Labor relations are labor relations, class struggle is class struggle—with its specificities in different fields, of course. I'm working towards fair labor relations. I fight precarity that I face every day and see in the art market just like any other labor market. You plant these seeds and create these spaces. In the end, the accumulation of the fruits of these struggles is a long-term process, just like any kind of activism. It's like climate change. Maybe some of us won't see the extreme effects of it in our immediate surroundings, maybe because of our age, but looking at it in a wholesome way, one should keep asking for fairness all over and fight environmental racism just like any other racism. In addition, because it becomes a very disempowering and depressing world if we only see our struggles in the short term. Then it looks like a single person or single collective or even a network of collectives has no power to change or challenge anything but in the long run that's only a limited vision, and this is what history tells us, too. It's all about how we organize, how we show solidarity, how we realize our privileges and stand with each other with a future perspective.

Cana:

Maybe "No" can only be meaningful in a sense of rejecting the injustice of what we face on a daily basis. So, "No" can be a starting point of changing that position. We should move beyond that and not become stuck there.

Banu:

In that sense, the "No" is a starting point for—to put it in your terms, Cana—"the conversation" about how we want to live and live together and for alternative politics. This needs to be a rigorous but "open-ended" conversation on how to move towards more justice and equity.

Cana:

Yes, it means moving from what life is to what life should be.

belit:

Or what life could be, the possibilities opening up in front of us.

Cana:

Yes, to say that another life is possible.

Banu:

I am still curious, Cana, how this works in your artistic practice though and in yours as well, belit?

belit:

In my practice it definitely points out a difference between the times I was more involved with video activism and the work I'm doing now, which is much more about contemplating on the issues, rather than reacting to issues head on. I'm a little wary of oversimplifying an earlier and very valuable practice with these words. With the political context and the urgency of human rights-based struggles, video-activist practice had to be sharp in order to fight certain discourses and false narratives that were circulating. It was so important to show that certain voices exist but they are erased, to show what's going on in the streets, that what is said is not what's going on for example. Doesn't it sound very similar to the current times? The practice itself was about underlining a clear position, it felt like there was no time to contemplate. Surely it would have been a different practice if I were to do it now. I wonder if it would still feel like there is no time. It is also about what stage of your life you are in. I guess I needed some time to figure out that you do not need to respond to everything all the time. You pick your own fight, how you want to fight, i.e. you pick how you want to live your life as well. If we were to put these practices next to each other, in my current practice I'm figuring out things as I do the work, and I'm curious to see the unfolding of thoughts and works. The practical everyday relations around the work is a constant fight with the art world standards, well, more the lack of it I'd say, and it is oftentimes a full-on fight. If I look at the content I'm creating, I see it as a slower way of doing activism, as part of different movements, in a longer term, as an extension of that earlier practice. I like how you defined it, Banu, "rigorous and open-ended conversation", these words feel close to what I aim to do with my current practice. How about you Cana?

Cana:

Maybe if we come back to the YouTube comments, for example, they show us the possibility of other kinds of thinking and living. My works and research or what I do is also not something against or for something, but of course it's important to position oneself, but in an artistic way, I think, that deals with certain topics, which are not visible in the "mainstream."

This makes me want to arrest the police

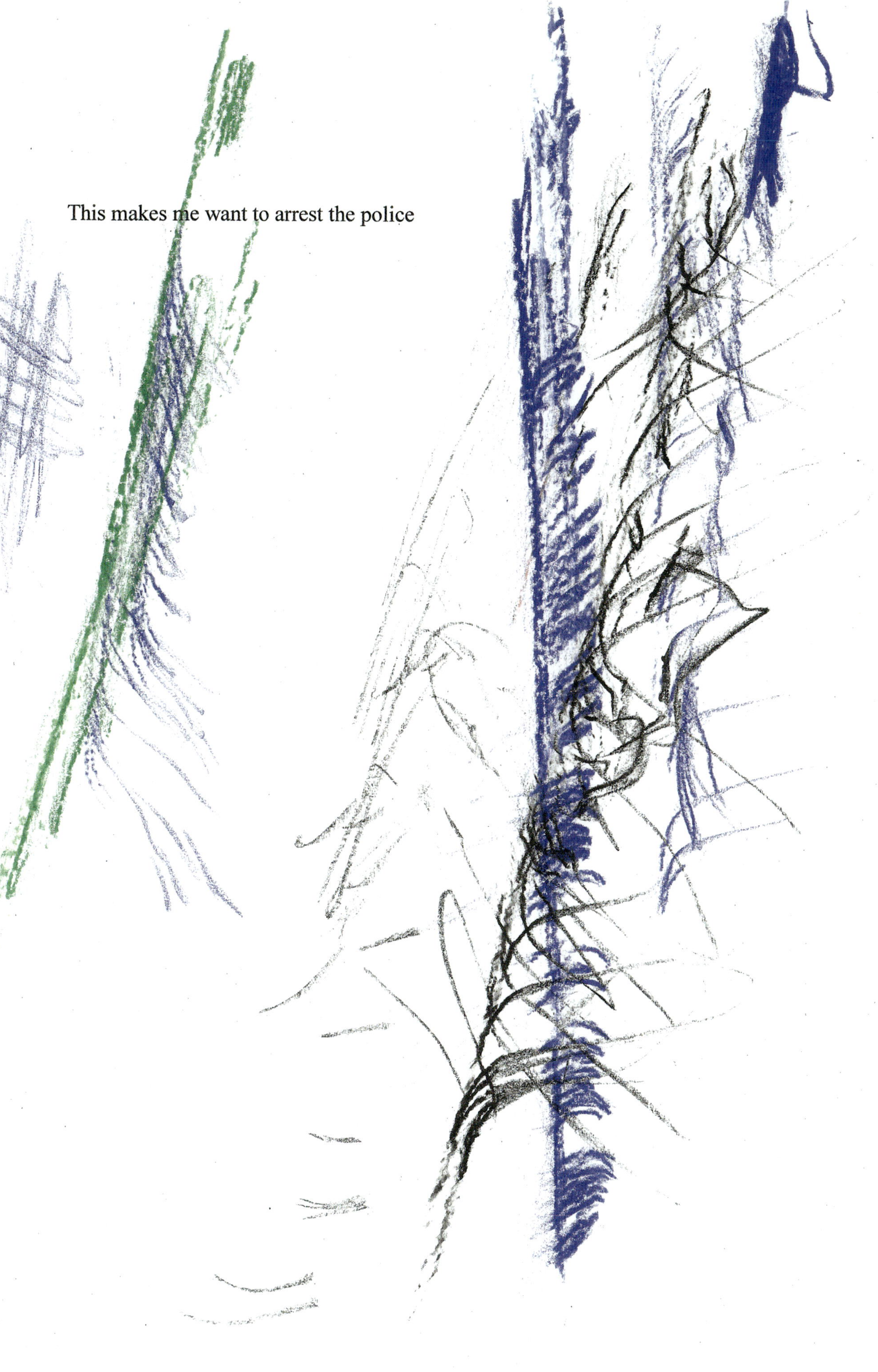

For example, with histor(ies) or memories of certain communities, which are also a way of showing another life.

"This makes me want to read a book from end to beginning," for example, is a comment of one user. So why not start over and read and remember the future anew, "predict the past" and combine fiction with dreams, reality with hopes, and wishes with facts in the vein of the notion, "I am no longer accepting the things I cannot change. I am changing the things I cannot accept", commonly attributed to African-American scholar and activist Angela Davis.

belit:

Exactly. The existing official narratives are unable to capture people's everyday experiences, and we need more intuitive connections in order to express the complexity of those and our own experiences. This is only meaningful alongside a fight for what we want to see happen in the world, changing the things we cannot accept, and the fight doesn't need to happen with an angry face. It comes in all shapes.

Cana:

I mean the knowledge that we are taught in schools and universities in the West sustains what the system wants us to learn. It's Eurocentric and deeply Orientalist and racist. That needs to be challenged and questioned. Young people all over the world are also taking to the streets for the *Fridays for Future* protests or *School Strike 4 Climate*, it's an international movement started by young people who decided not to attend school and protest against climate change every Friday. They demand equality and a better life for everyone and they are also questioning dominant narratives and knowledge production that create injustice in our society.

With your art, belit, and also what you do, Banu, I think you show us new perspectives and possibilities.

Banu:

I am thinking about what both of you have been saying and want to come back to your remarks, belit. Do you use the notion of unfolding as a way to work through something in order to understand?

belit:

Not only to understand but also maybe to feel, as Ulus Baker says,[8] to expand the possibilities of relating and experiencing. So, we can say, the notion of unfolding becomes a process of working through diverse ways of relating, thus diverse ways of knowledge production without centralizing understanding as the main form of relating, breaking that hierarchy and shaking the primary place given to the notion of understanding. We do not need to understand in order to relate. We are capable of relating in diverse ways, and otherwise it only flattens our capabilities of relating to the world. This also goes back to what I meant by the mainstream logic of this world, the forms that are recognized, the archiving practice, it all connects.

Banu:

Let me briefly think about how to put it. Cana points out very well that one of our shared concerns lies in the production of knowledge. So, it's not a coincidence that we are all working on different kinds of archives and state violence, which are not only "disciplining" tools but also generate certain kinds of knowledge. But, there is something more in belit's notion of "not just to understand but to feel" that I would like to know more about and connect to what Cana is saying.

belit:

I'd like to insert the term *embodied experience* here and connect our discussion to a, I think, relevant field for all of our practices, the archive. To make it more complete: the issues and challenges of archiving embodied experiences as archival practices are currently understood. I'm talking about experiences that I am working on and I think the two of you are as well. How do we need to think about archival practices, how fundamentally different do archival practices need to be thought of in order to develop the possibility of archiving these experiences, like the experience of state violence, for example. Maybe we need to call this not archiving, but something else. Diana Taylor calls them "repertoire."[9] Those experiences are primarily felt and experienced through the body rather than understood, and thus need other forms and thoughts, and a "rigorous and open-ended" conversation around it.

Banu:

belit's point strikes me as very important and brings different issues to mind. The first is the question of the relationship between archives and knowledge production. Archives are already set up to answer specific questions and always already express certain preferences as to what is deemed preservable and what is not. Given that we do not think about archives as "objective" repositories how do you make them work in your art practice?

Cana:

Yes, I agree that the official archives are linked to the power of the oppressor. So we should think about the mechanism of bringing out hidden archives to challenge the official ones. And art can play the role of a bridge between past and present and reviving that which has been hidden.

belit:

I think it is important too to think of archives as changing and dynamic structures. They might not be formed in order to define something in a certain way. In this case, I'm not talking about state archives that are mainly continuations of certain oppressive structures made to conform to official narratives. I'm talking about other archives, neither state nor necessarily oppositional nor alternative—let's say other institutional archives. These other archives might start with "good intentions," but under an unengaged administration and due to a lack of understanding of its power and its functions, they might end up in oppressive structures, erasing histories. Isn't this often the source of daily racisms too, i.e. being un-engaged and not understanding power structures? At least it is a very common form of racism in the Netherlands that Gloria Wekker refers to as "white innocence".[10]

An archive that is unaware of what is not included in it, participates in the erasure of those that it excludes. As Banu was saying, archives are never "objective," but they can be aware of what they are, they can define what they are, define what they do, clarify what they aim to do and communicate. Well, state archives do that and it is exactly through those definitions and communications that they erase. So there are different erasures at work in different cases. Archives are also responsible and should be accountable for how their collection is presented, how it is framed. They have to respond to a set of ethical codes and they often don't.

When I work with official or institutional archives, I'm interested in the narratives that are presented by those archives, the language and the framing that try to define and solidify histories. I'm interested in decoding structures that are not supported by different elements, structures that are imposed but may appear natural or act as if they are naturally there. I question this gesture and its internal mechanisms. I pull the pieces apart and try to put them back together and see where they actually don't fit each other in order to figure out the mechanics of that performance. I also engage with archives that are not recognized as archives; I insist on calling them archives until another term is coined. What can be archived and how an archive is defined through its practice? These definitions have to expand over time.

Banu:

You have already answered parts of my second question: can we even think of alternative archives and what they could look like? Is there a way to conceive of them as open-ended interrogations, for example? In the past few decades, feminist theory has moved away from the idea of revealing marginalized people's/women's voices, that is, from revealing voids in knowledge to transforming what is considered knowledge and what is not. In my research on how lost and dispossessed artworks and the erasure of non-Muslim artists have shaped both the writing of Ottoman and Islamic art history and the art history of present day Turkey, I have found that you cannot simply "plug in" their stories to already existing historical narratives. Instead, these narratives need to be transformed—or rather we have to work to transform them while acknowledging that any new narrative will also be incomplete, that some losses cannot be recovered and yet are formative for the past. I see Cana's earlier comments as entailing not just the uncovering of what has been obscured or erased but also as a search for ways to make such knowledge productive in the present.

Cana:

I think the question of the archive is linked to the question of understanding history as well. As we all know, state violence erases or puts aside the history of people who fought against that state violence. So maybe we also need to bring back the history that has been oppressed/erased by the state and connect it to our own experiences. State history means the history of the dominant class. It's bringing back the history of the oppressed people to learn from that history in order to produce another form of knowledge.

134

1
https://www.youtube.com/watch?v=Kp7eSUU9°y8.
Accessed 4/21/2019.
2
https://www.nytimes.com/2018/08/23/aarts/
design/john-akomfrah-review-new-museum.html.
Accessed 8/23/2018.
3
belit sağ, Cana Bilir-Meier, *Documentaristics—Documentation and their Characteristics*, in: Manfred Grübel, Linda Klösel (eds.), *Version Nr. 03*, Vienna: Verlag für Moderne Kunst, 2017.
4
The NSU was a Neo-Nazi network active from the mid-1990s onward. According to official sources, it killed at least ten people and planted at least two nail bombs in migrant neighborhoods over the course of eight years (2000-2007) throughout Germany. While one of its surviving members, Beate Zschäpe, has been sentenced to "life in prison," a full investigation of the network and the involvement of German intelligence and security forces must still be undertaken.
5
See Martha Woodmansee, *Art, the Author and the Market: Rereading the History of Aesthetics*, New York: Columbia University Press, 1994.
6
Silvia Federici, *Wages against Housework*, Bristol: Falling Wall Press Ltd and Power of Woman Collective, 1975, p. 3.
7
Ibid., p. 2.
8
See Ulus Baker, *Sanat ve Arzu*, İstanbul: İletişim Press, 2014.
9
See Diana Taylor, *The Archive and The Repertoire: Performing Cultural Memory in the Americas*, Durham: Duke University Press, 2003.
10
See Gloria Wekker, *White Innocence: Paradoxes of Colonialism and Race*, Durham: Duke University Press, 2016.

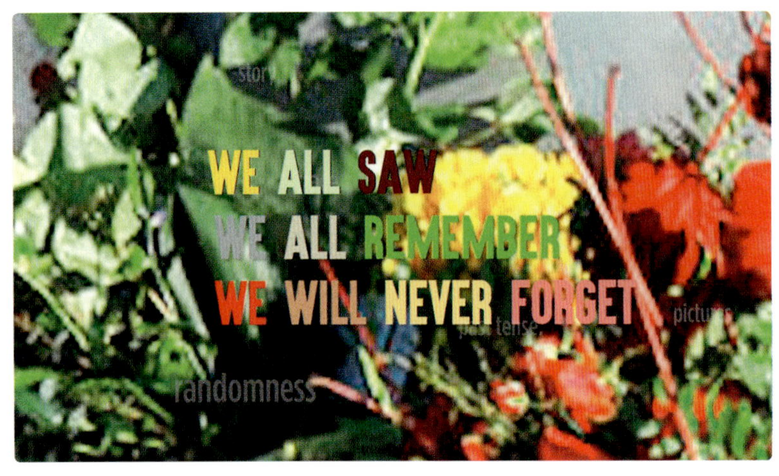
story
WE ALL SAW
WE ALL REMEMBER
WE WILL NEVER FORGET
past tense
pictures
randomness

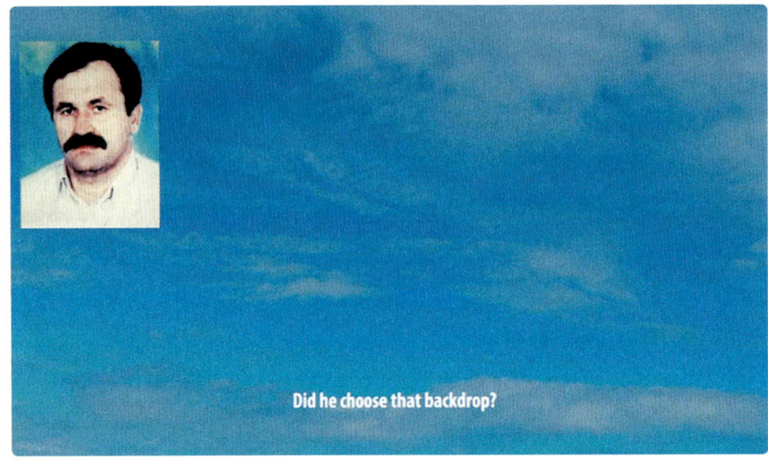
Did he choose that backdrop?

Wir wollen uns eine andere Art von Politik ausmalen:

Eine Unterhaltung mit offenem Ende

Cana Bilir-Meier im Gespräch mit
Banu Karaca und belit sağ

Der folgende Text dokumentiert ein Gespräch, das belit sağ, Banu Karaca und ich auf der Grundlage meiner aus einem Super-8-Film und Frottagen bestehenden Arbeit *This makes me want to predict the past* (2019) begonnen haben.

Die Frottagen und der Film entstanden im Münchner Olympia-Einkaufszentrum. Das Werk befasst sich mit Themen des Gedenkens und mit Erinnerungen an den rassistisch motivierten Anschlag auf das Einkaufszentrum im Jahr 2016. Es stellt sie mit Szenen aus dem Theaterstück *Düşler Ülkesi* (*Land der Träume*, Erman Okay, 1982), das die Alltagserfahrungen, Hoffnungen und Wünsche von Einwanderern in Deutschland betrachtet, in einen Dialog. Neun junge Menschen wurden

137

bei diesem Anschlag getötet und 36 weitere verletzt, vier davon durch Schüsse. Bei fast allen Opfern handelte es sich um Menschen mit Migrationshintergrund: sie waren türkischer oder kurdischer Abstammung, Roma und Sinti.

Der Titel des Films und die Frottagen basieren auf einem Zitat, das von einer/einem anonymen YouTube-Nutzer*in unter den Kommentaren zum Video *Redbone* des afroamerikanischen Musikers, Comedians, Autors und Filmregisseurs Donald Glover, der auch unter dem Namen Childish Gambino bekannt ist, geposted wurde.

Kommentare von YouTube-Nutzern zu Childish Gambinos Song *Redbone*[1]

This makes me want to brush my toothbrush.
This makes me want to predict the past.
This makes me want to tell my non biological parents that they're adopted.
This makes me want to sit on my TV and watch the couch.
This makes me want to rob my own bank account.
This makes me want to listen to my therapists problems.
This makes me want to arrest the police.
This makes me want to put on a pair of books and read glasses.
This makes me want to cut my barber's hair.
This makes me want to tell depression to kill itself.
This makes me wanna let the door open me.
This makes me want to sell myself on craigslist.
This makes me want to call two cab companies to see who arrives
        first then take the bus.
This makes me want to wake my alarm up.
This wants me to ask Burger King where the closest McDonald's is.
This makes me want to tell my boss to "get a job".
This makes me wanna let the elevator ride me.
This makes me want to read a book from end to beginning.
This makes me want to put milk in my cereal bowl, then the cereal.
This makes me want the homework to eat my dog.
This makes me want to give birth to my mom.
This make me wanna call in sick to my doctors appointment.
This makes me want to play on the Xbox with a PlayStation controller.
This makes me want to let my clothes wear me.
This makes me want to spy on my FBI agent.
This makes me want to put on my shoes before my sock.
This makes me wanna fall asleep before I close my eyes.
This makes me want to ask my dog to take me for a walk.
This makes me want to write with paper on a pencil.
This makes me wanna tell my boss he's fired.
This makes me want to tell my crush I have a girlfriend.
This makes me want to put on a pair of books and read glasses.
        I showed this to my dog, now he is a cat.
This makes me want to Google Bing.
This makes me wanna tell Aliens that humans are real…!
This makes me want to give mosquitoes malaria.
This makes me want to drive my parents to school.
This makes me want to kill two stones with one bird.
This makes me want to read a coloring book.
This makes me want to let the light turn me on.

This makes me wanna call my friend and tell him I can't talk right now
        call you later.
This makes me let my food eat me.
The makes me fall and hurt the ground.
This makes me want to do my desk on my homework.
This makes me want to take a bath with a unicorn.
This makes me wanna tell the weekend its Monday.
This makes me want to let my earphones wear my ear.
This makes me want to put my toaster in my toast.
This makes me want to remember the future.
This makes me want to tell my teacher to raise her hand if she wants
        to speak to me.
This makes me want to give my fish a bath.
This makes me want to steal money out of my own wallet.
This makes me want to drink vampire's blood.
This makes me want to ask the hotel's reception if they want a room
        with a beach view.
This makes me want to tell Monday to wake up.
This makes me want to be a vacuum to clean my house.
This makes me want to tell the clock what time it is.
This song makes me wanna threaten to call my teachers parents.
This makes me wanna call someone and say I can't talk.
This reminds me of spending time with people I love. Time sure does fly.
This makes me want to forget what I can't remember.
This makes me fly like I can feel.
This makes me want to walk on a fly!
This makes me want to pass a test and study for it afterwards.
This makes me want to put numbers in alphabetical order.
This makes me want to break into someone's house and install
        a security system.
This makes me want to end things I haven't started yet.

Die meisten meiner künstlerischen Arbeiten drehen sich um Fragen der offiziellen Wissensproduktion, oft durch Dekodierung. Jedes neue Bild erzeugt weitere neue Bilder und verdeckt dabei andere. Diese Fragen und Verfahren sind alle Teil davon, wie Macht konstituiert wird. Wenn der Kulturtheoretiker Stuart Hall erklärt, dass Identität „ein nie-abgeschlossenes Gespräch"[2] sei, dann lässt sich dies – meiner Meinung nach – auf die Kommentare von YouTube Nutzern beziehen, die über Dinge schreiben, die in der Realität nicht funktionieren können und die doch zugleich die Konstruktion eben dieser Realität aufzeigen. Unter einem Gespräch versteht man gewöhnlich etwas mit einem Anfang und einem Ende, aber wie könnte ein unabgeschlossenes Gespräch aussehen?

Für diesen Text habe ich mich entschieden, Banu Karaca und belit sağ zu einer Diskussion von Themen einzuladen, die für unsere Werke und in theoretischer Hinsicht wichtig sind, so wie die Mechanismen des strukturellen Rassismus, die Frage der Intersektionalität, Machtverhältnisse, die sich in Sprache sowie in persönlichen und öffentlichen Archiven ausdrücken, Migration, die Spannung zwischen offizieller und subalterner Geschichtsschreibung und die Politik von Sichtbarkeit und Zensur.

Die Anthropologin Banu Karaca arbeitet an den Schnittstellen von politischer Anthropologie, Kunst und Ästhetik, Nationalismus und Kulturpolitik,

Museen und Praktiken des Gedenkens in Deutschland und der Türkei. Sie ist Mitgründerin von Siyah Bant, einer Forschungsplattform, die die Zensur von Kunst in der Türkei dokumentiert. Ihre laufende Forschung befasst sich mit der Praxis des Verfassens von Kunstgeschichte vor dem Hintergrund der Enteignungspolitik in der Spätzeit des Osmanischen Reiches und der jungen türkischen Republik.

belit sağ ist Videomacherin, bildende Künstlerin und Kunstarbeiterin mit Wohnsitz in Amsterdam. Sie studierte Mathematik in der Türkei und bildende Kunst in den Niederlanden. Ihr Background im Film ist aus ihrer Arbeit mit Kreisen von Videoaktivisten in Ankara und Istanbul erwachsen, wo sie Gruppen wie VideA, Karahaber und bak.ma mit ins Leben rief. Arbeitsaufenthalte führten sie im Rahmen des International Studio & Curatorial Program (ISCP) nach New York und an die Rijksakademie van Beeldende Kunsten in Amsterdam. In ihrer laufenden künstlerischen und filmischen Praxis konzentriert sie sich auf die Rolle der visuellen Repräsentation bei der Erfahrung von politischen Konflikten in der Türkei, in Deutschland und in den Niederlanden.

In einem Interview mit mir sagte belit sağ einmal: „Bei allem, was ich tue, versuche ich, Stellung zu beziehen. Es ist wichtig, woher ich komme, weshalb ich mich für ein bestimmtes Thema interessiere und was ich damit tun werde. Und ich versuche, das transparent zu machen. Diejenige, die die Arbeit ediert und formuliert, bin immer ich, und es ist wichtig, offenzulegen, dass ich es bin, die hinter der Arbeit steht. In der Zeit des Videoaktivismus war die Sichtbarkeit von Menschen und Problemen unsere Taktik; ich denke, auch Unsichtbarkeit kann eine Taktik für Bewegungen sein. Es ist wichtig, sich einer Vielfalt von Taktiken zu bedienen."[3]

Banu:

Wenn man sich das Material anschaut, das du gerade geteilt hast, dann ist das echt beeindruckend. Mir war nicht bewusst, dass es solche Kommentare zu diesem Song gibt. Weißt du, wie das angefangen hat?

Cana:

Wie es angefangen hat, weiß ich nicht genau. Aber so, wie ich das verstehe, hinterfragt Childish Gambino mit *Redbone* den Status quo von alltäglichen Strukturen, so wie auch schon vorher mit seinem Lied (und Video) *This is America*. Die Texte enthalten eine starke Botschaft und sind besonders für junge Leute zu einem wichtigen Transportmittel zum Ausdruck ihrer Wünsche und ihres Bedürfnisses nach Veränderung geworden. Ich habe diese Kommentare mit dem Thema des rassistischen Anschlags verbunden, der 2016 am Olympia-Einkaufszentrum stattfand. Diese Kommentare zeigen uns, wie junge Menschen sich eine andere Gesellschaft vorstellen, indem sie aufdecken, wie Diskurse und Sprache in Machtverhältnissen verortet sind. Der Titel des Werks, *This makes me want to predict the past*, zeigt die in der Dichotomie von Vergangenheit und Gegenwart oder Geschichte und Erinnerung liegenden Widersprüche.

Banu:

Wie all diese Anschläge ist der Münchner Fall einzigartig und folgt doch einem vertrauten Muster. Als klar wurde, dass die meisten Opfer einen Migrationshintergrund hatten, wurde der Täter als „einsamer Wolf" beschrieben, als jemand mit psychischen Problemen. Die Behörden haben den Anschlag rasch als „nicht terroristisch" und, was bedeutsamer ist, als nicht rassistisch motiviert etikettiert. Und, das ist vielleicht am allerwichtigsten, sie haben den Anschlag von der Geschichte des Rassismus in Deutschland getrennt.

belit:

Wenn ich mir deine Arbeit und die Kommentare betrachte, Cana, dann erinnert mich das wieder daran, wie beschränkt es ist, Rassismus in Diskussionen am Runden Tisch zu besprechen, und dass die vorgegebene lineare Logik bestimmter Formate nicht ausreicht, um verschiedene Aspekte bestimmter Probleme anzugehen. Und es bringt mich auf den Gedanken, wie dringend es ist, bestimmte Erfahrungen und Ausdrucksformen als eine Quelle der Wissensproduktion ernst zu nehmen. Die Erfahrung von Rassismus zum Beispiel wird oft durch ihre Übersetzungen in Formen kommuniziert, die körperliche Erfahrungen nicht vollständig erfassen. Ich denke hier auch an Archive; Formen wie Bilder, Filme, Texte usw. werden archiviert, sind „archivierbar". Meine Frage geht dahin, wie man die Erfahrung als eine eigenständige Form beachten und wertschätzen kann. Es ist so, dass, selbst wenn es sich bei diesen Übersetzungen, die ich vorhin erwähnte, um solche Formate wie Texte handelt, oft nur solche Texte als gültige Wissensproduktion oder Quellen betrachtet werden, die einer linearen Logik folgen. Dann ist meine zweite Frage, wie man das Wissen, das durch körperliche Erfahrung erzeugt wird, (an-)erkennen kann und wie sich die Erfahrung mit anderen teilen lässt. Anti-Rassismus Gruppen pochen hartnäckig darauf, dass migrantisch situiertes Wissen in den Vordergrund gerückt wird, da bestimmte Erfahrungen für wertvoll gehalten und im System der Wissenserzeugung als Ressource geschätzt und gewisse andere ausgeblendet werden. Es besteht ein direkter Zusammenhang zu dem Ausblenden, von dem Banu spricht. Die Art und Weise, wie über diesen Angriff berichtet wurde, löscht die Erfahrung der Opfer aus, indem sie diese Erfahrung verbreitet und durch eine andere ersetzt, die den Täter schützt. Ich denke, wir alle drei arbeiten auf die eine oder andere Weise an solchen Erfahrungen, die von offiziellen Narrativen ignoriert, daraus gelöscht und/oder absichtlich verborgen werden.

Mir fällt dabei das Tribunal NSU-Komplex Auflösen ein. Zweck des Tribunals war es, migrantische Erfahrungen in den Mittelpunkt zu rücken, und es wurde von Graswurzel-Aktivisten*innen und Migrant*innengruppen in Zusammenarbeit mit den Familien der Opfer organisiert. Cana und ich haben kurze Videospots zum Fall des NSU (Nationalsozialistischer Untergrund)[4] gedreht, die diese Erfahrungen in den Blick nehmen. Ich denke, dass wir durch unsere Praktiken ständig versuchen, Formen und Ausdrucksmöglichkeiten in Bezug auf diese Erfahrungen zu finden. (siehe Bild: (Against) Randomness. 2017)

Banu:

Wenn ich mir deine Arbeiten anschaue, Cana, und bei deinem letzten Kommentar, belit, erinnere ich mich an ein Gefühl, das ich hatte und das zunehmend stärker geworden ist, nicht nur beim Thema Rassismus, sondern allgemein, wenn man etwas macht – Kunst, Politik, Wissenschaft – wie bedeutsam es tatsächlich ist, immer „Nein" zu sagen, als reine Umkehrung von Machtdiskursen. Zum Teil stammt mein Unbehagen aus meiner Arbeit mit Siyah Bant. Als wir damit angefangen haben, war es unser Ziel, die Zensur der Künste in der Türkei zu erforschen und zu dokumentieren, die verschiedenen Modalitäten der Zensur zu verstehen und aufzuzeigen, wie verschiedene Akteur*innen im Wechselspiel innerhalb und außerhalb des Kunstbetriebs kollektiv die Zensur ermöglichen.

Und wir waren daran interessiert, Räume zu fördern, in denen man über verschiedene Strategien und Taktiken zur Bekämpfung von Zensur und das Engagement für die Meinungsfreiheit nachdenken und diskutieren kann.

Diese Themen sind zwar nach wie vor relevant, aber es ist auch wichtig, die Debatte über den reinen Protest gegen die Zensur hinauszubewegen und die Diskussion über die Annahme, dass die freie Meinungsäußerung eine klar definierte „Sache für sich" oder ein bestimmbarer Endpunkt sei, auszudehnen und stattdessen an einen Bereich zu denken, auf dem gerungen wird, auf dem die freie Meinungsäußerung in ihrem Verhältnis zu Macht, Ort und Geschichte in Not ist. Die freie Meinungsäußerung liegt also nicht nur im Widerspruch zur Zensur, sondern auch im Ringen darum, die Bedingungen für eine Debatte, die diesen Parametern folgt, zu schaffen.

Versteht mich nicht falsch. Protest ist natürlich wichtig, aber wenn man darin verhaftet bleibt, dann heißt das, dass man der Logik der Macht verhaftet bleibt. Ich habe das Gefühl, dass wir angesichts der momentanen politischen Umstände allzu leicht in die Falle tappen, soviel zu protestieren, dass uns die Zeit dafür fehlt, herauszuarbeiten, *wofür* wir eigentlich sind. Es gibt natürlich auch Ausnahmen, wie zum Beispiel die Frauenbewegung und die Umwelt-/ Klimawandel-Bewegung. In diesem Sinn betrachtet zeigen uns die absurden Kommentare andere Möglichkeitshorizonte und unterschiedliche Vorstellungen, in denen das Potenzial für eine ganz andere Art von Politik liegt.

Cana:

Ja, dem stimme ich zu, denn „Nein" zu sagen ist auch eine Form der Stellungnahme oder Ablehnung und wenn man in dieser Haltung steckenbleibt, dann wird Veränderung sehr schwierig – und der rassistische Diskurs ist eine Sammlung starrer Worte, die als Waffe zur Abwertung von Menschen mit dunkler Hautfarbe (BPoC/Black People of Color), Migrant*innen, Geflüchteten dienen. Um uns dagegen zu wehren, müssen wir uns also gegen den verwendeten Diskurs wehren: gegen die Sprache. Und auch sind diese Kommentare Imaginationen einer Welt, sie malen uns etwas aus, anstatt [nur] gegen etwas zu sein! Anstatt immer „Nein" zu sagen, bieten sie etwas Stärkendes an. Und Wandel beginnt mit der Veränderung der Sprache und von Vorstellungen – Vorstellungen, die manchmal utopisch sein müssen.

belit:

Das ist auch, was wir überall sehen, oder? Die Polarisation und das Feststecken in einer Position, die von dem, wogegen man ist, diktiert wird. Es ist im Grunde entmündigend, wenn man seine Position davon bestimmen lässt, wogegen man ist. Obwohl es natürlich viele Momente, Orte, Zeiten gibt, wo man sagen muss „Das ist einfach unrecht", auch wenn es simpel und offensichtlich ist, dass diese Sache unrecht ist, und es auszusprechen deine Intelligenz und Existenz unterminiert, aber man ist in eine Position gedrängt, wo man das einfach aussprechen muss. Damit man sich in eine Umgebung begeben kann, in der man einen Raum für Diskussionen schaffen kann, wie Banu erwähnt hat, aber auch einen Raum, in dem man sich eine Welt, eine bestimmte Veränderung vorstellt und formuliert, wonach man strebt. Es geht auch um die Notwendigkeit, sich etwas auszumalen und über diese Vorstellungen eine Welt zu schaffen, die eigene Werte enthält. Um den Ausblick auf eine Welt, die den Reaktionismus hinter sich lässt, und wie man es schafft, diese Werte und diese Welt, die die Worte der Mehrheitslogik unserer heutigen Welt hinter sich lässt, zu kommunizieren; mit einer Sprache, die diese Imagination einschließt. Childish Gambino tut das. Er kommuniziert seine eigene Erfahrung und wie es sich anfühlt, in der heutigen Welt zu leben. Auf diesem Weg eröffnen sich auch Möglichkeiten, sich eine andere Welt auszumalen, und durch die YouTube-Kommentare wird diese Vorstellung zu einer kollektiven – und das ist unglaublich inspirierend!

Banu:

Ich würde von euch gerne hören, wie die allgemeine Situation, die belit gerade beschrieben hat, den aktuellen Kunstbetrieb formt, d.h. ob ihr das Gefühl habt, dass eure künstlerische Arbeit davon betroffen ist oder eure Auswahl von Ausstellungsorten? Um es anders auszudrücken: Glaubt ihr, dass die gegenwärtige Situation auch das Verhältnis zwischen Kunst und Politik neu konfiguriert?

Cana:

Ich glaube, wenn wir die Rolle der Kunst in der gegenwärtigen Situation sehen wollen, dann sollten wir sie mit der Frage analysieren, wie der Kapitalismus die Kunst zu einer Ware gemacht hat. Das heißt, wir sollten das in Frage stellen und versuchen, neue Kunstformen zu schaffen, die nach Veränderung streben und die Bedeutung von Kunst und ihre Beziehung zur Politik wiederherstellen. In diesem Kontext steht zum Beispiel der Film über Semra Ertan. Dasselbe habe ich auch mit meinem Projekt über die Moschee *Grundstein* in München zu erreichen versucht. *Semra Ertan* (2013) ist ein Film über die Schriftstellerin und Dichterin Semra Ertan, die in der Türkei geboren wurde, als Tochter von Gastarbeitern in den 1970er Jahren nach Deutschland kam und über 350 Gedichte schrieb. Sie protestierte gegen den Rassismus, der Einwanderern entgegengebracht wurde, und verbrannte sich 1982 in Hamburg in einer Form des öffentlichen Protests. Der Film dient dazu, ihre Geschichte neu zu schreiben – als die eines Menschen, der gegen Unrecht aufbegehrt, nicht als die eines Opfers. Das andere Projekt in der Moschee in Freimann in München, an dem ich 2017-18 gearbeitet habe, befasst sich mit den Architekt*innen der Moschee, Necla Gürel und Osman Edip Gürel, und zeigt eine andere Version von Geschichte, die antimuslimischen Rassismus und orientalistische Betrachtungsweisen in der deutschen Gesellschaft hinterfragt. Das Architektenehepaar Osman Edip und Necla Gürel wird in der Münchner Stadtgeschichte nicht erwähnt, obwohl die beiden viele bedeutende Gebäude entworfen haben.

belit:

Was du da gerade gesagt hast, Cana, ist wirklich so wichtig. Das heißt, nicht zulassen, dass eine Erzählung singulär wird, auch nicht, um sie durch eine andere Erzählung zu ersetzen, sondern um die Dinge zu verkomplizieren, weil diese Erzählungen, diese Leben immer vielschichtig sind. Es bedeutet im Grunde, zu erkennen, welche Macht in der Erzeugung und Verbreitung von vielschichtigen Narrativen liegt. Das ist eine fruchtbare Art, „Nein" zu sagen, die einen Weg über ein einzelnes „Nein" hinaus öffnet. Deine Arbeiten sind ein deutliches Beispiel für diesen Weg.

In dem Maße, wie die Polarisierung zunimmt, bin ich plötzlich direkter und entrüsteter und auch meine Arbeiten haben einen klareren Fokus, insbesondere seit 2013, als das Klima in der Türkei nach und nach immer gewalttätiger wurde. Diese Polarisierung und die Normalisierung der Sprache des Rassismus bringen ein Dringlichkeitsbewusstsein mit sich. Ich reagiere auch zunehmend empfindlicher und schärfer darauf, wie meine Arbeiten von anderen kontextualisiert werden. Als eine in Westeuropa lebende Person of Color mit Migrationshintergrund, deren Arbeiten sich primär mit den Problemen des Landes befassen, in dem sie geboren wurde und aufgewachsen ist, muss ich sorgfältig darauf achten, wie meine Arbeiten instrumentalisiert werden. Ich spüre zudem eine größere Distanz zur Kommerzialisierung meiner Werke, eine klare Distanz zu den Anforderungen des Kunstmarktes. Auf diese Weise kann ich meine Arbeitsabläufe schützen und mich auf das konzentrieren, was ich schaffen möchte, und der Erzeugungsprozess der Werke bleibt, so gut es geht, von den Anforderungen des Marktes und der damit einhergehenden Instrumentalisierung weit entfernt. Letztendlich finde ich dieses Bewusstsein wichtig und es ist ein Fragezeichen, das ich in meine Praxis einbringe. Bestimmte Auseinandersetzungen enden nie, sie gehören zum Charakter meiner Beziehung zum Feld. Das heißt nicht, dass diese Auseinandersetzungen bedeutungslos wären, oder dass wir aufgeben und sie beilegen sollten. Im Gegenteil, sie sind essentieller Teil meiner Arbeit.

Cana:

Dem stimme ich zu, weil das kapitalistische System auf Hierarchien und Klassen aufbaut, die den weißen Privilegien dienen. Deshalb werden Menschen anderer Hautfarbe und ihre Werke nicht ernst genommen.

belit:

Neben dem Aspekt, dass sie nicht ernst genommen werden, wollte ich darauf hinweisen, auf welche Art diese Werke und Menschen positioniert werden, vor allem von den Institutionen, um damit bestimmte Agenden zu unterstützen... Zum Beispiel laden Institutionen, die sich innerhalb ihres eigenen Betriebs weigern, rassistische Strukturen zu hinterfragen, das heißt Institutionen, die solche Strukturen unterhalten, indem sie sich selektiv unwissend oder einfach fördernd verhalten, PoC-Künstler*innen ein und/oder binden Werke mit klaren anti-rassistischen Botschaften ein, damit sie behaupten können, dass sie ein anti-rassistisches Programm verfolgen. Solche Instrumentalisierungen stellen eine echte alltägliche Herausforderung dar. Das ist „art-washing" – Kunstfärberei, mit der die rassistische Einstellung und die Doppelmoral einer Institution legitimiert werden. In der Praxis wird es sehr komplex, diese zu hinterfragen, hauptsächlich aufgrund von fehlender Solidarität und Organisation. Infolgedessen isolieren diese Erfahrungen oft diejenigen, die gegen sie kämpfen. Eine weitere Herausforderung sehe ich für mich in Bezug auf meine eigene Empörung. Das heißt, ich frage mich, wie ich diese Energie in Werke lenken kann, die ich als bildende Künstlerin, als Publikum und in allen Positionen dazwischen und darüber hinaus spannend fände. Für mich besteht die Herausforderung darin, diese Energie zu verlagern und in etwas zu verwandeln, das für unsere Zeit, für uns selbst und unsere Kämpfe Bedeutung hat, ohne zu vergessen, bei alledem auch Spaß zu haben.

Cana:

Der Herstellungsdruck auf dem Kunstmarkt führt bei mir manchmal zu einem Gefühl der innerlichen Entfremdung zu meinen eigenen künstlerischen Produktionsbedingungen. Ich denke, dass der Kunstmarkt nicht unabhängig von ökonomischen und politischen Strukturen analysiert werden kann. Der Markt, in dem Kunst produziert wird, ist auch Teil dieses sozio-ökonomischen Systems und viele Künstler*innen, die ich kenne, stehen unter dem Druck, fortlaufend und immer weiter künstlerische Arbeiten zu produzieren, denn sonst wird man sehr schnell ausgeschlossen. Dieses Gefühl der Entfremdung scheint persönlich, aber das ist es nicht, es ist ein strukturelles Problem.

Banu:

Ich möchte hier kurz eingreifen, bevor ich zum Thema des Imaginierens von Möglichkeiten und der Möglichkeiten des Imaginierens zurückkomme. Ich denke, es ist wichtig, bei der Beobachtung innezuhalten, dass die Struktur des Kunstmarktes die Produktion von „alternativer" Kunst nicht unberührt lässt. Vielleicht müssen wir berücksichtigen, dass bereits der Begriff der Kunst im späten 18. Jahrhundert in Bezug auf den Markt entwickelt wurde. Die Kunsttheoretikerin Martha Woodmansee zum Beispiel argumentiert, dass die Vorstellung von Künstler*innen oder Autor*innen als individuelle Schöpfer*innen (oder als „Genies") in jener Zeit entstand, und zwar teilweise, um den Künstlern zu erlauben, mit ihren Schöpfungen Geld zu verdienen (das Urheberrecht entstand zu genau jenem Zeitpunkt – zum Schutz der Künstler).[5] Aber zur selben Zeit entstanden auch Theorien über die Autonomie der Kunst, wodurch fundamentale Spannungen etabliert wurden, die uns bis heute begleiten: also ist Kunst, so wie wir sie allgemein auffassen, sowohl (in ihrer idealisierten Form) autonom, als doch auch eine Ware. Und so wie ich deine beiden Kommentare verstehe, sind diese Spannungen im gegenwärtigen Stadium des Kapitalismus noch sichtbarer geworden.

Cana:

Damit sprichst du einen sehr wichtigen Punkt an, nämlich den Konflikt der Kunst als Utopie, die danach strebt, sich eine neue Gesellschaft zu imaginieren und generell in Frage zu stellen, und gleichzeitig die Logik des Marktes, auf dem die Forderungen erfüllbar sein müssen und somit das System wiederrum legitimiert wird. Ich glaube auch, dass unter anderem die Renaissance dem Einzelnen mehr Rechte in einigen Gesellschaftsbereichen gab und dies damals auch die Kunstproduktion beeinflusste. Aber im Augenblick dominiert aus meiner Erfahrung und Perspektive immer noch sehr der Markt die sozialen und politischen Bereiche, was sich auch auf die Arbeitsumstände von Künstler*innen und Produktionsbedingungen von Kunst auswirkt. Ich denke, die Schriften der Frankfurter Schule, oder auch wie du, Banu, ansprichst, die von Martha Woodmansee haben dann später viel zur Analyse der Kommerzialisierung des Sozialen und der Kunst im Zeitalter des fortgeschrittenen Kapitalismus beigetragen.

Zum Thema der Prekarisierung von Arbeitsbedingungen im Kunstbetrieb muss ich auch an meine Erfahrung vor und während meines Studiums an der Akademie der bildenden Künste in Wien denken, als ich unbedingt ein paar Praktika beim Film oder in Kunstgalerien machen wollte. Während der ersten Jahre meines Studiums habe ich ein Praktikum bei einem Symposium, bei dem es um politische Kunst ging, gemacht und die Arbeitsbedingungen waren ungeheuer prekär. Mir wurde klar, dass vor allem viele Frauen in diesem Bereich unbezahlte Arbeit leisten. In diesem Fall müssen wir auch erwähnen, dass die feministische Bewegung *Lohn für Hausarbeit* 1972 in Europa begann und eine öffentliche Debatte über Themen wie Hausarbeit, Sexarbeit und Reproduktionsarbeit anstieß, die Teil des kapitalistischen Systems ist. Silvia Federici schreibt 1975 dazu in ihrem Essay *Lohn gegen Hausarbeit*: „Wir müssen einräumen, dass es dem Kapital mit großem Erfolg gelungen ist, unsere Arbeit zu verbergen. Es hat auf Kosten der Frauen ein echtes Meisterwerk geschaffen. Indem es einen Lohn für die Arbeit im Haushalt verweigerte und sie in eine aus Liebe verrichtete Handlung verwandelte, hat das Kapital viele Fliegen mit einer Klappe geschlagen."[6] Wir müssen an der unbezahlten Arbeit in den Künsten und an der Arbeit von Frauen im Haushalt, von der die Frauenbewegung und *Lohn für Hausarbeit* sprechen, Kritik üben. Beides ist fest miteinander verknüpft, denn, wie Federici schreibt: „Es stimmt, dass im kapitalistischen System jede/r Arbeiter/in manipuliert und ausgebeutet und seine/ihre Beziehung zum Kapital vollständig verborgen wird. Der Lohn lässt den Eindruck entstehen, es handele sich um ein faires Geschäft: man arbeitet und man wird bezahlt, man selbst und der Boss sind also gleichberechtigt: während der Lohn in Wirklichkeit, anstatt dich für die Arbeit, die du verrichtest,

zu entlohnen, all die unbezahlte Arbeit, die in den Profit einfließt, verbirgt.
Aber zumindest erkennt der Lohn dich als Arbeiter/in an und du kannst verhandeln und dich gegen die Bedingungen und die Lohnsumme wehren.“[7] The
Carrot Workers Collective und die Precarious Workers Brigade in London, die
sich seit Jahren mit diesem Thema beschäftigen, zeigen, womit wir es zu tun
haben, machen diese Verbindung von unbezahlter Arbeit in den Künsten
sichtbar und bekämpfen sie. Für meine Kolleg*innen und mich waren sie
enorm bestärkend. Trotzdem habe ich immer noch viel mit unbezahlter und
prekärer Arbeit in den Künsten zu kämpfen und ich nenne mich also lieber
Kunstarbeiterin als Künstlerin.

belit:

Ich glaube, die Spannungen, die zwischen
der Autonomie der Kunst und dem Kunstmarkt bestehen, sind zu verschiedenen Zeiten in verschiedenen Regionen am stärksten vom politischen Klima
außerhalb und dem politischen Bewusstsein innerhalb des Kunstfeldes betroffen gewesen, und jeder Augenblick scheint denjenigen, die diese Zeiten
durchleben, der jeweils spannungsreichste zu sein. Ich bezweifle, dass die
Spannungen im jetzigen Moment am sichtbarsten sind oder dass dies der mit
den stärksten Spannungen beladene Moment ist. Man betrachte nur einmal
die Entstehung des Urheberrechts und seine Entwicklung bis heute, von der
Idee, dass Künstler*innen Geld verdienen und die Rechte an ihren Schöpfungen schützen, bis dahin, dass Firmen wie Disney große Summen am Urheberrecht verdienen, ganze Abteilungen nur zum Zweck der Prozessführung unterhalten und Inhalte mit dem Copyright schützen, die nicht aus ihren eigenen
Schöpfungen stammen, sondern aus dem öffentlichen Bereich gestohlen
und privatisiert werden. Ein multinationales Unternehmen wie zum Beispiel
Disney zielt darauf ab, das gesamte Feld zu definieren und erschafft die
dominanten, ich würde sagen offiziellen, Narrative mit durch das Urheberrecht geschützten, angeeigneten Inhalten. Das heißt, es schreibt diese Narrative um, wie es ihm passt. Letztlich werden offizielle Narrative nicht nur
durch Staaten, sondern in den letzten 20 Jahren ebenso durch multinationale
Konzerne definiert. Zudem möchte ich hier noch anmerken, dass, wenn die
Kunstgeschichte erwähnt wird, hauptsächlich die westliche Kunstgeschichte
gemeint ist, die stärker mit dem Markt verknüpft ist als andere Kunstgeschichten. Wir können Disney mit Gagosian oder Christie's austauschen und
deren Praktiken in den Blick nehmen.

Ich glaube, dass wir als Kunstarbeiter*innen die Möglichkeit haben,
unser Feld durch unsere Arbeit und unsere Haltungen neu zu definieren, die
Möglichkeit, einen Raum zu eröffnen, wo bestimmte Werte gelebt werden
und eine bestimmte Einstellung dem Markt gegenüber eingenommen wird,
die seine Geschichte und sein Verhältnis zur Macht anerkennt und gleichzeitig durch unsere Praxis hinterfragt. Ich meine dabei nicht nur durch den Inhalt
der Werke, sondern durch den gesamten Prozess, was heißt, die Vorstellung
von Genie und Urheberrecht zu hinterfragen, prekäre Arbeitsverhältnisse,
Hierarchien, Elitedenken, inhärenten Sexismus und Rassismus zu hinterfragen, und die Macht dieser Unternehmen, Galerien und Auktionshäuser zu
hinterfragen, indem man lokale Praktiken schafft, die das Ziel haben, global
vernetzt zu sein. Ich frage mich ständig, in was für einer Gesellschaft ich
leben möchte und stelle mir diese Gesellschaft vor. Weshalb sollte der Kunst-
bereich in dieser Vorstellung eine Ausnahme sein? Arbeitsverhältnisse sind
Arbeitsverhältnisse, der Klassenkampf ist derselbe Klassenkampf. Ich setze
mich für gerechte Arbeitsverhältnisse ein. Ich kämpfe gegen prekäre Zustände,

denen ich jeden Tag begegne, und betrachte den Kunstmarkt als einen Arbeitsmarkt unter vielen. Man sät diese Saat und schafft diese Räume. Letztendlich ist die Akkumulation der Früchte dieser Bemühungen ein langfristiger Prozess, genau wie jede andere Form des Aktivismus. Es ist wie beim Klimawandel. Vielleicht werden einige von uns die extremen Folgen nicht in unserer unmittelbaren Umgebung erleben, vielleicht aufgrund unseres Alters, aber wenn man es auf gesunde Weise betrachtet, dann sollte man für Gerechtigkeit überall eintreten und den Umwelt-Rassismus genau wie jeden anderen Rassismus bekämpfen. Auch weil unsere Welt sehr entmutigend und deprimierend wird, wenn wir unsere Bemühungen nur kurzfristig betrachten. Dann sieht es so aus, als haben ein einzelner Mensch oder ein einzelnes Kollektiv oder selbst ein Netzwerk von Kollektiven nicht die Macht, etwas zu ändern oder zu hinterfragen, aber auf Dauer ist das nur eine beschränkte Sichtweise, und auch das sagt uns die Geschichte. Es geht darum, wie wir uns organisieren, wie wir Solidarität zeigen, wie wir unsere Privilegien realisieren und zukunftsorientiert füreinander einstehen.

Cana:

Vielleicht kann das „Nein" nur in dem Sinne eine Bedeutung haben, als es die Ungerechtigkeit dessen, dem wir tagtäglich ausgesetzt sind, zurückweist. „Nein" kann also ein Ausgangspunkt für die Veränderung dieser Position sein. Aber wir sollten es hinter uns lassen und nicht dort stecken bleiben.

Banu:

In diesem Sinne ist das „Nein" ein Ausgangspunkt für – um deinen Begriff zu verwenden, Cana – das Gespräch darüber, wie wir leben und zusammenleben möchten und für eine alternative Politik. Es muss ein gründliches Gespräch darüber sein, wie man sich in die Richtung von größerer Gerechtigkeit und Fairness bewegt, dessen Ende aber offenbleibt.

Cana:

Ja, das bedeutet, sich vom Leben, wie es ist, zum Leben, wie es sein sollte, zu bewegen.

belit:

Oder wie es sein könnte, mit den Möglichkeiten, die sich uns eröffnen.

Cana:

Ja, zu sagen, dass ein anderes Leben möglich ist.

Banu:

Ich bin trotzdem immer noch neugierig, Cana, wie sich dies in deiner künstlerischen Arbeit niederschlägt, und auch in deiner, belit?

belit:

In meiner bedeutet es definitiv einen Unterschied zwischen den Zeiten, in denen ich mich mit Videoaktivismus beschäftigt habe, und der Arbeit, die ich jetzt mache, bei der es eher darum geht, über Themen nachzudenken, als darum, wofür oder wogegen ich bin. Ich muss ein bisschen aufpassen, damit ich mit diesen Worten eine frühere, äußerst wertvolle Praxis nicht übermäßig simplifiziere. Angesichts der politischen Rahmenbedingungen und der Dringlichkeit des Kampfes um Menschenrechte musste die Praxis des Videoaktivismus klar und unmissverständlich sein, um bestimmte Diskurse und falsche Narrative zu bekämpfen, die verbreitet wurden. Es war so wichtig zu zeigen, dass es bestimmte Stimmen gibt, die ausradiert werden; zu zeigen, was auf den Straßen vor sich geht, dass das, was gesagt wird, nicht das ist, was tatsächlich passiert. Klingt das nicht ganz ähnlich wie die Situation heutzutage? Bei dieser Praxis ging es darum, eine klare Position zu unterstreichen. Man hatte das Gefühl, keine Zeit zum Nachdenken zu haben. Bestimmt wäre meine Praxis anders, wenn ich es heute machen würde. Ich frage mich, ob ich immer noch das Gefühl hätte, keine Zeit zu haben. Es geht auch darum, in welcher Phase deines Lebens du dich befindest. Ich schätze, ich brauchte etwas Zeit, um herauszufinden, dass man nicht immer auf alles reagieren muss. Man wählt seinen eigenen Kampf, wie man kämpfen will, das heißt man wählt auch, wie man sein Leben leben will. Es gilt, dass ich, wenn wir diese Formen der Kunstausübung nebeneinander betrachten würden, mir in meiner gegenwärtigen Praxis über Dinge klarwerde, während ich am Werk arbeite, und dass ich die Entfaltung der Gedanken und Werke mit Neugier beobachte. Die praktischen Alltagsbeziehungen rund um die Arbeit sind ein ständiger Kampf mit den Standards der Kunstwelt, naja, eher das Fehlen davon würde ich sagen, und es ist oft ein heftiger Kampf. Wenn ich mir den Inhalt ansehe, den ich schaffe, sehe ich ihn als eine langsamere Art, Aktivismus als Teil verschiedener Bewegungen auf längere Sicht zu betreiben, als eine Erweiterung dieser früheren Praxis. Ich mag es, wie du es definiert hast, Banu, „rigoroses und offenes Gespräch", diese Worte fühlen sich nah zu dem an, was ich mit meiner aktuellen Praxis erreichen möchte. Wie ist es bei dir, Cana?

Cana:

Wenn wir vielleicht wieder auf zum Beispiel die YouTube-Kommentare zurückkommen, dann zeigen sie uns, dass es andere Formen des Denkens und Lebens geben könnte. Meine Arbeiten und Recherchen oder das, was ich mache, sind auch nicht für oder gegen etwas, aber es ist natürlich wichtig, Stellung zu beziehen, eben auch auf künstlerische Weise. Ich glaube, so lassen sich bestimmte Themen behandeln, die im „Mainstream" nicht sichtbar sind. Zum Beispiel die Geschichte/n oder Erinnerungen bestimmter Gemeinschaften; auch auf diesem Weg lässt sich ein anderes Leben zeigen.

„This makes me want to read a book from end to beginning" [Deshalb will ich ein Buch vom Ende bis zum Anfang lesen], so lautet beispielsweise der Kommentar einer/eines Nutzerin/Nutzers. Also, warum fangen wir nicht einfach neu an, lesen und erinnern uns aufs Neue an die Zukunft, sagen die Vergangenheit voraus und verbinden Fiktionen mit Träumen, die Realität mit Hoffnung, Wünsche mit Fakten – im Sinne der afroamerikanischen Wissenschaftlerin und Aktivistin Angela Davis, der folgender Ausspruch zugeschrieben wird: „Ich akzeptiere nicht länger die Dinge, die ich nicht ändern kann. Ich ändere die Dinge, die ich nicht akzeptieren kann."

belit:

Genau. Die bestehenden offiziellen Narrative sind nicht in der Lage, die alltäglichen Erfahrungen der Menschen einzufangen, und wir brauchen intuitivere Verbindungen, um ihre Komplexität und die unserer eigenen Erfahrungen auszudrücken. Das hat nur Sinn, wenn es mit dem Kampf für das, von dem wir möchten, dass es auf der Welt geschieht, einhergeht, der Veränderung der Dinge, die wir nicht akzeptieren können. Und der Kampf muss kein wütender sein. Er kann viele Formen annehmen.

Cana:

Ich denke, das Wissen, das man uns in den Schulen und Universitäten der westlichen Welt beigebracht hat, hält aufrecht, was uns das System beibringen möchte. Und das ist eurozentrisch, zutiefst orientalistisch und rassistisch. Das muss angefochten und hinterfragt werden. Auf der ganzen Welt gehen junge Menschen außerdem auf die Straße, um an den Demos

Fridays for Future oder *Schulstreik fürs Klima* teilzunehmen. Das ist eine internationale Bewegung, die von Jugendlichen angestoßen wurde, die beschlossen haben, freitags nicht zur Schule zu gehen und stattdessen gegen den Klimawandel zu protestieren. Sie fordern Gleichberechtigung und ein besseres Leben für alle und stellen auch die herrschenden Narrative und die Wissensproduktion in Frage, die zur Ungerechtigkeit in unserer Gesellschaft führt.

Und mit deiner Kunst, belit, und auch damit, was du machst, Banu, zeigt ihr uns, wie ich finde, neue Perspektiven und Möglichkeiten.

Banu:

Ich denke darüber nach, was ihr beiden gesagt habt, und möchte noch einmal auf deine Bemerkungen zurückkommen, belit. Nutzt du den Gedanken des Entfaltens als ein Verfahren, bei dem du etwas durcharbeitest, um es zu verstehen…?

belit:

Nicht nur um zu verstehen, aber vielleicht auch um zu spüren, wie Ulus Baker sagt,[8] um die Möglichkeiten des Wissens, neben dem Verstehen, zu erweitern, das heißt Möglichkeiten für verschiedene Arten des Sich-Beziehens und des Erfahrens zu eröffnen. Also können wir sagen, der Gedanke der Entfaltung wird zu einem Verfahren zur Durcharbeitung verschiedener Arten des Bezugs, also unterschiedlicher Methoden der Wissensproduktion, ohne dabei das Verstehen als die Hauptform des Zugangs ins Zentrum zu stellen. Es geht darum, diese Hierarchie zu durchbrechen und den primären Platz zu erschüttern, der dem Begriff des Verstehens gegeben ist. Wir müssen nicht verstehen, um uns auf etwas zu beziehen. Wir sind in der Lage, uns auf verschiedene Weise mit etwas in Verbindung zu setzen, und andernfalls wird dadurch unsere Fähigkeit, die Welt nachzuvollziehen, nur eingeschränkt. Das geht auch auf das zurück, was ich mit der Mainstream-Logik dieser Welt gemeint habe; die Formen, die anerkannt werden, die Archivierungspraxis, das alles steht in Verbindung.

Banu:

Lasst mich kurz darüber nachdenken, wie ich es ausdrücken soll. Ich glaube, Cana betont sehr richtig, dass die Produktion von Wissen eines unserer gemeinsamen Anliegen ist. Es ist also kein Zufall, dass wir uns alle mit verschiedenen Arten von Archiven und staatlicher Gewalt befassen, wobei es sich dabei nicht nur um Instrumente der „Disziplinierung" handelt, sondern diese auch bestimmte Formen des Wissens hervorbringen… Aber belits Gedanke, „nicht nur zu verstehen, sondern auch zu spüren", enthält noch etwas, worüber ich gerne mehr erfahren würde, um es mit dem von Cana Gesagten zu verbinden.

belit:

An dieser Stelle möchte ich den Begriff der „verkörperten Erfahrung" einbringen und unsere Diskussion mit einem Bereich verknüpfen, der, wie ich denke, für die Praxis von uns allen relevant ist – dem Archiv. Um es vollständiger auszudrücken: den Problemen und Herausforderungen, die angesichts der gegenwärtigen Auffassung von archivarischen Verfahren mit der Archivierung verkörperter Erfahrungen einhergehen.

Ich spreche von Erfahrungen, die ich gerade verarbeite, und ihr beiden wohl auch. Wie müssen wir archivarische Verfahren verstehen, wie grundlegend anders müssen wir archivarische Verfahren auffassen, damit wir die Möglichkeit bekommen, solche Erfahrungen, wie zum Beispiel die Erfahrung staatlicher Gewaltausübung, zu archivieren? Vielleicht ist es nötig, das nicht als „archivieren" zu bezeichnen, sondern es anders zu nennen. Diana Taylor nennt es „Repertoire".[9] Eher als verstanden, werden solche Erfahrungen primär

149

körperlich gespürt und durchlebt und sie bedürfen daher einer anderen archivarischen Form. Sie benötigen daher andere Formen und Gedanken sowie ein „rigoroses und offenes" Gespräch.

Banu:

belits Punkt erscheint mir auch sehr wichtig und er rückt verschiedene Themen ins Bewusstsein. Das erste betrifft die Frage nach dem Verhältnis von Archiven und Wissenserzeugung. Archive sind bereits in ihrem Aufbau darauf ausgerichtet, spezifische Fragen zu beantworten, und in ihnen drücken sich bestimmte Präferenzen hinsichtlich dessen aus, was man für erhaltenswert erachtet und was nicht. Wenn wir also davon ausgehen, dass Archive keine „objektiven" Aufbewahrungsorte sind, wie schafft ihr es, sie für eure künstlerische Praxis nutzbar zu machen?

Cana:

Ja, ich sehe es auch so, dass die offiziellen Archive mit der Macht der Unterdrücker*innen verknüpft sind. Also sollten wir über einen Mechanismus nachdenken, mit dem sich verborgene Archive ans Licht bringen lassen, um die offiziellen zu hinterfragen. Und die Rolle der Kunst kann es sein, als Brücke zwischen Geschichte und Gegenwart zu dienen und das neu zu beleben, was verborgen war.

belit:

Meiner Meinung nach ist es wichtig, Archive als sich wandelnde und dynamische Strukturen zu begreifen. Möglicherweise wurden sie nicht geschaffen, um etwas auf bestimmte Weise zu definieren. Ich spreche jetzt nicht von staatlichen Archiven, bei denen es sich hauptsächlich um die Fortschreibung bestimmter oppressiver Strukturen handelt und die so eingerichtet wurden, dass sie sich den offiziellen Narrativen anpassen. Ich spreche von anderen Archiven, die weder staatlich, noch notwendigerweise oppositionell oder alternativ sind, aber institutionell sein können. Solche anderen Archive haben anfangs vielleicht „gute Absichten", enden aber womöglich unter einer unengagierten Verwaltung und aufgrund mangelnder Einsichten in ihre Macht und Funktionen in unterdrückerischen Strukturen und löschen Historien aus. Ist das nicht auch oft die Quelle des alltäglichen Rassismus, das heißt unengagiert zu sein und Machtstrukturen nicht zu verstehen? Zumindest ist es in den Niederlanden eine sehr verbreitete Form des Rassismus, die Gloria Wekker als „white innocence" bezeichnet.[10]

Ein Archiv, das sich nicht dessen bewusst ist, was es nicht erfasst, hat an der Ausradierung derjenigen, die es ausschließt, Anteil. Wie Banu gesagt hat, sind Archive nie „objektiv", aber sie können sich dessen bewusst sein, was sie sind. Sie können definieren, was sie sind, definieren, was sie tun, klarstellen, was sie bezwecken und kommunizieren. Nun, staatliche Archive tun das und genau durch diese Definitionen und Kommunikationen löschen sie Namen und Personen mit ihren Geschichten. Es sind also in verschiedenen Fällen verschiedene Löschungen am Werk. Archive tragen auch Verantwortung und sollten Rechenschaft darüber ablegen, wie sie ihre Sammlung präsentieren, in welchem Rahmen sie steht. Sie müssen einem Satz ethischer Leitlinien entsprechen, und oft tun sie das nicht.

Wenn ich mit offiziellen oder institutionellen Archiven arbeite, dann ist es mein Ziel, die von den Archiven angebotenen Narrative, die Sprachen und das Framing, welche die Dinge zu definieren und zu verfestigen versuchen, zu hinterfragen. Ich bin daran interessiert, Strukturen zu dekodieren, die nicht durch andere Elemente gestützt werden, Strukturen, die auferlegt sind, aber vielleicht natürlich aussehen, oder sich so verhalten, als seien sie natürlicherweise dort. Ich stelle diese Geste und ihre internen Mechanismen in Frage. Ich nehme ihre Einzelteile auseinander und versuche, sie wieder zusammenzusetzen und festzustellen, wo sie eigentlich nicht ineinanderpassen. Ich befasse mich auch mit Archiven, die nicht als Archive anerkannt sind; ich bestehe darauf, sie Archive zu nennen. Was bewahrt werden kann und wie ein Archiv durch seine Praxis definiert wird – diese Definitionen müssen geändert und erweitert werden.

Banu:

Zum Teil hast du meine zweite Frage schon beantwortet: Können wir uns alternative Archive und ihr Aussehen überhaupt vorstellen? Gibt es eine Möglichkeit, sie als Befragungen mit offenem Ende zu konzipieren? In den letzten paar Jahrzehnten hat sich die feministische Theorie von der Vorstellung, „die Stimmen marginalisierter Völker/Frauen hörbar zu machen", das heißt davon, Leerstellen in unserem Wissen aufzudecken, fortbewegt, hin zu einer Transformation dessen, was als Wissen betrachtet wird und was nicht. Bei meinen Recherchen dazu, wie verlorengegangene und enteignete Kunstwerke und die Löschung nicht-muslimischer Künstler*innen sowohl die Schriften der osmanischen und islamischen Kunstgeschichte als auch der heutigen Türkei geformt haben, habe ich festgestellt, dass man ihre Geschichten nicht einfach in die bestehenden historischen Narrative einschieben kann. Diese Narrative müssen stattdessen verwandelt werden – oder vielmehr, wir müssen daran arbeiten, sie zu transformieren, während wir uns zugleich dessen bewusst sind, dass jedes neue Narrativ ebenfalls immer unvollständig sein wird, dass mancher Schaden nicht wiedergutgemacht werden kann, aber dennoch als prägender Bestandteil der Vergangenheit verstanden werden muss. Also verstehe ich Canas vorherige Kommentare so, dass sie nicht nur die Aufdeckung des zuvor Verborgenen oder Gelöschten mit sich bringen, sondern auch eine Suche nach Wegen, auf denen sich solches Wissen für die Gegenwart produktiv machen lässt.

Cana:

Meiner Meinung nach ist die Frage des Archivs auch mit der Frage des Geschichtsverständnisses verknüpft. Wir alle wissen, dass die staatliche Gewaltausübung die Geschichte der Menschen, die gegen diese staatliche Gewaltausübung gekämpft haben, löscht oder beiseiteschiebt. Also müssen wir vielleicht die Geschichte, die vom Staat unterdrückt/gelöscht wurde, zurückholen und mit unseren eigenen Erfahrungen verbinden. Staatliche Geschichte bedeutet die Geschichte der herrschenden Klasse. Es geht darum, die Geschichte der unterdrückten Menschen zurückzuholen, um von dieser Geschichte zu lernen und dadurch eine andere Form des Wissens zu erzeugen.

151

1
https://www.youtube.com/watch?v=Kp7eSUU9°y8.
Zugriff: 21.4.2019.
2
https://www.nytimes.com/2018/08/23/arts/design/
john-akomfrah-review-new-museum.html. Zugriff:
23.8.2018.
3
belit sağ, Cana Bilir-Meier: *Documentaristics—Documentation and their Characteristics,* in: Manfred
Grübel, Linda Klösel (Hg.), *Version Nr. 03*, Verlag für
Moderne Kunst, Wien 2017.
4
Der NSU war ein ab Mitte der 1990er aktives neo-
nazistisches Netzwerk. Offiziellen Quellen zufolge er-
mordete es in ganz Deutschland innerhalb von acht
Jahren (2000-2007) mindestens zehn Menschen und
legte mindestens zwei Nagelbomben in von Migran-
ten bewohnten Stadtvierteln. Zwar wurde Beate
Zschäpe als ein überlebendes Mitglied zu lebenslan-
ger Haft verurteilt, doch eine vollständige Untersu-
chung des Netzwerks und der Verstrickung von deutschen Geheimdienst- und Sicherheitskräften steht
noch aus.
5
Martha Woodmansee: *Art, the Author and the Market:
Rereading the History of Aesthetics*, Columbia University Press, New York 1994.
6
Silvia Federici: Wages against Housework, Falling Wall
Press Ltd und Power of Woman Collective, Bristol 1975,
S.3. [Übersetzungen von Anja Welle]
7
Ebd., S.2.
8
Ulus Baker: *Sanat ve Arzu*, İletişim Press, İstanbul 2014.
9
Diana Taylor: *The Archive and The Repertoire: Performing Cultural Memory in the Americas*, Duke University Press, Durham 2003.
10
Gloria Wekker: *White Innocence: Paradoxes of Colonialism and Race*, Duke University Press, Durham 2016.

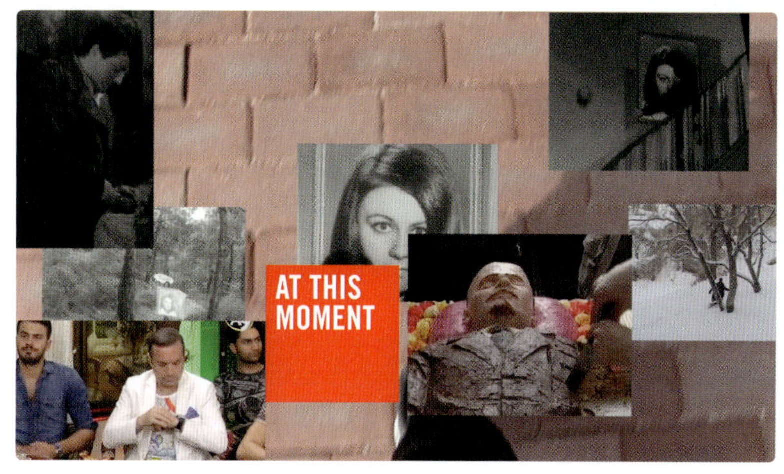

AT THIS
MOMENT

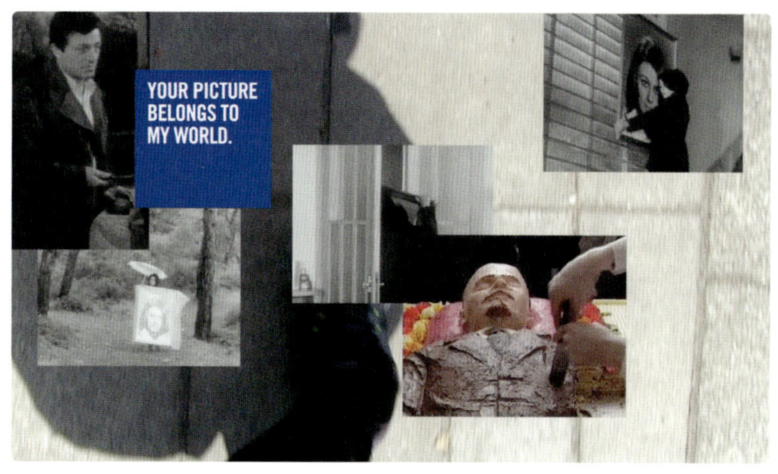

YOUR PICTURE
BELONGS TO
MY WORLD.

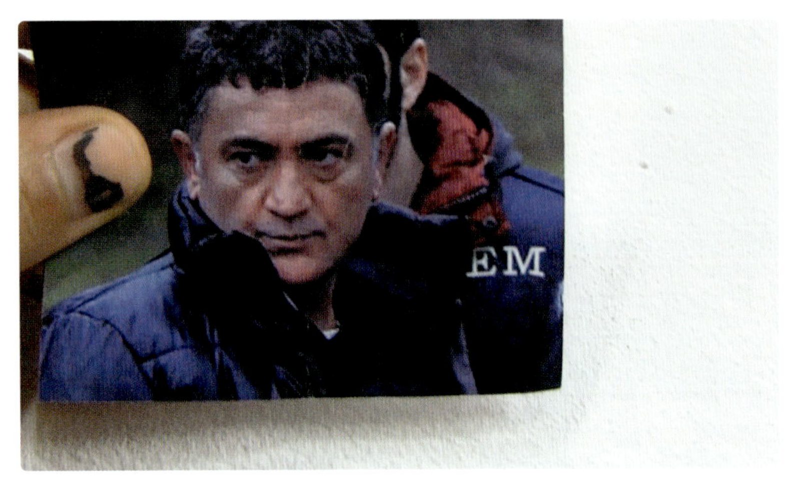

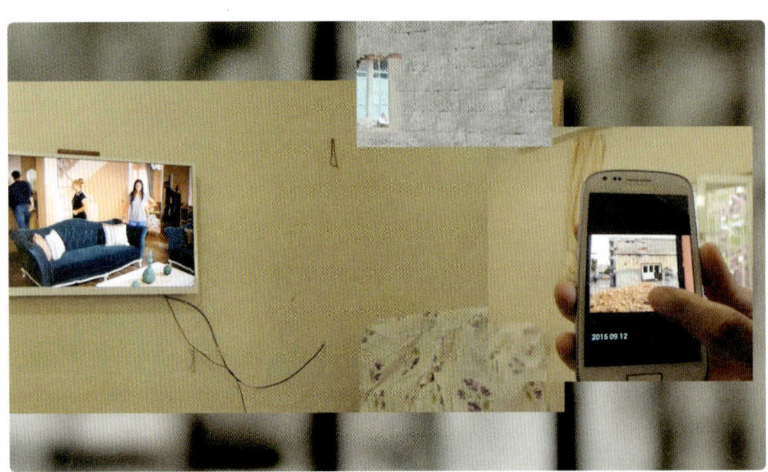

Başka bir siyaset tarzı tasavvur edelim:

Sonu açık olan bir sohbet

Cana Bilir-Meier, Banu Karaca
ve belit sağ ile sohbette

Aşağıdaki yazı belit sağ, Banu Karaca ve benim, süper 8 filmi ve frotajlardan oluşan yeni çalışmam, *This makes me want to predict the past* (2019) üzerine, yaptığımız sohbetin dökümüdür.

Frotajlar ve film, Münih Olympia Alışveriş Merkezinde ortaya çıktı. Eser, alışveriş merkezine 2016 yılında düzenlenen ırkçı saldırıyı, göçmenlerin günlük tecrübelerini, umutlarını ve arzularını konu alan tiyatro oyunu *Düşler Ülkesi*'nden *(Land der Träume, Erman Okay, 1982)* kesitlerle diyaloğa girerek irdeliyor. Bu saldırıda dokuz genç insan öldürüldü ve dördü ateşli silahla olmak üzere otuzaltısı yaralandı. Neredeyse tüm kurbanlar göçmen kökenli insanlardı: Türk, Kürt, Roman ve Sinti kökenliydiler.

155

Filmin adında ve frotajların temelinde, Childish Gambino adıyla tanınan Afro-Amerikan müzisyen, komedyen, rejisör, yazar ve film yönetmeni Donald Glover'in videosu *Redbone*'un altındaki yorumlar arasında bulunan, anonim bir YouTube kullanıcısına ait bir alıntı yatıyor.

YouTube kullanıcılarının Childish Gambino'nun şarkısı *Redbone*'a yaptığı yorumlar[1]

This makes me want to brush my toothbrush.
This makes me want to predict the past.
This makes me want to tell my non biological parents that they're adopted.
This makes me want to sit on my TV and watch the couch.
This makes me want to rob my own bank account.
This makes me want to listen to my therapists problems.
This makes me want to arrest the police.
This makes me want to put on a pair of books and read glasses.
This makes me want to cut my barber's hair.
This makes me want to tell depression to kill itself.
This makes me wanna let the door open me.
This makes me want to sell myself on craigslist.
This makes me want to call two cab companies to see who arrives
      first then take the bus.
This makes me want to wake my alarm up.
This wants me to ask Burger King where the closest McDonald's is.
This makes me want to tell my boss to "get a job".
This makes me wanna let the elevator ride me.
This makes me want to read a book from end to beginning.
This makes me want to put milk in my cereal bowl, then the cereal.
This makes me want the homework to eat my dog.
This makes me want to give birth to my mom.
This make me wanna call in sick to my doctors appointment.
This makes me want to play on the Xbox with a PlayStation controller.
This makes me want to let my clothes wear me.
This makes me want to spy on my FBI agent.
This makes me want to put on my shoes before my sock.
This makes me wanna fall asleep before I close my eyes.
This makes me want to ask my dog to take me for a walk.
This makes me want to write with paper on a pencil.
This makes me wanna tell my boss he's fired.
This makes me want to tell my crush I have a girlfriend.
This makes me want to put on a pair of books and read glasses.
      I showed this to my dog, now he is a cat.
This makes me want to Google Bing.
This makes me wanna tell Aliens that humans are real…!
This makes me want to give mosquitoes malaria.
This makes me want to drive my parents to school.
This makes me want to kill two stones with one bird.
This makes me want to read a coloring book.
This makes me want to let the light turn me on.
This makes me wanna call my friend and tell him I can't talk right now
      call you later.
This makes me let my food eat me.
The makes me fall and hurt the ground.

This makes me want to do my desk on my homework.
This makes me want to take a bath with a unicorn.
This makes me wanna tell the weekend its Monday.
This makes me want to let my earphones wear my ear.
This makes me want to put my toaster in my toast.
This makes me want to remember the future.
This makes me want to tell my teacher to raise her hand if she wants
    to speak to me.
This makes me want to give my fish a bath.
This makes me want to steal money out of my own wallet.
This makes me want to drink vampire's blood.
This makes me want to ask the hotel's reception if they want a room
    with a beach view.
This makes me want to tell Monday to wake up.
This makes me want to be a vacuum to clean my house.
This makes me want to tell the clock what time it is.
This song makes me wanna threaten to call my teachers parents.
This makes me wanna call someone and say I can't talk.
This reminds me of spending time with people I love. Time sure does fly.
This makes me want to forget what I can't remember.
This makes me fly like I can feel.
This makes me want to walk on a fly!
This makes me want to pass a test and study for it afterwards.
This makes me want to put numbers in alphabetical order.
This makes me want to break into someone's house and install
    a security system.
This makes me want to end things I haven't started yet.

Sanat çalışmalarımın çoğu, genellikle deşifre yoluyla, resmi bilgi üretimi ile ilgili sorulara odaklanıyor. Her yeni görüntü, başkalarını gizleyerek daha fazla yeni görüntü üretir. Bu sorular ve süreçler, iktidarın nasıl oluştuğunun bir parçasıdır. Kültür teorisyeni Stuart Hall kimliği, "hiç bitmemiş bir sohbet"[2] şeklinde tanımlıyor. Bence bu, gerçekte işlemesi mümkün olmayan şeyler üzerine yazan ve aynı zamanda tam da bu gerçeğin yapısını gösteren YouTube kullanıcılarının yorumları üzerine de söylenebilir. Genelde bir sohbetten anladığımız, belli bir başı ve sonu olması. Bitmemiş bir sohbet nasıl tasavvur edilebilir?

Bu metin için Banu Karaca ve belit sağ'ı, kendi eserlerimiz, kuramsal açıdan önemli olan ve kendini dilde, özel ve kamusal arşivlerde gösteren kurumsal ırkçılığın mekanizmaları, çoklu ayrımcılık, güç orantıları, göç, resmi ve subaltern tarihyazımı arasındaki gerilim, görünür olmanın ve sansürün siyasiliği gibi konular üzerine tartışmaya davet ettim.

Antropolog Banu Karaca siyasal antropoloji, sanat ve estetik, milliyetçilik ve kültürel politikalar, müzeler ve Almanya ile Türkiye'deki anma uygulamaları gibi alanlarda çalışıyor. Kendisi Siyah Bant isimli, Türkiye'de sanata uygulanan sansürü belgeleyen bir araştırma platformunun kurucularından. Şu an Osmanlı İmparatorluğunun son dönemi ve genç Türk Cumhuriyetindeki kamulaştırma politikası arka planında sanat tarihyazımının pratiği üzerine çalışıyor.

belit sağ, video yapımcısı, sanatçı ve sanat emekçisi, Amsterdam'da yaşıyor. Türkiye'de matematik, Hollanda'da Güzel Sanatlar okudu. Filmcilik kökleri Ankara ve İstanbul'da, VideA, Karahaber ve bak.ma gibi gruplar kurduğu, video eylemci çevrelerle yaptığı çalışmalara dayanıyor. Çalışmaları kapsamında New York'taki International Studio & Curatorial Program'da (ISCP) ve

Amsterdam'daki Rijksakademie van Beeldende Kunsten'de bulundu. Devam etmekte olduğu sanat ve film çalışmalarında Türkiye, Almanya ve Hollanda'da siyasi ihtilaf tecrübelerinde görsel temsilin etkisine odaklanıyor.

belit ve benle yapılan bir röportajda belit bana şöyle söylemişti: "Yaptığım her şeyde bir duruş ortaya koymaya çalışıyorum. Nereden geldiğim, neden belirli bir konu ile ilgilendiğim ve bununla ne yapacağım önemli. Ve ben bunu şeffaf şekilde yapmaya çalışıyorum. Çalışmayı gözden geçiren, değerlendiren ve formüle eden benim ve bu çalışmanın arkasında duranın bizzat kendim olduğunu açıklamam önemli. Video eylemciliği döneminde taktığımız insanların ve sorunların görünür hale gelmeseydi; görünmez olmak da eylemciler için bir taktik olabilir. Günün sonunda önemli olan pek çok farklı taktiği kullanabilmektir."³

Banu:
Şimdi paylaştığın malzemeye bakıldığında bu gerçekten çok etkileyici. Ben bu şarkı hakkında böyle yorumlar yapıldığının bilincinde değildim. Nasıl başladığını biliyor musun?

Cana:
Nasıl başladığını tam olarak bilmiyorum. Ama benim anladığım kadarıyla, Childish Gambino *Redbone* şarkısıyla, daha önce de *This is America* şarkısıyla (ve videosuyla) yaptığı gibi, günlük yaşam düzeninin statükosunu sorguluyor. Şarkı sözleri çok önemli mesajlar içeriyor ve özellikle genç insanların değişim arzularının ifadesi için önemli vasıta oldu. Ben bu yorumları, 2016'da Olympia Alışveriş Merkezinde yaşanan ırkçı saldırı konusuyla bağladım. Yorumlar bize genç insanların farklı bir toplumu nasıl kurguladıklarını, tartışmaların ve dilin güç ilişkisindeki yerini belirterek gösteriyor. Eserin adı, *This makes me want to predict the past*, geçmiş ve gelecek veya tarih ve anı ikileminde yatan çelişkileri gösteriyor.

Banu:
Tüm diğer saldırılar gibi Münih saldırısı da tekil, ama yine de bilindik bir şablonu takip ediyor. Kurbanlarının çoğunun göçmen kökenli olduğu anlaşılınca, katil psikolojik sorunlu, "yalnız bir kurt" olarak tarif edildi. Resmi makamlar alelacele saldırıyı "terör saldırısı değil" ve daha önemlisi; ırkçı nedenle işlenmemiş saldırı olarak etiketlediler. Ve belki de en önemlisi; saldırıyı Almanya'daki ırkçılık tarihinden kopardılar.

belit:
Cana, senin çalışmana ve yorumlarına baktığımda, ırkçılığı yuvarlak masa tartışmalarında konuşmanın ne kadar verimsiz olduğunu hatırlıyorum ve belirli formatların önceden belirlenmiş düz mantığının, belirli sorunlara farklı bakış açılarıyla yaklaşmaya yetmediği görüyorum. Ve bu beni belli tecrübelerin ve ifade şekillerinin, bilgi üretimi kaynağı olarak acilen ciddiye alınması gerektiği fikrine götürüyor. Örneğin ırkçılık tecrübesi çok kez, fiziki tecrübeyi tümüyle kavramayan biçimlere çevrilerek anlatılıyor. Bunu arşivleri de göz önünde bulundurarak söylüyorum; fotoğraf, film, metin vs. gibi şekiller arşivleniyor, yani "arşivlenmeye uygun". Benim sorum şu; tecrübe kendine özgü bir şekil olarak nasıl dikkate alınıp değerlendirilebilir? Diğer yandan az önce bahsettiğim çeviriler, metin formatında olan, düz mantığı takip eden metinler dahi, sanki geçerli bir bilgi üretimi ve kaynak gibi görülüyor. O zaman ikinci sorum şu: Fiziki tecrübe ile oluşmuş bilgi nasıl idrak edilir, kabul ettirilir ve bu tecrübe nasıl başkalarıyla paylaşılabilir? Irkçılık karşıtı gruplar ısrarla göçmenlerin sahip olduğu bilginin ön plana çıkarılması gerektiğini vurguluyorlar, çünkü belli tecrübeler değerli ve bilgi üretiminde kaynak olarak görülürken,

başka tecrübeler yok sayılıyor. Banu'nun bahsettiği yok sayma ile doğrudan bir bağlantı var. Bu saldırının haberleştirilme tarzı ve şekli, bu tecrübeyi yayarak ve suçluyu koruyan bir tecrübeyi öne sürerek, kurbanların tecrübelerini siliyor. Kanımca üçümüz de şu veya bu şekilde, resmi anlatımın görmezden geldiği, sildiği ve/veya kasıtlı gizlediği bu tecrübeler üzerine çalışıyoruz.

Aklıma *NSU-Komplex auflösen* (NSU Kompleksi Dağıtılsın) Tribünali geliyor. Tribünalin amacı bu tarz tecrübeleri ön plana çıkarmaktı. Graswurzel eylemcileri ve göçmen dernekleri tarafından, kurbanların aileleriyle iş birliği halinde ortaya çıktı. Cana ve ben NSU (Nasyonal Sosyalist Yeraltı)[4] olayı ile ilgili, bu bakış açısını dikkate alan kısa video spotları çektik. Çalışmalarımızla bu tecrübelere ilişkin biçim ve ifade imkanları bulmaya çalıştığımızı düşünüyorum. (örneğin: (Against) Randomness, 2017)

Banu:

Cana senin eserlerine baktığımda ve belit senin son yorumunda, yaşadığım ve giderek güçlenen bir hissi anımsadım; sadece ırkçılık konusunda değil, genel olarak insan bir şey yaptığında; sanat, siyaset, bilim olsun, güç tartışmalarının tersi mahiyetinde "hayır" demesi ne kadar anlamlı. Benim huzursuzluğum kısmen Siyah Bant çalışma dönemimden kaynaklı. Başladığımızda amacımız Türkiye'de, sanattaki sansürü araştırmak ve belgelemek, sansürün farklı biçimlerini anlamak, ortaya çıkarmak ve farklı aktörlerin karşılıklı etkileşimle, sanat aleminin içinde ve dışında kolektif olarak sansüre nasıl olanak sağladığını göstermekti. Bizim amacımız, sansürle mücadelede ve fikir özgürlüğü angajmanında, farklı stratejiler ve taktiklerin üzerine düşünülüp tartışılacağı ortamları teşvik etmekti. Bu konular tabii ki halen önemli, ama tartışmayı sansüre karşı yalın protestonun ötesine çekmek de önemli. Tartışmayı, fikir özgürlüğünün net "tarif edilmiş bir şey" veya son bir nokta olduğu kabulünün ötesine taşımak, mücadelenin yaşandığı, fikir özgürlüğünün, güç, mekan ve tarih bağlantılarında hep sıkıntıda olduğu bir alan olarak şekillendirmek gerek. Yani fikir özgürlüğü sadece sansürle değil, bu parametreler doğrultusunda bir tartışma yaratma mücadelesiyle de çelişki içinde.

Beni yanlış anlamayın. Protesto elbette önemli, ama ona bağlı kalmak iktidarın mantığına da bağlı kalmak anlamına geliyor. Benim kanımca, şu anki siyasi durumlar karşısında, aslında *ne* için mücadele ettiğimizi ortaya çıkarmaya vakit bırakmayan, çok fazla protesto etme tuzağına düşüyoruz. Elbette istisnalar var; mesela kadın hareketi ve çevre/iklim değişimi hareketi gibi. Bu açıdan bakıldığında absürt yorumlar, çok farklı bir siyaset potansiyeli olan diğer olasılık ufuklarını ve farklı hayalleri ortaya koymaktadır.

Cana:

Katılıyorum, çünkü "hayır" demek de bir tavır ve reddetmedir. Bu duruşun içinde sıkışıp kalındığı zaman değişim zorlaşıyor. Irkçı söylemler, koyu tenli insanları (BPoC/Black People of Color), göçmenleri, mültecileri aşağılamak için kullanılan sabit söylemlerin derlemesidir. Ona karşı kendimizi savunmak için, nihayetinde kullanılan söyleme karşı savunma yapmamız lazım; yani kullanılan dile karşı. Ve bu yorumlar, tasavvur edilen, [sadece] bir şeye karşı olmanın ötesindeki bir dünyanın hayali. Sadece sürekli "hayır" demek yerine, daha güçlü bir şey sunuyor. Ve değişim, dildeki ve düşüncedeki değişimle başlar. Düşünceler bazen ütopik olmak zorundadır.

belit:

Zaten her yerde gördüğümüz bu değil mi? Kutuplaşma ve bir görüşte sabit kalma, insana tepki gösterdiği şey tarafından dikta ediliyor. İnsanın duruşunun karşı olduğu şey tarafından belirlenmesi, aslen aşağılayıcı bir durum. Dile getirmenin, akıl ve varoluşunla dalga geçmek gibi geldiği alenilikteki haksızlıklara karşı çıkmak zorunda kaldığın pek çok yer ve zaman var. Bu Banu'nun söylediği gibi bir tartışma ortamı yaratma amacıyla girebileceğin çevre için gerekli. Ama aynı zamanda senin kendi tasarladığın dünya için, belli fikirleri kurgulayıp niçin çabaladığını ifade etmek için de gerekli. Bir şeyi hayal etmek ve bu fikir üzerinden senin değerlerini de içeren bir dünya yaratmakla alakalı bir gereksinim bu. Gericiliği arkasında bırakan bir dünyayı tasarlamak ve günümüzün dünyasındaki çoğunluk mantığını geride bırakan bir dünya ve onun değerleri nasıl hayal edilebilir; ancak bu hayal gücünü içeren bir dille; işte Childish Gambino bunu yapıyor. O kendi tecrübelerini aktarıyor ve bugünün dünyasında yaşamanın nasıl bir duygu olduğunu anlatıyor. Bu yolla başka bir dünyayı hayal etme olanakları açılıyor ve YouTube yorumlarında bu fikir toplumsal bir hal alıyor. Bu inanılmaz derecede ilham verici!

Banu:

belit'in tarif ettiği genel durumun günümüzdeki sanat alemini nasıl etkilediğini sizlerden dinlemek isterim. Yani sizlerin sanatsal çalışması veya mekan seçimleriniz de bundan etkileniyor mu? Başka şekilde ifade etmek gerekirse, şimdiki durumun, sanat ve siyaset arasındaki ilişkiyi yeniden derlediğine inanıyor musunuz?

Cana:

Sanatın şimdiki durumdaki rolünü görmek istiyorsak, buna ilişkin olarak kapitalizmin sanatı nasıl bir meta haline getirdiğini analiz etmek gerektiğine inanıyorum. Demek ki bunu irdelememiz lazım ve değişim için çabalayan yeni sanat şekilleri yaratmaya çalışarak, sanatın önemini ve sanatın siyasetle ilişkisini tekrar kurmak lazım. Örneğin Semra Ertan üzerine çektiğim film bu bağlamda. Aynısını Münih'teki cami projesi çalışmamda da hedefledim. *Semra Ertan* (2013), Türkiye'de doğan, Gastarbeiter ailesinin kızı olarak yetmişli yıllarda Almanya'ya gelen ve 350'den fazla şiir yazan, bir yazar ve şair. Göçmenlere yönelik ırkçılığı protesto etti ve 1982'de Hamburg'da kendini bir açık protesto niteliğinde yaktı. Film onun hikayesini, kurban olarak değil, haksızlığa karşı isyan eden birinin hikayesi olarak yeniden yazdı. 2017-18'de çalıştığım Münih Freimann'daki cami projesi ise, caminin mimarları Necla Gürel ve Osman Edip Gürel ile ilgili ve hikayenin başka, Alman toplumundaki İslam fobisini ve doğuya bakış açısını sorgulayan bir versiyonu. Mimar çiftten, çok sayıda önemli yapı tasarlamalarına rağmen, Münih kent tarihinde hiç bahsedilmiyor.

belit:

Şu söylediğin şey o kadar önemli ki Cana. Anlatımın tek anlatım olmasına müsaade etmemeli; onun yerine başka tekil anlatımlar konsun diye değil, onu daha da karmaşıklaştırmak için. Çünkü bu anlatımlar ve hayat hep çok katmanlı. Aslında bu, çok katmanlı anlatımların üretiminde ve yayımında ne kadar büyük bir gücün yattığını kavramak demek. Bu, tek bir "hayır"ın ötesinde, yeni bir yol açan, çok verimli bir "hayır" deme şekli. Senin çalışmaların bu yol için bariz bir örnek. Kutuplaşma arttıkça ben de daha açıksözlü ve sert olmaya başladım. Özellikle Türkiye'de şiddet havasının peyderpey arttığı 2013'ten itibaren çalışmalarımın daha net bir odak noktası var. Kutuplaşma ve ırkçılık dilinin normalleşmesi ivedilik bilincini de beraberinde getiriyor. Çalışmalarımın başkaları tarafından değerlendirilmesi konusunda giderek daha da hassaslaşıyor ve keskin tepki veriyorum. Batı Avrupa'da yaşayan, beyaz olmayan ve öncelikle doğduğu ve büyüdüğü ülkelerdeki meseleler üzerinde çalışma yapan göçmen kökenli bir kişi olarak, insanın çalışmalarının nasıl araçsallaştırıldığı konusunda dikkatli olması gerekiyor. Eserlerimin ticari bir nesneye dönüştürülmesi fikrine ve sanat piyasasının şartlarına karşı mesafeliyim. Bu benim çalışma sürecimi korumamın bir yolu. Bu sayede ne yapmak istediğime odaklanıyorum ve yaratım süreci piyasanın taleplerinden ve beraberinde gelen araç olma sorunundan kurtulmuş oluyor. Sonuç olarak bu farkındalığı önemli buluyorum ve pratiğime getirdiğim bir soru işareti olarak çalışmama dahil ediyorum. Bazı ihtilaflar hiç bitmez, bunlar benim sanatla ilişki tarzımın bir ifadesi. Bu onların anlamsız olduğu veya pes edip bırakmamız gerektiği anlamına gelmez. Tersine bu ihtilaflar çalışmamın önemli bir parçasıdır.

Cana:

Katılıyorum. Kapitalist sistem, beyazların çıkarları yönünde hiyerarşi ve sınıflar üzerine kurulu olduğu için, başka ten rengindeki insanlar ve eserleri ciddiye alınmıyor.

belit:

Ciddiye alınmama olgusunun yanı sıra, bu eserlerin ve insanların, özellikle kurumlar tarafından belirli bir ajandaya hizmet için, hangi şekilde konumlandırıldıklarına işaret etmek istedim... Mesela kendi bünyelerinde ırkçı yapıları sorgulamayı reddeden kurumlar, yani böyle yapıları içeren kurumlar, seçici davranarak, bilmeden veya teşvik etmek için, beyaz olmayan [People of Color] sanatçıları davet ediyorlar ve/veya net ırkçılık karşıtı mesaj veren eserleri kullanıyorlar ki, ırkçılık karşıtı bir çalışma programı izlediklerini öne sürebilsinler. Bu şekilde alet edilmemek ciddi bir mücadele gerektiriyor. Bu bir kurumun ırkçı tavırlarının ve çifte standardının meşrulaştırıldığı, bir nevi "art-washing" – sanat yıkama. Pratikte bunları sorgulamak, dayanışma ve örgütlenme olmadığı için, çok zor. Sonuçta bu tecrübeler çoğu kez; bunlara karşı mücadele edenleri izole ediyor. Rahatsızlığımı ve öfkemi kanalize etmek de benim için bir mücadele konusu. Bu enerjiyi sanatçı, izleyici veya bunun ötesindeki çeşitli roller içinde heyecan verici bulacağım eserlere nasıl yansıtabilirim sorusunu kendime sık sık soruyorum. Bu süreçte benim için önemli olan, yaşadığımız zaman dilimi, mücadelemiz ve kendimiz için anlamlı birşeyler ortaya çıkarmak ve bundan keyif almak.

Cana:

Sanat piyasasındaki üretim baskısı bende zaman zaman kendi öz sanatsal üretim şartlarıma karşı içsel bir yabancılaşma duygusuna yol açıyor. Sanat pazarının ekonomik ve siyasi yapılardan bağımsız analiz edilemeyeceğini düşünüyorum. Sanatın üretildiği pazar da, bu sosyo-ekonomik sistemin bir parçası ve tanıdığım birçok sanatçı sürekli ve her daim sanatsal çalışma üretme baskısı altında; aksi takdirde insan çok çabuk dışlanıyor. Bu yabancılaşma duygusu bireysel görünüyor, ama öyle değil, bu yapısal bir sorun.

Banu:

Burada, tasarımsal olanaklar ve tasarım olanakları konusuna gelmeden önce, bir şey söylemek istiyorum. Sanat piyasası yapısının "alternatif" sanata dokunmadığı gözlemi konusunda bir durup düşünmek gerektiğine inanıyorum. Belki bu tanımlamanın 18. yüzyıl sanat piyasasına ilişkin geliştirildiğini dikkate almak gerekli. Örneğin sanat teorisyeni Martha Woodmansee, bireysel yaratıcı (veya "dahi") olarak sanatçı ve yazar fikrinin o dönemde oluştuğunu ve kısmen sanatçılara yarattıklarıyla para kazanma (telif yasası tam o zamanda, sanatçıyı korumak için çıkarıldı)[5] imkanı vermek için ortaya çıktığı argümanını öne sürüyor. Ama aynı zaman diliminde sanatın özerkliği üzerine günümüze uzanan ve köklü gerilimler yaratan kuramlar geliştirildi. Genel anlayış şekliyle sanat hem özerk (ideal durumda), hem de bir mal. Yorumlarınızdan anladığım kadarıyla, bu gerilim kapitalizmin şimdiki aşamasında daha da belirginleşiyor.

Cana:

Bununla, çok önemli bir noktaya, yani yeni bir toplumu hayal etmeye ve sorgulamaya çabalayan sanatın bir ütopya olarak yarattığı heyecana ve aynı zamanda taleplerin karşılanabilir olması şartını koyan pazar mantığına, dolayısıyla sistemin tekrar meşrulaştırılmasına, değiniyorsun. Ben de diğerlerinin yanı sıra Rönesans'ın bireye bazı toplum alanlarında daha fazla hak getirdiğine ve bunun o dönemde sanat üretimini de etkilediğine inanıyorum. Ama benim deneyimlerime ve bakış açıma göre şu an pazar halen sosyal ve siyasi alanlara hakim; bu da sanatçıların yaşam durumlarını ve üretim şartlarını etkiliyor. Frankfurt Okulunun yazıları veya Banu senin de değindiğin gibi Martha Woodmansee'nin yazıları, daha sonra ileri kapitalizm çağında sosyal olanın ve sanatın ticarileştirilmesinin analizine çok şey kattı.

Sanat alanında güvencesiz çalışma koşulları konusunda Viyana Güzel Sanatlar Akademisi'ndeki üniversite eğitimim öncesinde ve sırasında film alanında veya sanat galerilerinde mutlaka birkaç staj yapmak istediğim dönem aklıma geldi. Üniversite eğitimimin ilk yıllarında, konusu siyasal sanat olan bir sempozyumda staj yaptım ve çalışma koşulları çok ağırdı. Her şeyden önce, bu alanda çok sayıda kadının ücretsiz çalıştığını anladım.

Bu bağlamda feminist hareket *Lohn gegen Hausarbeit*'ın (Ev İşine Maaş) 1972'de kapitalist sistemin bir parçası olan ev işi, seks işi ve üretim işi konularında Avrupa'da bir tartışma başlattığını söylememiz lazım. Silvia Federici[6] 1975'de *Lohn gegen Hausarbeit* makalesinde, "İtiraf etmeliyiz ki, sermaye büyük bir başarıyla bizim emeğimizi gizledi. Kadınların sırtından gerçekten bir şaheser yarattı. Evde yapılan işe maaş ödemeyi reddederek ve bunu aşktan kaynaklanan bir davranışa dönüştürerek, sermaye bir taşla iki kuş vurdu"[7] diye yazıyor. Feminist hareketin ve *Lohn gegen Hausarbeit*'ın bahsettiği, sanatta ve ev işlerinde ödenmeyen işgücü konularına eleştirel yaklaşmak zorundayız. İkisi sımsıkı birbirine bağlı, çünkü, Federici'nin yazdığı gibi, "Kapitalist sistemde her işçinin manipüle edildiği, sömürüldüğü ve sermayeyle olan ilişkisinin tamamen saklandığı bir gerçek. Maaş, kafalarda adil bir ticaret ilişkisi olduğunu, insanın çalıştığı ve parasının ödendiği, patronla çalışanın eşit olduğu intibasını yaratıyor. Gerçekte maaş, yaptığınız işin bedelini ödemek yerine, kara dönüşen tüm ücretsiz işleri gizler. Ama maaş seni en azından işçi olarak kabul ediyor ve pazarlık yapma, kendini çalışma şartlarına ve maaş miktarına karşı savunma imkanı doğuruyor."[8] Londra'da yıllardır bu konularla uğraşan The Carrot Workers Collective ve Precarious Workers, bu bağlantıları ortaya koyarak neyin ne olduğunu gösteriyor. Sanat alanında karşılığı ödenmeyen işleri görünür kılarak, bu durumla mücadele ediyor. Arkadaşlarım ve benim için onların bu çalışmaları müthiş güç vericiydi. Yine de sanatta ödenmeyen veya çok düşük ödenen işlerle mücadele ediyorum ve bundan dolayı da kendimi sanatçı değil, sanat işçisi olarak tanımlıyorum.

belit:

Ben sanatın özerkliği ile sanat piyasası arasında var olan gerilimin, farklı zamanlarda farklı bölgelerde, en çok sanatın dışındaki siyasi iklimden ve sanat alanı içindeki siyasi bilinçten etkilenmiş olduğuna inanıyorum. Ve bu zamanları yaşayanlar için her bir anın gerilim dolu olduğu görünüyor. Gerilimin şimdiki anda en görünür halde olduğundan veya şimdiki anın en çok gerilimli an olduğundan şüphe duyuyorum. Sadece telif yasasının oluşmasını ve onun bugüne kadarki gelişimini göz önünde bulunduralım; sanatçıların para kazanmaları gerektiği fikrinden ve onların eser haklarını korumaktan, Disney gibi şirketlerin telif haklarından büyük miktarlar kazanmalarına ve sırf dava yürütme amacıyla kurulan birimlerine, kendi yaratmadıkları, kamusal alandan çaldıkları ve özelleştirdikleri içerikleri copyright ile korumalarına dönüştüğünü görürüz. Mesela Disney gibi çok uluslu bir şirket, tüm alanı belirliyor, resmi anlatı ve telif hakkıyla korunan, çalınmış içerikler üzerinde hakimiyet kurmayı hedefliyor. Yani bu anlatıları nasıl işine gelirse değiştiriyor. Sonuçta resmi anlatı sadece ülkeler tarafından değil, son 20 yılda bu çok uluslu holdingler tarafından belirleniyor. Ayrıca şunu da belirtmek isterim; sanat tarihinden bahsedildiğinde, en başta, piyasa ile diğerlerinden daha güçlü bir bağı olan Batı'nın sanat tarihi kastediliyor. Disney'in yerine, Gagosian veya Christie's'i koyup onların uygulamalarını da inceleyebiliriz.

Diğer yandan sanat emekçileri olarak çalışmalarımız ve duruşumuzla, sanat alanını yeniden tanımlama imkanına sahip olduğumuzu düşünüyorum: Belli değerlerin yaşatıldığı, piyasaya karşı belli bir yaklaşımın sergilendiği ve bu süreçte tarih ve iktidarla olan ilişkisinin bilincinde olan, kendi pratiklerini sorgulayan bir alan. Bununla sadece eserlerimizin içeriğini değil, tüm süreci; dahi ve telif hakkı kavramlarını, düşük ücretli işleri, hiyerarşiyi, elit düşünceyi, mevcut cinsiyetçiliği, ırkçılığı ve global ağlar kurma hedefi güden kuruluş, galeri ve müzayede evlerini yerel pratikler aracılığıyla sorgulamayı kastediyorum. Sürekli kendime şunu soruyorum; nasıl bir toplumda yaşamak istiyorum ve bu toplumu nasıl tasavvur ediyorum? Neden sanat alanı bu tasavvurda bir istisna olsun? İş ilişkileri, iş ilişkisidir, sınıf mücadelesi de aynı sınıf mücadelesidir. Ben adil iş ilişkileri için uğraşıyorum. Her gün karşıma çıkan nahoş durumlarla mücadele ediyorum ve sanat piyasasını, diğer iş piyasalarından biri olarak görüyorum. Tohumlar ekilip, alanlar yaratılır. Nihayetinde bu uğraşların meyvelerinin toplanması uzun soluklu bir süreç, aynı diğer eylem şekillerinde olduğu gibi. İklim değişikliği gibi. Belki iklim değişikliğinin radikal sonuçlarını, biz yaşımızdan ötürü hayatımızda pek hissetmeyeceğiz, ama olaya sağlıklı bir şekilde baktığımızda, adaleti her yerde savunmamız gerekir. Çevre ırkçılığıyla, aynı diğer ırkçılık çeşitleriyle olduğu gibi mücadele etmemiz gerekir. Ayrıca mücadelelerimizi sadece kısa vadeli görürsek dünyamız çok cesaret kırıcı ve bunaltıcı bir yer olur. O zaman bir insanın, bir kolektifin veya bir kolektif ağının bir şeyler değiştirmeye veya sorgulamaya gücü yetmediği tablosu ortaya çıkıyor, ama uzun vaadede bu çok kısıtlı bir görüş. Tarih de bize bunu gösteriyor. Mevzu nasıl örgütleneceğimiz, dayanışma göstereceğimiz, imtiyazlarımızı elde edeceğimiz ve geleceğe yönelik birbirimize sahip çıkacağımız ile alakalı.

Cana:

"Hayır" demek belki her gün yaşadığımız haksızlıklara karşı durma anlamında önemli. Öyleyse "hayır" bu durumu değiştirmek için bir başlangıç noktası olabilir. Ama orada takılıp kalmamalıyız, arkamızda bırakmalıyız.

Banu:

Senin ifadenle Cana, "hayır" demek, nasıl bir yaşam ve ortak yaşam istediğimiz üzerine sohbet etmek için bir başlangıç noktası olabilir. Adalet ve hakkaniyet konusunda nasıl hareket edilmesi gerektiği ile ilgili, ama sonu açık bırakılan bir sohbet olmalı.

Cana:

Evet, bu yaşadığımız hayattan, yaşamak istediğimiz hayata doğru hareket etmek anlamına geliyor.

belit:

Veya yaşamın bize açılan imkanlarla nasıl olabileceği.

Cana:

Evet, başka bir yaşamın mümkün olduğunu söyleyebilmek.

Banu:

Ben yine de merak ediyorum Cana ve belit, bu, sizin çalışmalarınızda kendini nasıl gösteriyor?

belit:

Benim video eylemciliğiyle uğraştığım dönemler ve bugün yaptıklarım arasında somut bir fark var; artık neye karşı olup olmadığıma değil, düşünce üretmeye odaklanıyorum. Bu sözlerle amacım, daha önce yer aldığım çok değerli çalışmaları basite indirgemek değil. Siyasi şartlar altında ve insan hakları mücadelesinin aciliyeti nedeniyle, video eylemciliği haksız söylem ve anlatılara karşı yanlış anlamaya fırsat vermeyecek netlikte olmalıydı.

Susturulmak istenen seslerin olduğunu, sokaklarda neler olup bittiğini, söylenenlerin gerçekte yaşananlarla örtüşmediğini göstermek çok önemliydi. Aynı bugünkü gibi değil mi? Bu çalışmada mesele net bir duruşun altını çizmekti. Düşünmeye fırsat kalmadığı hissindeydik. O çalışmaları bugün yapsam, uygulamalarım kesinlikle farklı olur. Kendi kendime soruyorum; acaba yine de düşünmeye zamanım olmadığı hissi oluşur muydu? Bu yaşamının hangi evresinde bulunduğun ile de alakalı. Benim her şeye her zaman bir reaksiyon göstermek zorunda olmadığımızı keşfetmek için biraz zamana ihtiyacım vardı diye tahmin ediyorum. İnsan kendi mücadelesini ve mücadele şeklini kendi seçiyor, hayatını nasıl yaşamak istediğini de. Bu iki sanat şeklini karşılaştırmam gerekirse, şu anki pratiğimde bazı şeyleri çalışma sürecinde daha iyi anlıyorum ve düşüncelerin gelişimini, ortaya çıkan eseri merakla izliyorum. Çalışmanın etrafında dönen pratik hayatın günlük temaslar sanat dünyasının standartlarıyla sonu olmayan bir çatışma içindedir. Hatta olmayan standartlarla demem daha doğru olur ve bu çok hararetli bir çatışmadır. Yarattığım içeriği daha önceki çalışmalarımın bir uzantısı, eylemciliğin daha yavaş, hareketi uzun süreye yayan bir versiyonu gibi görüyorum. Banu, senin "sert ve açık sohbet" ifadeni beğendim. Bu tanımın, benim güncel çalışmalarımla hedeflediklerime yakın bir tınısı var. Sende nasıl Cana?

Cana:

Tekrar You-Tube yorumlarına geri dönecek olursak, onlar bize, düşünmenin ve yaşamın başka şekilleri olabileceğini gösteriyor. Benim çalışmalarım, araştırmalarım veya yaptıklarım bir şeyin lehine ya da aleyhine değil, ama sanatsal biçimde tavır almak tabii ki önemli. Bu şekilde "mainstream"de görünür olmayan konuları irdelemenin mümkün olduğuna inanıyorum. Mesela belirli toplumların tarihi veya anıları ile de başka bir yaşam gösterilebilir.

Mesela bir kullanıcının yorumu şöyle: "This makes me want to read a book from end to beginning" [Bu bende bir kitabı sonundan başına doğru okuma isteği uyandırıyor.]. Öyleyse neden yeniden başlamayalım, geleceği yeniden okuyup hatırlamayalım, geçmiş hakkında kehanette bulunmayalım ve hayalleri rüyalarımızla, gerçeği umutla, arzularımızı hakikatle, Afro-Amerikan bilim kadını ve aktivist Angela Davis'in "Ben değiştiremediğim şeyleri artık kabul etmiyorum. Kabul edemeyeceğim şeyleri değiştiriyorum" şeklindeki söylem doğrultusunda, birleştirmeyelim.

belit:

Aynen. Mevcut resmi anlatılar insanların günlük tecrübelerini kavrayacak durumda değil ve bizim, onların karmaşıklığını ve kendi tecrübelerimizi ifade etmek için sezgisel bağlantılara ihtiyacımız var. Bu sadece dünyada gerçekleşmesini istediğimiz şeyler adına mücadeleyle ve kabul etmediğimiz şeyleri değiştirmekle anlam kazanıyor. Ve bu mücadele öfkeli olmalı. Bir çok şekil alabilir.

This makes me want to remember the future

Cana:

Bence batı dünyasının okullarında ve üniversitelerinde bize öğretilenler, sistemin bize öğretmek istediğini ayakta tutmaya yarıyor. Bu da Avrupa merkezci, temelden oryantalist ve ırkçı. Buna karşı mücadele edilmeli ve sorgulanmalı. Ayrıca tüm dünyada genç insanlar *Fridays for Future* veya *İklim için okul boykotu* yürüyüşlerine katılmak için sokaklara dökülüyor. Cuma günleri okula gitmeyip, onun yerine iklim değişikliğine karşı eylem yapmaya karar veren gençler tarafından başlatılan uluslararası bir hareket. Gençler eşitlik ve herkes için daha iyi bir yaşam istiyor ve toplumumuzda haksızlılığa neden olan, hakim anlatıları ve bilgi üretimini sorguluyorlar. belit sen sanatınla, Banu, sen de çalışmalarınla bizlere yeni perspektifler ve olanaklar gösteriyorsun.

Banu:

İkinizin söyledikleri hakkında düşünüyorum ve belit tekrar senin açıklamalarına geri dönmek istiyorum. Geliştirme fikrini, üzerinde çalıştığın şeyi anlamak için bir yöntem olarak mı kullanıyorsun?

belit:

Anlamak için değil, ama Ulus Baker'in dediği[9] gibi, anlamanın yanında bilgi imkanlarını hissetmek, genişletmek, yani farklı tecrübeleri ve ilişkilendirme imkanlarını açmak için. Öyleyse geliştirme fikrinin farklı ilişkilendirme biçimlerinin baştan sona incelenmesi için bir yöntem olduğunu söyleyebiliriz, yani konuya giriş için anlamayı ana merkeze koymayan, değişik bilgi üretim metotları olduğunu... Mevzu hiyerarşiyi kırmak ve anlamak kavramına verilen asli yeri sarsmaktır diyebiliriz. Biz bir şeyle bağ kurmak için anlamak zorunda değiliz. Biz farklı biçimlerde bir şey ile bağ kurmaya vakıfız, zaten aksi takdirde dünyayı kavrama yeteneğimiz kısıtlı kalırdı. Bunun temelinde mainstream mantığı ile kastettiğim de yatıyor: Kabul edilen şekiller, arşiv uygulamaları, bunların hepsi bağlantı içinde.

Banu:

Nasıl ifade edeceğimi bir düşüneyim. Bence Cana bilgi üretiminin ortak ilgi alanlarımızdan biri olduğunu doğru tespit etti. Her birimizin farklı türde arşivlerle ve devlet şiddetiyle ilgileniyor olmamız tesadüf değil , bunlar sadece "disipline sokma" işlevi görmüyor, halihazırda belirli bilgi şekillerini üretiyorlar. Ama belit'in "sadece anlamak değil, bilhassa hissetmek" düşüncesinde, Cana'nın söyledikleriyle bağlamak istediğim ve daha fazlasını öğrenmek isteğim şeyler var.

belit: Burada "vücutlaşmış tecrübe" kavramını konuya dahil etmek ve tartışmayı hepimizin uygulamaları için önemli olduğunu düşündüğüm arşiv ile birleştirmek isterim. Daha doğrusu; vücutlaşmış tecrübelerin günümüzdeki arşiv yöntemleri ile arşivlenmesinin beraberinde getirdiği sorunları ve yükümlülükleri kastediyorum. Tam şimdi üzerine düşündüğüm, muhtemelen siz ikinizin de düşündüğü, tecrübelerden bahsediyorum. Arşiv yöntemlerini nasıl anlamalı ve sorgulamalıyız ki, devlet şiddeti tecrübesini arşivleyebilme olanağımız olsun? Belki olayı "arşivleme" olarak değil, başka bir şekilde tanımlamak gerekiyor. Diana Taylor bunu "Repertoire"[10]. diye tanımlıyor. Bu tecrübeler anlaşılmıyor, ilk etapta vücut tarafından hissedilip, yaşanıyorlar. Bu nedenden başka biçimlere, fikirlere ve de "sert ve ucu açık" sohbete gereksinim duyuyorlar.

Banu:

belit'in değindiği nokta bana da çok önemli geliyor ve akla başka konular da getiriyor. İlki arşivler ve bilim üretimin arasındaki bağlantıya ilişkin soru. Arşivler kuruluş aşamalarından itibaren belli soruları yanıtlamayı amaçlıyorlar ve neyin muhafaza etmeye değer, neyin değer olmadığını ifade eden bir tercih söz konusu. Arşivlerin "objektif" bir muhafaza mekanı olmadığından yola çıkarsak, onları sanat çalışmalarınız için nasıl kullanılabilir hale getiriyorsunuz?

Cana:

Resmi arşivlerin baskı kurucuların iktidarıyla bağlantılı olduğunu ben de görüyorum. Öyleyse resmi arşivleri sorgulamak için, gizlenmiş arşivleri gün ışığına çıkarma mekanizmaları üzerine kafa yormamız gerekir. Sanatın rolü geçmiş ve şimdiki zaman arasında köprü görevi görüp, gizleneni tekrar canlandırmak olabilir.

belit:

Kanımca arşivleri değişken ve dinamik yapılar olarak kavramak gerekli. Muhtemelen bir şeyi, belirli şekilde tanımlamak için kurulmadılar. Esasen baskıcı yapıların devam eden ve resmi anlatıma uyum sağlayan devlet arşivlerinden bahsetmiyorum. Devlete ait olmayan ama muhalif/alternatif olarak da tanımlanamayacak kurumsal arşivlerden bahsediyorum. Böyle arşivlerin belki "iyi gayeleri" olabilir, ama muhtemelen düşük angajmanlı idari mekanizmalar nedeniyle, ellerindeki güç ve işlevleri idrak edemediklerinden, baskıcı yapılarda son buluyorlar ve tarihin silinmesinde rol oynuyorlar. Vurdumduymazlık ve iktidar yapılarını anlayamamak, çoğu kez günlük ırkçılığın kaynağı değil mi? En azından bu Hollanda'da, Gloria Wekker'in "white innocence" olarak tanımladığı ırkçılığın çok yaygın bir şekli.

Neyi kapsamadığının bilincinde olmayan bir arşivin, dışladıklarının silinmesinde payı var. Banu'nun da söylediği gibi arşivler "objektif" olamaz, ama bunun bilincinde olabilirler, ne olduklarını ve yaptıklarını tanımlayabilir, ne amaçladıklarını netleştirip açıklayabilirler. Devlet arşivleri bunu yapıyor ve tam bu açıklama ile de siliyorlar. Yani farklı durumlarda farklı silme mekanizmaları iş başında. Arşivler aynı zamanda sorumluluk taşıyorlar ve seçkileri nasıl sundukları, hangi kapsamda konumladıkları hakkında hesap vermeliler. Etik temellerine uymalılar, ama çoğu kez bunu yapmıyorlar.

Ben resmi ve kurumsal arşivlerle çalıştığım zaman, tarihi tanımlayan ve sabitlemeye çalışan anlatımı, dili ve çerçeveyi sorgulamayı kendime hedef ediniyorum. Başka ögeler tarafından desteklenmeyen, ama doğal görünen veya doğal olarak oradaymış hissi uyandıran, empoze edilmiş yapıları deşifre etmek ilgimi çekiyor. Bu yapıların iç mekanizmalarına şüpheyle yaklaşıyorum. Onları tek tek parçalara ayırıyor ve tekrar birleştirmeye, parçaların nerede birbirlerine uymadıklarını tespit etmeye çalışıyorum. Ben arşiv olarak kabul edilmeyen arşivlerle de ve onların arşiv olarak kabul edilmesinde ısrar ediyorum. Neyin muhafaza edilebileceği ve arşivin pratikleri üzerinden işleyen tanımlamalar değiştirilmeli ve genişletilmeli.

Banu:

İkinci sorumu kısmen yanıtladın bile: Alternatif arşivler ve onların muhtemel görünümünü hayal edebilir miyiz? Bunları sonu açık bir derleme olarak tasarlamak mümkün mü? Son bir kaç onyılda feminist teori "marjinal halkların/kadınların sesini duyulur hale getirme", yani bilgimizdeki eksik yerleri ortaya çıkarma fikrinden uzaklaşarak, neyin bilgi olarak görülüp, görülmeyeceği yönünde bir dönüşüme uğradı. Kaybolan, kamulaştırılan sanat eserleri ve hem Osmanlı ve İslam sanat tarihi hem de bugünkü Türkiye'nin sanat tarihi metinlerini şekillendiren gayrimüslim sanatçıların tarihten silinmesiyle ilgili araştırma yaparken, onların hikayelerinin mevcut tarihi anlatılara kolayca yerleştirilemeyeceğini tespit ettim. Bu hikayeler dönüştürülmeli, daha ziyade biz bunları dönüştürmek için çalışmalıyız. Aynı zamanda her yeni anlatımın eksik kalacağının ve bazı hasarların telafi edilemeyeceğinin ama yine de geçmişin belirleyici bir bölümü olarak algılanmak zorunda olduğunun bilincindeyiz. Bu bağlamda Cana'nın deminki yorumlarını, sadece daha önce gizli kalanın veya silinenin ortaya çıkarılması olarak değil, bilhassa bu tip bilginin şimdiki zaman için yararlı hale getirilmesi için bir arayış olarak anlıyorum.

Cana:

Kanımca arşiv ve tarih anlayışı yakından ilişkili. Hepimiz biliyoruz ki, devletin şiddeti, bu şiddete karşı mücadele eden insanların tarihini siliyor veya kenara itiyor. Öyleyse devlet tarafından baskıya uğrayan / silinen tarihi alıp, kendi tecrübelerimizle birleştirmeliyiz. Resmi tarih iktidarda olan sınıfın tarihi anlamına geliyor. Mevzu, ezilenlerin tarihini, bu tarihten birşeyler öğrenmek ve başka bir bilgi biçimi oluşturmak için, geri almaktır.

1
https://www.youtube.com/watch?v=Kp7eSUU9°y8.
Erişim: 21.4.2019.
2
https://www.nytimes.com/2018/08/23/arts/design/
john-akomfrah-review-new-museum.html. Erişim:
23.8.2018.
3
belit sağ, Cana Bilir-Meier: *Documentaristics—Documentation and their Characteristics*, içinde: Manfred Grübel, Linda Klösel (ed.), Version Nr. 03, Verlag für Moderne Kunst, Wien 2017.
4
NSU 1990'lı yılların ortalarında faal bir Neonazi ağıydı. Resmi kaynaklara göre NSU tüm Almanya'da sekiz yıl içinde (2000-2007) en az 10 insanı öldürdü ve göçmenlerin yaşadığı semtlerde en az iki çivi bomba patlattılar. Örgütün hayatta kalan üyesi Beate Zschäpe ömür boyu hapis cezasına çarptırıldı ama, ağın araştırılması ve Alman gizli servislerinin ve emniyet güçlerinin rolünün bütünüyle incelenmesi şimdiye kadar gerçekleşmedi.
5
Martha Woodmansee: *Art, the Author and the Market: Rereading the History of Aesthetics*, Columbia University Press, New York 1994.
6
Silvia Federici: *Wages against Housework*, Falling Wall Press Ltd und Power of Woman Collective, Bristol 1975, S.3.
7
Aynı yerde, S.2.
8
Ulus Baker: *Sanat ve Arzu*, İletişim Press, İstanbul 2014.
9
Diana Taylor: *The Archive and The Repertoire: Performing Cultural Memory in the Americas*, Duke University Press, Durham 2003.
10
Gloria Wekker: *White Innocence: Paradoxes of Colonialism and Race*, Duke University Press, Durham 2016.

This makes me want to rob my own bank account

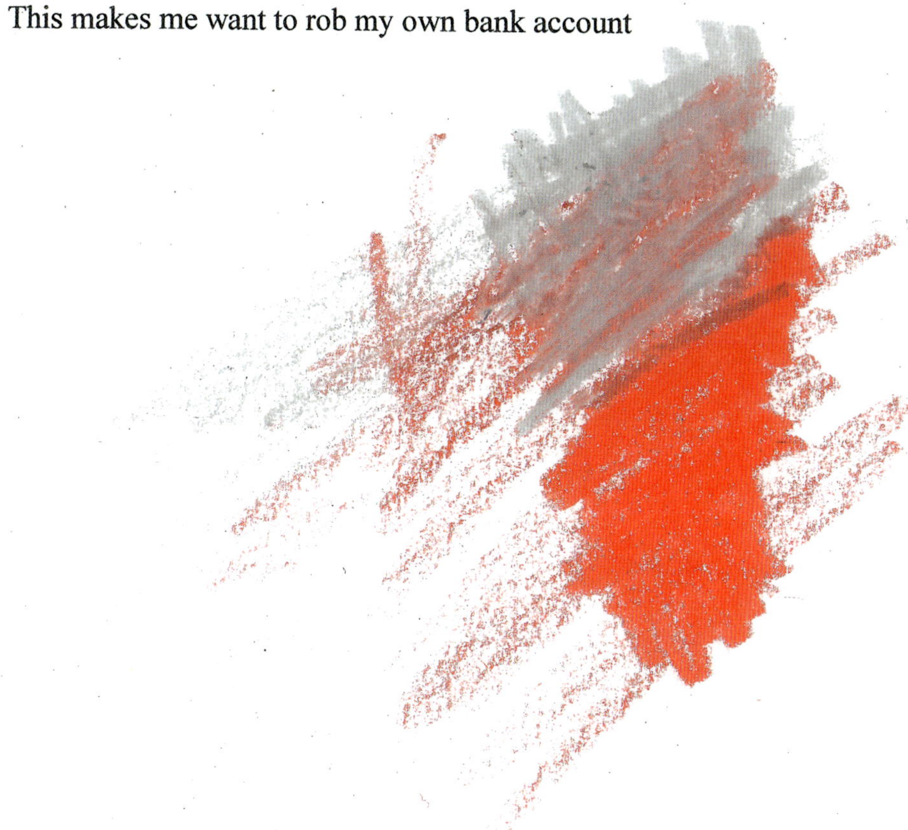

This makes me want to listen to my therapists problems

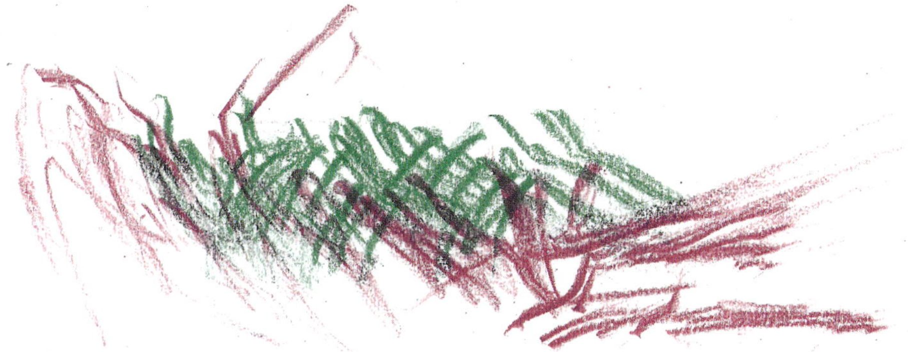

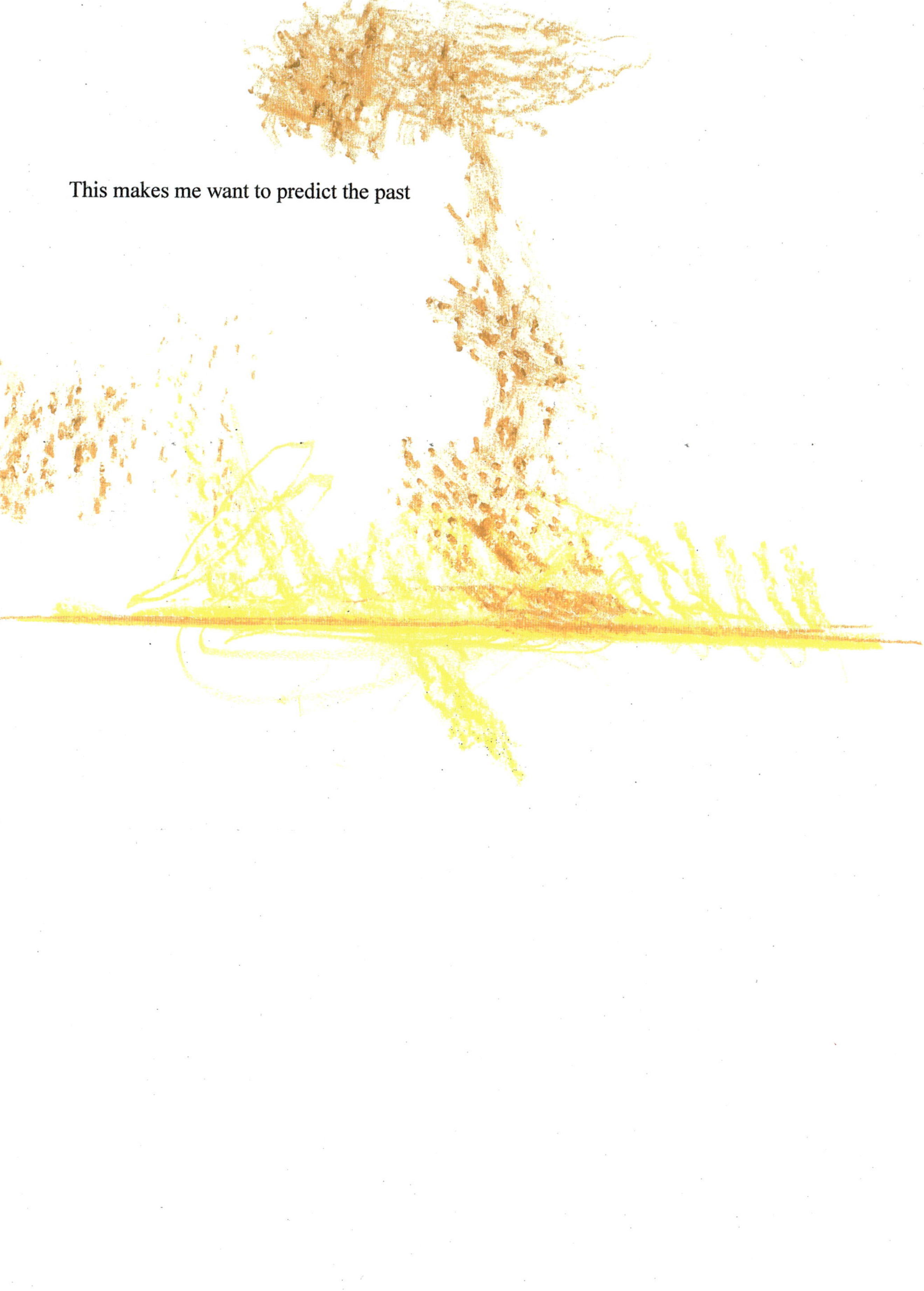

This makes me want to predict the past

This makes me want to tell depression to kill itself

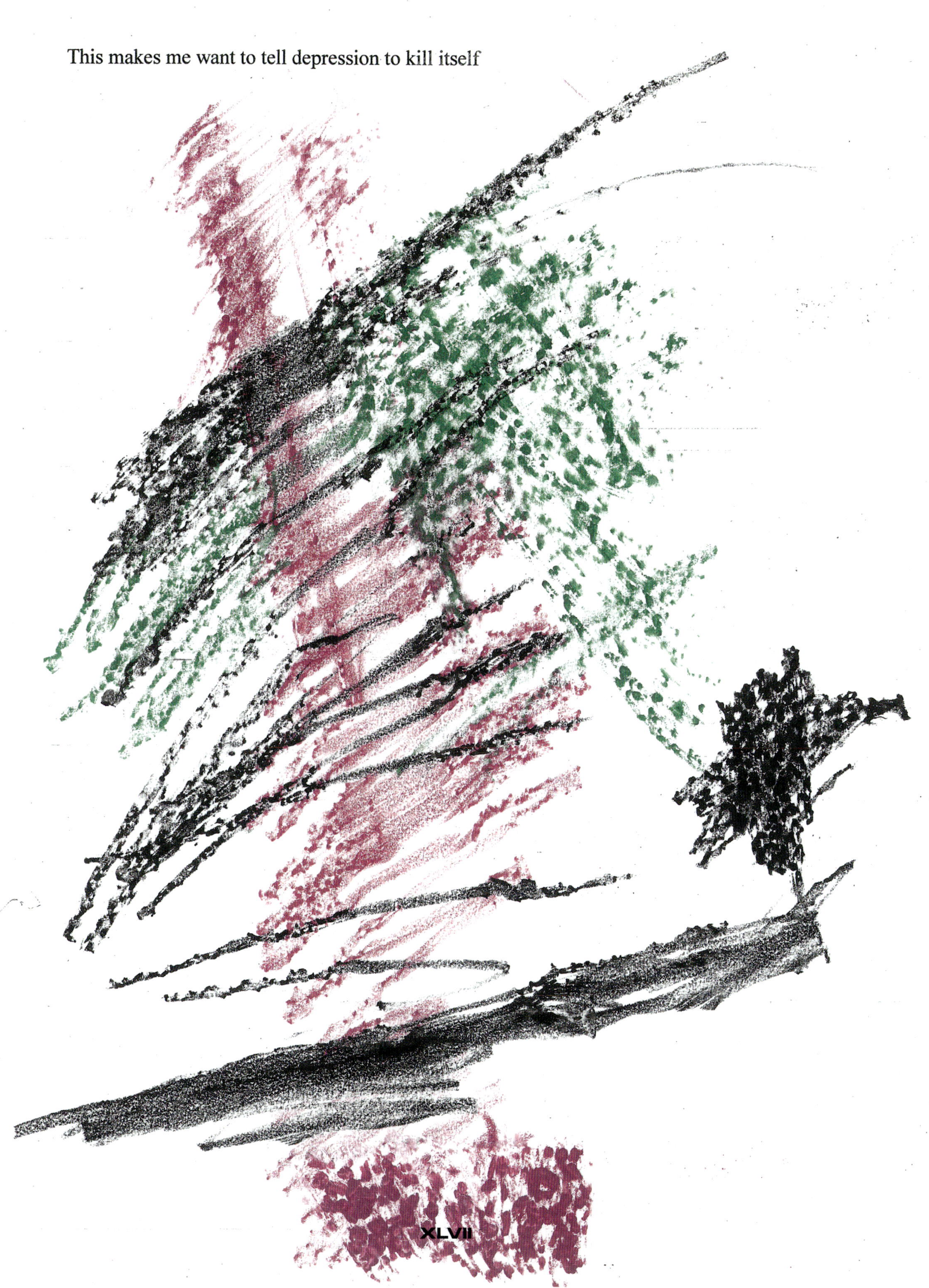

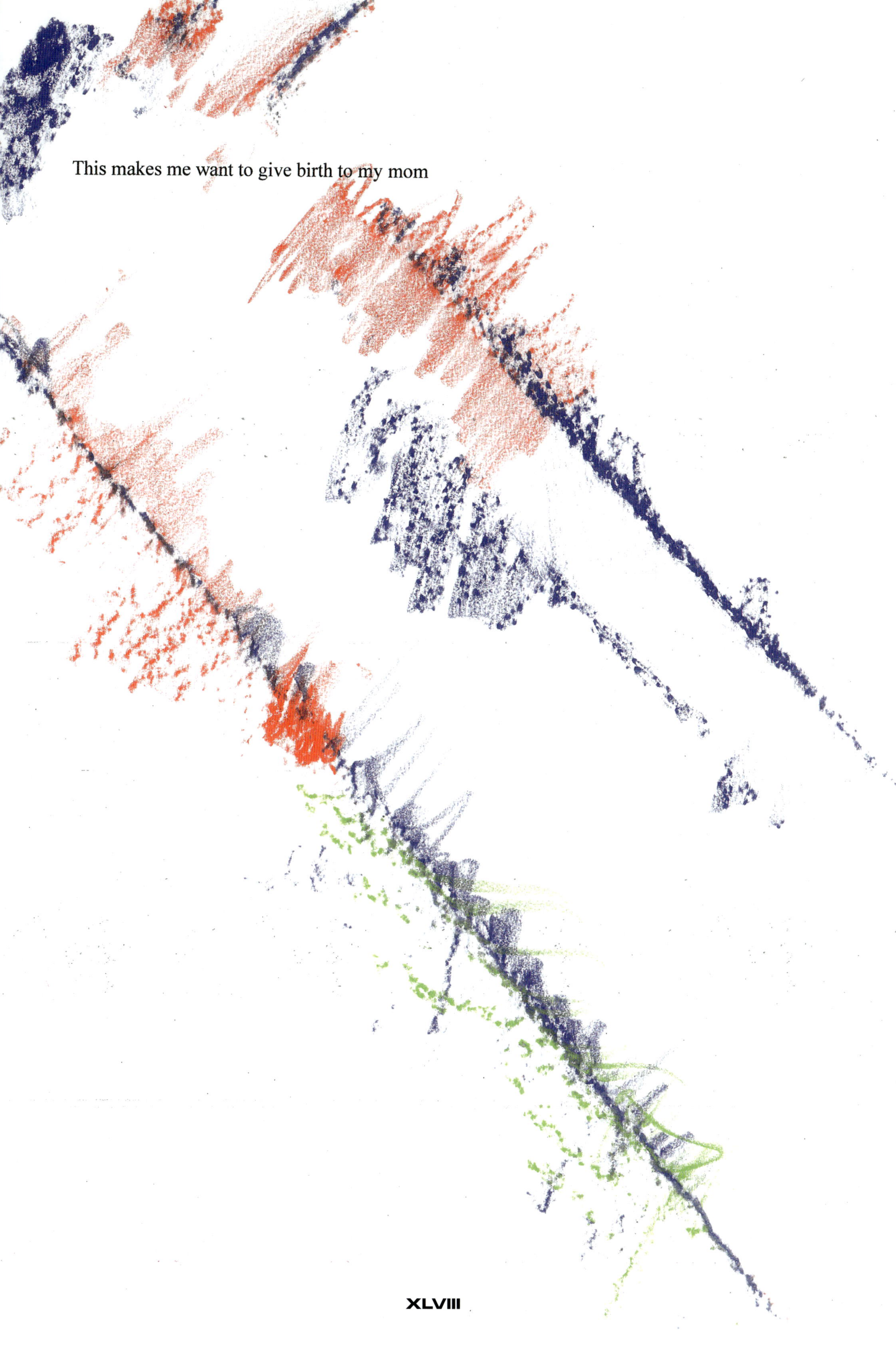

This makes me want to give birth to my mom

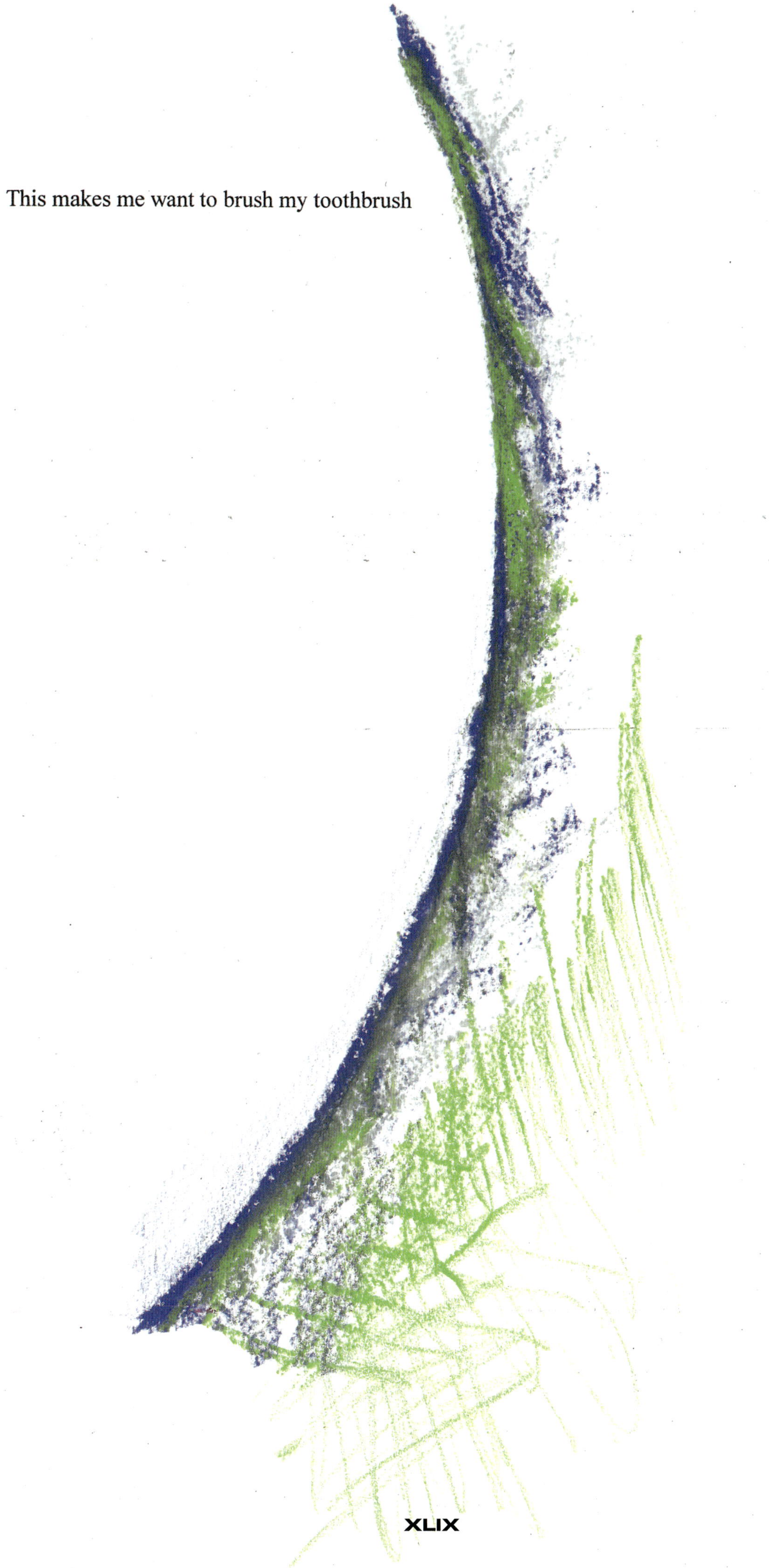

This makes me want to brush my toothbrush

This reminds me of spending time with people I love, time sure does fly

L

This makes me want to tell the clock what time it is

This makes me want to steal money out of my own wallet

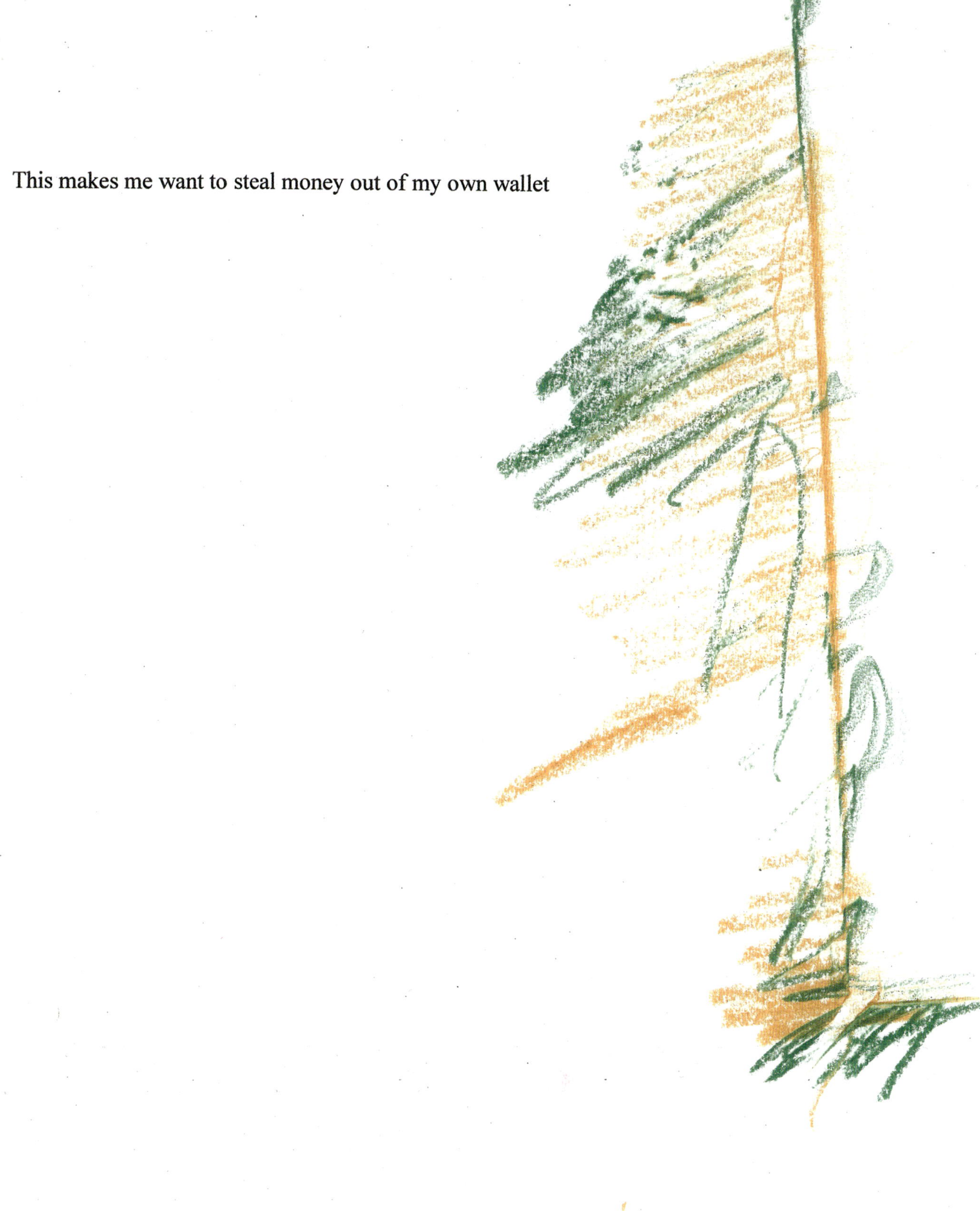

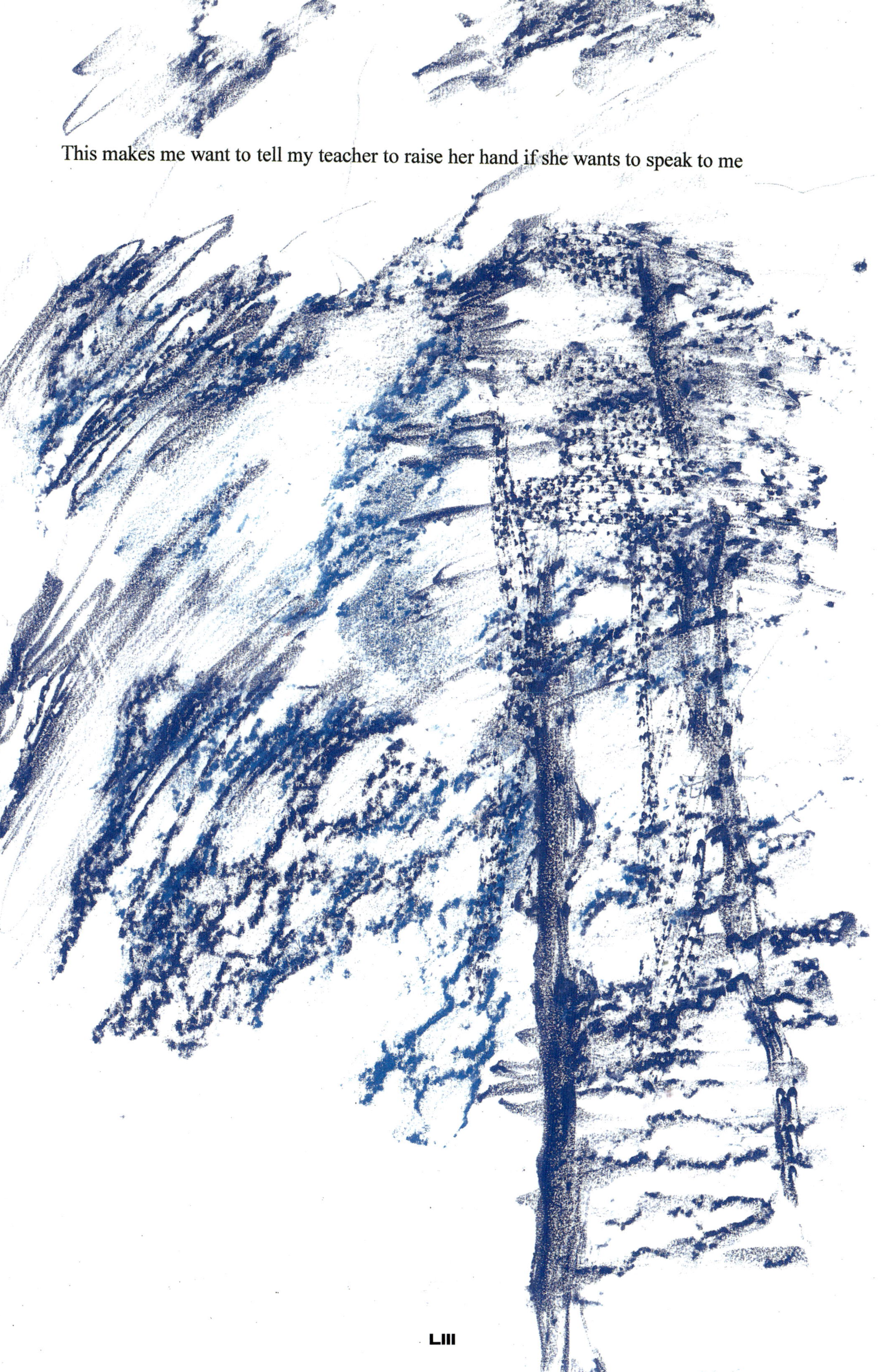

This makes me want to tell my teacher to raise her hand if she wants to speak to me

This makes me want to walk on a fly

This makes me want to call two cab companies to see who arrives first then take the bus

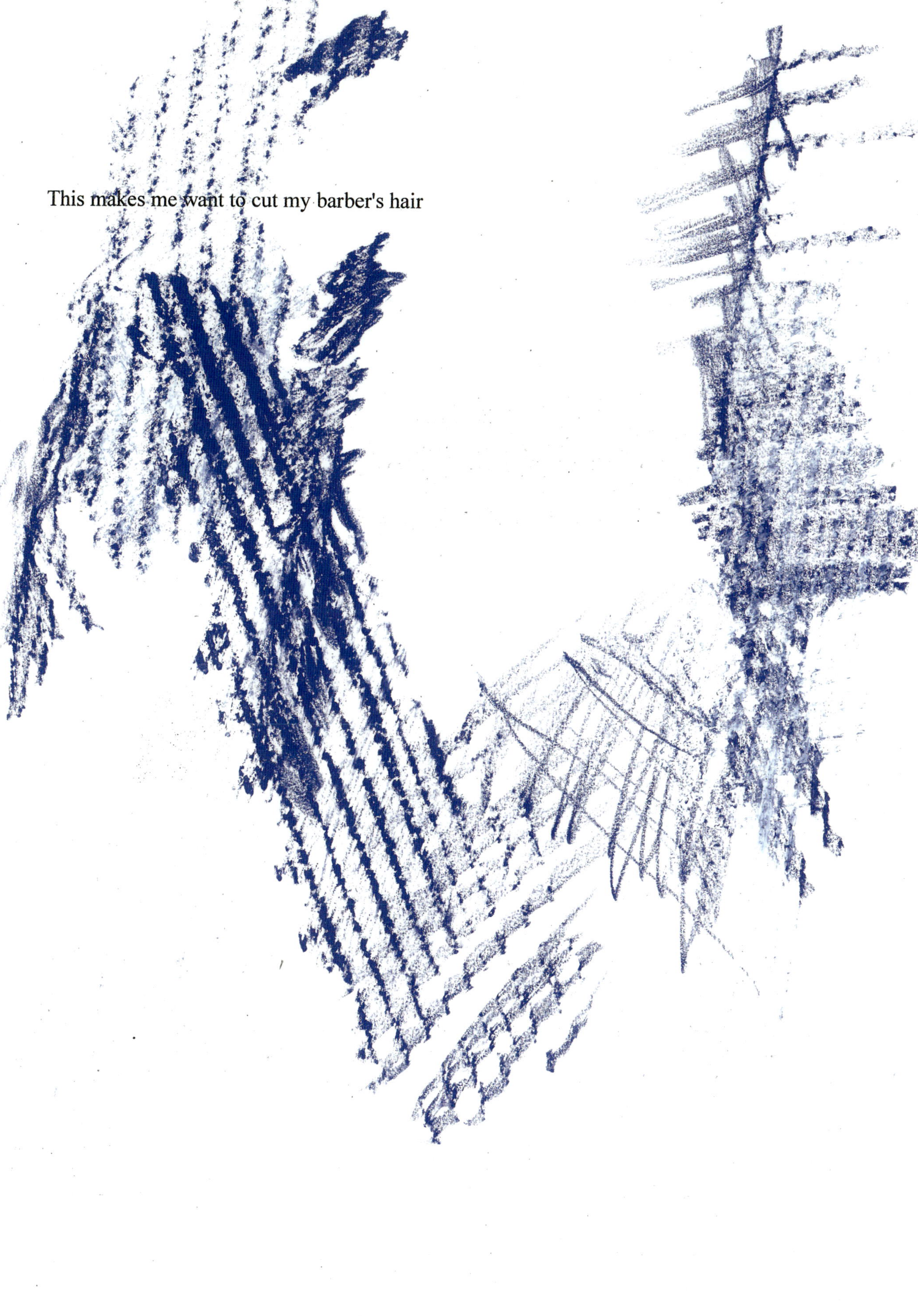

This makes me want to cut my barber's hair

This makes me want to let my clothes wear me

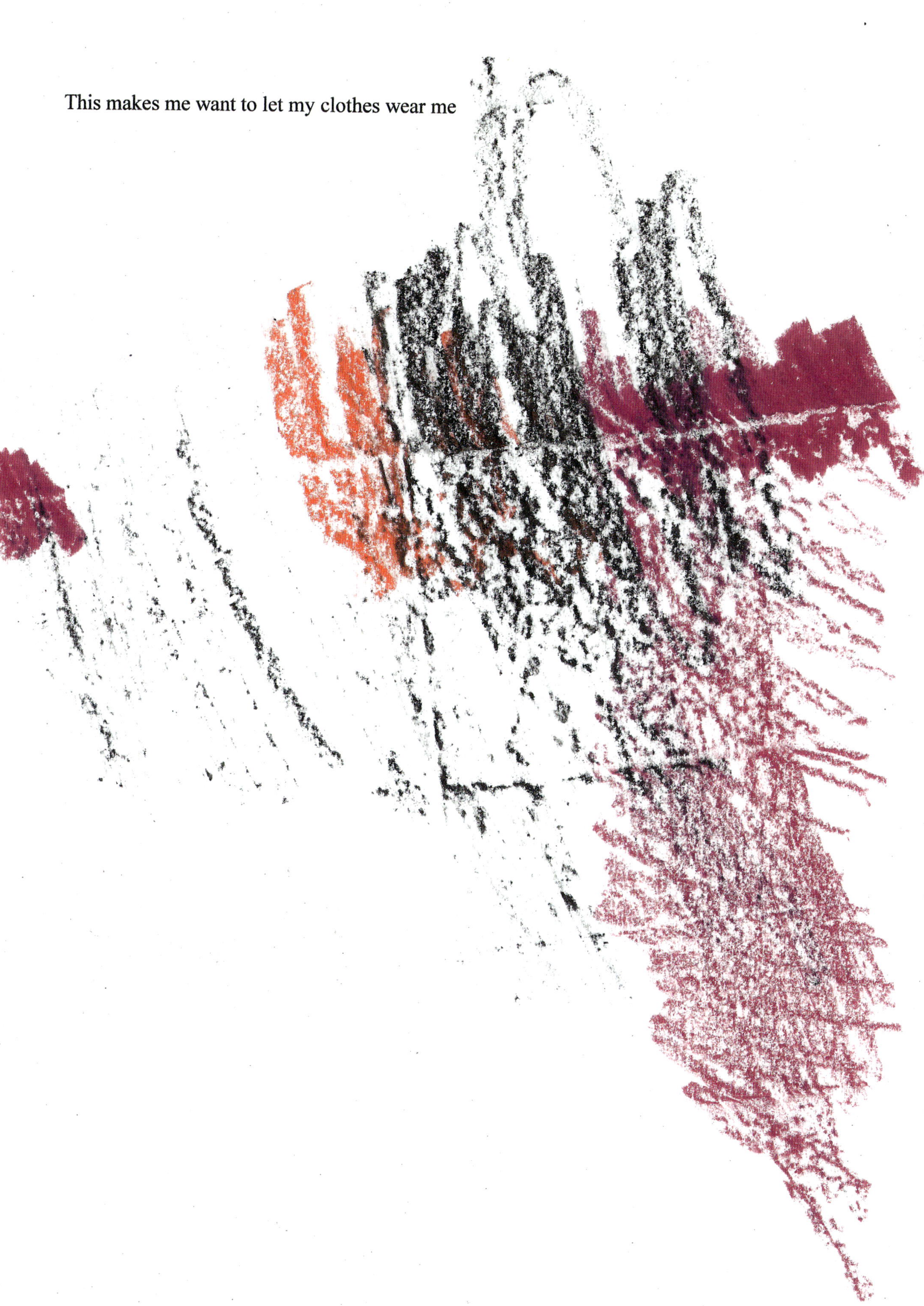

This makes me want to drive my parents to school

LVIII

This makes me wanna fall asleep before I close my eyes

LIX

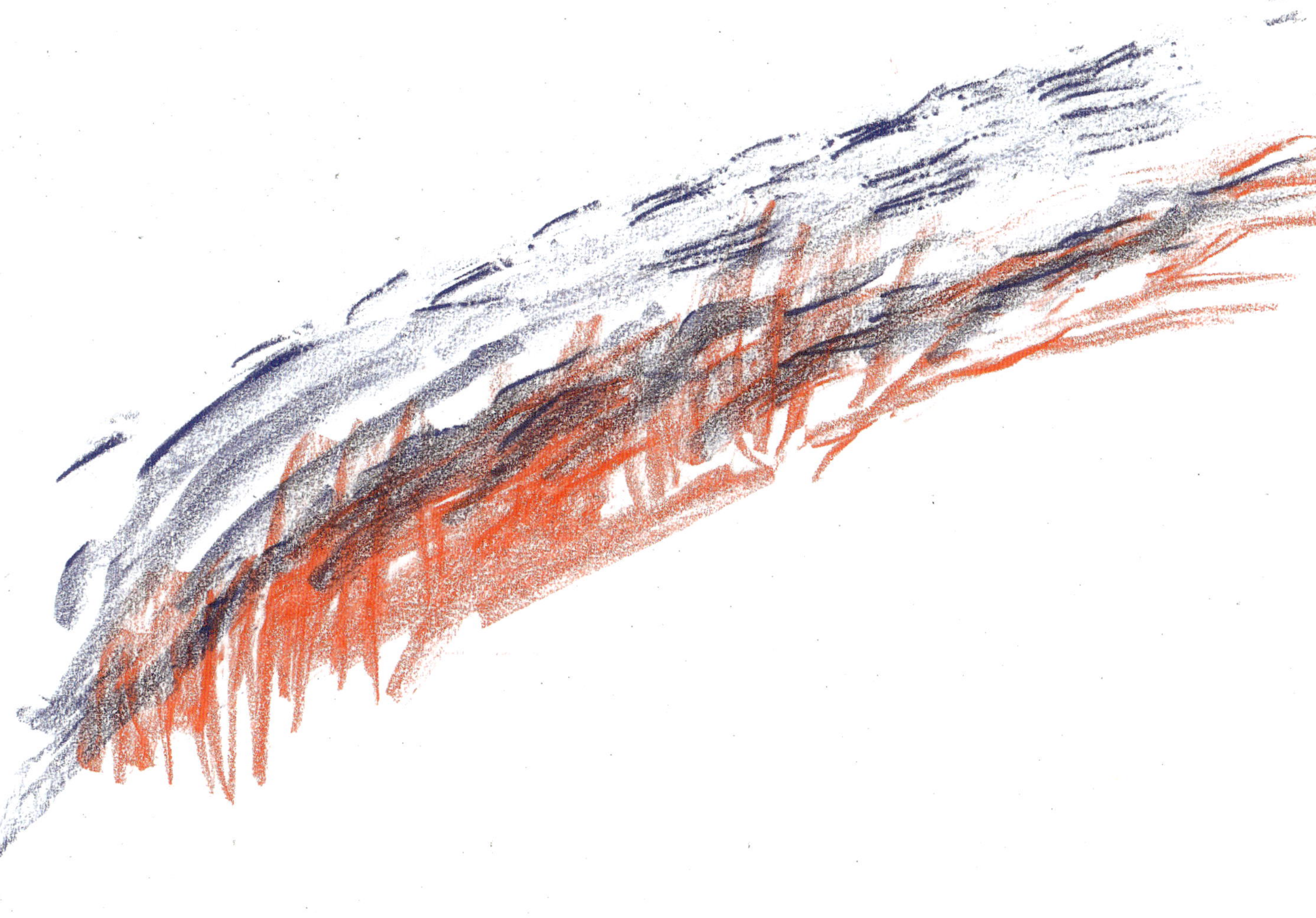

This makes me want to tell my boss to "get a job"

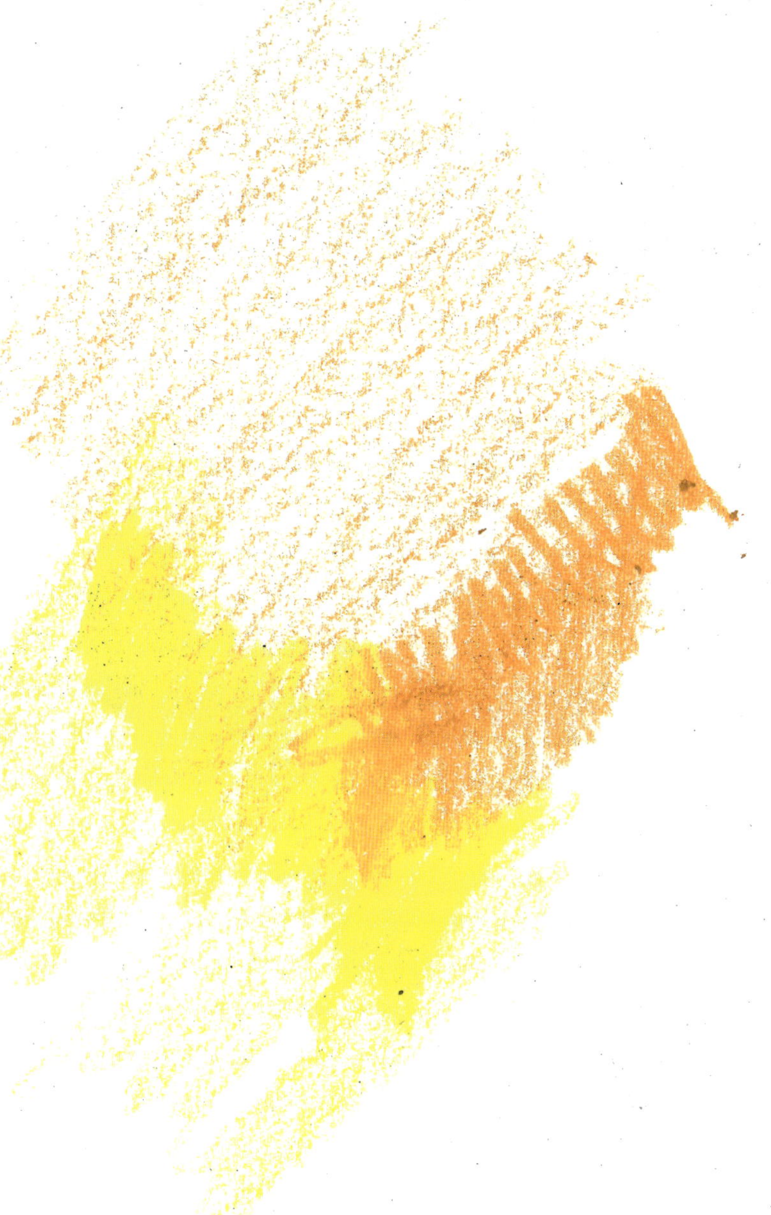

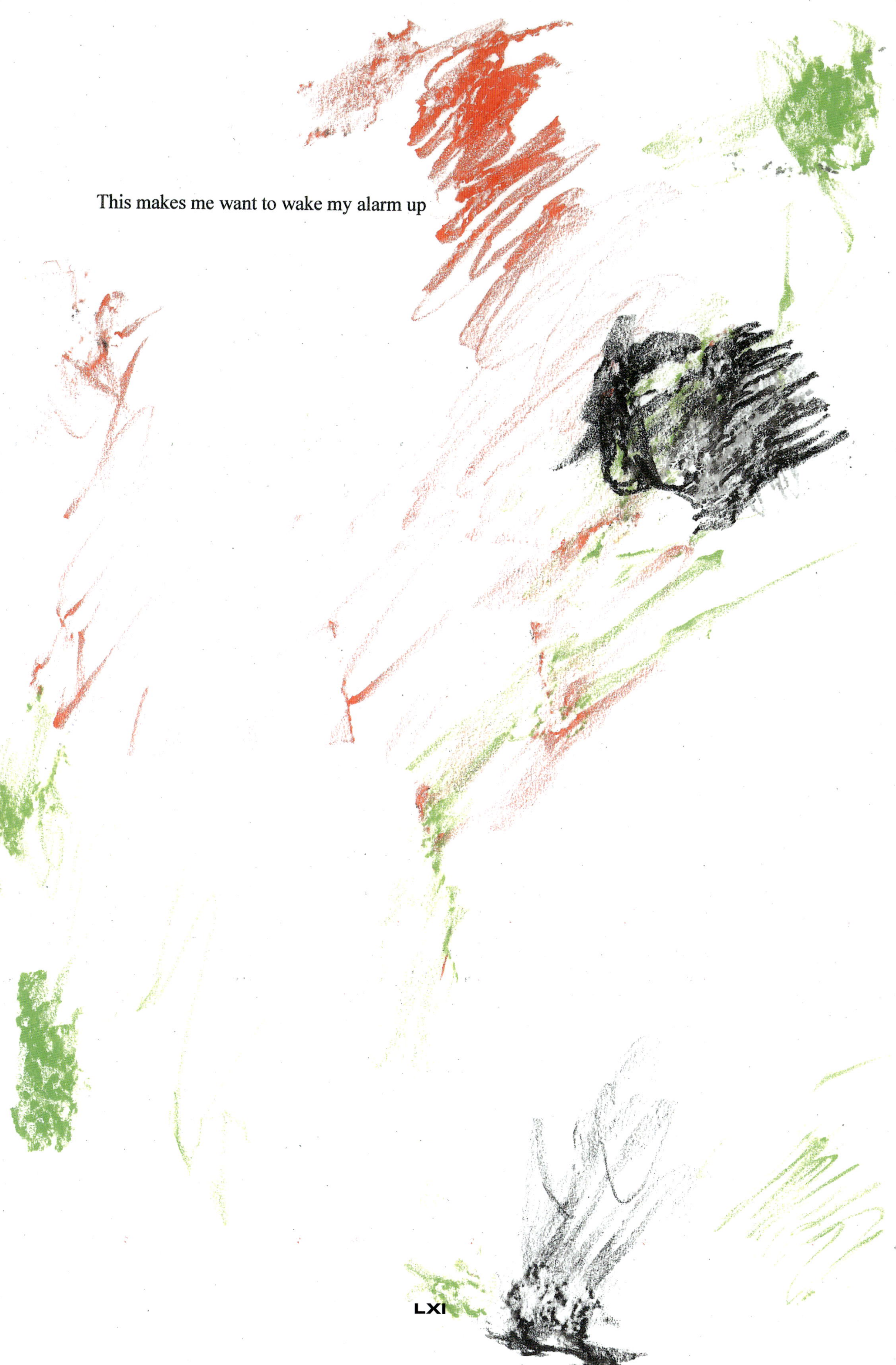
This makes me want to wake my alarm up
LXI

Seventy-four

Ronya Othmann

August 2014, I'm sitting in front of the television. I see women dressed like my grandmother, my aunt, my cousins; I see men like my grandfather, my uncle, my cousins running for their lives. Summer is at its height. In the mountains, infants, old people and the sick are dying of thirst. Shingal is surrounded. They kill the men and the older women, who have not managed to flee; they take the younger women and the children as spoils of war, selling them on at the slave markets for ISIS fighters. Women with the same name as me, as my sister, my cousin.

I can't remember August 2014 any more. Later on, I write: I'm sitting in front of the television. Because I know I was sitting in front of the television. I also know what I saw. But I can't remember what it was I saw any longer. I'm writing about how I'm sitting on the sofa in my parent's living room, that I don't take a shower or eat anything, until I realize how long it's been since I've done that. Each piece of writing is fiction to me. Whether I'm writing about myself, my father, my grandmother or a figure to whom I give a name and a story.

In 2014, I saw the Yazidi MP, Vian Dakhil, speaking before the Iraqi parliament, saw how she was trying to capture in words what happened in Shingal and then collapsed in the middle of her speech and was carried out of the chamber by two women MP's. I saw on Kurdish television the presenter and the commenting reporter, who, instead of reporting about Shingal, both began weeping.

The speechlessness is manifest here. In the face of the atrocities, and I cross out the word atrocities in the face of the crimes and I cross out the word crimes, because neither the word atrocities nor the word crimes are enough. In the face of what happened in Shingal in 2014, and what the United Nations and the European Parliament later called genocide, words fail.

Later I'm writing: I leave the aircraft, go down the steps, the hot air hits me. I breathe in the first draught of it, like I breathed as a child, long and deeply. I'm also writing: home, although I don't know if that's true. Passport control. I put my German passport on the table. The official smiles when he reads my name. He pronounces it as it is spoken in my family. Ronya with a soft "r" and a drawn-out "o". Uncle Xalef is waiting for me on the carpark. We embrace. We drive out of the city, a four-lane road. On the lefthand side, Ainkawa with its church towers, on the righthand, Erbil with the minarets. Past Nechirvan Barzani's palace. The city stops. Then mountains. We pass one checkpoint after another. I stop counting. The photos of the martyrs on the side of the road. I write: larger than life and I mean gigantic. Sometime or other we stop at a reservoir. We get out, drink tea and smoke. We're standing by the reservoir. Young people are racing across the lake in motorboats. Uncle Xalef takes a photo of me. We're sitting in the car again. I'm thinking what I've already thought on the plane, that I'm not just home but also in the country where they killed Yazidis because they were Yazidis.

You're hungry, Aunt Adar says. There is flatbread, meat with paprika, tomatoes in a dressing and lettuce on the table. Dew with mint to drink. We eat, Uncle Xalef, Aunt Adar, my cousins, the girls Lava and Lara, and the boy, Lorans, and I. We tear pieces out of the bread, reach across the table. I write: I have missed eating like this. I take a photo of the water melons and send it to my father.
After the food, tea, then sweets, then biscuits, then fruit. Salted sunflower seeds. Arabian coffee. Eat, eat, says Aunt Adar. I'm full, I say, and carry on eating. She once had guests, so she says, an old man. He broke out in tears at the meal. When she asked him what was the matter, he said it tasted like at his mother's.

We drive to the Ashti Camp, about half an hour from Sulaymaniyah, on the Iranian border. I'm writing I'm sitting next to Lara and Lava on the back seat. Lara and Lava are in a bad mood and are looking out of the window. Lara says, she doesn't want to, they're always driving us into the camp. We get closer, turn off, gravel road in the middle of a wide and flat landscape surrounded by mountains. Under the blue morning sky, there is a checkpoint. They know us here and wave us through. It's not until we drive into the camp that I see it is actually two camps, which are divided off from each other by a broad road and fences down the middle. On our side is the Yazidi-Kurdish camp, and on the other the Arab-Muslim one. We visit friends in the camp, drink tea and go further. In one tent, there are two boys, perhaps seven or eight years old, who are sitting there mutely, more so than I have ever seen before in children of their age. Their mother, who shows me photos of their abducted father, of her abducted daughter and breaks out in loud weeping. My cousin, who is sitting next to me and picks up her mother's smartphone and looks fixedly at cat videos. And I, who pulls down the arms of my jacket over my wrists when I see that the woman and her children are wearing the same watch as I am. Look at this woman, says my aunt and points to a woman, who is sitting in the corner of the tent, with her white hair, white headscarf and dress. Her shoulders and her head drawn in. I can scarcely see her face. Since ISIS came into her village, this old woman has not spoken one word. And not only not spoken any more, she couldn't be spoken to any more. Speechlessness has inscribed itself into this woman's body. She does not look up, not when we enter the tent, not when we're sitting there and not when we go. In her left hand, she is holding—something I only see when we say goodbye—a pebble.

A few days later, we visit our family's Sheikh. The Sheikh relates the story of a boy who was seven when ISIS fighters cut his father's head off in front of him, after the latter refused to convert to Islam. They force the head of his father into the seven-year-old's hands and say, now you've seen what we've done with your father, you'll convert to Islam.

The Sheikh pauses briefly and then relates a second story. After the second story, he relates a third. After the third story, he falls silent and then says, we could sit here for twenty-four hours, and I could relate such stories to you twenty-four hours long.

The MP, who collapsed during her speech, the reporters, who began to weep, the old woman, who turned mute, and the Sheikh who said, he could carry on relating for twenty-four hours, without coming to an end, show that there are no words for what happened in August 2014. Even assembling the facts, counting the dead, even the date, 8/3/2014, or the 74th Ferman, as we Yazidis call the genocide, are all a placeholder for something, for which we have no words.

The speechlessness underlies the language, even when a text exists. The speechlessness structures the written text, determines its grammar, its form, its words. I'm writing: I've been in a landscape. In the landscape was a camp. In the camp was a tent and in the tent, an old woman. And in the old woman's hand was a pebble.

I'm writing: I've seen. The "I" is a witness. It speaks, yet it has no language.

We take the car up the mountain behind the city. Twenty minutes, then we're at the top. We stand on the mountain and take photos. Twilight. The light is fading, and the city at our feet is illuminated with streetlights, neon signs, cars. On the way back, we stop at a kiosk beside the road. What would you like to drink, Uncle Xalef asks. We've everything you want. Beer, wine, whisky, vodka and raki!

This isn't Erbil, this isn't Duhok or Bagdhad. This is Sulaymaniyah. Sulaymaniyah is free and safe, Uncle Xalef says. Tourists come from all over the country. They're brought here in buses from Bagdhad. They're running away from the heat. We sit in the living room, smoke, drink beer from cans and eat salted sunflower seeds. We don't tell anyone we're Yazidis, says Aunt Adar. No-one here knows we're Yazidis.

On her cellphone, Aunt Adar shows me photos of people she knows. She swipes from right to left with her finger and says, she lost her hearing in captivity. Then she swipes again, the next picture, but I'm not looking at the picture, I'm looking at her hand, at her fingers, with the roughened skin from the housework, with her wedding ring. She says, they beheaded her husband and her sons in front of her. And swipes again. Next picture. I look briefly, then look away. She says, they blinded him, and swipes again.

I'm writing: if Aunt Adar, Uncle Xalef, Lava, Lara and Lorans hadn't lived in Sulaymaniyah in 2014, but 400 kilometres further in Shingal, and don't finish writing the sentence.

The house of Koçere and Sadun is an empty house. Have you enough blankets, Koçere asks, when I lie down to sleep alongside Lava and Lara. I'd like to give you more blankets, Koçere says, but ISIS has got mine. The car that saved Koçere and her family in 2014 is standing in front of the house. But her son with the driver's license is on the way to Germany with his wife. They've left the child here. It's too little, Koçere says. She doesn't say anything about the route. She only says: Germany.

When Koçere and her family fled from Shingal in 2014, they moved onto a building site. What they lived in was a shell, without windows and doors until the family, meaning our family—Sadun and us, we're related—sent money, and they could move into this empty house. Sadun says, in Duhok we're safe, but people don't buy anything from Yazidis. People say that what the Yazidis sell isn't clean.

When we go to bed, Sadun takes a pistol from the little cupboard and puts it next to his pillow. Nobody looks up, and it is not the first weapon I'm seeing. I can remember the Kalashnikov, with which my Uncle Hemo in Newroz was shooting into the air. But the way Sadun takes the pistol out of the little cupboard, as if it were a toothbrush. I say to Aunt Adar, why does Sadun have a pistol, and Aunt Adar laughs, ah, Ronya, she says, it's only twenty minutes from here to Mosul.

Koçere shuts the doors, she leaves the key in the lock. I wake up in the night, once, twice, because the child has begun crying. Then it's morning, we sit outside and have breakfast.

After eating, we drive to a cemetery, and in the middle of the cemetery is a shrine. In front of the shrine, we meet Sheikh Hassan. It's an old cemetery, some graves are several hundred years old, says Sheikh Hassan. You can make out little birds on the weathered gravestones, ships and other engraved ornamentation. It's the first time I've seen such a thing. In my grandparents' village, you kept your Yazidi identity hidden. You would never have dared to build a Yazidi temple, recognizable from a distance, with the typical conical roof and the sun emblem at the peak. I've never seen such gravestones either. ISIS is reported to have destroyed 92 Yazidi sites. And not only our sites but also the memory of them ever having existed. Time and time again, I've watched the video of how they move through the museum in Mosul with pneumatic hammers and sledgehammers, topple one statue after another from their plinths, destroy what has lasted for more than two thousand years. I knew when the music comes in, when the image falters, when the the fighters draw back their sledgehammers, synchronically, and freeze in mid-movement, pound the fallen statues at their feet with their hammers in slow motion, until the video is running at normal tempo again. So much the less can I believe what I'm now seeing before me. These gravestones bear witness to us having been here for a long time. That our ancestors already lived in this landscape, tended their fields, raised sheep and buried their dead in this earth.

Much of what I'm writing has no order. Sentences, words that break off, run away into nothingness. I put things together. That something begins with capitals and ends with a full stop. In between a comma perhaps, a half sentence that refers to what has just been said. Capitals again, subject, verb, object up to the next full stop. Paragraph by paragraph. I've no language for writing in. I've saved my journey in document files in my laptop, the sound recordings in my cellphone. I look at a documentary. A man from the Commission for International Justice and Accountability says ISIS advanced into Shingal on three fronts. Two fronts from the south, one out of Syria, from the north. Here they start to round up the Yazidis, the man says and points to a map. They separate the men from the women. It's the same pattern in every occupied village.

I'm reading: "the notorious ISIS executioner, Jihadi John", I'm reading: "sex slaves of ISIS", "ISIS wives". I don't read perpetrators. I don't read survivors. I say, I have to think about the interview that the Canadian radio presenter did with Nadia Murad. I have to think about how the presenter asked Nadia Murad how it feels when you are treated like an object? How did you feel when they used you like that? How did they share you out and what did they do to you? Did they beat you? And then you were raped. They repeatedly grabbed you. How did you bear all that?

That, I say to my mother is what they want to hear. Then they don't need to go to the movies any more, I say. My father says, when the ox collapses, there are a lot of knives.

I'm sitting with Aunt Adar and Uncle Xalef on their sofa, the laptop on my knees, the earphones on my ears. I'm writing: Xatê says, welcome among the Yazidis. I'm writing: Xatê receives us in uniform. She got the day off. But as a general, she's only allowed to talk to us in uniform. I sit next to her parents in the living room. I'm writing: it's a bare living room; like most of the living rooms I was in, it's the living room of refugees. Xatê says, I'm also a daughter of Shingal. I was born in Shingal, she says. You know what happened on 8/3/2014, when ISIS came. We were trapped in the mountains for twelve days, says Xatê. I'm sitting and writing: Xatê says, I heard about a woman from Koço. She was abducted with her child. They kept her captive for three days and three nights on the airfield in Tal Afar. The child was young, it was still at the breast, it wasn't a year old. The child was hungry and screamed. For three days, Xatê says: the child screamed so loudly that ISIS amir could not sleep. The amir said to the woman, give me the child, then it will stop crying. The woman gave him the child, because she thought, he would give it something to eat and drink. The amir took the child and went with it to the kitchen. In the kitchen, he took a big knife and cut the child's head off. He cooked the child's flesh and presented it to the mother. The mother did not immediately understand, says Xatê, until she saw the child's hand. She lost her mind.

I'm sitting on the sofa at Aunt Adar and Uncle Xalef's place. I'm writing that that was the last thing the mother understood before she lost her mind. I stop the recording.

Whilst Xatê is talking, she begins to weep. Tears run down her face; Xatê goes on speaking. I'm writing: Xatê is stting in her uniform and weeping. And while Xatê is sitting her in her uniform and weeping, I begin weeping too. And again, when I'm sitting on the sofa, play the recording back and write: Xatê is weeping.

Xatê says: I was a singer, like my father. She shows us a video on YouTube. Uploaded on 4/9/2013, sixteen months before ISIS came to Shingal. Xatê is wearing a red dress and jewelry. She is sitting with her saz and playing and singing, the mountains of Shingal behind her. Xatê begins weeping again. I'm writing: Xatê is weeping.

Xatê says: I had a lot of CD's, but I've left them behind. Xatê says: after we fled from Shingal, I said to my parents, I don't want a saz any more, I want a rocket. Xatê shows us a second video. Xatê with her unit, on the border to Mosul. They're kneeling behind sandbags and pointing their weapons into the wide landscape. Xatê is singing.

There is one point in the recording, when Faruk says to Xatê, I'm a Yazidi too. After Faruk has said that, Xatê wants to know what family I hail from. I say, my father is a Yazidi, from Hasake, we're Murid, Xatltî, from Xûdan der Mend, I say. My mother is German, I say. Xatê stands up, goes to the door and calls out, is anyone bringing us some tea. Xatê looks at me, otherwise you'll tell them in Germany, you were at Xatê's and didn't even get any tea.

Xatê calls me sister. Xatê says, you are a sister too. Are you hungry, Xatê asks, We have to go, says Faruk. I switch off the recorder. It's already late, Faruk says, and we've still got to go to Duhok today. I stand up and kiss the hands of Xatê's mother and Xatê's father.

I've often wondered why they do that to us. How can they do such things. But that is not a question. When I was walking through Kivax with Cana, I asked myself that. Past the ruins, which were once her village and past the three-legged dog, which was still here for some reason. And was sitting in front of the old school house and raised its head, looked at us as we walked past it.

When the Turkish soldiers were still here and were guarding the empty village, so that PKK fighters couldn't hide in the ruins. And Cana pointed to the hill behind the village, where the sacred trees stood until a year ago. Whether they came in the day or at night, the Turkish soldiers must have seen them. Why, I ask Cana, isn't it enough for them that there aren't any Yazidis here anymore. What did these trees do to them.

Not that they were interested in the wood, the felled trunks were still lying there, next to the stumps. Just that they, then, came here sometime, one day or one night, and the Turkish soldiers guarding the village day and night watched how they felled the sacred trees.

I wondered, after we'd been in the camp, and I was sitting back at Uncle Xalef and Aunt Adar's place on the Hollywood swing and looking for cigarettes in my bag, my lighter and still doing that a while after I'd found it. When I was sitting in Lalish on the flat roof in front of the temple, eating sandwiches with Sheikh Hassan, Faruk and the children from the Kaniya sipi school, and Faruk is saying, the girl next to you had been sold. She'd been sold this or that many times. I've forgotten the number, and the girl and I are eating our sandwiches. The boy sitting opposite you, says Faruk, they beheaded his father before his eyes. Since he's been teaching the children, he can't sleep any more at night, the Sheikh says. Faruk says, what is that, cutting off a head. Why do they do that, cut off a head.

My mother says, they are really brutal, so brutal. And she takes a breath and says, that, with this brutality, my mother is saying, with this brutality, and is looking for some comparison, by which you can measure this brutality. But, my mother takes a breath and is saying, really. They are not human beings, says my father. Someone who does something like that is not a human being. How can someone who does such a thing be a human being. No, my father is saying, they're not human beings.

My mother's friend, she's a Christian from Mosul,—we visit her in Erbil—says, she knows a woman, a doctor and a Sunni, who was working in the Mosul hospital. My mother's friend says that they brought the doctor a Yasidi girl, nine years old, whom they had repeatedly raped, so that it was so badly injured. And when the doctor saw the girl, she said, how could you do something like that. And that they, following her question, which wasn't a question, beheaded the doctor.

They think they are going to paradise, my mother says.

In March 2019, after ISIS has been defeated militarily, the suicide attempts in the camps increase. I say to my mother on the phone, we're dead. They've destroyed us. I'm in the university canteen. I take the quick service plate. I sit down at a table. I'm eating and I'm alone. I want to go to the library after lunch. I'm reading the news on my cellphone. A special unit of the British army has found the heads of 50 Yazidi women. They found the heads in garbage bins. I get up and bring my tray to the dirty dishes return. On my way to the library, I ring up my mother, it doesn't make sense, I say. Why, they've been defeated and the last thing they do, when it's long been clear they can't win, they're defeated, is to behead Yazidi women. Right up to their end, they didn't stop destroying us.

I'm saying, the Yazidis are destroyed. My mother is saying, you can't say that. That's something you can't say. You can't say it like this. I'm saying, we're the ones who are still there. When they came to Shingal to destroy us, I'm saying, we were in Europe. When they came to murder my great-grandfather, I wasn't born. But my grandmother was already born. If my grandmother hadn't been

213

born by then, I wouldn't be here. They came to Shingal to destroy all Yazidis. We were in Europe, when they came to Shingal. We're the ones they haven't killed. We're not alive. We've just not been killed, I say. That's the difference, I say. The others are there, because they're there, they're alive but not, because they weren't killed.

I'm saying, our relatives from Shingal are alive because they had a car. But, between being alive and living, there is a difference. The question about the why is not a question. It is formulated speechlessness. I can't answer it. If I could answer it, I'd have to either be ISIS or I'd be ISIS speaking or I'd speak like ISIS or ISIS was speaking through me. Because we're infidels, Kafir, would be the answer. And because that is not an answer to it. And the question about the why not a question. I have to think about how my grandmother was, to her dying day, asking herself why they murdered her father. What had he done for them to murder him. And I, when she asked that, was thinking right up to her death, nothing. He hadn't done anything. There is no reason for it. And because my grandmother's question wasn't a question, I said nothing.

We drive up onto a hill behind Xhanke with Faruk. You can see the Mosul dam from up on the hill. And the Mosul dam is lying there—I say how beautiful—in the twilight.

Blue water, lights on the other side. ISIS was over there, Faruk says, the Mosul dam, the border. We park behind a Yazidi shrine, white stone and sun emblem on the roof peak. How beautiful, I say. I take a photo. That they were firing across here in 2014. And only the Mosul dam between the Yazidi village and ISIS. So narrow, that you can see across it. Faruk goes towards a wall. The branches of an olive tree reach over it. Faruk shifts the barbed wire, which serves as a door here, to one side. Because of the animals, he says, the graves of my uncles. He switches on his cellphone torch and shines it on the gravestones.

It's not the first time that Faruk has shown me graves. And Faruk is not the only one. Sometime or other we'll have more dead here than living. And already, sometime or other is almost now. My great-grandparents' garden in Tel Khatoun has burned down. The trees my father planted too. What was once a home is a battlefield trench today. Somebody sent my aunt photos and a video: someone is going through our garden. From one fence to the other, the picture wobbles, it hisses. My mother is showing it to me on her cellphone and saying, those were the trees your father planted forty years ago. My father is saying, how many years it's taken for these trees to grow so tall.

Someone also sent us a video of the hill where they buried my grandmother. That no-one from the family could be there, that we couldn't bury her. And my cousin drove with the coffin, in which my grandmother lay, into Turkey, as far as the Syrian border, where people took over the dead woman, for a little money, so that my grandmother could be buried on the hill next to my grandfather.

When I'm standing at the graves of Faruk's uncles, and he's lighting up the gravestones with the torch, I wonder if I'd one day stand like this at my grand-parents' grave. And kiss their gravestones, as Faruk does now.

I have to think about how I stood behind the garden fence in my grandparents' village and watched the trucks, which were driving along the Turkish border into Iraq or were coming out of Iraq. That they travelled along the roads I travelled along too, were in the towns, where I was too. Kobanê, Raqqa, Palmyra.

That's all, I'm thinking. Along the roads with the trucks, turn off once, towards Bajid, across the Tigris, which is a narrow arm here and not as wide as the Mosul dam. And also on the other side of the border. I can remember trips, with the family, how my father as a schoolboy had already taken trips to the Tigris. How we, my siblings, my cousins and I, played on the bank, ate kebabs in a restaurant. There are photos of it, which my uncle took of us. It could've all happened so quickly, I'm thinking, as I stand in Derabûn and look at the road. Twelve kilometres. How far are twelve kilometres. Fifteen minutes perhaps. We would have been sitting at breakfast, as we are doing now, in the house of Faruk's cousin, we would have drunk tea, in a house like this one, only twelve kilometres further, in 2014.

In September 2018, I fly to Izmir and further east. I'm writing: I want to visit the village where my grandmother grew up and from which my family was driven away, when she was still a child. The surrounded us, my father says, they wanted to kill us. Our family fled overnight, left everything behind, first to Shingal, then to Syria. I'm writing: my grandmother had to flee four times. The last time in 2014, and every time because she was a Yazidi. I'm writing: whoever flees once, is always fleeing. My grandmother is sitting in my parents' house. When we give her something to eat, she says, you want to poison me. When she goes upstairs, she says, look out, they've set a trap for us. She says, we're surrounded.

I ring up my father and say I'm going to Bazîvan.
I say I can't find it on Google Maps, My father says, I'll write to you, when I've found out the Turkish name. My mother rings me up and says, my father said Cîndî was there a few years ago. He said Muslims are now living in the village. If you say you're a Yazidi, they'll kill you. My mother says, you mustn't tell anyone that you're a Yazidi. My father writes, I've found out what the village is called. My mother says, Uncle Hemo gave me a phone number, of a Hadjji. My father says, the Hadjji is a Sunni, but our ancestors knew each other. I'm in Diyarbakir when my father rings up and says, the Hadjji's been told. He said, you don't have to be afraid.

215

Malan barkir lê lê çûne waran lê
Dînê lê dînê lê Dînara min
Goştê me xwar lê lê mişk û maran lê
Dînê lê dînê lê Dînara min
Goştê me xwar lê lê mişk û maran lê
Kecê lê rîndê lê Hewala min
Ez sewî me lo lo ber desta me lo
Hewalo hewalo hewalê min
Brîndar im lo lo bê xwedî me lo
Hewalo hewalo hewalê min
Brîndar im lo lo bê xwedî me lo
Delalo delalo delalê min
Malan bar kir lê lê koç bi rê ket lê

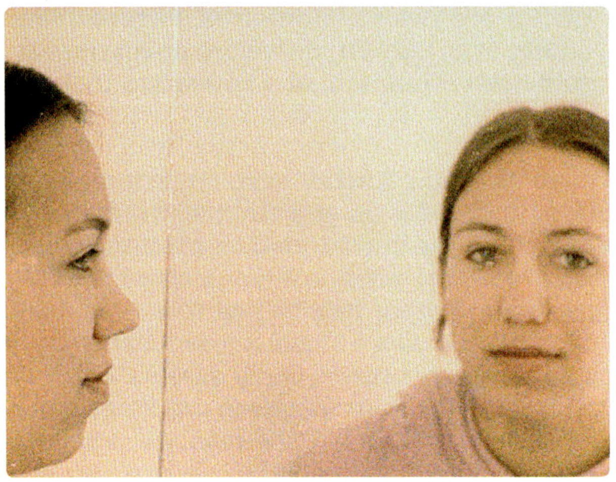

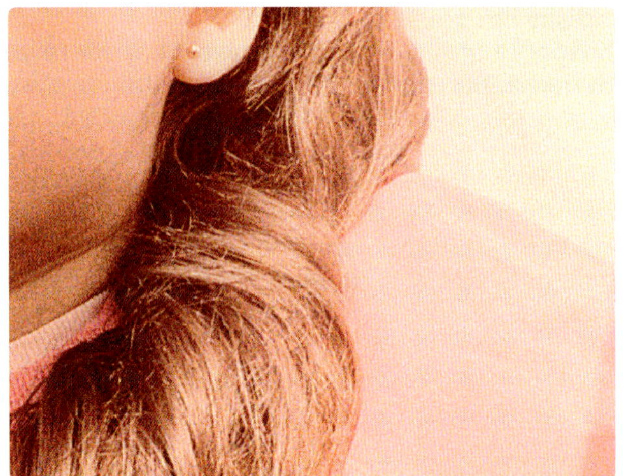

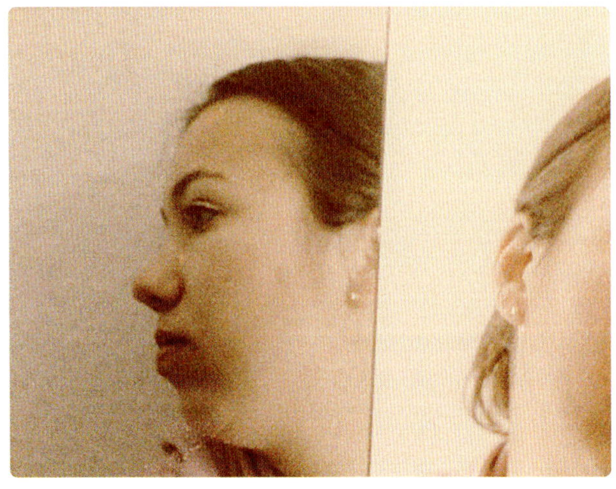

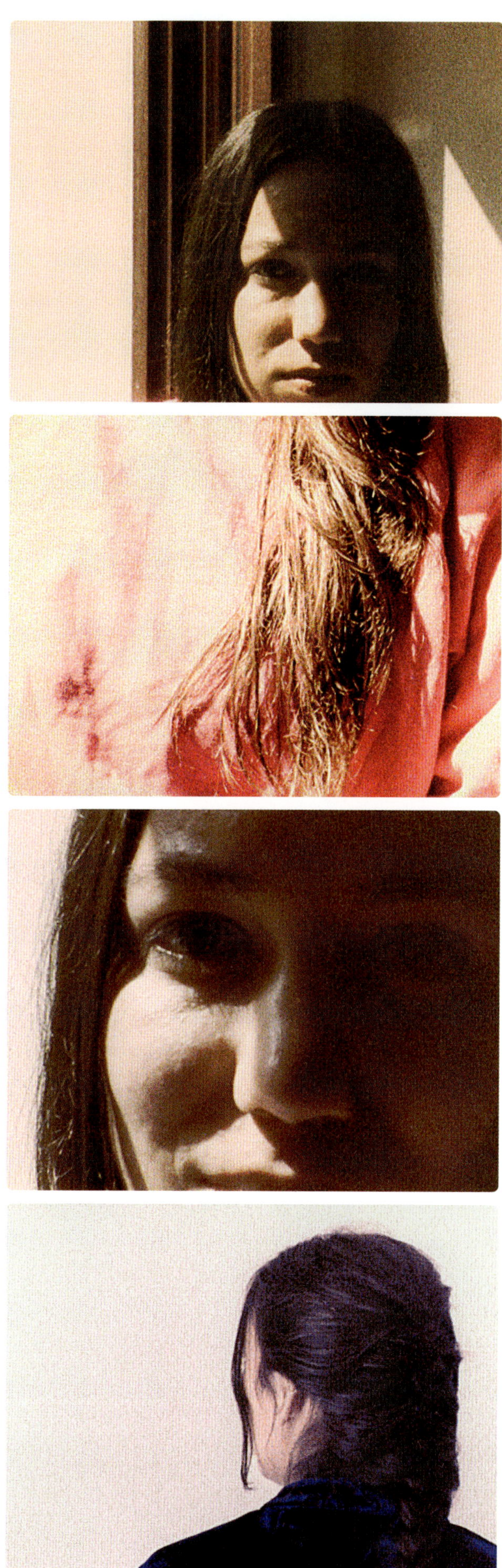

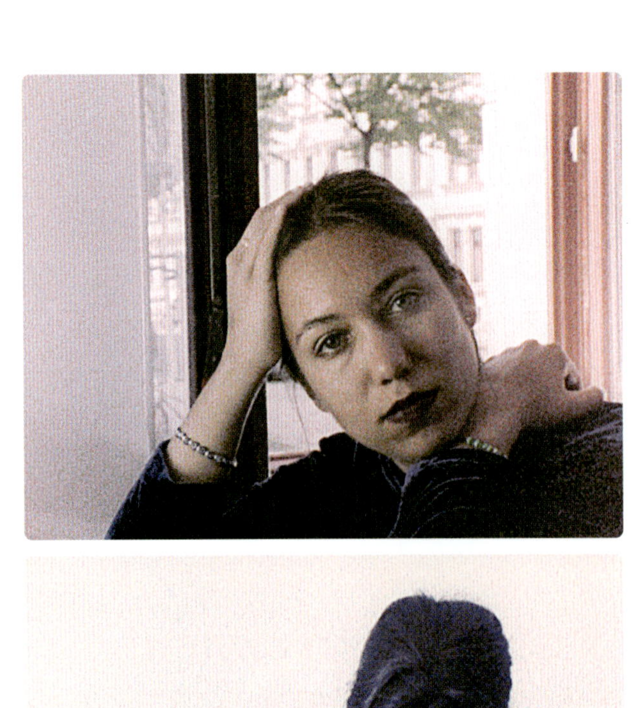

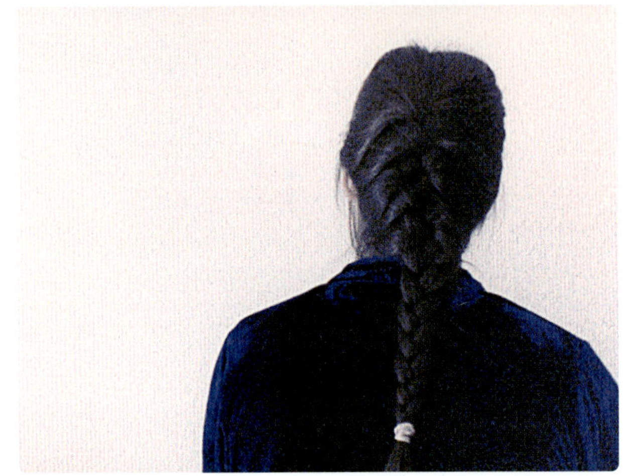

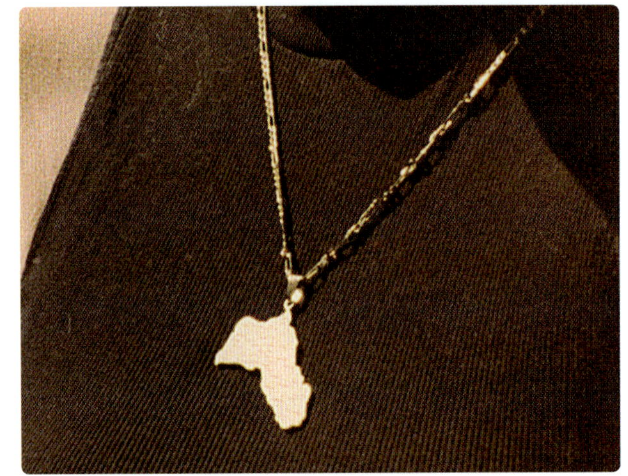

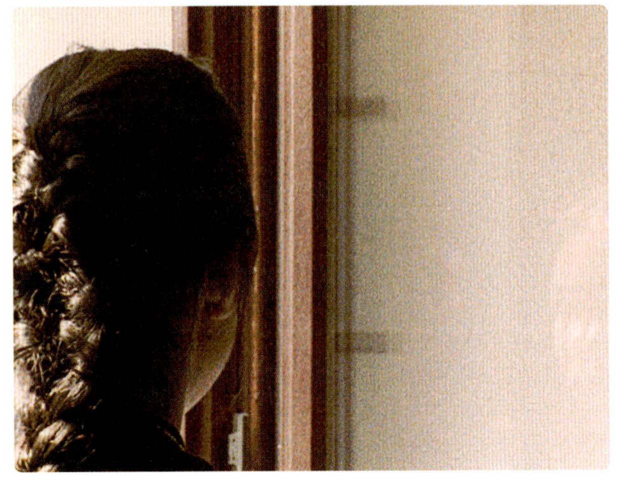

Vierundsiebzig

Ronya Othmann

August 2014 sitze ich vor dem Fernseher. Ich sehe Frauen in den Kleidern meiner Großmutter, meiner Tante, meiner Cousinen, sehe Männer wie meinen Großvater, meinen Vater, Onkel, meine Cousins um ihr Leben rennen. Es ist Hochsommer. In den Bergen verdursten Kleinkinder, Alte, Kranke. Shingal ist umzingelt. Die Männer und die älteren Frauen, die es nicht schaffen zu fliehen, töten sie, die jüngeren Frauen und Kinder nehmen sie mit als Kriegsbeute, verkaufen sie weiter auf den Sklavenmärkten für die Kämpfer des IS. Frauen, die meinen Namen tragen, den meiner Schwester, meiner Cousine.

An den August 2014 kann ich mich nicht mehr erinnern. Später schreibe ich, ich sitze vor dem Fernseher. Weil ich weiß, dass ich vor dem Fernseher saß. Ich weiß auch, was ich sah. Aber an das, was ich sah, kann ich mich nicht mehr erinnern.

Ich schreibe, wie ich auf dem Sofa im Wohnzimmer meiner Eltern sitze, dass ich erst dusche oder esse, wenn mir auffällt, wie lange ich es nicht mehr getan habe.
Jedes Schreiben ist für mich Fiktion. Ob ich über mich schreibe, meinen Vater, meine Großmutter oder eine Figur, der ich einen Namen gebe und eine Geschichte.

2014 habe ich die êzîdische Abgeordnete Vian Dakhil bei ihrer Rede vor dem irakischen Parlament gesehen, wie sie versuchte, das, was in Shingal geschah, in Worte zu fassen, dann mitten in ihrer Rede zusammenbrach und von zwei Parlamentarierinnen aus dem Saal getragen wurde.
Ich habe den Moderator und den zugeschalteten Reporter im kurdischen Fernsehen gesehen, die, anstatt von Shingal zu berichten, zu weinen anfingen.
Die Sprachlosigkeit ist hier offensichtlich. Angesichts der Gräueltaten und ich streiche das Wort Gräueltaten angesichts der Verbrechen und ich streiche das Wort Verbrechen, weil sowohl das Wort Gräueltaten als auch das Wort Verbrechen nicht tragen. Angesichts dessen, was 2014 in Shingal geschah und was die Vereinten Nationen und das Europäische Parlament später Völkermord nannten, versagt die Sprache.

Später schreibe ich: Ich steige aus dem Flugzeug, gehe die Treppe hinunter, heiße Luft schlägt mir entgegen. Ich atme, wie ich als Kind geatmet habe, den ersten Atemzug, lang und tief.
Ich schreibe auch: zuhause, obwohl ich nicht weiß, ob das stimmt.
Passkontrolle. Ich lege meinen deutschen Pass auf den Tisch. Der Beamte lächelt, als er meinen Namen liest. Er spricht ihn aus, wie er in meiner Familie ausgesprochen wird. Ronya mit weichem R und langem O.
Onkel Xalef wartet auf dem Parkplatz auf mich. Wir umarmen uns.
Wir fahren aus der Stadt, eine vierspurige Straße. Auf der linken Seite Ainkawa mit seinen Kirchtürmen, auf der rechten Erbil mit den Minaretten. Am Palast von Nêçîrvan Barzanî vorbei. Die Stadt endet. Dann Berge. Wir passieren Checkpoint um Checkpoint. Ich höre auf zu zählen. Am Straßenrand die Fotos der Märtyrer. Ich schreibe: überlebensgroß, und meine riesig.
Irgendwann halten wir an einem Stausee. Wir steigen aus, trinken Tee und rauchen. Wir stehen am Stausee. Jugendliche rasen in Motorbooten über den See. Onkel Xalef macht ein Foto von mir.
Wir sitzen wieder im Auto. Ich denke das, was ich im Flugzeug schon gedacht habe, dass ich nicht nur zuhause bin, sondern, in dem Land, in dem man Ezîden tötete, weil sie Ezîden waren.

Du hast sicher Hunger, sagt Tante Adar. Auf dem Tisch steht Fladenbrot, Fleisch mit Paprika, Tomaten in Soße und Salat. Zum Trinken Dew mit Minze.
Wir essen, Onkel Xalef, Tante Adar, meine Cousinen Lava und Lara und mein Cousin Lorans und ich. Wir reißen das Brot in Stücke, greifen über den Tisch. Ich schreibe: ich habe es vermisst, so zu essen. Ich mache ein Foto von den Wassermelonen und schicke es meinem Vater.
Nach dem Essen Tee, dann Bonbons, dann Kekse, dann Obst. Gesalzene Sonnenblumenkerne. Arabischer Kaffee. Iss, iss, sagt Tante Adar. Ich bin satt, sage ich und esse weiter. Einmal habe sie Gäste gehabt, sagt sie, ein alter Mann. Er sei beim Essen in Tränen ausgebrochen. Als sie fragte, was los sei, habe er gesagt, es schmecke wie bei seiner Mutter.

Wir fahren in das Camp Ashti, etwa eine halbe Stunde von Sulaymaniyah entfernt, an der iranischen Grenze. Ich schreibe, ich sitze neben Lara und Lava auf der Rückbank. Lara und Lava sind schlecht gelaunt und sehen aus dem Fenster. Lara sagt, sie habe keine Lust, ständig würden sie ins Camp fahren. Wir nähern uns, eine Straße, biegen ab, Schotterweg, inmitten einer weiten flachen, von Bergen umgebenen Landschaft. Unter dem blauen Vormittagshimmel ein Checkpoint. Man kennt uns hier und winkt uns durch. Erst als wir durch das Camp fahren, sehe ich, dass es eigentlich zwei Camps sind, die in der Mitte durch eine breite Straße und Zäune voneinander abgetrennt sind. Auf unserer Seite, das êzîdisch-kurdische Camp und auf der anderen, das arabisch-muslimische.
Wir besuchen Freunde im Camp, trinken Tee und gehen weiter.
In einem der Zelte zwei Jungen, vielleicht sieben oder acht Jahre alt, die so stumm dasitzen, wie ich es bei Kindern in ihrem Alter noch nie gesehen habe. Ihre Mutter, die mir die Fotos ihres verschleppten Vaters, ihrer verschleppten Tochter zeigt und in ein lautes Weinen ausbricht. Meine Cousine, die neben mir sitzt und das Smartphone ihrer Mutter in die Hand nimmt und sich angestrengt Katzenvideos ansieht. Und ich, die sich die Ärmel der Jacke über das Handgelenk zieht, nachdem ich sehe, dass die Frau und ihre Kinder dasselbe Armband tragen wie ich.
Sieh dir diese Frau an, sagt meine Tante und zeigt auf eine Frau, die in der Ecke des Zeltes sitzt mit weißem Haar, weißem Kopftuch und Kleid. Die Schultern, der Kopf eingesunken. Ich kann ihr Gesicht kaum sehen. Seitdem der IS in ihr Dorf kam, hat diese alte Frau kein einziges Wort mehr gesprochen. Und nicht nur nicht mehr gesprochen, sie war auch nicht mehr ansprechbar.
Die Sprachlosigkeit hat sich in den Körper dieser Frau eingeschrieben. Sie sieht kein einziges Mal auf, nicht als wir das Zelt betreten, nicht als wir sitzen und nicht als wir gehen. In ihrer linken Hand hält sie, und das sehe ich erst, als wir uns verabschieden, einen Kieselstein.

Ein paar Tage später sind wir bei dem Sheikh unserer Familie zu Besuch. Der Sheikh erzählt die Geschichte von einem Jungen, der sieben Jahre alt war, als IS-Kämpfer seinen Vater vor seinen Augen köpften, nachdem dieser sich geweigert hatte, zum Islam überzutreten. Dem siebenjährigen Jungen drücken sie den Kopf seines Vaters in die Hand und sagen, nun da du gesehen hast, was wir mit deinem Vater gemacht haben, willst du zum Islam übertreten.
Der Sheikh macht eine kurze Pause und erzählt dann eine zweite Geschichte. Nach der zweiten Geschichte erzählt er eine dritte. Nach der dritten Geschichte verstummt er und sagt, vierundzwanzig Stunden können wir hier sitzen und ich könnte euch vierundzwanzig Stunden solche Geschichten erzählen.

Die Parlamentarierin, die bei ihrer Rede zusammengebrochen ist, die Reporter, die angefangen haben zu weinen, die alte Frau, die verstummt war, und der Sheikh, der sagte, er könnte vierundzwanzig Stunden weiter erzählen, ohne zu einem Ende zu kommen, zeigen, dass es keine Sprache gibt für das, was im August 2014 geschah. Selbst das Aneinanderreihen der Fakten, das Zählen der Toten, selbst das Datum 3.8.2014, oder der 74. Ferman, wie wir Ezîden den Genozid nennen, bleibt ein Platzhalter für etwas, wofür wir keine Worte haben.
Die Sprachlosigkeit liegt noch unter der Sprache, selbst wenn ein Text da ist.
Die Sprachlosigkeit strukturiert den geschrieben Text, legt seine Grammatik fest, seine Form, seine Worte.

Ich schreibe: Ich bin in einer Landschaft gewesen. In der Landschaft war ein Camp. In dem Camp ein Zelt und in dem Zelt eine alte Frau. Und in der Hand der alten Frau war ein Kieselstein.
Ich schreibe: Ich habe gesehen. Das Ich ist ein Zeuge. Es spricht und doch hat es keine Sprache.

Wir fahren mit dem Auto den Berg hinter der Stadt hinauf. Zwanzig Minuten, dann sind wir oben.
Wir stehen auf dem Berg und machen Fotos. Abenddämmerung. Das Licht schwindet, und die Stadt zu unseren Füßen erleuchtet von Straßenlaternen, Leuchtreklamen, Autos.
Auf dem Rückweg halten wir an einem Kiosk am Straßenrand. Was willst du trinken, fragt Onkel Xalef. Wir haben alles, was du willst. Bier, Wein, Whisky, Wodka und Raki!
Das ist nicht Erbil, das ist nicht Duhok oder Bagdad. Das ist Sulaymaniyah. Sulaymaniyah ist frei und sicher, sagt Onkel Xalef. Aus dem ganzen Land kommen Touristen. Aus Bagdad werden sie in Bussen hierhergebracht. Sie fliehen vor der Hitze.
Wir sitzen im Wohnzimmer, rauchen, trinken Dosenbier und essen gesalzene Sonnenblumenkerne.
Niemandem sagen wir, dass wir Ezîden sind, sagt Tante Adar. Niemand hier weiß, dass wir Ezîden sind.

Tante Adar zeigt mir auf ihrem Handy Fotos von Leuten, die sie kennt. Sie wischt mit dem Finger von rechts nach links und sagt, sie hat ihr Gehör verloren in der Gefangenschaft. Dann wischt sie wieder, nächstes Bild, aber ich sehe nicht auf das Bild, ich sehe auf ihre Hand, auf ihre Finger, mit der von der Hausarbeit rissigen Haut, mit ihrem Ehering. Sie sagt, sie haben ihren Mann und ihre Söhne vor ihren Augen enthauptet. Und wischt wieder. Nächstes Bild. Ich sehe kurz hin, dann sehe ich weg. Sie sagt, ihm haben sie die Augen ausgestochen und wischt wieder.
Ich schreibe: wenn Tante Adar, Onkel Xalef, Lava, Lara und Lorans 2014 nicht in Sulaymaniyah gelebt hätten, sondern 400 Kilometer weiter in Shingal, und schreibe diesen Satz nicht zu Ende.

Das Haus von Koçere und Sadun ist ein leeres Haus. Reichen dir die Decken, fragt Koçere, als ich mich zum Schlafen neben Lava und Lara lege. Ich würde dir gerne mehr Decken geben, sagt Koçere, aber meine Decken hat der IS. Das Auto, das Koçere und ihrer Familie 2014 das Leben rettete, steht vor dem Haus. Aber der Sohn mit dem Führerschein ist mit seiner Frau auf dem Weg nach Deutschland. Das Kind haben sie hiergelassen. Es ist zu klein, sagt Koçere. Über die Route sagt sie nichts. Sie sagt nur: Deutschland.
Als Koçere und ihre Familie 2014 aus Shingal flohen, bezogen sie eine Baustelle. Es war ein Rohbau, in dem sie wohnten, ohne Fenster und ohne Türen, bis die Familie, also unsere Familie, Sadun und wir, wir sind Verwandte, Geld schickte, und sie in dieses leere Haus ziehen konnten.
Sadun sagt, in Duhok sind wir sicher, aber die Leute kaufen nicht bei Ezîden. Die Leute sagen, dass das, was die Ezîden verkaufen, unrein ist.
Als wir schlafen gehen, nimmt Sadun eine Pistole aus dem Schrankkästchen und legt sie neben sein Kopfkissen. Niemand sieht auf, und es ist nicht die erste Waffe, die ich sehe. Ich kann mich an die Kalaschnikow erinnern, mit der mein Onkel Hemo zu Newroz in die Luft schoss. Aber die Art, wie Sadun die Pistole

aus dem Schrankkästchen nimmt, als sei sie eine Zahnbürste. Ich sage zu
Tante Adar, warum hat Sadun eine Pistole, und Tante Adar lacht, ach Ronya,
sagt sie, von hier nach Mossul sind es nur zwanzig Minuten.
Koçere schließt die Türe, sie lässt den Schlüssel im Schloss stecken.
Ich werde nachts wach, einmal, zweimal, weil das Kind zu weinen anfängt.
Dann ist es Morgen, wir sitzen draußen und frühstücken.

Nach dem Essen fahren wir auf einen Friedhof und inmitten des Friedhofs gibt
es einen Schrein. Vor dem Schrein treffen wir Sheikh Hassan. Es ist ein alter
Friedhof, manche Gräber sind mehrere hundert Jahre alt, sagt Sheikh Hassan.
Auf den verwitterten Grabsteinen sind kleine Vögel zu erkennen, Schiffe und
andere eingravierte Ornamente. Es ist das erste Mal, dass ich so etwas sehe.
Im Dorf meiner Großeltern hielt man sein Ezîdentum versteckt. Nie hätte man
es gewagt, einen êzîdischen Tempel zu bauen, von Weitem erkennbar, mit dem
typischen kegelförmigen Dach und dem Sonnenemblem auf der Spitze. Auch
solche Grabsteine habe ich nie gesehen.
92 êzîdische Stätten soll der IS zerstört haben. Und nicht nur unsere Stätten,
sondern auch die Erinnerung daran, dass es sie jemals gegeben hat. Das Video,
wie sie mit Pressluft- und Vorschlaghammer durch das Museum in Mossul ziehen, eine Statue nach der anderen vom Sockel stürzen, zertrümmern, was
mehr als zweitausend Jahre gehalten hatte, habe ich mir wieder und wieder
angesehen. Ich wusste, wann die Musik einsetzt, wann das Bild ins Stocken
gerät, wann die Kämpfer mit ihrem Vorschlaghammer ausholen, synchron,
und in ihren Bewegungen einfrieren, in Zeitlupe, mit den Hämmern auf die um-
gestürzte Statue zu ihren Füßen einschlagen, bis das Video wieder in norma-
lem Tempo läuft.
Desto weniger kann ich glauben, was ich jetzt vor mir sehe. Diese Grabsteine
zeugen davon, dass wir schon lange hier sind. Dass schon unsere Vorfahren in
dieser Landschaft lebten, ihre Felder bestellten, Schafe züchteten und in dieser Erde ihre Toten bestatteten.

Vieles von dem, was ich schreibe, hat keine Ordnung. Sätze, Worte, die abbre-
chen, im Nichts verlaufen. Ich füge zusammen. Dass etwas mit Großbuchstaben anfängt und mit einem Punkt endet. Dazwischen ein Komma vielleicht, ein
Halbsatz, der sich auf das eben Gesagte bezieht. Wieder Großbuchstaben,
Subjekt, Verb, Objekt bis zum nächsten Punkt. Absatz für Absatz. Ich habe
keine Sprache, in der ich schreibe. Ich habe meine Reise in Dokumentenord-
nern auf meinem Laptop gespeichert, die Tonaufnahmen auf meinem Handy.
Ich sehe mir eine Dokumentation an. Ein Mann von der Commission for International Justice und Accountability sagt, der IS sei auf drei Achsen in den
Shingal vorgerückt. Zwei Achsen aus dem Süden, eine aus Syrien, aus dem
Norden. Hier fangen sie an, die Ezîden zusammenzutreiben, sagt der Mann
und zeigt auf eine Karte. Sie trennen die Männer von den Frauen. Es ist das
gleiche Muster in jedem besetzten Dorf.

Ich lese „der berüchtigte IS-Henker Jihadi John", ich lese „Sexsklavinnen des
IS", „IS-wives". Ich lese nicht Täter und Täterinnen. Ich lese nicht Überlebende.
Ich sage, ich muss an das Interview denken, dass die kanadische Radiomode-
ratorin mit Nadia Murad gemacht hat. Ich muss daran denken, wie die Modera-
torin Nadia Murad gefragt hat, wie fühlt es sich an, wenn man wie ein Objekt
behandelt wird? Wie haben Sie sich gefühlt, als sie Sie so benutzt haben?
Wie haben sie Euch verteilt und was haben sie Ihnen angetan? Haben sie Sie

geschlagen? Und dann wurden Sie vergewaltigt. Sie haben Sie immer wieder angefasst. Wie haben Sie alles ertragen?
Das, sage ich meiner Mutter, wollen sie hören. Dann brauchen sie nicht mehr ins Kino, sage ich.
Mein Vater sagt, wenn der Ochse umfällt, gibt es viele Messer.

Ich sitze bei Tante Adar und Onkel Xalef auf dem Sofa, den Laptop auf meinen Knien, die Kopfhörer in den Ohren. Ich schreibe: Xatê sagt, willkommen bei den Ezîden. Ich schreibe: Xatê empfängt uns in Uniform. Sie hat heute frei. Aber als Generalin darf sie nur in Uniform zu uns sprechen. Ich sitze neben ihren Eltern im Wohnzimmer. Ich schreibe: Es ist ein kahles Wohnzimmer, wie die meisten Wohnzimmer, in denen ich war, ist es ein Wohnzimmer von Flüchtlingen.
Xatê sagt, auch ich bin eine Tochter von Shingal. Ich bin in Shingal geboren, sagt sie. Sie wissen, was passiert ist, am 3.8.2014, als der IS kam. Zwölf Tage waren wir in den Bergen eingeschlossen, sagte Xatê.
Ich sitze und schreibe: Xatê sagt, ich habe von einer Frau aus Koço gehört. Sie ist mit ihrem Kind verschleppt worden. Drei Tage und drei Nächte hielt man sie auf dem Flughafen in Tal Afar gefangen. Das Kind war klein, es trank noch Milch, kein Jahr war es alt. Das Kind war hungrig und schrie. Drei Tage lang. Xatê sagt: Das Kind schrie so laut, dass der Amir des IS nicht schlafen konnte. Der Amir sagte zu der Frau, gib mir das Kind, dann hört es auf zu weinen. Die Frau gab ihm das Kind, weil sie dachte, er würde ihm zu essen geben und zu trinken. Der Amir nahm das Kind und ging mit dem Kind in die Küche. In der Küche nahm er ein großes Messer und schnitt dem Kind den Kopf ab. Das Fleisch des Kindes kochte er und setzte es der Mutter vor. Die Mutter begriff nicht sofort, sagt Xatê, erst als sie die Hand des Kindes sah. Sie verlor den Verstand.

Ich sitze auf dem Sofa bei Tante Adar und Onkel Xalef. Ich schreibe, dass es das Letzte war, was die Mutter begriff, bevor sie den Verstand verlor.
Ich stoppe die Tonaufnahme.

Während Xatê spricht, fängt sie an zu weinen. Tränen laufen über ihr Gesicht, Xatê spricht weiter.
Ich schreibe: Xatê sitzt in Uniform und weint. Und während Xatê in Uniform sitzt und weint, fange auch ich an zu weinen. Und wieder, als ich auf dem Sofa sitze, die Tonaufnahme abspiele und schreibe: Xatê weint.
Xatê sagt: ich war eine Sängerin, wie mein Vater. Sie zeigt uns ein Video, auf YouTube. Hochgeladen am 9.4.2013, sechzehn Monate, bevor der IS nach Shingal kam. Xatê trägt ein rotes Kleid und Schmuck. Sie sitzt mit ihrer Saz und spielt und singt und hinter ihr die Berge von Shingal. Xatê fängt wieder an zu weinen. Ich schreibe: Xatê weint.
Xatê sagt: ich hatte viele CDs, aber die habe ich zurückgelassen.
Xatê sagt: Nachdem wir aus Shingal flohen, habe ich zu meinen Eltern gesagt, ich will keine Saz mehr, ich will eine Rakete.
Xatê zeigt uns ein zweites Video. Xatê mit ihrer Einheit, an der Grenze zu Mossul. Sie knien hinter Sandsäcken und haben ihre Waffen in das weite Land gerichtet. Xatê singt.

Es gibt eine Stelle in der Tonaufnahme, als Faruk zu Xatê sagt, auch ich wäre Ezîdin. Nachdem Faruk das gesagt hat, will Xatê wissen, aus welcher Familie ich sei. Ich sage, mein Vater ist Ezîde aus Hasake, wir sind Murid, Xatltî, vom Xûdan der Mend sage ich. Meine Mutter ist Deutsche, sage ich.

Xatê steht auf, geht zur Tür und ruft, bringt uns jemand Tee. Xatê sieht mich an, sonst erzählst du noch in Deutschland, du wärst bei Xatê gewesen und hättest nicht einmal einen Tee bekommen.
Xatê nennt mich Schwester. Xatê sagt, auch du bist eine Schwester.
Habt ihr Hunger, fragt Xatê.
Wir müssen los, sagt Faruk. Ich schalte das Aufnahmegerät aus.
Es ist schon spät, sagt Faruk, und wir müssen heute noch nach Duhok.
Ich stehe auf und küsse die Hände von Xatês Mutter und die Hände von Xatês Vater.

Ich habe mich oft gefragt, warum tun sie uns das an. Wie können sie so etwas tun. Aber es ist keine Frage. Als ich mit Cana durch Kivax lief, habe ich mich das gefragt. An den Ruinen vorbei, die einmal ihr Dorf waren und an dem dreibeinigen Hund, der aus irgendeinem Grund noch immer hier war. Und vor dem alten Schulhaus saß und den Kopf hob, uns ansah, als wir an ihm vorbeiliefen. Als die türkischen Soldaten immer noch hier waren und das menschenleere Dorf bewachten, damit sich in den Ruinen keine PKK Kämpfer*innen versteckten. Und Cana auf den Hügel hinter dem Dorf zeigte, wo bis vor einem Jahr die heiligen Bäume standen. Kamen sie tagsüber oder kamen sie nachts, die türkischen Soldaten müssen sie gesehen haben. Warum, frage ich Cana, reicht es ihnen nicht, dass hier keine Ezîden mehr sind. Was haben ihnen diese Bäume getan.
Dass es ihnen nicht um das Holz ging, die abgeholzten Stämme lagen immer noch da, neben den Stümpfen. Dass sie also hierher kamen zu einer Tag- oder Nachtzeit und die zu jeder Tag- und Nachtzeit das Dorf bewachenden türkischen Soldaten ihnen dabei zusahen, wie sie die heiligen Bäumen fällten.
Ich fragte mich, nachdem wir im Camp gewesen sind, und ich bei Onkel Xalef und Tante Adar zuhause auf der Hollywoodschaukel saß und in meiner Tasche nach den Zigaretten suchte, mein Feuerzeug, und immer noch, als ich es längst gefunden hatte. Als ich in Lalish auf dem Flachdach vor dem Tempel saß, mit Sheikh Hassan, Faruk und den Kindern der Kaniya sipi Schule Sandwiches aß und Faruk sagt, das Mädchen neben dir ist verkauft worden. So und so viel Mal ist sie verkauft worden. Ich habe die Zahl vergessen, und das Mädchen und ich essen unser Sandwich. Der Junge, der dir gegenüber sitzt, sagt Faruk, seinen Vater haben sie vor seinen Augen enthauptet.
Seitdem er die Kinder unterrichte, könne er nachts nicht mehr schlafen, sagt der Sheikh. Faruk sagt, was ist das, Kopf abschneiden. Warum machen sie das, Kopf abschneiden.
Meine Mutter sagt, sie sind wirklich brutal. So brutal. Und atmet ein und sagt, dass man mit dieser Brutalität, sagt meine Mutter, mit solch einer Brutalität und sucht nach einem Vergleich, an dem sich diese Brutalität messen kann. Aber, meine Mutter atmet ein und sagt, wirklich.
Sie sind keine Menschen, sagt mein Vater. Jemand, der so etwas tut, ist kein Mensch. Wie kann einer, der so etwas tut, ein Mensch sein. Nein, sagt mein Vater, das ist kein Mensch.
Die Freundin von meiner Mutter, sie ist Christin aus Mossul, – wir besuchen sie in Erbil, sagt, sie kenne eine Ärztin, eine Sunnitin, die im Mossuler Krankenhaus arbeitete. Dass sie der Ärztin ein êzîdisches Mädchen brachten, sagt die Freundin meiner Mutter, neun Jahre alt, das sie wieder und wieder vergewaltigt haben, dass es so zugerichtet war. Und die Ärztin, als sie das Mädchen sah, sagte, wie könnt ihr so etwas tun. Und dass sie die Ärztin auf ihre Frage hin, die keine Frage war, enthaupteten.
Sie denken, sie kommen ins Paradies, sagt meine Mutter.

Im März 2019, nachdem der IS militärisch besiegt ist, steigen die Selbstmord-
versuche in den Camps. Meiner Mutter sage ich am Telefon, wir sind tot. Sie
haben uns vernichtet.
Ich bin in der Mensa. Ich nehme den schnellen Teller. Ich setze mich an einen
Tisch. Ich esse und bin alleine. Ich will noch in die Bibliothek gehen nach dem
Mittagessen. Auf meinem Handy lese ich die Nachrichten. Eine Spezialeinheit
der britischen Armee, hat die Köpfe von 50 Ezîdinnen gefunden. Die Köpfe
haben sie in Mülltonnen gefunden. Ich stehe auf, bringe mein Tablett zu der
Geschirrrückgabe. Auf dem Weg in die Bibliothek rufe ich meine Mutter an, es
macht keinen Sinn, sage ich. Warum, sage ich, sie sind besiegt und das Letzte,
was sie tun, als längst feststeht, sie können nicht mehr gewinnen, als sie
längst besiegt sind, ist, Ezîdinnen zu köpfen. Bis zu ihrem Ende haben sie
nicht aufgehört, uns zu vernichten.
Die Ezîden sind vernichtet, sage ich.
Meine Mutter sagt, das kannst du nicht sagen. So etwas kannst du nicht sagen.
Du kannst das nicht so sagen.
Wir sind die, die noch da sind, sage ich. Als sie nach Shingal kamen, um uns zu
vernichten, sage ich, waren wir in Europa. Als sie kamen, um meinen Urgroß-
vater zu ermorden, war ich noch nicht geboren. Aber meine Großmutter war
schon geboren. Wäre meine Großmutter noch nicht geboren worden, sage ich,
wäre ich nicht hier.
Sie kamen nach Shingal, um alle Ezîden zu vernichten. Wir waren in Europa, als
sie nach Shingal kamen. Wir sind die, die sie nicht getötet haben. Wir leben
nicht. Wir sind nur nicht getötet worden, sage ich. Das ist der Unterschied,
sage ich. Die anderen sind da, weil sie da sind, sie sind am Leben, aber nicht,
weil sie nicht getötet wurden.

Unsere Verwandten aus Shingal sind am Leben, weil sie ein Auto hatten, sage ich.
Aber zwischen am Leben sein und leben ist ein Unterschied.
Die Frage nach dem Warum ist keine Frage. Sie ist ausformulierte Sprachlosig-
keit. Ich kann sie nicht beantworten. Wenn ich sie beantworten könnte, müsste
ich entweder der IS sein oder ich wäre der IS oder ich spräche wie der IS oder
aus mir spräche der IS.
Weil wir Ungläubige sind, Kafir, wäre die Antwort. Aber weil das darauf keine
Antwort ist. Und die Frage nach dem Warum keine Frage.
Ich muss daran denken, wie meine Großmutter bis zu ihrem Tod gefragt hat,
warum haben sie meinen Vater ermordet. Was hat er denn getan, dass sie ihn
ermordeten.
Und ich, wenn sie das fragte, bis zu ihrem Tod gedacht habe, nichts. Er hat
nichts getan. Es gibt dafür keinen Grund. Und weil die Frage meiner Großmutter keine Frage war, habe ich nichts gesagt.

Mit Faruk fahren wir auf einen Hügel hinter Xhanke. Vom Hügel aus kann man
auf den Mossul-Damm sehen. Und der Mossul-Damm liegt da, wie schön sage
ich, in der Abenddämmerung. Blaues Wasser, auf der anderen Seite Lichter.
Dort war der IS, sagt Faruk. Der Mossul-Damm die Grenze.
Wir parken hinter einem êzîdischen Schrein, weißer Stein und Sonnenemblem
auf der Spitze. Wie schön, sage ich. Ich mache ein Foto. Dass sie 2014 rüber
geschossen haben. Und nur der Mossul-Damm zwischen dem êzîdischen Dorf
und dem IS. So schmal, das man hinüber sehen kann.
Faruk geht auf eine Mauer zu. Über die Mauer ragen die Äste eines Oliven-
baums. Faruk nimmt den Stacheldraht beiseite, der hier eine Tür ist. Wegen der

Tiere, sagt er, die Gräber meiner Onkel. Er schaltet die Handytaschenlampe ein und leuchtet auf die Grabsteine.
Es ist nicht das erste Mal, dass mir Faruk Gräber zeigt. Und Faruk ist nicht der einzige. Irgendwann haben wir hier mehr Tote als Lebende. Und irgendwann ist fast schon jetzt.
Der Garten meiner Großeltern in Tel Khatoun ist abgebrannt. Auch die Bäume, die mein Vater gepflanzt hat. Das, was einmal ein Zuhause war, ist heute ein Schützengraben. Jemand hat meiner Tante Fotos geschickt und ein Video: jemand geht durch unseren Garten. Von Zaun zu Zaun, das Bild wackelt, es rauscht. Meine Mutter zeigt es mir auf ihrem Handy und sagt, das waren die Bäume, die dein Vater vor vierzig Jahren gepflanzt hat. Mein Vater sagt, wie viele Jahre hat es gedauert, bis diese Bäume so groß geworden sind.
Jemand hat uns auch ein Video geschickt von dem Hügel, auf dem sie meine Großmutter begraben haben. Dass niemand von der Familie dabei sein konnte, dass nicht wir sie begraben konnten. Und mein Cousin mit dem Sarg, in dem meine Großmutter lag, in die Türkei fuhr, bis zur syrischen Grenze, wo Leute die Tote entgegennahmen, mit etwas Geld, damit meine Großmutter auf dem Hügel neben meinem Großvater begraben werden konnte.
Als ich an den Gräbern von Faruks Onkel stehe, und er mit der Taschenlampe die Grabsteine beleuchtet, frage ich mich, ob auch ich einmal so an dem Grab meiner Großeltern stehen würde. Und wie Faruk jetzt ihre Grabsteine küsse.

Ich muss daran denken, wie ich als Kind hinter dem Gartenzaun im Dorf meiner Großeltern gestanden und den LKWs nachgesehen habe, die an der türkischen Grenze entlang in den Irak fuhren oder aus dem Irak kamen. Dass sie auf Straßen fuhren, auf denen ich auch gefahren bin, in Städten waren, in denen ich auch war. Kobanê, Raqqa, Palmyra.
Das ist alles, denke ich. Die Straße mit den LKWs entlang, einmal abbiegen, Richtung Bajid, über den Tigris, der hier ein dünner Arm ist und nicht so breit wie der Mossul-Damm. Und auch auf der anderen Seite der Grenze. Ich kann mich an Ausflüge erinnern, mit der Familie, wie schon mein Vater als Schüler Ausflüge an den Tigris gemacht hatte. Wie wir, meine Geschwister, meine Cousins, meine Cousine und ich am Ufer spielten, in einem Restaurant Kebab aßen. Es gibt Fotos davon, die mein Onkel von uns machte.
Es hätte so schnell gehen können, denke ich, als ich in Derabûn stehe und auf die Straße sehe. Zwölf Kilometer. Wie viel sind zwölf Kilometer. Fünfzehn Minuten vielleicht. Wir säßen beim Frühstück wie jetzt im Haus von Faruks Cousine, tränken Tee, in einem Haus wie diesem, nur zwölf Kilometer weiter, 2014.

September 2018 fliege ich nach Izmir und weiter in den Osten. Ich schreibe: Ich will das Dorf besuchen, in dem meine Großmutter aufgewachsen ist, aus dem unsere Familie vertrieben wurde, als sie noch ein Kind war. Sie haben uns umzingelt, sagt mein Vater, sie wollten uns töten. Unsere Familie floh über Nacht, ließ alles zurück, erst in den Shingal, dann nach Syrien. Ich schreibe: viermal musste meine Großmutter fliehen. Das letzte Mal 2014 und jedes Mal, weil sie Ezîdin war. Ich schreibe: wer ein Mal geflüchtet ist, bleibt geflüchtet.
Meine Großmutter sitzt im Haus meiner Eltern. Wenn wir ihr etwas zu essen geben, sagt sie, ihr wollt mich vergiften. Wenn sie die Treppe hinauf steigt, sagt sie, passt auf, sie haben uns eine Falle gestellt. Sie sagt, wir sind umzingelt.

Ich rufe meinen Vater an und sage, ich fahre nach Bazîvan.
Ich sage, ich kann es nicht auf Google Maps finden.

Mein Vater sagt, ich schreibe dir, wenn ich den türkischen Namen herausgefunden habe.

Meine Mutter ruft mich an und sagt, mein Vater habe gesagt, Cîndî sei vor ein paar Jahren dort gewesen. Er habe gesagt, im Dorf wohnen jetzt Muslime. Wenn du sagst, dass du Ezîdin bist, bringen sie dich um.

Meine Mutter sagt, du darfst niemandem sagen, dass du Ezîdin bist.

Mein Vater schreibt, ich habe rausgefunden, wie das Dorf heißt.

Meine Mutter sagt, Onkel Hemo hat mir eine Telefonnummer gegeben, von einem Hadschi.

Mein Vater sagt, der Hadschi ist Sunnit, aber unsere Vorfahren kennen sich.

Ich bin in Diyarbakir, als mein Vater anruft und sagt, der Hadschi weiß Bescheid.

Er hat gesagt, du musst keine Angst haben.

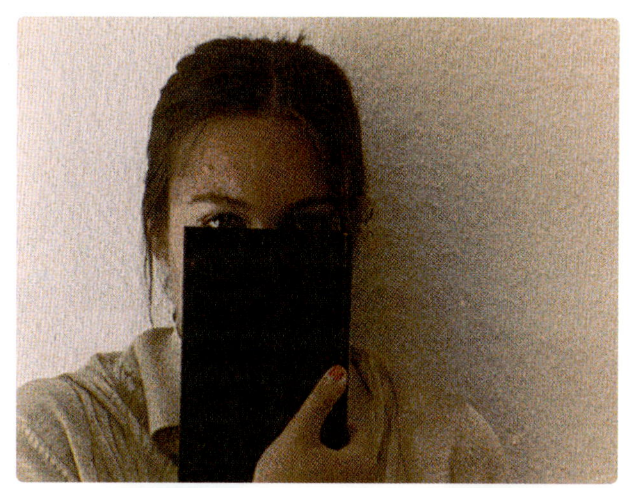

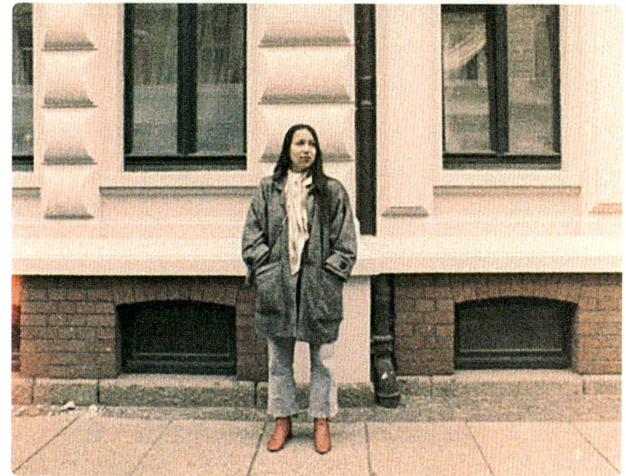

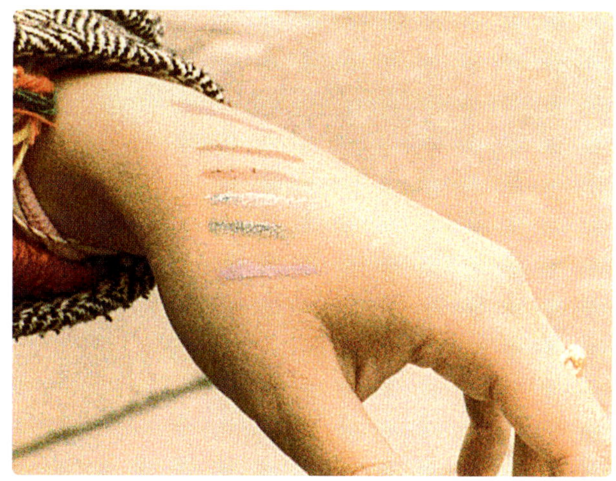

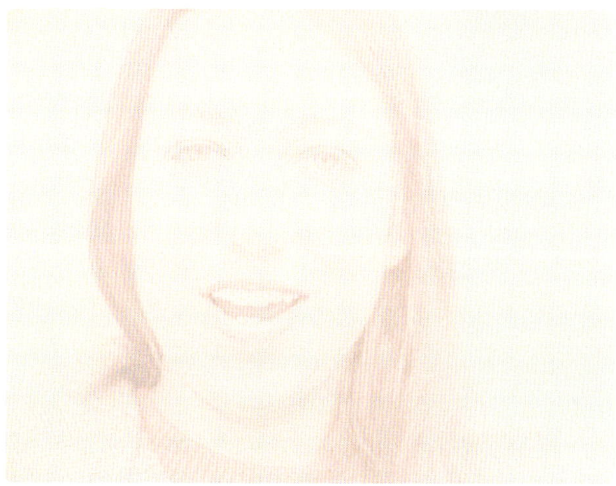

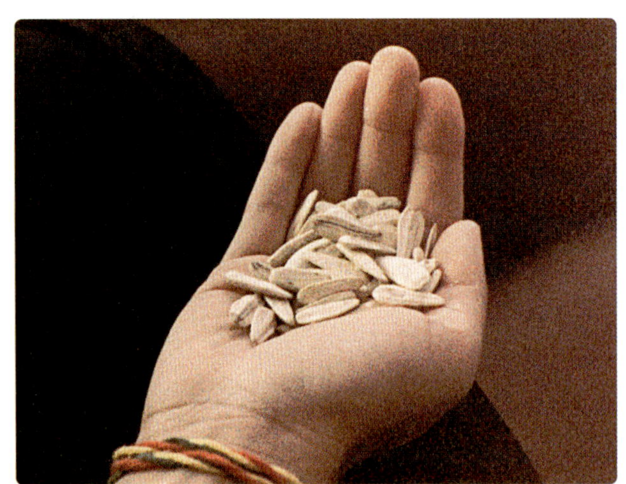

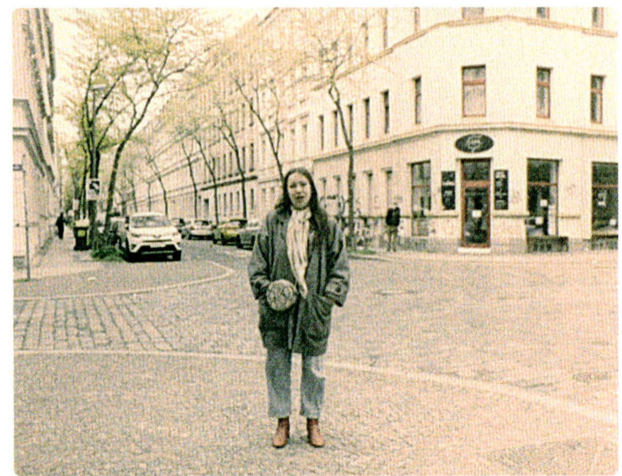

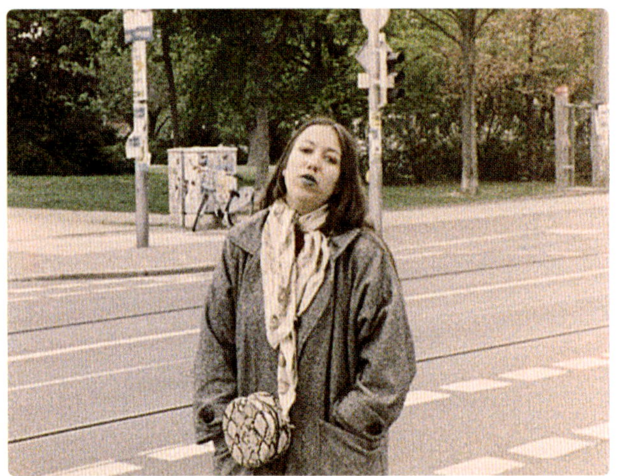

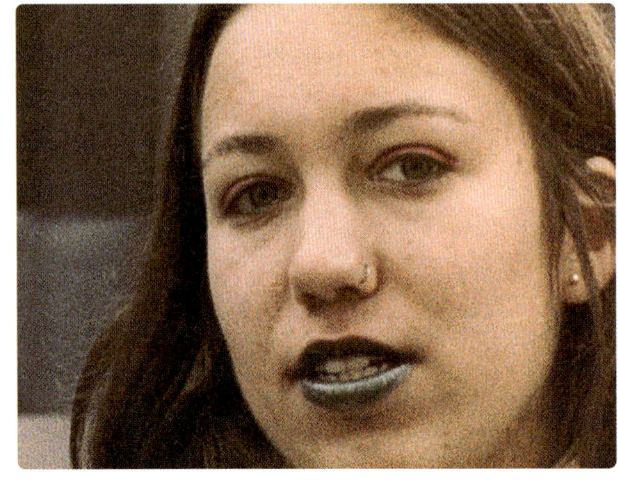

Heftê û çar

Ronya Othmann

Tebax 2014'an ez li pêşiya televîzyonê rû-
niştim. Ez jinan di cilên dapîra xwe de,
xaltîka xwe de, dotmamên xwe de dibînim,
mêran dibînim mîna bapîrê xwe, bavê xwe,
pismamên xwe, ji bo jiyana xwe xelas bikin
dibezin. Kelkela havînê ye. Li çîyan zarok,
kal û nexweş ji tîna dimirin. Şingal hate
dorpêç kirin. Zilam û jinên pîr, yên ku nikarî
bûn xwe xelas bikin, hate kuştin, jinên
ciwan û zarokên biçûk wek mîna xenîmen-
ta şerî tên girtin û li bazarên koleyan ji
bo milîtanên Daîşê tên firotin. Jin, yên ku
navê min, yên xwişka min, pismamê min
wergirtin.

Tebaxa 2014'an êdî ez nikarim bînim bîra
xwe. Piştre ez dinivîsim, ez li pêşiya televîzyonê rûdinim. Ji ber ku ez dizanim, ez li ber
televîzyonê rûniştî bûm. Ez dizanim min çi
jî dît. Lê tiştên ku min dît, êdî ez nikarim
bîn bîra xwe.

231

Ez dinivîsim, çawa ez di odeya dêûbavê xwe ya rûniştinê li ser dîwanê rûniştî-
me, ka ez pêşve xwe dişom anjî ez dixwum. Ew bala min bikşîne ku ev çend
deme min ew tişt êdî wer nekirîye.
Her nivîsîn ji bo min xeyalî ye. Yanî ez di derbarê xwe, bavê xwe, dapîra xwe anjî
fîgûrekê kû ez navekî û çîrokekê bidimê de binivîsim jî .

Di 2014'an de min parlementera êzîdî Vîyan Dakhil li pêşiya Parlamentoya Îraqê
dît, wê çawa hewldida, bûyerên ku li Şîngalê çêbûbûn vebêje, vêca di nav axaftina xwe de hilweşî û du parlementeran ew ji odeyê derxistin.
Min pêşkeşvan û nûçevanê li ser televîzyona Kurdî dît ku ew li şûna behsa Şingalê bikin, dest bi gîrînê kirin.

Lalbûyîn li ber çavan e. Ji ber wê zordarîyê ez peyva zordarîyê, ji ber wê sûcê jî
ez peyva sûcê binxêz dikim. Ji ber ku him peyva zordariyê him jî peyva sûcê
şûna wê bûyerê nagirin. Ji bo bûyerê ku di 2014ªn de li Şingalê çêbûye Parlamentoya Ewrûpa û Yekîtîya Netewan pişt re navê jenosîd lêkirine, ew biserne-
ketina zimanê ye.

Piştre ez dinivîsim: Ez ji Balefirê dadikevim, li ser pêlikan dadikevim, bayekî
germ ji hember tê li ser rûyê min. Ez bêhn digirim, wek mîna min di zarokatîya
xwe de bêhn digirt , bêhngirtina yekemîn, dirêj û bi kûr.
Ez herweha dinivîsim: li malê, tevî ku ez nizanim, ku ew rast e.
Kontrola pasaportê. Ez pasaporta xwe ya almanî datînim ser maseyê. Kesê kar-
mend dikene, gava ew navê min dixwîne. Ew wî bi lêvdike,wek mîna ew di malbata min de tê bilêvkirin. Ronya bi R ya nerm û O ya dirêj.
Apê Xelef li cîhe parkê benda min e. Em hevdû bi hembêz dikin.
Em ji bajêr derdikevin, li ser rê a bi çar şopan. Li ser milê çepê Ainkawa bi bircên
dêran, li ser milê rastê Erbîl bi Mînareyan. Di ber qesra Nêçîrvan Barzanî re derbas dibin. Bajar diqede. Piştre çîya. Em di nuqteya kontrolan re, ên ku paş hev
re dihatin, derbas dikin. Ez ji dev jimartinê berdidim. Li kêlaka rê de wêneyên
pakrewanan.
Ez dinivîsim: Girs, yanê gir.
Di demekê de em li kêleka bendavekê radiwestin. Em ji wesayetê dadikevin,
çay veduxwin û cixarê dikêşînin. Em li kêleka bendavê disekinin. Ciwan li ser
golê motorên avê dibezînin. Apê Xelef wêneyeka min digire. Em dîsa wesayetê
siwar dibin. Ez tiştek difikirim, tiştek yê ku ez di Balafirê de berê li ser fikirî bûm
ku ne ez tenê li malê me, lê belê, li welatekî ku mirov êzîdî tên kûştin, ji ber ku
ew êzîdî bûn.

Xaltîka Adar got, bawerim birçî bûna te heye. Li ser maseyê nanê vekirî, goşt bi
Îsot, bacanê sor di nava sosê de û selete hene. Ji bo vexwarinê dewê bi nah-
neyê heye.
Em dixwun, ez, apê Xelef, xaltîka Adar, dotmamên min Lava û Lara û pismamê
min Lorans. Em nan perçe dikin, datînin ser maseyê. Ez dinîvîsim: Min bêri kirî
bû, wûsa bixwum. Ez wêneyekî ji zebeşan digirim û ji bavê xwe re dişînim.

Piştî xwarinê çay, dûre şekirok, piştre kek, piştre fêkî. Dendikê bi xoykirî. Kahwe-
ya Erebî. Xaltikâ Adar dibêje bixwe, bixwe. Ez dibêjim ez têr bûm û lê xwarinê
berdewam dikim. Ew dibêje, carekê mêvanên wê hebûne, mêrekî kal. Li ber
xwarinê hêstirên çavên wî hatine xwarê. Gava wê pirsîya, gelo çi bûye, wî gotîye, xwarin wek mîna xwarina dîya wî bûye.

Em bi ber kampa Aştî re diçin, nêzî nîv saet ji Silêmanî dûr e, li sînorê Îranê. Ez dinivîsim, ez li kêleka Lara û Lava li ser paldanka paş erebeyê da rûdinim. Lara û Lava bêkêf in û ji avê jî tê xuyakirin. Lara dibêje, kêfa min tune ye, em her tim ber bi Kampê re biçin. Em nêzîk dibin, cadeyekê , dizîvirin, rêya bê asfalt, di navendeka dûr û pahn, cîhekî bi çîyan dorpêç bûye. Di bin ezmanên pêşnîvro yên şîn kontrolek. Li vir em tên naskirin û derbaskirin. Gava ku em di kampê re derbas dibin, min dît ku ew du kamp in, di navbera wan da cadeyeka fireh heye û bi du çeperan ji hev hatine veqetandin. Ji mile me ve, kampa êzîdîyên kurd û milê din yên ereb yê musliman.

Li Kampê em serlêdana hevalan dikin, çay vedixwun û berdewam dikin diçin. Di çadirekê de du xort, dibik ku temenê wan heft an jî heşt be, li wir bêdeng rûdinim, di wî temenî de li ba zarokan min hîn qet tiştê wusa nedîtîye. Dêya wan, wêneyên bavê xwe, ê têyî revandin, ya keça xwe,ya tê revandin nîşanî min dide û bi girîyakî bilind hestirên wê tê xwarê. Dotmama min, ya ku li kêleka min rûniştî ye û telefona dêya xwe dike destê xwe û hewl dide vîdeoyek pisîkan temaşe bike. Û ez, ya ku deve pîyê çakêtê jorî zendê xwe dikişîne, piştî ku min dît ku ew jin û zarokên wê jî eynî bazbend di zenda de ne, wek ya min.

Xaltîka min jinekê nîşan dide û dibêje, li wê jinê binêre, ya ku li kêleka çadirê rûniştî ye, bi porê sipî, kitana sipî û kirasê sipî.Perîşan, mil û serî daketî. Ez dikarim rûyê wê bi zorê bibînim. Ji hatina Daîş ya gûndê wê vir ve, vê jina pîr qet peyvek jî neanîye ziman. Û ne tenê ne peyvek got, êdî tevahî mirov nikare xwe bigêhejînê.
Bêaxaftin xwe di bedena vê jinê de nivîsandîye. Ew qet carekê jî li me nanêre, ne gava em dikevin hûndirê çadirê, ne jî gava em rûdinin û ne jî gava em diçin. Di destê wê yê çepê de kevirekî biçûk digire, û ez nû dibînim, dema em xatir ji hevdû dixwazin.

Pişt çend rojan şunde em mêvandarên şêxê malbata xwe ne. Şêx behsa çiroka cîwanekî dike, yekî heft salî bû, dema îslamê qebul nake, dema mîlîtanê Daîşê li ber çavên wî sere bavê wî jêdikin. Wî serîyî jêkirî dikin destê zarokê heft salî û ji wî re dibêjin, te dît ,me çi li bavê te kir, tu dixwazî bê ser dîne îslamê.

Şêx navbereke biçûk didê û pitşre qala çîroka duyemîn dike.
Piştî çîroka duyemîn behsa çîroka sêyemîn dike. Pişt çîroka sêyemîn bêdeng dimîne û dibêje, bîst û çar saetan em dikarin li vir rûnin û ez dikarim bîst û çar saetan behsa çîrokên wusa bikim.

Parlementer, ya di nav axaftina xwe de hilweşîya, nûçegîhan, ên ku dest bi girî kirî bûn, ew jina pîr, ya ku lal bû, û şêxê ku digot, ew bikare bîst û çar saetan behsa çîrokên wiha bike, bê ku ew wan bi dawî bîne, xûya ye, tu gotin têrê bûyera Tebaxa 2014'an nake. Pişthev rêzkirina sedeman jî, hejmartina mirîyan jî, ev bûyera 3.8.2014'an jî, fermana 74min jî, wek em yên êzîdî wê qirkirinê binav dikin, dîsa jî cîhek vala dimîne, ji bo wê peyvên me tune ne.

Bi xwe heger nivîsek li wir be jî, matmayî hîn jî di bin zimanî de ye. Matmayî nivîsandina tekstekê pêk tîne, rêzimana wê, forma wê, gotinên wê bi cîh dike,
Ez dinivîsim: Ez li cîhekî bûm. Li wî cîhî kampek hebû. Li kampê konek û di kon de jî jineka pîr. Û di destên wê jina pîr de kevirekî biçûk hebû.

Ez dinivîsim: Min dît. Ez bi xwe dîtarek im. Ew diaxive û lê belê ew axaftin bê ziman e.

Em bi erebê diçin ser çîyayê bajarî. Bîst deqîqe, piştre em li jor in.
Em li ser çîyayî disekinin û wêneyan dikişînin. Roj diçe ava. Ronahî kêm dibe, û ronahîya lambeyên cadan, çirûskên ereban, çirrûsîna tabeleyên reklaman, bajar ber bi lingên me diçûrisin
Di vegerê de em cîhekî li kêlaka cadeyê li ba dikanek biçûk disekinin. Tu dixwazî çi vexwî, apê Xelef dipirse. Hemû tişt hene, tu çi bixwazî. Bîra, şerab, vîskî, vodka û araq!

Ev ne Erbîl e, ev ne Dûhok e, an jî ne Bexda ye. Ev der Silêmanî ye. Silêmanî azad û ewle ye, apê Xelef dibêje. Ji hemû bajaran turîst tên. Ji Baxdayê bi otobûsan wan tînin vir. Ji ber germê direvin.
Em li odaya rûniştinê rûdinin, cixarê dikêşînin, bîrayê di qutîkan de vedixwun û dendikê bi xoykirî dixwun.
Xaltîka Adar dibêje, em ji kesekî re nabêjin ku em êzîdî ne. Kesek jî li vir nizane ku em êzîdî ne.

Xaltîlka Adar ji telefona xwe hinek wêneyan nîşanî min dide, yên ku ew nasdike. Bi pêçîyê xwe ji rastê ber bi çepê re digûherîne û dibêje, guhê xwe di girtigehê de kerr bûye. Piştre dîsa digûherîne, wêneyê din, lê ez ne li ser wêneyê dinêrim, ez li ser destê wê dinêrim, bi çermên mezin, li ser pêçîyên wê, bi gûstirkê zewacê. Ew dibêje, wan zilamê wê û kurê wê li ber çavên wê ser jê kirin. Û dîsa digûherîne. Wêneyê din. Demeke kin lê dinêrim, piştre ez berê xwe digûherînim. Ew dibêje, çavên wî derxistine û dîsa digûherîne.
Ez dinîvîsîm: heger xaltîka Adar, apê Xelef, Lava, Lara û Lorans 2014'an ne li Silêmanî jîyanbûna, lêbelê 400 kîlometre durtir li Şingalê bûna, û ez nivîsandina vê hevokê bi dawî naînim

Xanîyê Koçerêyê û Sadûnî, xaniyekî vala ye. Koçerê lihêfan dirêj dike û dipirse, gava ku ez ji bo razanê li kêlaka Lava û Lara xwe dirêjdikim. Min bi hezkirinê hinek lihêfên din jî bidana te, Koçerê dibêje, lê hêmû lihêfên min Daîşê bir. Erebe, ya ku Koçerêyê û malbata wê di sala 2014'an de jîyana wan xelas kiribû, li ber malê ye. Lê kûrê wê, yê bi ehlîyet bi jina xwe re di rêde ye û ber bi Almanya ve diçe. Wan zarok li vir hiştin. Ew pirr biçûk e, Koçerêyê dibêje. Di der heqê rê de tiştekî nabêje. Ew tenê dibêje: Almanya.
Gava Koçerê û malbata wê 2014'an de ji Şingalê revîn, ketin avahîyeka nîvçe. Ew îskelata avahîyê bû, ya ku ew têde rûdiniştin, bê pace û bê derî, heta ku malbat, yanî malbata me, Sadûn û em, em merivê hevin, pere şand, û ew di vî xanîyê vala têde karibin rûnin.
Sadûn dibêje, li Dûhokê em bi ewle ne, lê civat ji êzîdîyan tiştekî nakirin. Civat dibêjin ku, çi tiştê êzîdî difiroşin, ne helal e.
Dema em diçin xewê, Sadûn ji dolabê demanceyekê radihêje û li kêleka balgîya xwe datîni. Kesek lênanêre, û ev ne çeka yekemîn e, ya ku ez dibînim. Ez dikarim wê keleşê bînim bîra xwe, ya ku apê min Hemo di Newrozê de bera hewa dida. Lê şêwe, çawa Sadûn dibance ji dolabê derdixe, wek tu dibê qey mîna firça dirana bû. Ez ji xaltîka Adar dibêm, çima Sadûnî dimançeyeke xwe heye, û xaltîka Adar dikene, Ronya, wê got, ji vir heta Misulê tenê bîst deqîqe ne.
Koçer derî digire, kilîdê di cihê niftê de dihêle.
Ez dê şev şîyar bivîm, yekcar, ducar, ji ber ku zarok dest bi girî dike. Piştre sibe ye, em li derve rûdinin û taştê dixwun.

Pişt xwarinê em ber bi goristanekê ve diçin û di navênda goristanê de gorek
heye.
Li ber gorê me şêx Hesen dît. Ew goristaneke kevn e, henek gor nêzî hezar salî
ne, dibêje şêx Hesen. Li ser kevirê goristanan wêneyê çûkan tê naskirin, keştî
û henek nexşeyên hatine kolandin. Ev cara yekemîn e, ez tiştekî wûsa dibînim.
Li gûndê bapîrê min parestgeha êzîdî tê veşartin. Mirov tu caran bawer nedi-
kir ku perestgeha êzîdî bê avakirin, ji dûrahîyake naskirî, bana wek mîna erdk-
lorê û li ser pozik de sembola rojê. Min tu carî kevirê Gorê nedîtin.
92 deverên Êzîdî divê ji terefî Daîşê hatîye hilweşandin. Tene ne deverên me,
bêrîyên me yên li wan deran, yên ku hebûn. Vîdeoya ku bi çaguçê betonan
dişkînin û çaguçê mezin muze ya Mûsilê de digerin û peykeran yek bi yek tînin
xware, hûrhûrî dikin, yên kû ji dusedhezar salî zêdetir de hatîye parastin, min
dîsa û dîsa lê temaşe kir. Min dizanîbû kengî mûzîk dest pê dike, kengî wêne
disekine, kengî leşkerên Daîşê bi çaguçê xwe yê mezin amade dikin, di heman
demê de wêne didine sekinandin û hêdî hêdî dide xuya kiri, bi çaguçan li pey-
kerê ku hatine xwarê dixin, heta ku vîdeo dîsa normal berdewam dike.
Ewqas hindik dikarim bawer bikim, tiştê ez li pêş xwe dibînim. Ev kevirên goristanê nîşane ku em demek dirêjin li vir in. Berê jî pêşîyên me li van deran, erd
dihajotin, pez xwedî dikirin û li ser vê axê mirîyên xwe vedişartin.
Piranî ji wan, tiştê ez dinivîsim, rêza xwe tune ye. Hevok, peyv, qutbûn, ber bi
tu tişt bûnê diçe. Ez wan digîhînim hev. Hinekî bi tîpên mezin dest pê dibe û bi
xalekê dawî dibe. Di navberê de belkî bêhnokek, hevokek nîvçe, peywendîyak
tiştê ku tê ser axavtin çêdike. Dîsa tîpên mezin, kirde, lêker, bireser heta xala
dawî. Ristbend bi ristbend. Zimanek nîne, ê ez têde dinivîsim. Min gera xwe li
ser kompîtirê di dosyayeya belgeyan de qeyt kirin, dengên qeyîtkirî, yên di
telefona min de.
Ez ji xwe re dokumentasyonekê temaşe dikim. Mirovek ji Komîsyona Navne-
teweyî ya Huquqî û Hesabdarîyê dibêje ku Daîş bi sê milan ve êrîşî Şingalê
kirin. Du mila ji başûr, yek jê Sûrî û ji bakur. Ji vir dest pê dikin, Êzîdîyan ji hev
diqetînin, ew mirov dibêje û li ser kartekê nîşan dide. Mêr û jinan ji hev diqetînin. Ev yek wek mînak li herderê gundê dagirkirî wek heve.

Ez dixwînim „Celadê rûrêş Jihadi John", ez dixwînim „Koleyên seksê yên
Daîşê", „Jinên Daîşê". Ez kujeran naxwînim. Ez kesên filitîne naxwînim.
Ez dibêjim, divê ez hevpeyivînê bifikirim ku moderatora radîyo ya kanadî bi
Nadia Murad çêkirî bû. Divê ez li ser bifikirim, çawa wê moderatorê ji Nadia
Murad pirs kir, çawa tê hîskirin, gava mirov wek mîna birêser nêzîkatî bibîne?
Te çawa hîskir, gava wan te wûsa bikaranîn? Wan çawa we ji hev qetan û li we
çi hate kirin? Wan li we dan? Û piştre hûn hatin tecawiz kirin. Wan her tim dest
we da. Çawa we dikarî bû hemû tişt ragirin?
Ev, ez ji dêya xwe dibêjim, hûn dixwazin bibîhîsin. Êdî pêwîstî tune ye hûn biçin
sînemayê, ez dibêjim. Bavê min dibêje, gava ga bikeve, gelek kêr hene.

Li kêlaka xaltîka Adar û apê Xelef li ser paldankê rûniştî me, laptopa min li ser
congê min, gûhik di gûhên min de. Ez dinîvîsim: Xatê dibêje, xêr hatin ba
êzîdîyan. Ez dinîvîsim: Xatê bi uniform me pêşwazî dike. Îro ew vala ye. Lê
wek fermandar bi mere dive tenê bi uniform biaxive. Ez dinîvîsim: Odeyek
rûniştandinê, wek piranî odeyê rûniştandinê , yên ku ez lê bûm, odeyek ji
penaberan.
Xatê dibêje, ez jî keceke ji Şingalê me. Ez li Şîngalê hatime cîhanê, ew dibêje.
Hûn dizanin, çi qewîmî ye, di 3.8.2014dan de, gava Daîş hatî bû. Em 12 rojan li
çîyan hatibûn girtin, got Xatê.

Ez rûdinim û dinîvîsim: Xatê dibêje, min ji jinekê ji Koço bihîst e. Ew bi zarokê
xwere hate revandin. Sê roj û sê şevan li Balefirgeha Tal Afar wek girtî tê girtin.
Ew zarok biçûk bû, hîn şîr vedixwar, hîn nebûbû yek salî jî. Ew zarok birçî bû û
digîrîya. Sê rojan. Xatê dibêje: Zarok ew qas bi deng digirîya ku serokê Daîşê
nikarî bû razayê. Serokê Daîşê ji jinikê re dibêje, ka zarok bide min, piştre zarok
nema digirî. Jinik zarok dide wî, ji ber ku ew difikirî, ewê xwarin û vexwarin bide
wî. Serokê Daîşê zarok digire û bi zarok re diçe xwaringehê. Li xwaringehê ew
radihêje kêreke mezin û sere zarok jê dike. Ew goştê yê zarok dikelîne û dide
ber dayîka zarok. Dayik di serî de fahm nake, Xatê dibêje, gava destê zarok di-
bîne şunde. Piştre êdî heşê xwe wenda dike.

Li kêlaka xaltîka Adar û apê Xelef li ser paldankê rûniştî me. Ez dinîvîsim ku ew
ya dawî bû, tiştê dayikê têgîhîşte, berî ku ew heşê xwe wenda bike.
Ez qeyda deng disekinînim.
 Dema ku Xatê diaxive, dest girî dike. Hêstirê wê li ser rûyê wê tên xwarê, Xatê
axaftina xwe berdewam dike.Ez dinîvîsim: Xatê bi uniformê xwe rûdinê û digirî,
ez jî dest bi girî dikim. Û dîsa ez li sel paldankê rûdinim, cîhazê deng qeytkirinê
qeyd digire û dinivîse: Xatê digirî.
Xatê dibêje: Ez hûnermendek bûm, wek mîna bavê min. Vîdeoyekê nîşanî me
dide, ji youtûbê. Barkirin di 9.4.2013 de, şazdeh Meh, berî ku Daîş bê Şengalê.
Xatê kirasekî sor û bazin û gûhar. Bi tembûra xwe rûniştî ye û lê dide û li pişt
çîyayê Şingalê. Xatê dîsa dest bi girî dike.Ez dinivîsim: Xatê digirî.
Xatê dibêje: gelek kaset min çêkirî bû, lê min hemû li pişt xwe hiştin.
Xatê dibêje:Piştî em ji Şingalê derketin, min ji dêûbavê xwe re got, êdî ez nema
tembûrê dixwazim, ez roketekê dixwazim.
Xate vîdeoya duyemîn nîşanî me dide. Xatê bi yekîne, nêzî Misûlê. Bi çong diçin
pişt kîsê kumê û çekên xwe li hemberî bajêr nîşan dide. Xatê distirê.
Di cîhêkî de, di cihazê dengqeyitkirinê de heye, gava Faruk ji Xatê re dibêje, ez
jî êzîdî me. Pîştî Faruk got, Xatê dixwaze bizanibe, ez ji kîjan malbatê têm. Ez
dibêjim, bavê min ji Hesekê ye, em mirud in, Xatltî, ji Xûdan Mend ez dibêjim.
Dêya min Alman e, dibêjim ez.
Xatê radibe li ser linga, diçe ba derî ,kesek ji mere çay bîne. Xatê li min dinêre,
wekî din tu ji mere qala Almanya bike, heger tu li ba Xatê ba û te qet çayek jî
nedigirt.
Xatê ji minre dibêje xweşkê. Xatê dibêje, dibêje tu jî xweşkeke.
Hûn birçî ne, dipirse Xatê.
Divê em biçin, dibêje Faruk. Ez cîhazê dengqeytkirinê digirim.
Dereng bûye, dibêje Faruk, û dive hîn em biçin Duhokê.
Ez radibim ser xwe û deste dîya Xatê maçî dikim û destên bavê Xate.
Min ji xwere her tim pirsî, çima li me wûsa dikin. Çawa dikarin tiştê wûlo bikin.
Lê ev ne pirs e. Gava ez bi Cana re li Kivaxê meşîyam, min ji xwere pirsî. Li ba
kavilan derbas bûn, ew carekê li gundê wan bû û kuçikê sê lingo, ji ber sede-
mekê li vir bû. Û li ber dibistina kevn rûniştî û serî rakirî jor, li me nerî bû, gava
em li ber wî dimeşîyan. Gava leşkerên tirka hîn li vir bûn û gundê vala dişopan-
din, Ji bo ku tu şervanên PKK`ê li xwe li wê derê veneşêre. Û Cana li ser gir li pişt
gund nîşan da, heta gava darên pîroz li wir bûn. Di nava rojê an jî di şevê de,
leşkerên tirka dive ew dîti bin. Çima, ez ji Cana re dipirsim, qey têra wan nake ku
êdî êzîdî li vir nemani. Van daran li wan çi kiri ne.
Meseleya wan ne text bûn, hîn qurmikên jêkirî niha li wir in, li kêlaka êzingan in.
Leşkeren tirk dihatin vir, rojekê an jî şevekê, an jî her roj û şev li gund nobed
digirtin û dixwaztin lê binêrin ku çawa ew darên pîroz tên qirkirin.

Gava em ji Kampê şûnve bûn, min ji xwe pirsî, û ez li ba apê Xelef û xaltîka
Adar li malê li ser hêlkana holîyvud bûm û di bêrika xwe de ez li cixarê digerî-
yam, hesteyê xwe, û hîn jî niha, dema ku min ji zûve ye ditî bû. Gava ez li Laleşê
li ser cîhe pahn li ber perestgehê rûniştî bûm, bi şêx Hesen, Faruk û zarokên
kanîya sipî dibistanê Sandiwîç dixwar û Faruk dibêje, keça li kêlaka te hatibû
firotan. Ew qas û ew qas car hatibû firotan. Min hejmar ji bîr kir, û Keç û ez em
Sandiwîça xwe dixwun. Ew xort, ê ku li hemberî te rûniştiye, Faruk dibêje, li
ber çavên wî serê bavê wî jêkirin. Ji wê virve ew zarok perwerde dike, dibêje
ew êdî şev nikare razê, dibêje şêx. Faruk dibêje, ew çi ye, serî jêkirin. Çima ew
wûsa dikin, serî jêkirin.
Dêya min dibêje, ew bi rastî jî hov in. Wusa hov. Û bêhnê vedide û dibêje ku hovîtîyak wûsa, dîya min dibêje, bi hovîtîyak wusa û dikeve lêgerina muqayesê,
tiştek dikaribe vê hovîtîye bipîvî ne. Lê, dîya min bêhnê vedide û dibêje, bi rastî.
Ew ne mirov in, bavê min dibêje. Kesek, tiştê wisa dike, ne mirov e. Çawa meri-
vek, tiştê wisa dike, karibe bibe Mirov. Na, dibêje bavê min, ew ne mirov e.
Hevala dîya min, ew mesîhîyê ji Musulê ye, li Erbîl em diçin serdana wê, dibêje,
ew bijîjkekê nasdike, yeke sunî, yeka di nexweşxaneya Musulê kar dike. Ji wê
bijîjkê re keçeke êzîdî dibin, dibêje hevala dîya min, neh salî, ew dîsa û dîsa
tecawuz kiri bûn, ku ew tişt wisa êyarkirî bû. Û bijîjk, gava wê ew keç dît, got,
hûn çawa dikarin tiştê wisa bikin. Û li ser pirsa bijîjkê, ew ne pirs bû, serî hati
bû jê kirin.
Ew difikirin, ew dê biçin bihiştê, dibêje dîya min.
Adara 2019dan de, pîştî Daîş di warê leşkerî dawî bû, li kampan hejmara kesê
xwekuştin zêde dibe. Li ser telefone ji dêya xwe re dibêjim, em mirin. Wan em
qir kirin.
Ez li xwaringehê me. Ez tabletekê digirim. Ez li ba maseyekê rûdinim. Ez dixwum
û ez tenê me. Ez dixwazim hîn biçim pirtûkxanê pîştî xwarina nîvroj. Ez di telefona xwe de nûçeyan dixwînim. Hêzen taybet yên leşkerên Birîtanî, 50 serî yên
êzîdîyan dîtîne. Serî di tenekeyê çopê de ditîne. Li ser rîya pirtûkxanê ez li dîya
xwe digerim, ev fikreke vala ye, ez dibêjim. Çima, ez dibêjim, ew hatin şikêna-
nindin û ya dawî, ya ku ew dikarin, ji demek dirêje dîyare, êdî ew nikarin serbike-
vin, ji zû de ew hatine şikênandin, dîsa serê êzîdîyan jê dikin. Heta dawîya wan
jî, wan dev ji tunekirina me berneda.
Êzîdî hatin qir kirin, dibêjim ez.
Dîya min dibêje, tu nikarî bivêje. Tiştê wisa tu nikarî bivêjî. Tu nikarî wisa
bivêje.
Em ew in, yê ku ê mayin in, dibêjim ez. Gava hatin Şingalê me tune bikin, dibêjim ez, em li ewropa bûn. Gava hatin kalikên me bikujin ez hîn çênebû bûm. Lê
bapîrê min hebû. Heger dapîrê min tune ba, dibêjim ez, ez dê ne li vir bam.
Ew hatin Şingalê, me êzîdîyan hemûyan qir bikin. Em li ewropa bûn, gava hatin
Şingalê. Em ew in, yên wan nekuştine. Em jîyan nakin. Em yên nehatine kuştin,
dibêjim ez. Ev cudahî ye, dibêjim ez. Yên din li virin, ji ber ku ew li virin, ew jîyan
dikin, lê na, ne ji ber ku ew nehatin kuştin.
Mervê me yên Şingalê jîyan dikin, ji ber ku erebeyek wan hebû, dibêjim ez.
Lê di navbera jiyanê de be û jîyan cuda ye.
Pirsa ji bo çi ne pirs e. Ew pênaskirina mat bûnê ye. Ez nikarim wê bibersivînim.
Heger ez karibim bibersivînim, dive ez an Daîş bim an jî diba ku ez Daîş bam an
jî ez wek mîna Daîşê diaxivim an jî di min de Daîş diaxive.
Ji ber ku em bê bawerî ne, kafir, diba ku bersiv. Lê ji ber ku li ser vêya ew ne
bersive. Û pirs ji bo çi ne pirse.
Divê ez li ser bifikirim, heta mirina bapîra min wê çawa dipirsîya, çima wan bavê
min kuştin. Wî çi kiri bû ku wî kuştin.

Û ez, heger min ji wê dipirsiyam, heta mirina xwe fikirî be, tiştek tune. Wî tu tişt nekiri bû. Jiber vêya tu sedem tune ye. Û ji ber ku pirsa dapîram ne pirs bû, li ser wê min tiştek negot.

Bi Faruk re li ser girekî em diçin Xhankê. Ji gir mirov dikare benda Musulê bivîne. Û benda Musulê li wure, ez çawa xweşik dibêjim, cîhê ku roj diçe ava.

Ava şîn, li ser pîyê din yê cadê Ronahî. Li wir Daîş lê bû, dibêje Faruk. Benda Musulê li sînor.

Em li pişt dolabeka bi motîva bawerîya êzîdîyan park dikin, kevirê Spî û sembola Rojê li ser pozikê wê. Çiqas xweşik, dibêjim ez. Ez wêneyekî dikşînim. Ku wan 2014 berda hember kiri bûn. Û tenê benda Musulê di navbera gundê êzîdîyan û Daîşê. Wisa nêzîk, mirov dikare hember bivîne. Faruk diçe li ser dîwarekî. Ji dîwaran gulîyê darek zeytûnê bilin dibe. Faruk radije têlê bi stirî dide kêlekekê, li vir derîyak e. Ji ber ajalan, ew dibêje, gorên apê min. Ew lampeya telefonê vêdixe û ronî dide kevirên tirban.

Ev ne cara yekemîne ku Faruk goran nîşanî min dide. Û Faruk ne yê tenê ye. Di demekê de li vir mirî ji zindîyan pirtir re. Û ew dem jî hema niha ye.

Baxçê yê dapîrûbapîrê min ê li Tel Khatounê şewitî ye. Dar jî, yên bavê min çandî bû. Ev, demekê Xanîyek bû, îro bûye parastinek gorê ye. Kesek ji xaltîka min re wêneyek û videoyek şande: Kesek diçe nava baxçe. Ji çeper bi çeper, wêne kil dibe, dişemite. Dîya min ji telefona xwe de nîşanî min dide û dibêje, ew wan dar bûn, yên ku bavê te berî çil sal berê çandî bu. Bavê min dibêje, çend sal berdewam kir, heta ew dar ewqas mezin bûn.

Kesek ji mere jî videoyek şande ji çeper, cihê ku li ser dapîra min vedişêrin. Kesek ji malbatê nikarî bû beşdar bibe, me nikarî bû wê veşêrin. Û dotmam ma min bi tabutê re, ya ku dapîra min di hundirê wê de bû, diçin Tirkî, heta sînorê Sûrî, cihê ku j i terefî gel de tê girtin, hinekî bi pere, da ku karibe dapîra min li ser wê çeperê li kêlaka bapîre min bê veşartin.

Gava ez li ber goran yên apê Faruk disekinim, û wî bi lampa bêrîkê kevirên goran ronî dikir, min ji xwe pirsî, gelo ezê jî wisa carekê li ber tirba dîya bisekinim û niha wek mîna Faruk kevirê gorê yê dîya xwe maç dike.

Divê ez li ser bifikirim, çawa, gava ez zarok li pişt dîwarê baxçe li gundê dapîr û bapîrên min disekinim û ereban min dû mêz dikir, yên ku li ber sînorê tirka ber bi iraqê diçûn an jî ji Iraqê dihatin. Li ser wan cadan diçin, ê liser yê ku ez jî li ser çibûm, li bajaran bûn, yên ez jî li wur bûm. Kobanê, Reqqa, Palmyra.

Hemû tişt ev bû, difikirim ez. Cade bi dirêjî bi erebeyen, carekê bizîvire, ber bi Bajid, li ser Dîcle, yê li vir destekî tengtire û ne wek bendava Misulê freh e. Û li pîyê din yê sînor jî. Ez dikarim hemû gerên me bînim bîra xwe, bi malbatê re, çawa baş e gava bavê min wek mîna xwendevan çu bû seyranê. Çawa em, ez, xweşk û birayê min, dotmamê min û pismamê min li ber çem dilîstin, li restorantekê xwarin dixwarin. Wêne ji wan hîn hene, yê ku apê min ji me kişandi bû.

Ew dikarîbû wisa zû li me jî biqewimîya, difikirim ez, gava ez li ber Derabûn disekinîm û li cadeyê dinerim. Dozdeh kîlomtre. Çiqasin dozdeh kîlomtre. Dibe ku pazdeh deqiqe. Em li ber taştê li malê dotmama Faruk, çayê vedixwin, li malekî wek vê malê, tenê dozdeh ji vir dûr, 2014.

Îlon 2018 de bi balafirê diçim Îzmîrê û ji wir difirim rojhilat. Ez dinivîsim: ez dixwazim wî gundî serlêdan bikim, wî yê ku dapîrê min tê de mezin bûye, yê malbata me jê hatîye derxistin, gava ew hîn zarok bûn. Wan em dorpêç kiri bûn, dibêje bavê min, wan dixwest me bikujin. Malbata me di nîvê şevê de koçber bûn, hemû tişt li pê xwe hişt, di serî de Şingal, piştre Sûrî. Ez dinivîsim: car caran dapîra min divê koçber biva. Cara dawî 2014 û her car, ji ber ku ew êzîdî bû. Ez dinivîsim: kî carekê bibe penaber, penaber dimîne.

Dapîra min li mala dêûbavê min rûniştî ye. Heger em tiştek ji bo xwarinê bidinê,
ew dibêje, hûn dixwazin min bi jahr bikin. Gava ew li ser pêlika dimeşe, dibêje
ew, balder be, wan li me feq vekirine. Ew dibêje, em hatin dorpêç kirin.
Ez telefonî bavê xwe dikim û dibêjim, ez diçim Bazîvanê.
Ez dibêjim, ez nikarim wê li ser Google Mapsê bivînim.
Bavê min dibêje, ez ji tere binîvîsînim, gava min navê wî yên tirkî dît.
Dêya min telefonî min dike û dibêje, bavê min gotîye, Cîndî bû berî çend sal
berê li wir buyî. Wî gotibû ku, li gund niha misliman dijîn. Heger tu bivêjî ku ez
êzîdî me, wê te bikujin.
Dêya min dibêje, dive tu ji kesekî re nebêje tu êzîdî ye.
Bavê min dinivîse, min dît nave wî gundi çîye.
Dêya min dibêje, apê Hemo numareyek daye min, ya yekî Hecî ye.
Bavê min dibêje, Hecî sunî ye, lê pêşîyên me hevdû nasdikin.
Ez li Amedê me, gava bavê min telefon dike û dibêje, Hecî hay jê heye. Wî got,
dîvê tirsa te tune
be.

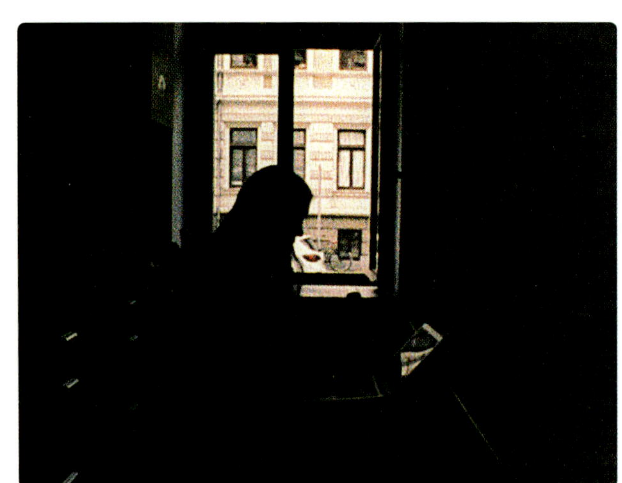

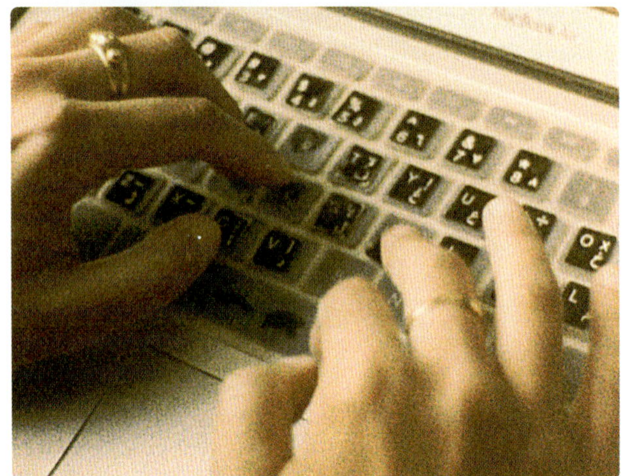

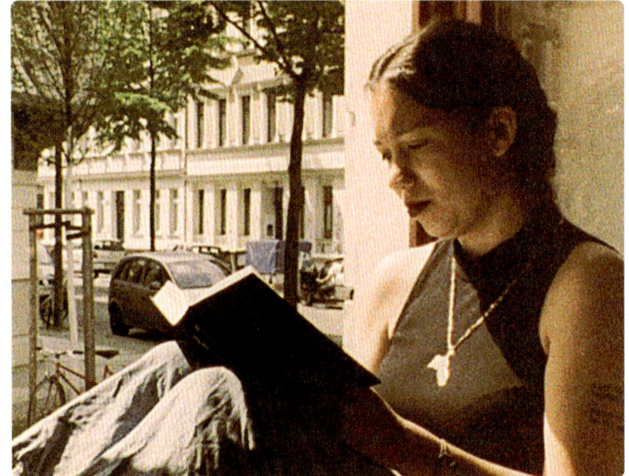

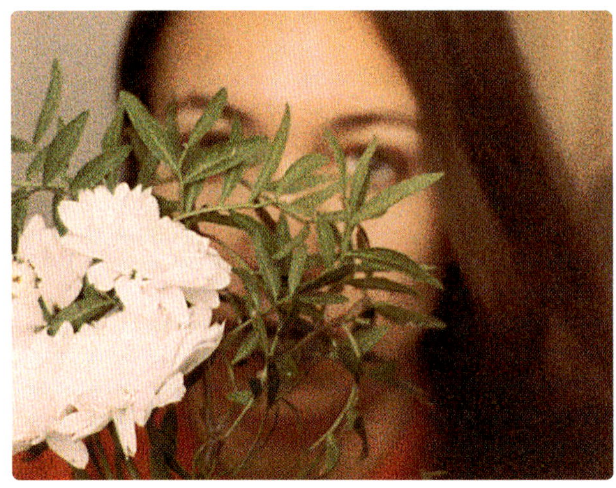

LXVII

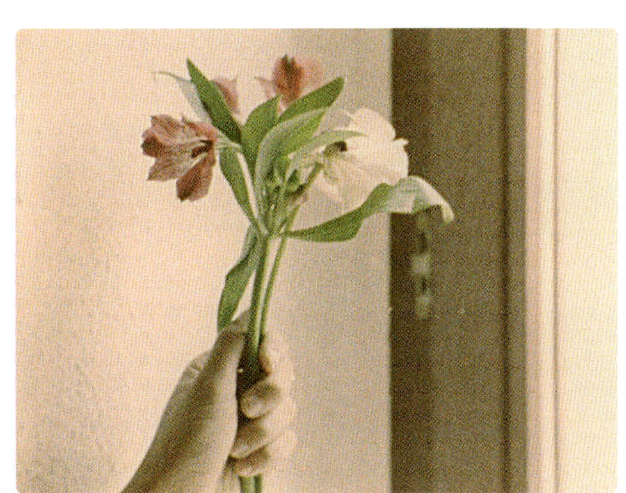

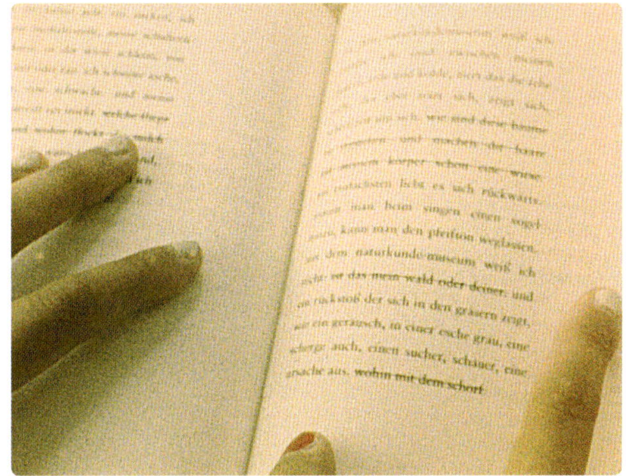

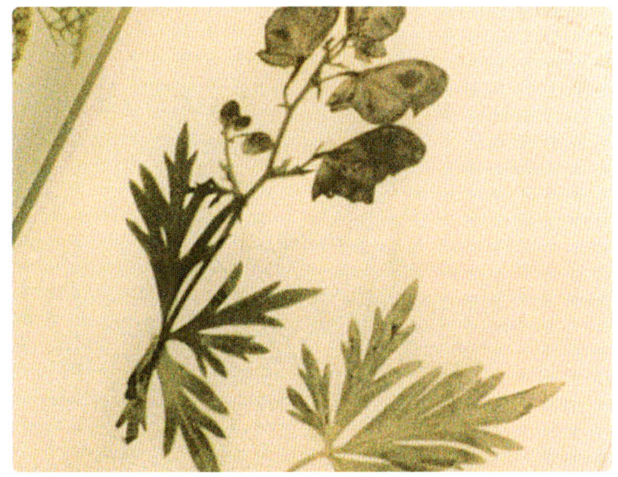

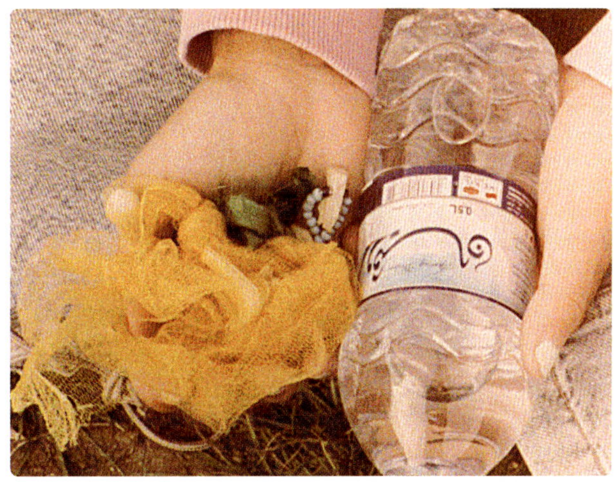

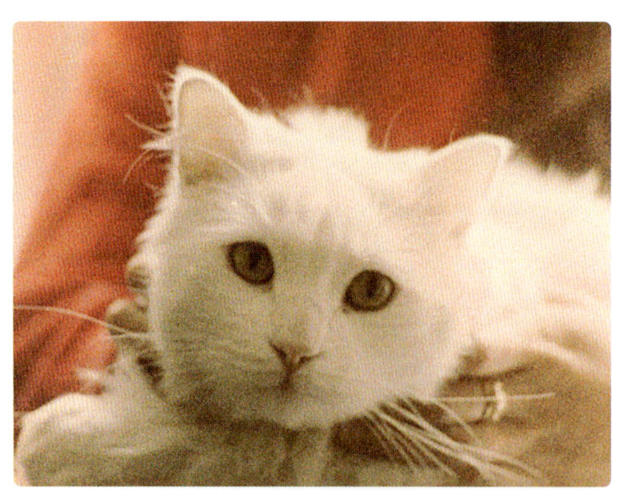

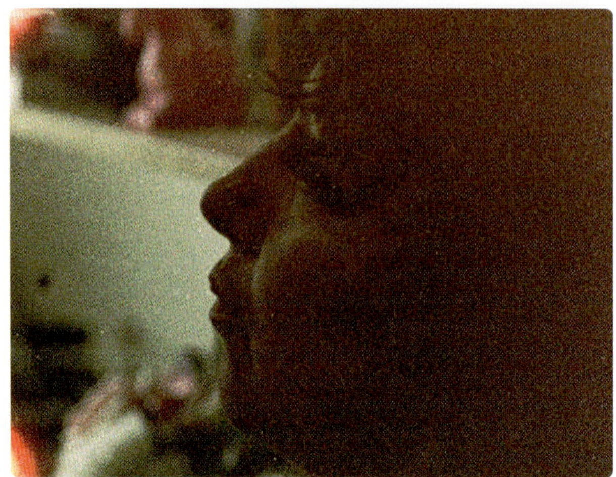

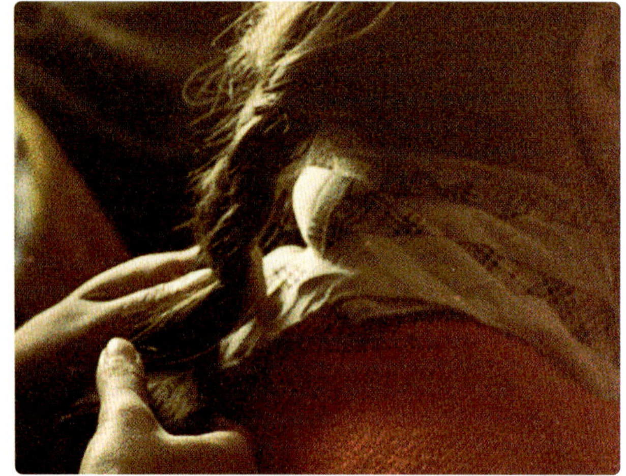

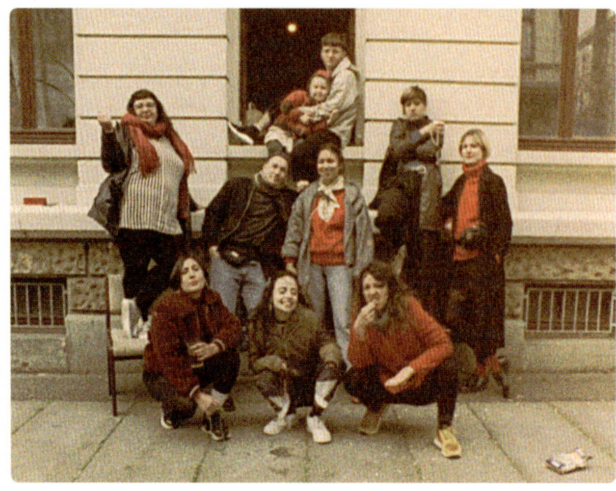

Cana Bilir-Meier

born 1986 in Munich, lives and works in Munich and Vienna, studied at the Academy of Fine Arts and the Friedl Kubelka School for Independent Film in Vienna as well as at the Sabancı University in Istanbul. Her works have been exhibited nationally and internationally, including at the Tensta Konsthall in Stockholm, the Kunsthalle Wien, the Public Art Munich Festival in Munich, the *Parlament der Körper* at documenta 14 in Kassel, Ankara International Film Festival, and many other venues. In 2018 she won the ars viva prize of the Kulturkreis der deutschen Wirtschaft and in 2016 Bilir-Meier won the Birgit-Jürgenssen-Prize among other awards and scholarships.

Burcu Dogramaci

is a Professor of Art History at the Ludwig-Maximilians-University Munich. She researches and publishes works on Art of the 20th century and present day, with a focus on exile and migration, photography, fashion, architecture, cities, modern sculpture and live art. Publications (selections): *Handbook of Art and Global Migration Theories, Practices and Challenges,* De Gruyter, Munich 2019 (ed. with B. Mersmann); *Nomadic Camera, Photography, Exile and Migration*, Special Issue of the magazine *Fotogeschichte*, H. 151/2019 (ed. with H. Roth); *Performance Photography, Live Art in the Age of Reproducibility*, Wilhelm Fink, Padeborn 2018; *Passages of Exile*, An International Yearbook, Exile research, vol. 35, edition text+kritik, Munich 2017 (ed. with E. Otto); *Reorientation. Context of Contemporary Art in Turkey and On The Road*, Kadmos, Berlin 2017 (ed. with M. Smolińska); Homeland. *An Artistic Search for Traces*, Böhlau, Cologne 2016; *Photographing and Researching. Scientific Expeditions with the Camera in Turkish Exile after 1933*, Jonas, Marburg 2013; *Migration and Artistic Production. New Perspectives*, (ed.) transcript, Bielefeld 2013.

geboren 1986 in München, lebt und arbeitet in München und Wien, studierte an der Akademie der bildenden Künste und der Schule Friedl Kubelka für unabhängigen Film in Wien sowie an der Sabancı-Universität in Istanbul. Ihre Arbeiten wurden national und international ausgestellt; u.a. in der Tensta Konsthall in Stockholm, in der Kunsthalle Wien, beim Public Art Munich Festival in München, im Programm *Parlament der Körper* der documenta 14 in Kassel, auf dem Ankara International Film Festival und an vielen weiteren Orten. 2018 war sie Preisträgerin des ars viva Preises vom Kulturkreis der deutschen Wirtschaft und 2016 gewann Bilir-Meier den Birgit-Jürgenssen-Preis neben weiteren Auszeichnungen und Stipendien.

ist Professorin für Kunstgeschichte an der Ludwig-Maximilians-Universität München. Sie forscht und publiziert zur Kunst des 20. Jahrhunderts und der Gegenwart mit einem Schwerpunkt auf Exil und Migration, Fotografie, Mode, Architektur, Stadt, Skulptur der Moderne und Live Art. Publikationen (Auswahl): *Handbook of Art and Global Migration Theories, Practices, and Challenges*, De Gruyter, München 2019 (hg. mit B. Mersmann); *Nomadic Camera. Fotografie, Exil und Migration*, Themenheft der Zeitschrift *Fotogeschichte*, H. 151/2019 (hg. mit H. Roth); *Fotografie der Performance. Live Art im Zeitalter ihrer Reproduzierbarkeit*, Wilhelm Fink, Paderborn 2018; *Passagen des Exils / Passages of Exile*, Ein Internationales Jahrbuch, Exilforschung 35, edition text+kritik, München 2017 (hg. mit E. Otto); *Re-Orientierung. Kontexte zeitgenössischer Kunst in der Türkei und unterwegs*, Kadmos, Berlin 2017 (hg. mit M. Smolińska); *Heimat. Eine künstlerische Spurensuche*, Böhlau, Köln 2016; *Fotografieren und Forschen. Wissenschaftliche Expeditionen mit der Kamera im türkischen Exil nach 1933*, Jonas, Marburg 2013; *Migration und künstlerische Produktion. Aktuelle Perspektiven*, (hg.) transcript, Bielefeld 2013.

(1986 Münih doğumlu, Münih ve Viyana'da yaşıyor ve çalışıyor) Viyana'da Güzel Sanatlar Akademisi'nde ve Friedl Kubelka Bağımsız Film Okulu'nda ve İstanbul'da Sabancı Üniversitesi'nde okudu. Çalışmaları ulusal ve uluslararası sergilerde gösterildi; Stockholm'deki Tensta Konsthall'de, Viyana Sanat Salonu'nda, Münih'teki Public Art Munich Festivali'nde, Kassel'deki documenta 14'te Vücutların Meclisi programında, Ankara Uluslararası Film Festivali'nde ve bir çok başka yerde Bilir-Meier, 2018'de Alman Ticareti Kültür Cemiyetinin ars viva Ödülü'nü kazandı ve 2016'da başka ödül ve bursların yanısıra, Birgit Jürgenssen Ödülü'ne layık görüldü.

Münih Ludwig-Maximilians Üniversitesi'nde sanat tarihi profesörü. 20. yüzyılın sanatı, ağırlıkla sürgün ve göç, fotoğrafçılık, moda, mimarlık, kent, çağdaş heykelcilik ve Live Art üzerine araştırıyor ve yazıyor. Yayınları (seçki): *Handbook of Art and Global Migration Theories, Practices, and Challenges*, De Gruyter, Münih 2019 (diğer yayıncı B. Mersmann); *Nomadic Camera. Fotografie, Exil und Migration (Fotoğrafçılık, Sürgün ve Göç)*, Fotogeschichte dergisinin ağırlık konulu yayını, H. 151/2019 (diğer yayıncı H. Roth); *Fotografie der Performance (Performans Fotoğrafçılığı) Live Art im Zeitalter ihrer Reproduzierbarkeit (Çoğaltılabirliği Döneminde Live Art)*, Wilhelm Fink, Paderborn 2018; *Passagen des Exils / Passages of Exile (Sürgün Dönemleri)*, Jahrbuch Exilforschung 35 (Sürgün Araştırmaları 35 Yıllığı), edition text+kritik, Münih 2017 (diğer yayıncı E. Otto); *Re-Orientierung. Kontexte zeitgenössischer Kunst in der Türkei und unterwegs (Yeniden Yönlenme. Türkiye'de ve Yolda Çağdaş Sanatın Bağlantıları)*, Kadmos, Berlin 2017 (diğer yayıncı M. Smolińska); *Heimat. Eine künstlerische Spurensuche (Vatan. Sanatsal Bir İz Sürüşü)*, Böhlau, Köln 2016; *Fotografieren und Forschen. Wissenschaftliche Expeditionen mit der Kamera im türkischen Exil nach 1933 (Fotoğrafçılık ve Araştırma. 1933 Sonrası Türkiye Sürgününde Kamerayla Bilimsel Keşif Gezisi)*, Jonas, Marburg 2013; *Migration und künstlerische Produktion. Aktuelle Perspektiven (Göç ve Sanatsal Üretim. Aktüel Bakış Açıları)*, transcript, Bielefeld 2013 (Yayıncı).

Banu Karaca

is an anthropologist working at the intersection of political anthropology, critical theory, art and aesthetics, nationalism and cultural policy, museums and feminist memory studies. She holds a Ph.D. from the Graduate Center, CUNY. Her recent publications interrogate freedom of expression in the arts, the visualization of gendered memories of war and political violence, and visual literacy. Her manuscript "The National Frame: State Violence and Aesthetic Practice in Turkey and Germany" analyzes the entrenchment of art in state violence, and she is co-editor of *Women Mobilizing Memory* (Columbia University Press). She is the co-founder of Siyah Bant, a research platform that documents arts censorship in Turkey. Karaca is a Faculty Fellow at Columbia University's Center for the Study of Social Difference and previously held fellowships in the "Art Histories and Aesthetics" and "Europe in the Middle East — The Middle East in Europe" Research Programs at the Forum Transregionale Studien, Berlin. Her current research on how dispossessed, looted and lost art works have shaped the writing of post-Ottoman art histories is supported by a grant from the Foundation for Arts Initiatives.

Ronya Othmann

born 1993 in Munich, began her studies in 2014 at the German Literature Institute Leipzig. She writes poetry, prose and essays, as well as journalistic works. She has been awarded the residency of the 2015 Künstlerhaus Lukas, and the MDR Literature Prize 2015, among others. In 2017, she won the Caroline Schlegel Prize for Essay and the Open Mike for Poetry. In 2018, she and Beliban zu Stolberg and Eser Aktay received the Cross-Border Scholarship for Turkey and Kurdistan. This year she is nominated for the Ingeborg Bachmann Prize. She organized the Kurdish Film Days in Leipzig, and in 2018, was on the jury of the International Film Festival in Duhok, the Kurdistan Region of Iraq. She is co-editor of the *Flexen, Flaneusen* schreiben Städte* which was published in June 2019 by Verbrecher Verlag. Publications in *edition text+kritik, taz*, the literature section of *DER SPIEGEL*, *Zeit Online*, *Zeit Campus*, *edit*, and the queer literature magazine *glitter*.

ist eine Anthropologin, die an der Schnittstelle von politischer Anthropologie, kritischer Theorie, Kunst und Ästhetik, Nationalismus und kultureller Politik, Museen und feministischen Erinnerungskulturen arbeitet. Sie promovierte am Graduate Center, CUNY. Ihre neuesten Publikationen fragen nach der Freiheit des Ausdrucks in der Kunst, der Visualisierung von geschlechtsspezifischen Erinnerungen an Krieg und politische Gewalt sowie nach visueller Literarität. Ihr Manuskript „The National Frame: State Violence and Aesthetic Practice in Turkey and Germany" analysiert die Verankerung von Kunst in der Staatsgewalt und sie ist Mitherausgeberin von *Women Mobilizing Memory* (Columbia University Press). Sie ist Mitgründerin von Siyah Bant, einer Forschungsplattform, die die Kunstzensur in der Türkei dokumentiert. Karaca ist Dozentin am Columbia University's Center for the Study of Social Difference und erhielt zuvor Stipendien in den Bereichen "Kunstgeschichte und Ästhetik" und in "Europa im Nahen Osten – Der Nahe Osten in Europa" am Forum Transregionale Studien, Berlin. Ihre aktuelle Forschung über die Frage, wie enteignete, geplünderte und verlorene Kunstwerke das Schreiben von postosmanischen Kunstgeschichten beeinflusst haben, wird unterstützt mit einem Stipendium der Foundation for Arts Initiatives.

geboren 1993 in München, studiert seit 2014 am Deutschen Literaturinstitut Leipzig. Sie schreibt Lyrik, Prosa und Essays und arbeitet als Journalistin. Sie erhielt u. a. das Aufenthaltsstipendium des Künstlerhaus Lukas 2015 und den MDR-Literaturpreis 2015. 2017 gewann sie den Caroline-Schlegel-Förderpreis für Essay und den Open Mike für Lyrik. 2018 erhielt sie mit Beliban zu Stolberg und Eser Aktay zusammen das Grenzgänger-Stipendium für die Türkei und Kurdistan. Dieses Jahr ist sie für den Ingeborg-Bachmann-Preis nominiert. Sie organisierte die kurdischen Filmtage in Leipzig und war 2018 in der Jury des Internationalen Filmfestivals in Duhok, der Autonomen Region Kurdistan, Irak. Sie ist Mitherausgeberin von *Flexen, Flaneusen* schreiben Städte*, die im Juni 2019 im Verbrecher Verlag erschienen ist. Veröffentlichungen u. a. in *edition text+kritik, taz*, Literaturbeilage von *DER SPIEGEL*, *Zeit Online*, *Zeit Campus*, *edit* und dem queeren Literaturmagazin *glitter*.

siyasal antropoloji, eleştirel teori, sanat ve estetik, milliyetçilik ve kültür politikası, müzeler ve feminist anı kültürünün kesiştiği alanlarda çalışan bir antropolog. Doktorasını Graduate Center, CUNY'de yaptı. Yeni yayınları sanatta özgür ifade şekilleri, cinsiyete özgü savaş ve siyasi şiddet anıları ve ayrıca yazımın görselleştirilmesi sorularını irdeliyor. *The National Frame: State Violence and Aesthetic Practice in Turkey and Germany* yazısında devlet hakimiyeti altındaki sanatı analiz ediyor ve kendisi *Women Mobilizing Memory*'nin (Columbia University Press) yayımcılarından. Kendisi ayrıca Siyah Bant isimli, Türkiye'de sanata uygulanan sansürü belgeleyen bir araştırma platformunun kurucularından. Karaca Columbia University's Center for the Study of Social Difference'de doçentlik yapıyor ve daha önce Berlin'deki Transbölgesel Araştırmalar Forumunda "Sanat ve Estetik" ve "Yakın Doğu'da Avrupa – Avrupa'da Yakın Doğu" alanında çalışmalar için burs almıştı. Şu an üzerine çalıştığı, Foundation for Arts Initiatives tarafından bursla desteklenen araştırma ise, kamulaştırılan, yağmalanan ve kayıp olan sanat eserlerinin Osmanlı sonrası sanat tarihyazımını nasıl etkilediği hakkında.

1993 Münih doğumlu. 2014'ten beri Leipzig Alman Edebiyat Enstitüsü'nde okuyor. Şiir, nesir ve denemeler yazıyor ve gazeteci olarak çalışıyor. Başka ödüllerin yanı sıra 2015'te Sanatçı Evi Lukas'ın İkamet Bursu'nu ve 2015 MDR Edebiyat Ödülü'nü kazandı. 2017'de Caroline Schlegel Deneme Yazılarını Teşvik Ödülünü ve Open Mike Şiir Ödülünü, 2018'de Beliban zu Stolberg ve Eser Aktay ile birlikte, Türkiye ve Kürdistan için Sınır Gezginleri Bursu'nu kazandı. Leipzig'deki Kürt Film Günleri'ni düzenledi ve 2018'de Irak Kürdistan Özerk Bölgesi Duhok'taki Uluslararası Film Festivalinin jüri heyetinde yer aldı. Haziran 2019'da Verbrecher Yayınevi'nde yayınlanan *Flexen, Flaneusen* schreiben Städte*'nin (Flexen, Flaneusen*Kentleri Yazıyor) yayıncılarındandır. Yazıları diğerlerinin yanı sıra, *edition text+kritik, taz, DER SPIEGEL* edebiyat ekinde, *Zeit Online*, *Zeit Campus*, *edit* ve queer edebiyat dergisi *glitter*'de yayınlandı.

Tobias Peper

born 1984, studied Art History, Sociology and German Philology in Cologne. He currently works as assistant curator at the Kunstverein in Hamburg, where he curated exhibitions with Prem Sahib, Katja Novitskova, Calla Henkel & Max Pitegoff, FORT, and others. Before, he was a trainee at the Migros Museum for Contemporary Art in Zurich and worked at the Museum Ludwig in Cologne. In 2012 and 2014, he was responsible for the art education at *new talents—biennale cologne*. He publishes regularly on the art of the 20th and 21st century, in recent years for example about Matheus Rocha Pitta, FORT, MOON & JEON or Xanti Schawinsky.

belit sağ

is a video maker, visual artist and art worker living in Amsterdam. She studied mathematics in Turkey and visual arts in the Netherlands. Her background in moving images is rooted in her work within video-activist groups in Ankara and Istanbul, where she co-initiated groups such as VideA, karahaber, and bak.ma. She has completed residencies at the International Studio & Curatorial Program (ISCP) in New York (2016) and at Rijksakademie van Beeldende Kunsten in Amsterdam (2014-2015) among others. Her ongoing artistic and moving image practice largely focuses on the role of visual representations of violence in the experience and perception of political conflicts in Turkey, Germany, and the Netherlands, and incorporates archival research and practice. She presented her work, among others, in MOCA, Taipei; Flaherty NYC; documenta 14, Kassel; LUX, London; Tabakalera, San Sebastian; Tütün Deposu, Istanbul; Toronto, Rotterdam, San Francisco and New York International Film Festivals; transmediale, Berlin; EYE Filmmuseum, Amsterdam. Her work is distributed by LIMA, and has been written about in *Frieze, Artforum, ArtSlant, The Brooklyn Rail, MUBI* and *Art Monthly UK* among others.

geboren 1984 studierte Kunstgeschichte, Soziologie und Deutsche Philologie in Köln. Derzeit arbeitet er als Assistenzkurator am Kunstverein in Hamburg, wo er Ausstellungen mit Prem Sahib, Katja Novitskova, Calla Henkel & Max Pitegoff, FORT und anderen kuratierte. Zuvor war er Volontär am Migros Museum für Gegenwartskunst in Zürich und arbeitete am Museum Ludwig in Köln. 2012 und 2014 war er unter anderem für die Kunstvermittlung der *new talents—biennale cologne* verantwortlich. Er veröffentlicht regelmäßig über die Kunst des 20. und 21. Jahrhunderts, in den letzten Jahren zum Beispiel über Matheus Rocha Pitta, FORT, MOON & JEON oder Xanti Schawinsky.

ist Videoproduzentin, bildende Künstlerin und Kunstarbeiterin und lebt in Amsterdam. Sie studierte Mathematik in der Türkei und bildende Künste in den Niederlanden. Hintergrund ihrer Auseinandersetzung mit dem Bewegtbild ist ihre Arbeit mit Video-Aktivist*innengruppen in Ankara und Istanbul, wo sie unter anderem VideA, karahaber und bak.ma mitinitiiert hat. Unter anderem war sie mit Stipendien im International Studio & Curatorial Program (ISCP) in New York (2016) und an der Rijksakademie van Beelende Kunsten in Amsterdam (2014-2015). Ihre kontinuierliche künstlerische und Bewegtbild-Praxis fokussiert sich größtenteils auf die Rolle der visuellen Repräsentation von Gewalt mit der Erfahrung und Wahrnehmung von politischen Konflikten in der Türkei, Deutschland und den Niederlanden und vereinigt archivarische Recherche und Praxis. Sie präsentierte ihre Arbeit unter anderem im MOCA, Taipei; Flaherty NYC; LUX, London; Tabakalera, San Sebastian; Tütün Deposu, Istanbul; EYE Filmmuseum, Amsterdam; auf der documenta 14, Kassel, und der transmediale Berlin sowie auf den Filmfestivals in Toronto, Rotterdam, San Francisco und New York. Ihre Arbeit wird über LIMA vertrieben und war Inhalt von Artikeln in: *Frieze, Artforum, ArtSlant, The Brooklyn Rail, MUBI, Art Monthly UK* und anderen.

doğum 1984. Köln'de sanat tarihi, sosyoloji ve Alman Dili okudu. Şu anda, Prem Sahib, Katja Novitskova, Calla Henkel & Max Pitegoff, FORT ve diğerlerinin sergilerine küratörlük yaptığı Kunstverein in Hamburg'da küratör asistanı olarak çalışıyor. Daha önce Zürih Migros Çağdaş Sanat Müzesi'nde stajyer idi ve Köln Ludwig Müzesinde çalıştı. 2012 ve 2014'te *new talents—biennale cologne* için sanat komisyonculuğu yaptı. 20. ve 21. yüzyılın sanatı üzerine (örneğin son yıllarda Matheus Rocha Pitta, FORT, MOON & JEON veya Xanti Schawinsky hakkında) düzenli yayınlar çıkarıyor.

video yapımcısı, güzel sanatlar sanatçısı ve sanat işçisi ve Amsterdam'da yaşıyor. Türkiye'de matematik ve Hollanda'da görsel sanatlar okudu. Hareketli görüntülerle çalışmasının fonunu Ankara ve İstanbul'da, VideA, karahaber ve bak.ma gibi grupların kurulmasına önayak olduğu, video eylemci gruplarla yaptığı çalışmalar oluşturuyor. Bu kapsamda New York'ta (2016) International Studio & Curatorial Program (ISCP) ve Amsterdam'da (2014-2015) Rijksakademie van Beelende Kunsten'de çalıştı. Devam etmekte olduğu sanat ve filmcilik çalışmasında, Türkiye, Almanya ve Hollanda'da siyasi ihtilaf ve şiddet tecrübelerinde görsel temsilin rolüne odaklanıyor ve arşiv araştırmasını ve pratiği birleştiriyor. Çalışmalarını MOCA, Taipei; Flaherty NYC; LUX, Londra; Tabakalera, San Sebastian; Tütün Deposu, İstanbul; EYE Film Müzesi, Amsterdam; documenta 14, Kassel ve transmediale Berlin, ayrıca Toronto, Rotterdam, San Francisco ve New York film festivallerinde sundu. *Frieze, ArtForum, ArtSlant, Brooklyn Rail, MUBI, Art Monthly UK* ve diğer yayınların haberlerine konu olan belit sağ'ın çalışmalarının sürümü ve pazarlaması LIMA üzerinden yapılmaktadır.

Bettina Steinbrügge

is the director of the Kunstverein in Hamburg. She was director of Halle für Kunst Lüneburg, curator at La Kunsthalle Mulhouse and Senior Curator at Belvedere, Vienna. She has taught at the University of Lüneburg and at the HEAD in Geneva. Since 2014, she is a professor of art theory at the Academy of Fine Arts in Hamburg. She has been a member of the programming team for Forum Expanded/International Film Festival in Berlin from 2007-2017.

ist Direktorin des Kunstverein in Hamburg. Sie hat die Halle für Kunst Lüneburg geleitet, war Kuratorin an La Kunsthalle Mulhouse und Seniorkuratorin und Sammlungsleiterin am Belvedere in Wien. Sie hat an der Universität Lüneburg und der HEAD in Genf unterrichtet. Seit 2014 ist sie Professorin für Kunsttheorie an der Hochschule für Bildende Künste (HFBK) in Hamburg. Von 2007–2017 war sie Mitglied des Programmteams des Forum Expanded der Internationalen Filmfestspiele Berlin.

Kunstverein in Hamburg'un müdürü. Daha önce Lüneburg'daki Halle für Kunst'u yönetti, Mulhouse La Kunsthalle'nin küratörü ve Viyana'daki Belvedere'nin baş küratörüydü. Lüneburg Üniversitesi'nde ve Cenevre'deki HEAD'de ders verdi. 2014'ten beri Hamburg Güzel Sanatlar Yüksekokulu'nda (HFBK) profesör. 2007–2017 arasında Berlin Film Festivali'nin Forum Expanded program ekibinin üyesiydi.

2   I
4   II
6   III
8   IV
10   V
12   VI
14   VII
16   VIII
18   IX
20   X
21   XI
22   XII, XIII
23   XIV, XV
24   XVI, XVII
25   XVIII, XIX
26   XX
Cana Bilir-Meier, *Düşler Ülkesi* Installation view / Ausstellungsansicht / Sergi düzeni, Kunstverein in Hamburg 2019, Photo / Foto / Foto: Fred Dott
55   XXI
77   XXII
Cana Bilir-Meier, *Frottagen 1–32, Olympia-Einkaufszentrum München*, 2019, Rubbings / Frottagen / Frotajlar, 29,7 × 21 cm
87   XXIII
Düşler Ülkesi, Written and directed by / Buch und Regie / Yazun ve yönetem: Erman Okay, Türkisches Theater München am Theater der Jugend, 1982, Open call / Aufruf / Çağrı, Archive / Archiv / Arşiv Zühal Bilir-Meier
88   XXIV
Düşler Ülkesi, Written and directed by / Buch und Regie / Yazun ve yönetem: Erman Okay, Türkisches Theater München am Theater der Jugend, 1982, Poster / Plakat / Poster, Archive / Archiv / Arşiv Zühal Bilir-Meier
90   XXV
91   XXVI
Düşler Ülkesi, Written and directed by / Buch und Regie / Yazun ve yönetem: Erman Okay, Türkisches Theater München am Theater der Jugend, 1982, Photo / Foto / Foto: Ali Kılıç, Archive / Archiv / Arşiv Zühal Bilir-Meier
92   XXVII
Düşler Ülkesi, Written and directed by / Buch und Regie / Yazun ve yönetem: Erman Okay, Türkisches Theater München am Theater der Jugend, 1982, Ticket / Eintrittskarte / Bilet, Archive / Archiv / Arşiv Zühal Bilir-Meier
101   XXVIII
102   XXIX
103   XXX
Cana Bilir-Meier, *This makes me want to predict the past*, 2019, Super-8-Film / Süper-8-Film (Digitalisiert, Schwarz-weiß, Ton / Digitized, B/W, Sound / Sayısallaştırmıst, Monokrom, Ses), 17 min. / dakika
111   XXXI
112   XXXII
113   XXXIII
114   XXXIV
115   XXXV
116   XXXVI
117   XXXVII
Cana Bilir-Meier, *Semra Ertan*, 2013, HD-Video / HD-Video (Farbe, Ton / Color, Sound / Renk, Ses) 7:30 min. / dakika
119   XXXVIII
131   XXXIX
Cana Bilir-Meier, *Frottagen 1–32, Olympia-Einkaufszentrum München*, 2019, Rubbings / Frottagen / Frotajlar, 29,7 × 21 cm
136   XL
belit sağ, *(Against) Randomness*, 2017, Single channel video / 1-Kanal-Video / 1-Kanal-Video, 2:20 min. / dakika
(below / unten / altında)
belit sağ, *cut-out*, 2018, Single channel video / 1-Kanal-Video / 1-Kanal-Video, 4 min. / dakika
153   XLI
belit sağ, *disruption*, 2016, Single channel video / 1-Kanal-Video / 1-Kanal Video, 5 min. / dakika

154   XLII
belit sağ, *Ayhan and me*, 2016, Single channel video / 1-Kanal-Video / 1-Kanal Video, 15 min. / dakika
(below / unten / altında)
belit sağ, *geriye kalanlar / what remains*, 2018, Single channel video / 1-Kanal-Video / 1-Kanal Video, 7 min. / dakika
165   XLIII
171   XLIV
173   XLV
175   XLVI
177   XLVII
179   XLVIII
181   XLIX
183   L
185   LI
187   LII
189   LIII
191   LIV
193   LV
195   LVI
197   LVII
199   LVIII
201   LIX
203   LX
205   LXI
Cana Bilir-Meier, *Frottagen 1–32, Olympia-Einkaufszentrum München*, 2019, Rubbings / Frottagen / Frotajlar, 29,7 × 21 cm
216   LXII
217   LXIII
218   LXIV
229   LXV
230   LXVI
240   LXVII
241   LXVIII
242   LXIX
Cana Bilir-Meier, *Porträt Ronya Othmann*, 2019, Single channel video / 1-Kanal-Video / 1-Kanal Video, 2:30 min. / dakika
255   LXX
Cana Bilir-Meier, *Frottagen 1–32, Olympia-Einkaufszentrum München*, 2019, Rubbings / Frottagen / Frotajlar, 29,7 × 21 cm

IMPRINT

KUNSTVEREIN IN HAMBURG

Klosterwall 23
20095 Hamburg
Germany

T +49 40 322157
F +49 40 322159

hamburg@kunstverein.de
www.kunstverein.de

Director
Bettina Steinbrügge

Head of Finances
Emek Ulusay

Assistant Curator
Tobias Peper

Registrar
Lydia Jung

Press and Public Relations
Dilara Kubitzki

Technical Manager
Robert Görß

Art Education
Corinna Koch

Patrons
Frauke Willems

Member support
Nils Grossien

Visitor Service
Maike Nuppnau
Max Fascher

Interns
Maximilian Langefeld
Thilo Schmahl

Installation Team
Suzana Cosic
Otis Dusör
Carlos Gutierrez
Hannes Heinrich
Simone Kessler
Alexander Pröpster

Tobias Sandberger
Joshua Sassmannshausen
Heinz Völlen
Björn Westphal

Exhibition Graphic Design
Bueronardin

Webdesign and Development
Büro Ballmann Weber

Board
Marie Becker
Sabine Bührich-Glasa
Tilman Mueller-Stöfen
Klaus Schockmann
Verena Schöttmer
Christoph Seibt
András Siebold
Timm Weber
Frauke Willems

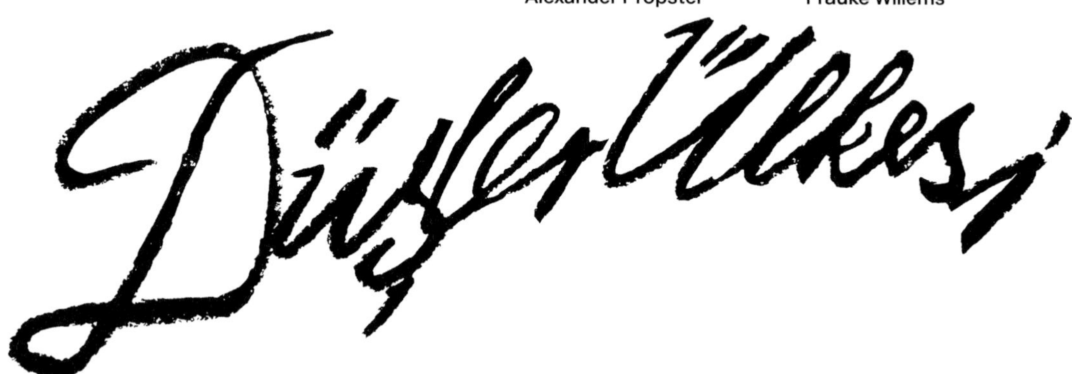

Cana Bilir-Meier

Published on the occasion of the exhibition *Düşler Ülkesi,* Kunstverein in Hamburg, 18 May—21 July 2019

Published by Kunstverein in Hamburg: Bettina Steinbrügge and Tobias Peper

Managing Editor
Tobias Peper

Copy editing and proofreading
Dilara Kubitzki
Tobias Peper
Thilo Schmahl
Bettina Steinbrügge

Translation
Cansu Beksan
Kemal Doğan
Karl Hoffmann
Arda Recep
Anja Welle

Graphic Design
Christian Lange Studio

Fonts
LL Riforma, Microgramma

Reproductions
Marc Teipel

Printing
KOPA, Lithuania

Published by
Spector Books
Harkortstraße 10
04107 Leipzig
www.spectorbooks.com

Distribution

Germany, Austria:
GVA, Gemeinsame Verlagsauslieferung Göttingen GmbH & Co. KG,
www.gva-verlage.de

Switzerland:
AVA Verlagsauslieferung AG,
www.ava.ch

France, Belgium:
Interart Paris,
www.interart.fr

UK:
Central Books Ltd,
www.centralbooks.com

USA, Canada, Central and South America, Africa:
ARTBOOK | D.A.P.,
www.artbook.com

Japan:
Twelvebooks,
www.twelve-books.com

South Korea:
The Book Society,
www.thebooksociety.org

Australia, New Zealand:
Perimeter Distribution,
www.perimeterdistribution.com

ISBN 978-3-95905-342-6

First Edition
Printed in the EU

All rights reserved.
No part of this publication may be reproduced, stored in a retrieval system, or transmitted in any form or by any means, electronic, mechanical, or otherwise without prior permission in writing from the publisher.

© 2019, the artist, the authors / Kunstverein in Hamburg; Spector Books, Leipzig.

Acknowledgements
Behörde für Kultur und Medien der Freien und Hansestadt Hamburg
Cansu Beksan
Cihan Bilir
Zühal Bilir-Meier
Burcu Dogramaci
Tamer Düzyol
Yasemin Göze
Hamburgische Kulturstiftung
Christian Lange
Cihad Hammy
Ronja Hesse
Belinda Kazeem-Kamiński
Banu Karaca
İpek Karacagil Kul
Katja Kobolt
Liesa Kovacs
Berit Köhler
Betül Küpeli
Justus Linz
Rebecca Lohse
Can-Peter Meier
Hans-Peter Meier
Aleyna Osmanoğlu
Ronya Othmann
Enes Özmen
Esra Özmen
belit sağ
Frauke Steinhäuser
Stiftung Kunstfonds
Lichun Tseng
Berfin Ünsal
Tobias Wollborn
Gürsel Yildirim
Sosuna Yildiz
Ünal Zeran

KUNSTVEREIN IN HAMBURG

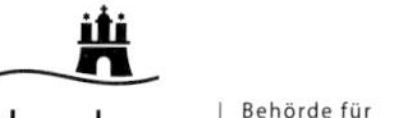

Hamburg | Behörde für Kultur und Medien

STIFTUNG KUNSTFONDS

LfA FÖRDERBANK BAYERN

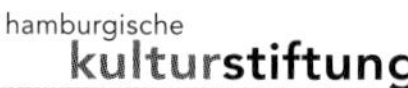

hamburgische kulturstiftung

IMPRESSUM

KUNSTVEREIN IN HAMBURG

Klosterwall 23
20095 Hamburg
Deutschland

T +49 40 322157
F +49 40 322159

hamburg@kunstverein.de
www.kunstverein.de

Direktorin
Bettina Steinbrügge

Kaufmännische Leitung
Emek Ulusay

Assistenzkurator
Tobias Peper

Registrarin
Lydia Jung

**Presse- und
Öffentlichkeitsarbeit**
Dilara Kubitzki

Technischer Leiter
Robert Görß

Kunstvermittlung
Corinna Koch

Fördermitgliedschaft
Frauke Willems

Mitgliederbetreuung
Nils Grossien

Kasse
Maike Nuppnau
Max Fascher

Praktikanten
Maximilian Langefeld
Thilo Schmahl

Aufbauteam
Suzana Cosic
Otis Dusör
Carlos Gutierrez
Hannes Heinrich
Simone Kessler
Alexander Pröpster

Tobias Sandberger
Joshua Sassmannshausen
Heinz Völlen
Björn Westphal

Grafik Ausstellung
Bueronardin

Webdesign und Umsetzung
Büro Ballmann Weber

Vorstand
Marie Becker
Sabine Bührich-Glasa
Tilman Mueller-Stöfen
Klaus Schockmann
Verena Schöttmer
Christoph Seibt
András Siebold
Timm Weber
Frauke Willems

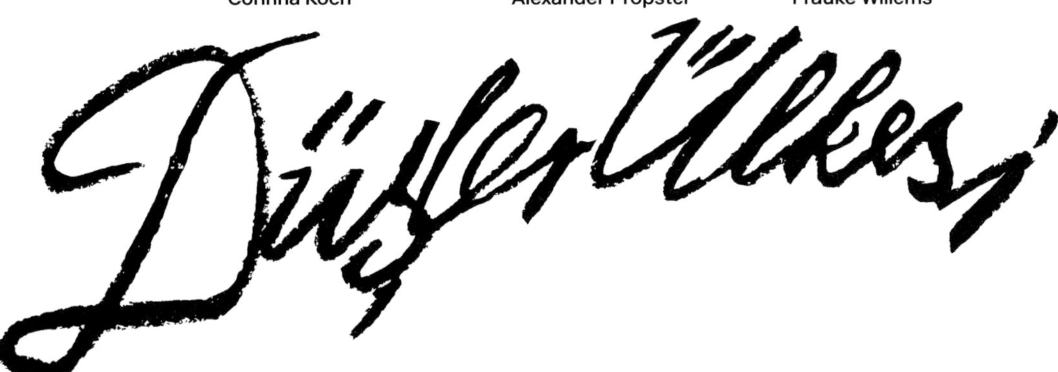

Cana Bilir-Meier

Erscheint anlässlich der
Ausstellung *Düşler Ülkesi*,
Kunstverein in Hamburg,
18.5. – 21.7.2019

**Herausgegeben von
Kunstverein in Hamburg:**
Bettina Steinbrügge
und Tobias Peper

Redaktion
Tobias Peper

Lektorat und Korrektur
Dilara Kubitzki
Tobias Peper
Thilo Schmahl
Bettina Steinbrügge

Übersetzung
Cansu Beksan
Kemal Doğan
Karl Hoffmann
Arda Recep
Anja Welle

Gestaltung
Christian Lange Studio

Schriften
LL Riforma, Microgramma

Lithografie
Marc Teipel

Druckerei
KOPA, Litauen

Erschienen bei
Spector Books
Harkortstraße 10
04107 Leipzig
www.spectorbooks.com

Distribution

Deutschland, Österreich:
GVA, Gemeinsame
Verlagsauslieferung
Göttingen GmbH & Co. KG,
www.gva-verlage.de

Schweiz:
AVA Verlagsauslieferung AG,
www.ava.ch

Frankreich, Belgien:
Interart Paris,
www.interart.fr

UK:
Central Books Ltd,
www.centralbooks.com

USA, Kanada, Mittel-
und Südamerika, Afrika:
ARTBOOK | D.A.P.,
www.artbook.com

Japan:
Twelvebooks,
www.twelve-books.com

Südkorea:
The Book Society,
www.thebooksociety.org

Australien, Neuseeland:
Perimeter Distribution,
www.perimeterdistribution.com

ISBN 978-3-95905-342-6

Erste Auflage
Gedruckt in der EU

Alle Rechte vorbehalten.
Kein Teil dieser Publikation
darf ohne vorherige schrift-
liche Genehmigung des
Herausgebers in irgendeiner
Form oder mit irgend-
welchen elektronischen,
mechanischen oder
sonstigen Mitteln
reproduziert, gespeichert
oder übertragen werden.

2019, die Künstlerin,
die Autor*innen,
Kunstverein in Hamburg;
Spector Books, Leipzig.

Danksagungen
Behörde für Kultur
und Medien der Freien und
Hansestadt Hamburg
Cansu Beksan
Cihan Bilir
Zühal Bilir-Meier
Burcu Dogramaci
Tamer Düzyol
Yasemin Göze
Hamburgische Kulturstiftung
Christian Lange
Cihad Hammy
Ronja Hesse
Belinda Kazeem-Kamiński
Banu Karaca
İpek Karacagil Kul
Katja Kobolt
Liesa Kovacs
Berit Köhler
Betül Küpeli
Justus Linz
Rebecca Lohse
Can-Peter Meier
Hans-Peter Meier
Aleyna Osmanoğlu
Ronya Othmann
Enes Özmen
Esra Özmen
belit sağ
Frauke Steinhäuser
Stiftung Kunstfonds
Lichun Tseng
Berfin Ünsal
Tobias Wollborn
Gürsel Yildirim
Sosuna Yildiz
Ünal Zeran

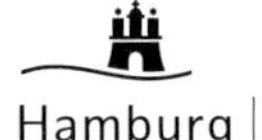

KÜNYE

KUNSTVEREIN IN HAMBURG

Klosterwall 23
20095 Hamburg
Almanya

T +49 40 322157
F +49 40 322159

hamburg@kunstverein.de
www.kunstverein.de

Direktör
Bettina Steinbrügge

Ticari Yönetim
Emek Ulusay

Asistan Kuratör
Tobias Peper

Kayıt Sorumlusu
Lydia Jung

Basın ve Halka İlişkiler
Dilara Kubitzki

Teknik Sorumlusu
Robert Görß

Sanat Arabulucusu
Corinna Koch

Destekci Üyelik
Frauke Willems

Üye Hizmetleri
Nils Grossien

Gişe
Maike Nuppnau
Max Fascher

Stajyer
Maximilian Langefeld
Thilo Schmahl

Enstelasyon Ekibi
Suzana Cosic
Otis Dusör
Carlos Gutierrez
Hannes Heinrich
Simone Kessler
Alexander Pröpster

Tobias Sandberger
Joshua Sassmannshausen
Heinz Völlen
Björn Westphal

Sergi Grafik Tasarımı
Bueronardin

Web Tasarımı ve Uygulama
Büro Ballmann Weber

Yönetim Kurulu
Marie Becker
Sabine Bührich-Glasa
Tilman Mueller-Stöfen
Klaus Schockmann
Verena Schöttmer
Christoph Seibt
András Siebold
Timm Weber
Frauke Willems

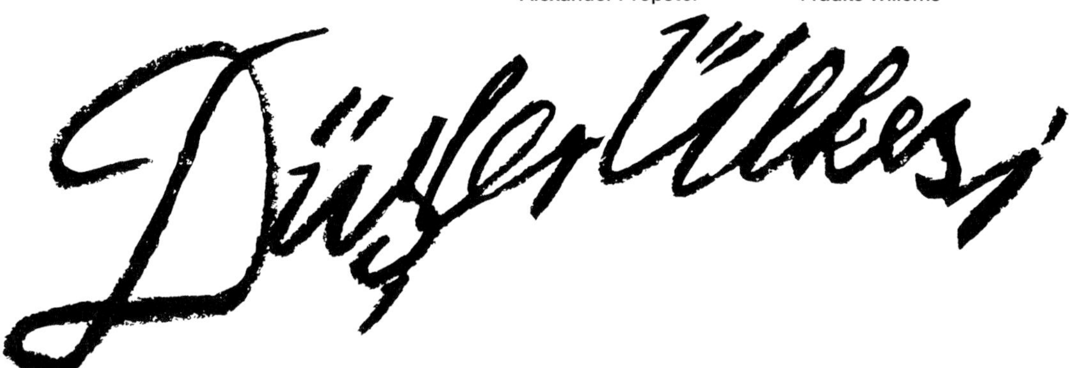

Cana Bilir-Meier

Kunstverein in Hamburg'da,
18.5.—21.7.2019 düzenle
nen *Düşler Ülkesi* sergisi
kapsamında yayınlanıyor,

Yayınlayan Kunstverein
in Hamburg: Bettina
Steinbrügge ve Tobias Peper

Editör
Tobias Peper

Redakte ve tashih
Dilara Kubitzki
Tobias Peper
Thilo Schmahl
Bettina Steinbrügge

Çeviri
Cansu Beksan
Kemal Doğan
Karl Hoffmann
Arda Recep
Anja Welle

Tasarım
Christian Lange Studio

Fontlar
LL Riforma, Microgramma

Litografi
Marc Teipel

Basımevi
KOPA, Litvanya

Yayınlayan
Spector Books
Harkortstraße 10
04107 Leipzig
www.spectorbooks.com

Dağıtım

Almanya, Avusturya:
GVA, Gemeinsame
Verlagsauslieferung
Göttingen GmbH & Co. KG,
www.gva-verlage.de

İsviçre:
AVA Verlagsauslieferung AG,
www.ava.ch

Fransa, Belçika:
Interart Paris,
www.interart.fr

Birleşik Krallık:
Central Books Ltd,
www.centralbooks.com

ABD, Kanada, Orta ve Güney
Amerika, Afrika:
ARTBOOK | D.A.P.,
www.artbook.com

Japonya:
Twelvebooks,
www.twelve-books.com

Güney Kore:
The Book Society,
www.thebooksociety.org

Avusturalya, Yeni Zelanda:
Perimeter Distribution,
www.perimeterdistribution.com

ISBN 978-3-95905-342-6

1. Basım
AB'de basılmıştır

Tüm hakları saklıdır.
Bu yayının hiçbir bölümü
yayıncının önceden alınan
yazılı izni olmadan hiçbir
biçimde veya elektronik,
mekanik veya diğer şekillerle
iktibas, kayıt yapılamaz veya
nakledilemez.

© 2019, Sanatçılar, Yazarlar /
Kunstverein in Hamburg,
Spector Books, Leipzig.

Teşekkürler
Behörde für Kultur
und Medien der Freien und
Hansestadt Hamburg
Cansu Beksan
Cihan Bilir
Zühal Bilir-Meier
Burcu Doğramacı
Tamer Düzyol
Yasemin Göze
Hamburgische Kulturstiftung
Christian Lange
Cihad Hammy
Ronja Hesse
Belinda Kazeem-Kamiński
Banu Karaca
İpek Karacagil Kul
Katja Kobolt
Liesa Kovacs
Berit Köhler
Betül Küpeli
Justus Linz
Rebecca Lohse
Can-Peter Meier
Hans-Peter Meier
Aleyna Osmanoğlu
Ronya Othmann
Enes Özmen
Esra Özmen
belit sağ
Frauke Steinhäuser
Stiftung Kunstfonds
Lichun Tseng
Berfin Ünsal
Tobias Wollborn
Gürsel Yildirim
Sosuna Yildiz
Ünal Zeran

KUNSTVEREIN IN HAMBURG

STIFTUNG KUNSTFONDS

LfA FÖRDERBANK BAYERN

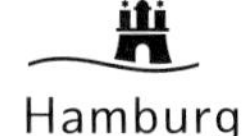
Hamburg | Behörde für Kultur und Medien

hamburgische kulturstiftung

This makes me want to read a book from end to beginning

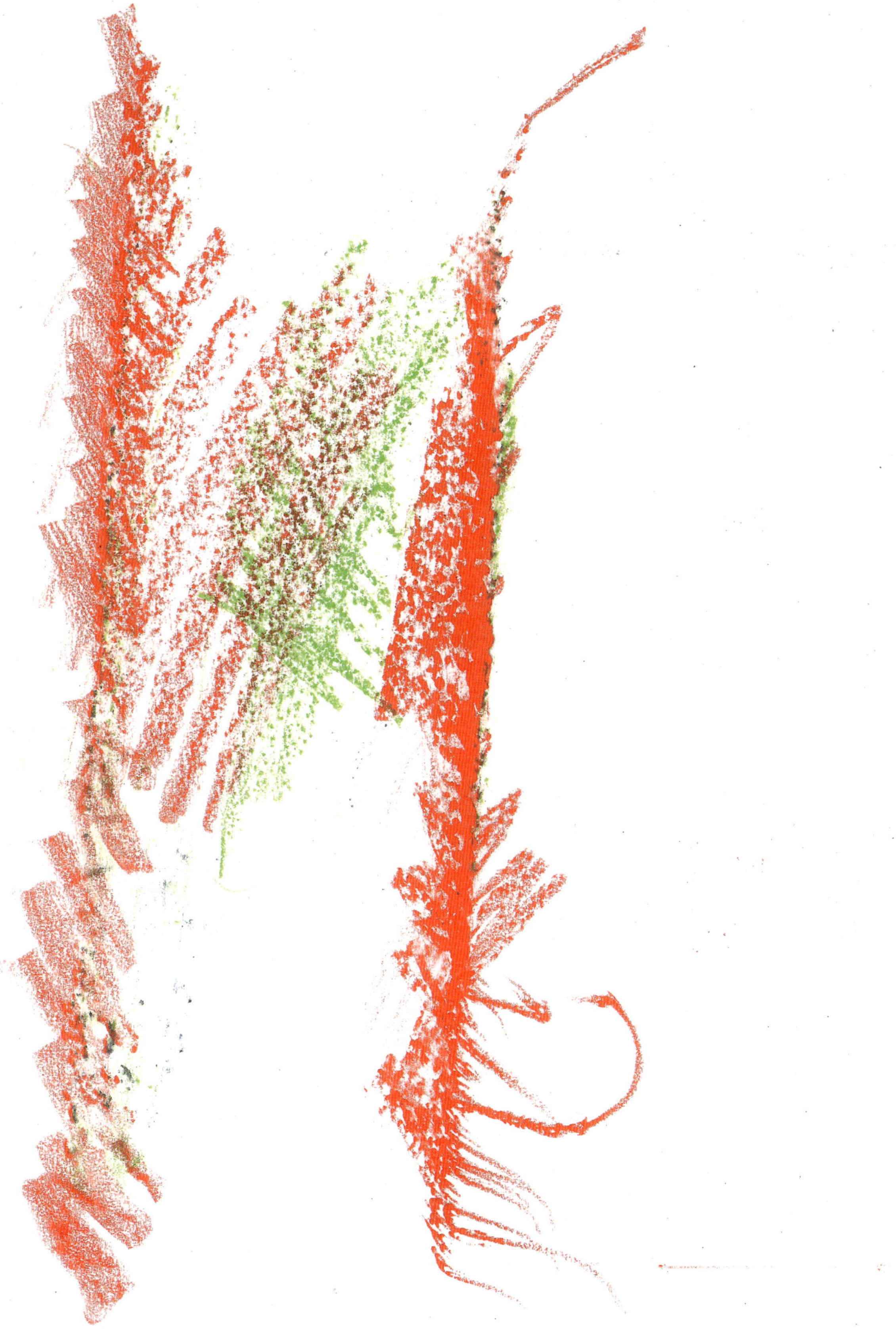